DE HAVILLAND
MOSQUITO

CROWOOD AVIATION SERIES

DE HAVILLAND
MOSQUITO

Martin W. Bowman

The Crowood Press

First published in 1997 by
The Crowood Press Ltd
Ramsbury, Marlborough
Wiltshire SN8 2HR

www.crowood.com

Paperback edition 2005

British Library Cataloguing-in-Publication Data
A catalogue record for this book is available from the British Library.

ISBN 1 86126 736 3

Photograph previous page: In memoriam: on 21 July 1996, RR299 crashed at Great Barton, Manchester, killing pilot, Kevin Moorhouse, and flight engineer, Steve Watson. *BAe*

Line drawings by Simon Peters

Typefaces used: Goudy (*text*),
Cheltenham (*headings*).

Typeset and designed by
D & N Publishing
Lambourn Woodlands, Hungerford, Berkshire.

Printed and bound in Great Britain by
Antony Rowe Ltd, Chippenham, Wiltshire

Acknowledgements

A great many people world-wide, all of them very special, have contributed their time, expertise and above all, generosity and a large selection of rare and previously unpublished photos, mainly from personal collections, to make this one of the most comprehensive books on the Mosquito yet. I would espeially like to thank Eric Atkins DFC* KW*, RAF Retd, Chairman, Mosquito Aircrew Association, for writing the foreword and for his kindness and help throughout. Graham M. Simons of GMS enterprises, author of *Mosquito, the original Multi-role Aircraft*, loaned many photos, all of which he gave freely for all the right reasons. Andrew D. Bird provided much expertise on Banff Strike Wing Mosquitoes, while Derek Carter in Copenhagen was especially helpful with valuable information and photos on the Shellhaus raid.

I am equally grateful to the following: Steve Adams; David Backhouse; Mike Bailey; Ron Bartley RAF Retd; Frank Baylis AFM RAF Retd; John B. Beeching; Taffy Bellis; Serge Blandin; Barry Blunt BA Hons; Dr Theo Boiten; Dennis Bolesworth; S/L Lewis Brandon DSO DFC* RAF Retd; S/L T.J. Broom DFC RAF Retd; Lt Cmdr Eric 'Winkle' Brown OBE DSC; W.W. Burke; Alan Carter; Bob Collis; Hank Cooper DSO RAF Retd; Alfred J. Cork DFM FLS FCollP RAF Retd; Vic Cramer; G/C John Cunningham DSO** DFC* RAF Retd; Des Curtis DFC RAF Retd; Tom Cushing; Joyce Dann, Hon. Sec. 613 Squadron; S/L Ian R. Dick RAF Retd; Richard Doleman RAF Retd; Grenville Eaton RAF Retd; Roy Edwards RAF Retd; John D.S. Garratt DFC* RAF Retd; Ken Godfrey; Ted Gomersall RAF Retd; Grp Capt J.R. 'Benny' Goodman DFC* AFC AE RAF Retd; Charles Harrold DFC* RAF Retd; Ron Mackay; Stuart Howe; A. 'Baron' Humphrey RAF Retd; Roy House RAF Retd; Leslie 'Dutch' Holland RAF Retd; Vic Hester RAF Retd; Ken Hyde, archivist, Shuttleworth Collection; Chris Jefferson; Ted Johnson; Rod Jones; George Lord RAF Retd; Allan Lupton RAeS; Ron Mackay; H. Mears RAF Retd; Basil McRae RAF Retd; Alan Morgan RAF Retd; John R. Myles DFC RCAF Retd; Grp Capt G.W.E. 'Bill' Newby RAF Retd; J.A. Padilla; Vic Parker RAF Retd; W/C D.A.G. Parry DSO DFC RAF Retd; Simon Parry, Air Research Publications; S/L Charles Patterson DSO DFC RAF Retd; Edwin R. Perry RAF Retd; Air Commodore G. Pitchfork; Ronnie Plunkett RAF Retd; Mike Ramsden; Harry Randall-Cutler RAF Retd; John Sampson RAF Retd; Alan Sanderson; George Sesler; E.T. Scheyer; Jerry Scutts; Jim Shortland; Alan V. Shufflebottom RAF Retd; the late W/C Joe Singleton DSO DFC AFC RAF Retd; Kevin Sloper, City of Norwich Aviation Museum; Dave Smith; Margaret Taplin; Ian Thirsk; F/L Andy Thomas RAF; Geoff Thomas; Peter Verney RAF Retd; Maj-Gen Karel Vervoort, Belgian Air Force; W/C C.M. Wight-Boycott DSO RAF Retd; Alan B. Webb RAF Retd; Dyson Webb RCAF Retd; the late J. Ralph Wood DFC CD RCAF Retd; Gerry R. Wooll RCAF Retd.

Contents

Glossary

AA	anti-aircraft
AI	Airborne Interception (radar)
AM	Air Marshal
ASH	AI Mk XV radar
AVM	Air Vice Marshal
BSDU	Bomber Support Development Unit
CRT	Cathode Ray Tube (C-scope)
Day Ranger	Operation to engage air and ground targets within a wide but specified area by day
Diver	Code-name for V-1 flying bomb operation
Düppel	German code name for *Window*
Firebash	Fire-bombing raids by Mosquitoes of 100 Group, 1945, using Napalm (Naphaline, Palm Oil and White Phosphorus), in 100-gallon drop tanks
FIU	Fighter Interception Unit
Flensburg	German device to enable their night-fighters to home onto *Monica*
Flower	British low-level night intruder patrol of German airfields
F/L	Flight Lieutenant
F/O	Flying Officer
F/Sgt	Flight Sergeant
Freelance	Patrol with the object of picking up a chance contact or visual of the enemy
ftr	failed to return
G/C	Group Captain
Gee	British navigational device involving a special aircraft radio receiver working on signals transmitted by two ground stations. Was limited to a range of about 400 miles (640km). By late 1942 *Gee* had been rendered almost ineffective by German jamming and was replaced by *Oboe*. G-H was a development of *Gee* giving more precise fixes
H2S	British 10cm navigational radar
IFF	Identification Friend or Foe
Instep	Air patrol over the Bay of Biscay and Atlantic
Intruder	Offensive night operation to fixed point or specified target
LAC	Leading Aircraftman
Lichtenstein	First form of German AI
Mahmoud	High level, bomber support sortie
Mandrel	airborne radar jamming device
Monica	tail-mounted warning radar device
MTU	Mosquito Training Unit
Night Ranger	Operation to engage air and ground targets within a wide but specified area by night
Noball	British code-name for Flying bomb (V-1) or rocket (V-2) site
Oboe	Ground-controlled radar system of blind bombing in which one station indicated track to be followed and another the bomb release point
Op	Operation
OTU	Operational Training Unit
Outstep	Patrol seeking enemy air activity off Norway
P/O	Pilot Officer
PFF	Pathfinder Force
PR	Photo reconnaissance
Rhubarb	Low-level daylight fighter sweep
R/T	Radio Telephony
Serrate	British equipment designed to home in on *Lichtenstein* radar
S/L	Squadron Leader
soc	struck off charge
Turbinlight	An aircraft-mounted searchlight system for night-fighting
W/C	Wing Commander
W/O	Warrant Officer

Foreword

The Latin for a fly is 'Musca', hence Mosquito, but this is about a different kind of 'fly' and mosquito! I don't know how far the 'Musca' type of mosquito can travel, but this one had a range of some 1,560 miles (2,510km)! It was the most successful multi-role combat aircraft of WWII; around 7,700 built, flown by more than 120 RAF squadrons in all commands, and over 45 different marks. Truly a 'fly' in both the sense of a noun or verb, of magnificent proportions.

Civilian air travel was still in its infancy when WWII began. The majority viewed the opportunity to fly with some trepidation. Most of the RAFVR had never flown before volunteering for the RAF. The most I had done was to ride a bicycle. In a Tiger Moth we were as one with the elements and the ground flew past at a speed slow enough to make it feel possible to build up a relation with it. In contrast, the Mosquito sped along over the ground at really low level like a bullet from a gun, calling for much more professional map reading and perception well ahead of position. At its ceiling it seemed to be 'master of all it surveyed' – a fly on the ceiling one moment, yet ready and able to turn and dive at a slight movement of the control stick, in its own element regardless of its relation to the ground. Even at ground level it seemed to operate in its open void, splendidly independent, and both pilot and navigator had to 'run to keep up with it'! Is it possible to build a close relationship with an aircraft – a mass of wood, instruments, engines? Yes, more so with a Mosquito! Pilot and navigator were so often immersed in their separate duties, sometimes we hardly spoke to one another throughout an operation, except to give directional instructions. There was a closer and more equal relationship though than in the bomber crews of heavier aircraft. Few Mosquito pilots were called 'Captain' or 'Skipper'.

The third member of the crew was the aircraft itself and it had an almost human relationship. Crews felt warm inside and friendly towards it, especially if it was one they had flown many times before. If they had to change from their usual Mosquito, they were sorry, but it was still a Mosquito and worthy of the legend and the squadron. It was the same with a good ground crew. You knew a strange one would be up to squadron efficiency, but you missed the last 'hand-shake' of your usual ground crew.

Night flying could be a battle of wits and experience between you and your mind. Your eyes could take everything in on the panel and yet you were flying blind in a black void around you. Clouds, and the base of moonlight, provided a chiaroscuro of shadows and light and down below there was a grey misty mantle of night over the ground with an occasional twinkle or beam quickly passing underneath. Being small, and light, the Mosquito could fall foul of adverse conditions but when caught in flak, searchlights or in an attack by enemy aircraft, it could be flung around the sky in almost impossible manoeuvres. It responded to the controls like a thoroughbred racehorse – with speed, precision and a sixth sense of judgement linked to that of the pilot.

In daylight, and at low level, the Mosquito excelled. It was ideal for operations like the Amiens prison raid, or on the Gestapo HQs at roof top height. Attacks on V-1 sites proved that the Mosquito could put them out of action more effectively and with less tonnage than any other aircraft. These sites and the type of operation were affectionately known as *Noball* – some say because you stood a good chance of losing your testicles, but the probable reason was the concrete pill box which shielded the ball bearing and magnetic link with the V-I which enabled it to find its target. Bomb this and the site could be put out of action. These were some of the most exacting and exciting operations I flew! Over back gardens with washing hanging out, up and down as various pylons, hills and spires got in the way, people waving down below, hugging the side of hills and down the valleys. (Map reading at this level had to be of a high order.) Then, up to 1,000ft (300m), nose down, target ahead, bomb doors open. With little time to take notice of the flak coming up, you threw the aircraft at the target. Bombs gone (bombing had to be visual and done by the pilot in a pre-emptive manner), steep, drastic climb up to 800ft (240m), wing down to see the damage, down on the deck again and away before the other aircraft threw their bombs at you!

The Mosquito inspired confidence in its crew. Despite its wooden construction, the Mosquito had strength and endurance and was easy to repair – you simply spliced another wing on when you landed with half a wing missing! It excelled at everything – army support, jamming and intruding, pathfinding and PR, weather finding, SAS parachute drops and anti-U-boat patrols. Mosquitoes even delivered newspapers, collected ball bearings from, and flew VIPs in and out of, Sweden, in the bomb bay! Had more Mosquitoes been available earlier the war might have been shortened! I'm proud of having had a Mosquito under the 'seat of my pants' and despite the *Noball* operations, glad to have come through it all intact!

Eric Atkins DFC* KW*
*464 & 305 Squadrons, Chairman,
Mosquito Aircrew Association*

7

Chronology

25 November 1940, W4050, the prototype, flies for the first time.

16 January 1941, W4050 outpaces a Spitfire at 6,000ft (1,830m).

10 June 1941, W4051, the PR prototype, flies for the first time.

13 December 1941, 157 Squadron, first Mosquito fighter squadron in Fighter Command.

15 May 1941, W4052, the night fighter prototype, flies for the first time.

17 September 1941, W4055, a PR. I, makes the first operational Mosquito flight, a daylight photo reconnaissance of Brest, La Pallice and Bordeaux.

19–19 July 1941, W4050, attains 433mph (697kph) at 28,500ft (8,690m).

16 November 1941, W4066 becomes first Mosquito bomber to enter RAF service, at 105 Squadron, Swanton Morley, Norfolk.

27/28 April 1942, 157 Squadron flies first AI Mk V radar equipped NF. II patrol.

31 May 1942, 105 Squadron fly first operation.

13 June 1942, 264 Squadron becomes first operational Mosquito intruder squadron.

2 July 1942, six B. IVs of 139 Squadron bomb the U-boat yards at Flensburg in the first mass low level strikes by the aircraft.

4 August 1942, first diplomatic flight to Sweden, by a 105 Squadron Mosquito, in a prelude to regular BOAC service between Scotland and Sweden.

19 September 1942, 105 Squadron makes first daylight Mosquito raid on Berlin.

25 September 1942, four 105 Squadron crews bomb Gestapo HG at Oslo.

6 December 1942, ten B. IVs of 105 and 139 Squadrons take part in 'Operation Oyster', the 2 Group daylight raid on the Philips works at Eindhoven.

20/21 December 1942, Oboe used for first time when six B. IVs of 109 Squadron are dispatched to bomb Lutterade power-station, Holland.

31 December 1942/1 January 1943, on a raid on Düsseldorf, sky-marking using *Oboe* tried for the first time, by two Mosquitoes of 109 Squadron, 8 Group, (PFF).

27 January 1943, nine Mk. IVs of 105 and 139 Squadrons make a daring low-level raid on the Burmeister and Wain Diesel engine works at Copenhagen.

30 January 1943, Mosquitoes bomb Berlin and disrupt live enemy broadcasts.

27 May 1943, final large-scale daylight Mk. IV raid in 2 Group, an attack on the Zeiss Optical factory, and the Schott Glass Works, at Jena.

24/25 July–2 August 1943, during nine days of Operation Gomorrah, the 'Battle of Hamburg', Mosquitoes fly 4,472 sorties, with the loss of just thirteen Mosquitoes.

4 December 1943, 141 Squadron first NF. II squadron to join 100 Group.

3 October 1943, first operation by FB. VIs of 2nd TAF.

15 October 1943, 138 Wing at Lasham re-equips with FB. VI.

18 February 1944, Operation Jericho, Amiens prison bombed by FB. VIs of 140 Wing.

23/24 February 1944, first Cookie to be dropped by a Mosquito is released by a Mk IV (modified) of 692 Squadron, during a raid on Düsseldorf.

25 March 1944, Cmdr Eric 'Winkle' Brown, lands and takes off from a carrier in a Mosquito, the first twin-engined aircraft to do so.

25 March 1944, Tsetse Mosquitoes become first Mosquitoes to sink U-boat.

25/26 March 1944, the Lyons engine factory marked by 8 Group Mosquitoes.

11 April 1944, Gestapo HQ in The Hague destroyed by 613 Squadron FB. VIs.

18/19 April 1944, Juvisy railway marshalling yards, Paris, marked at each end by seven Mosquitoes of Nos 5 and 8 Groups are bombed so effectively that the

yards are not brought back into service until 1947.

14 July 1944, Bonneuil Matours barracks destroyed by FB. VIs of 140 Wing.

6 August 1944, 604 Squadron first Mosquito fighter squadron to move to France.

19 August 1944, fifteen FB. VIs of 613 Squadron destroyed Egletons SS barracks.

17 September 1944, 138 Wing FB. VIs attack barracks at Arnhem and Nijmegen ahead of the 'Market-garden' airborne invasion.

26 October 1944, Banff Strike Wing Mosquitoes use RPs for the first time.

31 December 1944, twelve Mosquitoes of 627 Squadron dive bomb the Oslo Gestapo HQ.

31 October 1944, twenty-five FB. VIs of 140 Wing 2nd TAF destroy the Gestapo HQ at Aarhus University, Denmark.

22 February 1945, twenty-one Mosquitoes lost and forty damaged during all out attacks on enemy transport system in Operation Clarion.

21 March 1945, Operation 'Carthage', Gestapo HQ Shellhaus building in Copenhagen bombed in daylight precision raid by eighteen FB. VIs of 140 Wing.

9 April 1945, Banff Wing Mosquitoes sink three U-boats.

17 April 1945, six FB. VIs of 140 Wing destroy the Gestapo HQ at Odense, Denmark.

2/3 May 1945, final Bomber Command raids are made and involve 179 Mosquitoes from Nos. 8 and 100 Groups.

15 November 1950, VX916, a NF. 38 built at Chester is the 7,781st and final Mosquito.

15 December 1955, PR. 34A of 81 Squadron at Seletar makes the final operational flight of a Mosquito in the RAF, a 'Firedog' sortie over Malaya.

CHAPTER ONE

Wood Against Steel

Birth and Production of the Wooden Wonder

By mid-1944 pin-point bombing by high speed Mosquitoes, hedge-hopping their way over enemy-occupied Europe in broad daylight, had become a common practice. Often, the sheer speed of the aircraft and the *élan* of their crews got them home again through flak and fighters. Over the previous three years more often than not this speed was their only escape from Luftwaffe interceptors and flak. Revered by its crews, loathed, yet respected by its enemies, the Mosquito eventually gained such a deserved reputation for achieving the impossible that at one stage the British press claimed that when one was shot down the Luftwaffe crew could count it as two victories. Apocryphal this may be but during four years of war the 'wooden wonder' was to prove the scourge of the Axis throughout Europe, the Mediterranean and the Far East. Such was the incisive contribution made by this remarkable aircraft, built largely of beech, spruce and ply, and the shattering effect it had on the Germans as a whole, that its very presence eventually caused 'Moskitopanic' throughout the Reich territory. Over 500 years earlier, at Agincourt, British archers using longbows honed from yew and firing fusillades of arrows from long distance, had panicked, then routed, another enemy. Equally, in WWII, Mosquitoes proved that they too could kill from long range, with minimal loss and deadly accuracy, as once again, wood triumphed decisively over steel.

The de Havilland Mosquito's birth and subsequent development was a difficult process in the precarious days of 1930s Europe. World War I (1914–18) had ended with victory for Great Britain and her allies, but at great cost. As the market for weapons stagnated, Britain's aircraft industries immediately reverted to the production of commercial airliners and the modification of bomber types for civilian use. Wood and wire construction was the order

of the day and for some, like the famous de Havilland company, it remained so well into the late 1930s.

Geoffrey de Havilland, one of the world's most famous aviation pioneers, was born the son of a clergyman in 1883. 'DH' as he was affectionately known, had built his first aircraft, with Frank Hearle, in 1908. It crashed, but DH taught himself to fly and he and Hearle built another. Both men were offered Government posts in the embryonic Royal Aircraft Factory at Farnborough, where Geoffrey de Havilland designed the B.E. (Blériot Experimental) No.1. In 1912 he was the prime mover in the development of the B.S.1, the first British single-seat scout of any note. Two years later DH joined the Aircraft Manufacturing Co. at Hendon as designer and test pilot. When war broke out in 1914 he was commissioned in the RFC as a second lieutenant, although he was too valuable to be sent to the front. DH spent the war designing aircraft, his best being the DH.4 biplane day bomber, the finest of its kind. On 25 September 1920 DH formed his own company, de Havilland Aircraft Co. Ltd, and rented a large field at Stag Lane in Edgware, North London. Frank Hearle became his general manager. They decided mainly to build commercial aircraft but were grateful for the odd RAF contract, such as that for the refurbishment of 150 DH.9As, to keep the money coming in. De Havilland owed its initial success to the use of simplified structures – the cabins of aircraft such as the DH.18, 29, 34 and 50 were literally plywood boxes, spacious, without any internal bracing. By 1925 the first of the DH.60 Moth series appeared, which led to one of the most successful light aeroplane families in the history of aviation. But the future was by no means secure, as the civil market ultimately was to suffer an inevitable downturn in line with the economy.

Ever the innovative designer, DH turned his attentions to the military market, but

his ambitions were restricted by the rigid adherence by the military mandarins to designs not far removed from those of WWI. Stag Lane was needed for redevelopment, so in 1930 de Havilland moved his operation to the green fields of Hatfield in Hertfordshire, but not before three DH.88 Comet racers had been built, amid great secrecy, before final assembly and testing at the new factory at Hatfield. Just as the Supermarine S6B influenced the design of the Spitfire, after the seaplane's success in the Schneider Trophy races, the DH.88 ultimately was to play a significant role in the development of the Mosquito. The Comet was a streamlined low-wing monoplane design with a small frontal area, all of which compensated for the low power of its two 230hp (171kW) de Havilland Gipsy Six R (Racing) engines. The aircraft had a span of 44ft (13.4m), was 29ft (8.8m) long and loaded, weighed 5,320lb (2,413kg). Wooden construction and stressed skin covering not only saved weight but also speeded up production. Later, these techniques were successfully applied in the late 1930s to the highly successful four-engined de Havilland DH.91 Albatross airliner, capable of cruising at 210mph (338kph) at 11,000ft (3,350m).

The first order for a Comet Racer was placed by Mr A.O. Edwards, Managing Director of the Grosvenor House Hotel, London. In 1934 this aircraft, now registered G–ACSS, and named *Grosvenor House*, together with G–ACSP *Black Magic*, and the third Comet, which was owned by racing driver, Bernard Rubin, were entered in the London–Melbourne Centenary Air Race, which took place in October. *Grosvenor House* was crewed by Tom Campbell Black and C.W.A. Scott, *Black Magic*, by Amy (neé Johnson) and Jim Mollinson, and the third, No.18, was flown by O. Cathcart Jones and Kenneth Waller. The Mollinsons retired from the race at Allahabad with piston trouble caused by

DH.88 Comet Racer Grosvenor House which won the London–Melbourne Air Race in 1934, its streamlined low-wing monoplane design with a small frontal area immediately apparent. Ultimately, the DH.88 was to play a significant role in the development of the Mosquito, whose 54ft 2in (16.5m) one-piece cantilever wing was built, like the Comet, around a stress-bearing box spar with a thick planking of spruce applied diagonally in two layers.
Martin W. Bowman

(Below) The initial DH.98 design was based on the DH.91 Albatross E-2 commercial monoplane, shown here in its initial form with inset fins, later to be registered G–AEVV. The Albatross flew for the first time on 20 May 1937 at Hatfield. Its manufacture was of mainly wood and stressed skin construction with laminations of cedar ply with a thick balsa sandwich between. Graham M. Simons

unsuitable fuel. Scott and Black pressed on and completed the 11,300 miles (18,180km) to the Flemington Racecourse in Melbourne with an elapsed time of 70hr 54min and 18sec to win the race. In 1935 two more DH.88 Comet Racers were built. A year later, on 8 September 1936, de Havilland took an interest in Air Ministry Specification P.13/36 which was issued by Air Commodore R.H. Verney on behalf of the RAF Directorate of Technical Development (DTD) and called for a 'twin-engined medium bomber for world-wide use'. Britain was at last emerging, albeit slowly, from its post-WWI complacency. Politicians, no doubt stirred by news of German rearmament, and upbraided in Parliament by Winston Churchill MP, brought a new found urgency which culminated in a long overdue expansion of the RAF. The DTD now wanted an aircraft that:

> could exploit the alternatives between the long range and very heavy bomber load which are made possible by catapult launching in heavily loaded condition. During all operations it is necessary to reduce time spent over enemy territory to a minimum. Therefore the highest possible cruising speed is necessary. It appears that there is a possibility of combining medium bomber, general reconnaissance and general purpose classes into one basic design, with possibly two 18 inch torpedoes carried.

In addition, DTD wanted two forward- and two rearward-firing Browning machine guns, horizontal bomb stowage, in tiers if necessary, suitability for outside maintenance at home or abroad, consideration of

remotely controlled guns and a top speed of not less than 275mph (442kph) at 15,000ft (4,570m) on two-thirds engine power and a range of 3,000 miles (4,830km) with a 4,000lb (1,810kg) bomb load.

At this time de Havilland was pinning his commercial hopes on the DH.91 Albatross commercial monoplane. Its manufacture was of mainly wood and stressed skin construction, with laminations of cedar ply with a thick balsa sandwich between. The layers were cemented under pressure on a retractable jig which permitted the whole fuselage shell to be lifted off in one piece. The 105ft (32m) one-piece cantilever wing was built, like that of the Comet, around a stress-bearing box spar with a thick planking of spruce applied diagonally in two layers. The Albatross flew for the first time on 20 May 1937 at Hatfield. Altogether, seven of these beautiful aircraft were built.

De Havilland had bad memories of submitting designs to the military in the 1920s, when all of his ideas had been considered too revolutionary. DH therefore proposed a

modified miniature version of the Albatross airliner design to meet the DTD specification. It could certainly carry a 6,000lb (2,720kg) bomb load to Berlin and back at 11,000ft (3,350m). Pacifists in Parliament were appalled and certainly Captain de Havilland's doubts were well-founded, but he persevered with the Albatross proposal. In April 1938 studies were conducted for a two-Rolls-Royce Merlin-powered version of the airliner. There was nothing radical about this but what would the DTD make of a wooden design being submitted to carry bombs 3,000 miles (4,830km) in war? On 7 July Geoffrey de Havilland sent a letter detailing the design to Air Marshal Sir Wilfred Freeman, an old friend of de Havilland's from WWI, now the Air Council's member for Research and Development. DH (eventually Sir Geoffrey) was to recall later in his autobiography, *Sky Fever* that:

> it only needed one meeting with this wise and far-sighted man to discuss our plans and get his full approval.

Design studies showed that the Merlin-engined Albatross would need at least a three man crew and the aircraft should have between six and eight forward-firing machine guns plus one, perhaps two, manually operated guns, with provision for a rear turret. All this would produce an all-up weight of 19,000lb (8,616kg). Top speed would be 300mph (483kph) and cruise, 268mph (431kph) at 22,500ft (6,860m). Not surprisingly therefore, the de Havilland Company considered that Specification P.13/36, which itself embraced a hotch-potch of requirements many companies would find hard to meet, would produce a less than satisfactory aircraft. In a way they were right. The two winning designs – the Avro Manchester, and the Handley Page HP.56, both to be powered by two Rolls-Royce Vulture engines – were failures. Plans for the Vulture-engined HP.56 were scrapped in 1937 while the unsuccessful Manchester only redeemed itself later when the design was converted into the very successful four-engined Lancaster.

A Radical Proposal

The weight restrictions prompted de Havillands to opt for a very radical approach to the design of a twin-engined bomber. They proposed deleting the gun armament altogether, as doing so would save about one-sixth of the total weight of the aircraft. As a consequence production would be easier and therefore faster with service delivery far in excess of any other bomber or fighter of the period. Equally importantly, if there was no armament (although Chief Designer, Ronald E. Bishop, looking ahead, made provision under the floor for four 20mm cannon), the crew could be reduced to a pilot and a navigator only. What the authors of Specification P.13/36 made of this is not hard to fathom. At this time the RAF was considering specifications for eight gun single-engine fighters along with heavily armed bombers.

If de Havilland's proposals were not already considered radical enough, on 27 July they distanced themselves still further by informing DTD that Specification P.13/36 could not be met by using just two Merlins, unless of course the Air Ministry wanted to carry only half the anticipated bomb load? If they stuck to the 4,000lb (1,810kg) bomb load, then a much larger and consequently slower bomber would be needed. In August de Havillands came up with a compromise, but to proceed would have been an admission of defeat in design principles, and the company soon rejected it.

The Munich Crisis of 1938 concentrated ministerial minds wonderfully and de Havillands went for broke. Their submission would no longer be a modified Albatross but a brand new design, with two crew, a pair of Rolls-Royce Merlins and no gun armament whatsoever. Speed, they reasoned, would be the new bomber's only defence. After all, the question of the unarmed bomber had been answered by Geoffrey de Havilland's experience in World War I, where the DH.4 bomber was able to outstrip the fighters of the day. And with war looming, a whole year normally taken up by the prototype stage could be saved by building the new bomber almost entirely of wood. Geoffrey de Havilland and C.C. Walker, Chief Engineer, went to London in October with the intention of convincing the Air Ministry of their radical proposal. Not surprisingly perhaps, their proposal was unceremoniously rejected; the Air Ministry wanted only conventionally built all-metal bombers bristling with armament to defend themselves against enemy fighters.

By December 1938 the company's all-metal DH.95 Flamingo four-engined airliner, had flown. The Flamingo was designed by Ronald E. Bishop, who had succeeded A.E. Hagg as Chief Designer in 1938. But even with conversion to a bomber and using Bristol Taurus engines in place of the Perseus powerplants, the Flamingo was never a serious contender owing to its lack of high-speed performance. That December another new bomber specification, B.18/38, was issued, but it was of no interest to de Havillands, who persevered well into 1939 with the idea of a fast unarmed bomber.

War with Germany was declared on Sunday 3 September 1939 and three days later de Havilland went to lobby the Air Ministry again. Still sceptical, but slightly less so, the Air Ministry could still find no reason to agree with de Havilland's proposal that their unarmed high speed bomber would get through. Of this, de Havilland had no doubts. He wrote to Sir Wilfred Freeman again:

> The existence of a type of bomber having the highest performance possible and capable within a year of going into production forms a kind of insurance against surprises emanating from the enemy's design resources. If a prototype were undergoing trials, in, say, nine months, without detracting from production plans, it would be a platform for future plans, the value of which can hardly be exaggerated.

At Hatfield other powerplants were considered. So too was the retrograde step of reintroducing armament, even to the extent of siting a two gun turret in the fuselage, but de Havillands would not compromise their design principles or their long-held beliefs. In a letter to Sir Wilfred Freeman, dated 20 September 1939, Geoffrey de Havilland wrote:

> We believe we can produce a twin-engined bomber which would have a performance so outstanding that little defensive equipment would be needed. This would employ the well tried out method of construction used in the Comet and Albatross and being of wood or composite construction would not encroach on the labour and material used in expanding the RAF. It is especially suited to really high speeds because all surfaces are smooth, free from rivets, overlapped plates and undulations and it also lends itself to very rapid and subsequent production.

In November various long-range and escort fighter developments, as well as bomber, fighter and reconnaissance versions, were looked at and a conference was called with Sir Wilfred Freeman to consider all the proposals. Richard Clarkson was of the opinion that the turret would spoil the design, since fighter speed could be achieved without it and almost all interceptions by the enemy could therefore be avoided. Sir Wilfred was in favour of having no armament at all but doubted de Havilland's performance estimates which claimed that the two-crewed unarmed wooden bomber powered by two Merlins could carry a 1,000lb (450kg) bombload for 1,500 miles (2,410km) and at a speed faster than that of the Spitfire. It could; by skilful design which obtained every ounce of power by cleverly using ducted radiators and faired propeller roots which produced more thrust than drag.

While the Air Ministry conceded that a two-man crew in any reconnaissance version put forward by de Havillands was acceptable (although the Ministry wanted them in tandem seating) there was still strong opposition to the two-crew complement in any bomber version. A third crew member aft of the wing was favoured because it was believed that he could relieve the other two of the high workload on operations. The pilot, it was argued, would have no relief at the controls and the navigator would have the added burden of operating the radio, looking out for enemy fighters and aiming and dropping the bombs. De Havillands came down in favour of side-by-side seating in a two-man cockpit and were still adamantly opposed to a three-man crew under any circumstances. Matters came to a head on 12 December at a conference attended by the Assistant Chief of the Air Staff, the Director-General of Research and Development, the Air Officer Commanding-in-Chief, Bomber Command and other high ranking officers. While the AOC-in-C could find no room in his heart for the unarmed bomber, he conceded that there was a need for a fast, unarmed reconnaissance aircraft equipped with three F24 cameras.

More talks were held before Christmas and on 29 December the project received official backing when the Air Ministry asked for a basic requirement for a bomber capable of carrying a 1,000lb (450kg) bomb load and with a range of 1,500 miles (2,410km). Finally, on 1 January 1940 a further meeting, chaired by Air Marshal Sir Wilfred Freeman, took place at the Air Ministry with Geoffrey de Havilland, John Buchanan, Deputy General of Aircraft Production and John Connolly, Buchanan's chief staff officer, present. DH placed his design drawings on the table and is reported to have simply said ; 'This is the fastest bomber in the world; it must be useful.' It was. Sir Wilfred backed de Havilland and ordered a single prototype of the unarmed bomber variant to specification B.1/40/dh and powered by two Merlin engines. The aircraft was to have a level speed of 397mph (639kph) at 23,700ft (7,220m), a cruising speed of 327mph (526kph) at 26,600ft (8,110m) with a 1,480 mile (2,380km) range at 24,900ft (8,500m) on full tanks. Service ceiling was to be 32,100ft (9,780m).

Project Go-ahead

The specification was approved by Roderick Hill on behalf of DTD on 1 March 1940 and a contract for fifty DH.98 Mosquito aircraft placed. This was jeopardized following the Dunkirk debacle of May 1940, when fears that Britain could be overrun prompted the Ministry of Aircraft Production to concentrate on established aircraft such as the Spitfire, Hurricane, Wellington and Blenheim. There was no

E-0234 nears completion at Salisbury Hall, October 1940. Mosquito Museum via Ian Thirsk

surplus capacity available for aircraft like the DH.98, which could not be expected to be in service by early 1941. Precious Merlin engines were in short supply, and when the Mosquito was deleted from the priority list altogether there were none allocated to the project at all. The Mosquito was only reinstated in July 1940, after de Havillands promised Lord Beaverbrook (the Minister of Aircraft Production) the fifty Mosquitoes by December 1941. They knew this was impossible in reality, and in fact only twenty machines were built that year.

Work began on three prototypes. One of the first problems to confront de Havillands was the lack of much needed materials. Their argument that the Mosquito would not need much in the way of special materials and would make little demand on labour now worked against them. Besides, the company had other important work required urgently by the hard-pressed Air Ministry. De Havillands had to continue producing much needed bomb racks for Tiger Moths for low level attacks on beaches should the Germans invade, then during that summer and autumn the company repaired Hurricanes and Merlin engines and modified over 1,000 Spitfires and Hurricanes to take constant speed propellers.

W4050, the Mosquito prototype, meanwhile, was built in strict secrecy in a small hangar at Salisbury Hall, not far from Hatfield where a team of nine designers led by Chief Designer, Ronald E. Bishop, wrestled with the problems of the DH.98 design.

'Bishop,' recalls Ralph Hare, who was responsible for aircraft overall loads and for stressing the wing, 'was not a hierarchy man, and the hours he personally put in were staggering.' Bishop had been raised in the de Havilland tradition of wooden structures, and under A.E. Hagg he had seen how the Comet Racer had made use of innovative diagonal planking to achieve a thin wing of high aspect ratio without external bracing. This form of construction had also been adopted for the very much larger 1937 DH.91 Albatross airliner for Imperial Airways. It was also looked at for the DH.98, but it became obvious that this form of construction was not going to take the loads. Mike Ramsden explains (from *The Mosquito Fifty Years on: A Report on the 50th Anniversary Symposium Held at BAe Hatfield, 24.11.90.* GMS Enterprises for Hatfield RAeS):

The bottom skin was not the problem; the top skin would take the compression loads without buckling and failing. It was found that a double plywood sandwich with spanwise stringers – first of spruce, later of Douglas fir – was by far the most effective structure. The size of the square section stringers was calculated by theory, varying with wing station and checked by testing. The top of the single-piece wing comprised three double-skin panels. Many panels were made for 'control tests', to measure the basic performance properties of the materials and the construction, to put numbers to allowable stresses in tension, compression and shear, and to measure elastic moduli, mean values being used to obtain stress distributions for design. Optimizing these properties for the wing – the most heavily loaded part of the structure – was the ultimate test of de Havilland's timber experience. Two spars with tip-to-tip top and bottom booms of the laminated spruce, boxed with plywood webs, were finally chosen. Canadian spruce was selected for construction of the 50ft [15.2m] spars, although only one in ten trees met the required standard laid down in Air Ministry Specification DTD 36B. [It is worth remembering that some of the Mosquito materials were home grown – approximately 6 million cubic feet of beech on Lord Bathurst's estate near Cirencester, for example, was extracted from three forests in three years to be made into plywood at Lydney, Glos.]

The forward booms were made of single-piece spruce lamination; the aft booms had to have forward sweep as well as dihedral, and were spliced. The front spar booms were originally made of three (later ten, to save more wood) horizontal laminations, and the aft spar of three vertical laminations to accommodate the forward sweep. The laminations and spar webs were glued in their jigs under pressure and, to

speed up glue setting, were heated. Electric mats kept the temperature of the whole production jig constant regardless of whether one end of the spar was near a draughty factory door or the other near a warm canteen. The accuracy of the spar over a length of 50ft [15.2m], was 0.04in [1mm] – a remarkable precision of 1 in 15,000 – not bad for mass production carpentry!

The glueing operation was critical. The laminated booms had to be at least as strong as single-piece booms. In fact, a well glued laminated spar could be stronger than a solid spar. Laminations also obviated the shrinkage and warping which single beams might suffer. The glue was at first casein, a milk-based adhesive with which de Havilland and other wooden aircraft manufacturers had had long experience, but which proved unsatisfactory because of fungal growth (later, when a damaged tailplane was removed and the inside found to be full of mushrooms, casein was replaced by synthetic 'Beetle', introduced in Britain in about 1942, made by Dr N.A. de Bruyne's Aero Research company at Duxford (now Ciba-Geigy). Testing and service experience was to show that the wood fibres tore before the Beetle glue did. Tests of Mosquito

spars – spruce booms boxed by plywood webs joined with glue and screws – showed that the booms nearly always failed before the glue). Beetle was also more resistant to humidity and to the temperature cycling suffered by Mosquitoes operating to high altitudes in all climates from the tropics of Asia to the arctic winter airfields of northern Europe. Mosquitoes glued with casein would have deteriorated sooner, and probably none would have survived in airworthy condition to this day. But even Beetle has its weathering limits.

Screws and Glue

In India in November 1944 all Mosquito operations were abruptly halted after there were instances of wings collapsing in flight. Glue failure was suspected as the cause of the accidents after extreme heat had caused the glue to crack and the upper surfaces to lift from the spar. An investigating team led by Major Hereward de Havilland blamed the structural failures on climatic conditions and all parts made with casein glue

Reproduced from Flight, **6 May 1943.**

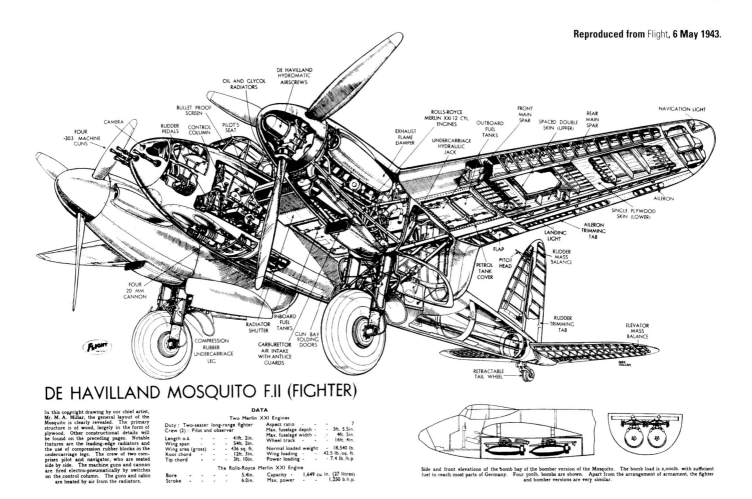

DE HAVILLAND MOSQUITO F.II (FIGHTER)

In this copyright drawing by our chief artist, Mr. M. A. Millar, the general layout of the Mosquito is clearly revealed. The primary structure is of wood, largely in the form of plywood. Other constructional details will be found on the preceding pages. Notable features are the leading-edge radiators and the use of compression rubber blocks in the undercarriage legs. The crew of two comprises pilot and navigator, who are seated side by side. The machine guns and cannon are fired electro-pneumatically by switches on the control column. The guns and cabin are heated by air from the radiators.

DATA

Two Merlin XXI Engines

Duty : Two-seater long-range fighter
Crew (2) : Pilot and observer

Length o.a.	- -	41ft. 2in.
Wing span	- -	54ft.
Wing area (gross)	-	436 sq. ft.
Root chord	- -	12ft. 3in.
Tip chord	- -	3ft. 10in.

Aspect ratio	- - - -	7
Max. fuselage depth -	-	5ft. 5.5in.
Max. fuselage width –	-	4ft. 5in.
Wheel track	- -	16ft. 4in.
Normal loaded weight	-	18,540 lb.
Wing loading - -	42.5 lb./sq. ft.
Power loading - -	- 7.4 lb./h.p.

The Rolls-Royce Merlin XXI Engine

Bore	- - -	5.4in.
Stroke	- - -	6.0in.

Capacity -	1,649 cu in. (27 litres)
Max. power -	1,250 b.h.p.

Side and front elevations of the bomb bay of the bomber version of the Mosquito. The bomb load is 2,000lb. with sufficient fuel to reach most parts of Germany. Four 500lb. bombs are shown. Apart from the arrangement of armament, the fighter and bomber versions are very similar.

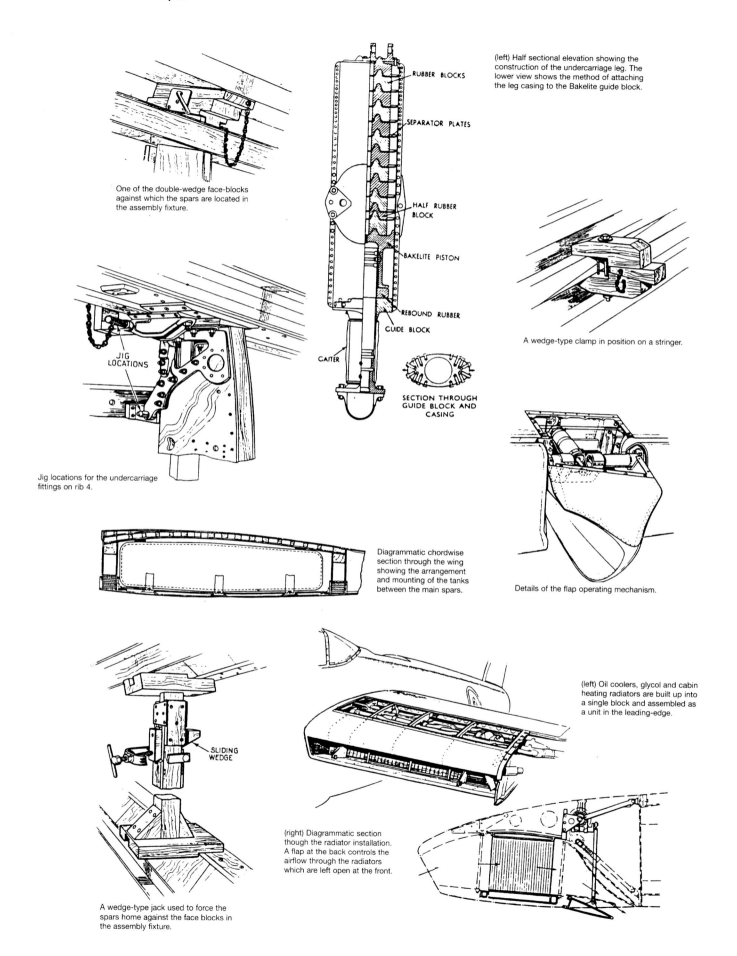

One of the double-wedge face-blocks against which the spars are located in the assembly fixture.

Jig locations for the undercarriage fittings on rib 4.

JIG LOCATIONS

RUBBER BLOCKS

SEPARATOR PLATES

HALF RUBBER BLOCK

BAKELITE PISTON

REBOUND RUBBER

GUIDE BLOCK

GAITER

SECTION THROUGH GUIDE BLOCK AND CASING

(left) Half sectional elevation showing the construction of the undercarriage leg. The lower view shows the method of attaching the leg casing to the Bakelite guide block.

A wedge-type clamp in position on a stringer.

Diagrammatic chordwise section through the wing showing the arrangement and mounting of the tanks between the main spars.

Details of the flap operating mechanism.

SLIDING WEDGE

A wedge-type jack used to force the spars home against the face blocks in the assembly fixture.

(right) Diagrammatic section though the radiator installation. A flap at the back controls the airflow through the radiators which are left open at the front.

(left) Oil coolers, glycol and cabin heating radiators are built up into a single block and assembled as a unit in the leading-edge.

14

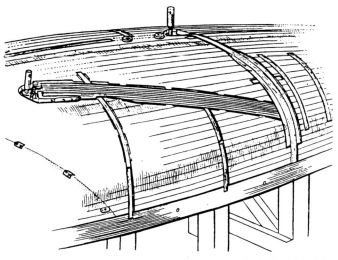

The two starboard-side wing pick-up fittings located with their support members in the fuselage mould.

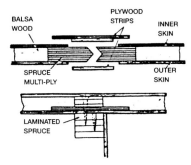

BALSA WOOD
PLYWOOD STRIPS
INNER SKIN
SPRUCE MULTI-PLY
OUTER SKIN
LAMINATED SPRUCE

(above) Details of the joint between the fuselage halves and (below) a typical section through the balsa plywood sandwich at one of the bulkhead stations.

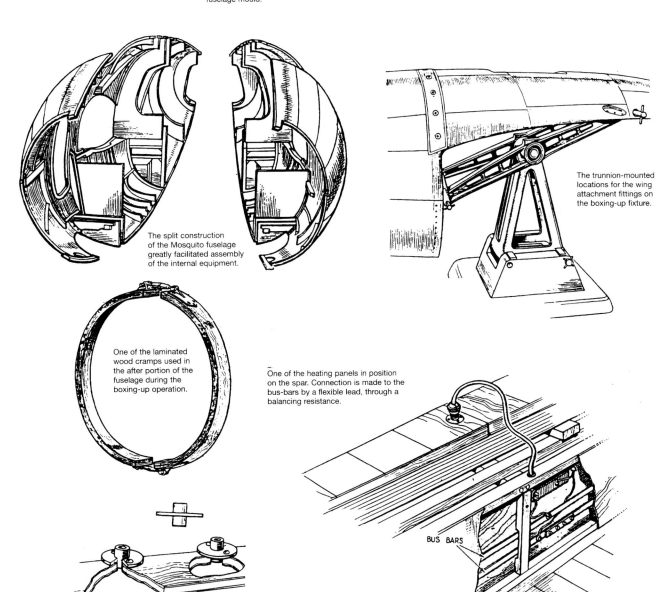

The split construction of the Mosquito fuselage greatly facilitated assembly of the internal equipment.

The trunnion-mounted locations for the wing attachment fittings on the boxing-up fixture.

One of the laminated wood cramps used in the after portion of the fuselage during the boxing-up operation.

One of the heating panels in position on the spar. Connection is made to the bus-bars by a flexible lead, through a balancing resistance.

BUS BARS

Wooden templates fitted with case-hardened mild-steel bushes used for drilling the plywood panels.

were ordered to be destroyed. Further investigation however, concluded that:

> the standard of glueing ... leaves much to be desired.

The failures were definitely due to faulty manufacture. Early in 1944 a series of fatal flying accidents among Mosquitoes of various marks was attributed to failure of the wing structure. Defects were found in Mk VI aircraft built by Standard Motors, and in Mosquitoes built at Hatfield. At a meeting at the Air Ministry on 1 January 1945 Maj. de Havilland still maintained that the wing failures in India were a result of the conditions there. It seems that the Air Ministry went along with this assertion to prevent any loss of confidence in the Mosquito squadrons. Modification 638, a plywood strip to be inserted along the span of the wing to seal the whole length of the skin joint along the main spar, was later applied to all Mosquitoes being produced in Australia but in India most Mosquitoes found to have skin defects were simply broken up. (In late 1945, during operations against Indonesian separatists, more faulty wing-structures were discovered in

some Mk VIs and they were again briefly grounded for inspection.)

Mike Ramsden again:

There was a saying in the old de Havilland days, possibly attributable to DH himself: 'You never glue without a screw'. There were more than 30,000 brass screws in a Mossie's wing, and I know not how many more in the fuselage and tail. If we say 50,000 screws per Mosquito and my arithmetic is right, then that's 400 million brass screws in 8,000 Mosquitoes – so the aircraft did require some metal! (Not forgetting of course the steel undercarriage, Merlins, DH propellers, engine and undercarriage mountings, elevators, canopy, wiring and plumbing.)

Birch plywood found to give the best results was made of three plies laid at 45 degrees to each other, so that when a shear load was applied, it was redistributed into a tension load along one ply grain and a compression load along the other two, the whole web taking a bigger load under compression. The lower wing skin was to be a single plywood panel stiffened with spruce stringers. The lower spar booms were reinforced round the tank door cutouts with strips of ash (originally compressed birch) to deal with the high concentration of tank door bolt loads. The bolt bearing edges of the tank doors were

similarly reinforced with the hard plastic impregnated laminated fabric called *Tufnol* – an ancestor of today's structural plastics.

Ash reinforcings extended along the bottom of each spar boom to the outboard tank rib – about two thirds of the span. Compared with compressed birch, ash was found on test to have better sensitivity to holes and other notches. The wing ribs were conventional; Rib One had a top boom of five spruce laminations with a bottom boom of Douglas Fir and a three ply web. Ribs Three and Four took metal fittings for the engines and undercarriage.

The Mosquito's fuselage, made in halves by stretching two skins of birch plywood over concrete moulds remains unique in aircraft construction. The plywood – three 1.5mm [.06in] to 2mm [.08in] 45 degree diagonal plies – were stretched cold over the concrete mould, into which the bulkheads and other structural members had been slotted. Steel straps then stretched the plywood to its double curvature shape. Before the second skin was applied, ⅜in [9.5mm] thick balsa fillings were inserted to stabilize the structural sandwich. Balsa had been the first choice for filling material, as it had worked well in the Albatross. Tests showed that the allowable stress of a birch plywood panel went up from 1,500lb per sq.in to 5,000lb per

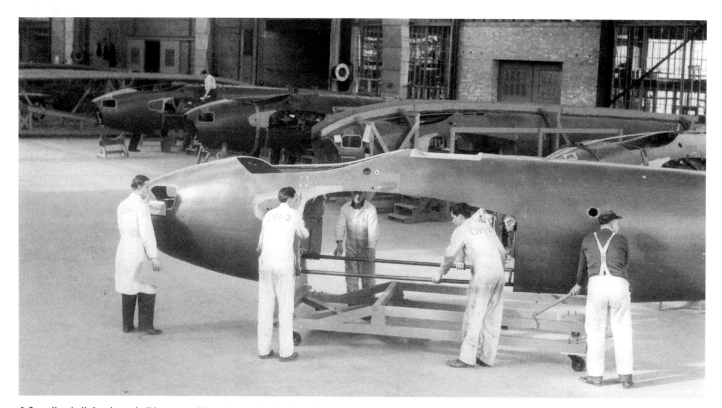

A Canadian-built fuselage shell is removed from the production line at Downsview for mating with the wing section. Note the temporary support rods where the wing centre section will go. The shells in the background still have straps wrapped around them while the vertical glue joints set. via Graham M. Simons

sq.in with a balsa sandwich core. The finished half fuselage shells were edged with male and female laminated spruce wedge joints, glued and screwed. Before the joining each shell was fitted with its wiring, plumbing and equipment.

The completed fuselage was covered with a fabric called Mandapolam. The outer skin was supported by seven bulkheads in the fuselage each made up of two plywood skins separated by spruce blocks. At the points where the bulkheads were attached the balsa skin core was replaced by a spruce ring. The fuselage underside was cut out to accommodate the wing, which was attached to four huge pick-up points, the lower portion of the cutout section being replaced after the wing was in position. Walnut, a strong hardwood, was used where the steel fuselage-to-wing attachment bolt loads had to be distributed. The walnut carried bearing loads from the bolts and these loads were transmitted to the supporting structure by the glued joints. The steel wing attachment fittings, like those carrying the engines and undercarriage, were remarkably economical of material and therefore weight.

The wings consisted of a one-piece two-spar mid-wing of Piercy Modified RAF 34 aerofoil section and contained ten fuel tanks of 539 Imp. gal. (2,450 litres) total capacity. The box spars had laminated spruce flanges and plywood webs, and there were spruce and plywood compression ribs between the spars. Later, No 8 rib in each wing was reinforced to carry drop tanks or underwing bombs. A false leading edge, built up of nose rib formers and a D-skin, was attached to the front spar. Span-wise spruce stringers supported the plywood wing skin, which, on the upper surface, was screwed, glued and pinned, and given an overall fabric covering. Wooden slotted flaps, slotted ailerons of light alloy frame and skin, with trim tabs, completed the wing structure. The centre portion of the wing carried welded steel tube engine mountings and wing radiators, the leading edge being extended forward by 22in (56cm) to accommodate the latter. Flap-controlled radiator outlets were sited ahead of the front spar on the wing undersides. Each radiator was divided into three parts; an oil cooler section outboard, the middle section forming the coolant radiator and the inboard section the cabin heater. The low drag nacelles for the 1,250hp (930kW) Merlin 21 engines housed the retractable undercarriage

Completed Mosquito wings ready for mating with their fuselages at Hatfield. via Graham M. Simons

Mosquitoes being assembled at Downsview, Toronto. De Havilland Canada turned out a total of 1,076 Mosquitoes. via Graham M. Simons

which had the de Havilland system of rubber blocks in compression shock absorbers in place of the more usual oleo-pneumatic shock-absorbers, to which end light alloy castings were used instead of forgings.

Bombs fell within a mile of the Hatfield factory one day in every five, but the only direct hit was on 3 October 1940 when a low flying Ju 88A of KG77 dropped four bombs on the old 94 shop (named after the production of the DH.94 Moth Minor), used as a busy sheet metal shop. Twenty-one people were killed and seventy wounded. Among the bomb wreckage was 80 per cent of the Mosquito work in progress. As a result, Mosquito production was widely dispersed to prevent any further major disruption by enemy action. Subcontractors included many well known furniture companies, such as Harris Lebus at Tottenham, and E. Gomme Ltd

made everything from simple parts to small components. The London bus refurbishment facility at Aldenham became a major Mosquito subcontractor, ESA in Stevenage produced complete wings and the smallest contractor was located in a garden shed in Welwyn!

The prototype, referred to originally as 'E-0234', the Company B-Condition marking, had a slightly smaller tailplane than the production Mosquitoes that followed. The fixed tail surfaces were all wood and ply-wood-covered while the rudder and elevators were made of aluminium and the elevators fabric-covered. (Later, in 1943, metal skinning of the elevators was introduced to give better performance in high speed dives). E-0234 was completed at Salisbury Hall and moved by road on two Queen Mary trailers to Hatfield on 3 November. In a hangar there it was assembled and the

The Mosquito Flies

Next day, just four days short of 11 months from the start of detailed design work, at 3.45pm, Geoffrey de Havilland Jr., with John E. Walker, Chief Engine Installation Designer, made the maiden flight. Take-off, de Havilland was to recall, was 'straightforward and easy'. The undercarriage was not retracted until considerable height had been gained and this was observed by John Walker through the nose windows. The aircraft reached a speed of 220mph (354kph) and the only real problem encountered was the inability of the undercarriage doors to fully close, and their opening, by some 12in (31cm), as speed was increased (a problem which would reoccur for a long time). Another difficulty that persisted for a long time was the inability of the tailwheel to castor properly – a problem which was to

E-0234 is prepared for an early flight at Hatfield, November 1940. It may even be the first, on 25 November 1940. Mosquito Museum via Ian Thirsk

and Dancer and Hearne Ltd in High Wycombe, who were making spars and wings, and Vanden Plas in Hendon, who were making wing coverings, as well as members of the exhibition stand and coach building industries. Detail parts were being manufactured by numerous other small companies, including bicycle manufacturers and a firm of craftsmen used to making ecclesiastical ironwork, while in homes, garages and church halls the length and breath of the country, women ranging from 'duchesses to charladies',

two Merlin 21s engines with two-speed single-stage superchargers installed. The aircraft emerged on 19 November for engine runs in overall trainer yellow with black spinners and de Havilland Hydromatic constant speed three-bladed airscrews. On the afternoon of Monday, 24 November, E-0234 began taxiing trials in the hands of Captain Geoffrey de Havilland Jr., who as Chief Test Pilot was to be responsible for the initial flight testing. Everything went well and the aircraft even made a short 'hop' in the process.

cause the fuselage to fracture when the wheel jammed in a rut at Boscombe during testing in 1941. (The castoring problem was finally cured in June–July 1941 by the fitting of a Dowty unit, evaluated at Benson). As E-0234 had flown a little left wing low, a rigging adjustment also had to be carried out before the next two flights, on 29 November. On the third flight the undercarriage would not come down and had to be pumped down by hand.

These short-term irritations are symptomatic of the problems that prototype

W4050, 10 December 1940, with fillet affixed to the rear section of the nacelle plus wool tufts to investigate airflow behaviour. Mosquito Museum via Ian Thirsk

that when the Mosquito was fitted with radar 'it would be a splendid replacement for the Beaufighter.'

On 16 January 1941, W4050 – a *bomber/photo-reconnaissance* aircraft, do not forget – outpaced a Spitfire in tests at 6,000ft (1,830m)! Over a period of a few days in early February, W4050 made a number of level speed trials, during which it reached a maximum speed of 390mph (627kph) at 22,000ft (6,700m). Official trials, which began at the A&AEE Boscombe Down on 19 February 1941, confirmed de Havilland's faith in the design and on 20 April 1941 the prototype was demonstrated to Lord Beaverbrook, Minister of Aircraft Production, and Major General Hap Arnold, Chief of the USAAF, and other senior officers. W4050, in the hands of Geoffrey de Havilland Jr., gave a dazzling performance, making rolling climbs on one engine. Major Elwood Queseda, General Arnold's aide, and later to control IX Fighter Command in England, told of his impressions:

> I do recall the first time I saw the Mosquito as being impressed by its performance, which (was something) we were aware of. We were impressed by the appearance of the airplane...all aviators are affected by the appearance of an airplane. An airplane that looks fast usually is fast, and the Mosquito was, by the standards of the time, an extremely well streamlined airplane, and it was highly regarded, highly respected!

Interest had already been growing during the official trials, turning the original blatant disinterest in the programme to outright enthusiasm. The official visit to Hatfield not only confirmed this, but gave the opportunity for setting up production in Canada and Australia. American interest, however, got no further. General Arnold

aircraft often encounter, but on 5 December E-0234, now officially serialled W4050, experienced tail buffeting at speeds of 240–255mph (386–410kph). The widespread shaking was particularly noticeable on the control column. Detailed investigations revealed that a stall was taking place away from the rear section of the engine nacelles and also on the undersurface of the wing. This disturbed airflow was striking the tailplane, thereby giving rise to the buffeting and general 'shake' throughout the aircraft. Extensive ground and airborne

testing, and experiments with aerodynamic 'slots' in an attempt to smooth out the disturbed air, failed to cure the problem. It was not until February 1941, after the engine nacelles were redesigned and finally extended beyond the trailing edge of the wing (although as a consequence, the flaps had to be split) that tail buffeting was virtually eliminated. On 9 February John Cunningham flew W4050 and was now greatly impressed by the lightness of the controls and 'generally pleasant handling characteristics'. Equally, it was clear to him

W4050 landing at Hatfield on the afternoon of 10 January 1941 during one of the four flights that were made that day. Mosquito Museum via Ian Thirsk

asked for, and received, plans data, and photos of the Mosquito, and engineers from Curtiss-Wright spent nearly a month visiting the de Havilland plant, but the Material Division of the AAC placed little importance on the plane, and expected that P-38 Lightnings would soon be available and capable of handling American photo-reconnaissance needs. Reports from Britain about the Mosquito emphasized only technical problems, or 'teething' problems. Nevertheless, Arnold was of the opinion that the design was being overlooked, and directed that the matter not be dropped. If the Americans were not to use

W4050 fitted with a mock-up of a rear turret immediately aft of the cockpit for drag tests during July 1941. Fortunately, the turret idea was not proceeded with by the Air Ministry.
Mosquito Museum via Ian Thirsk

(Below) The first version of the segmented Youngman frill airbrake as fitted to W4052, the fighter prototype, when the aircraft was at Salisbury Hall. The 'frill' could be opened by a bellows and venturi arrangement to provide a rapid deceleration during interceptions and was tested in a number of different forms between January–August 1942 but the idea was shelved when it was found that lowering the undercarriage in flight had the same effect.
Mosquito Museum via Ian Thirsk

the Mosquito, he felt that there was much to learn from the design. Within weeks, a request was sent to Britain for one airframe to evaluate at Wright Field, but this request was only three days old before the US declaration of war. Events had caught up with the US photo-reconnaissance programme and the US entered WWII without a single combat worthy photo-plane.

W4051, the photo-reconnaissance prototype, the second Mosquito completed at Salisbury Hall, was not the second to fly. The fuselage originally intended for W4051 was used to replace W4050's fuselage, which had fractured at Boscombe in the tail wheel incident. W4051 received a production fuselage instead, a factor which enabled this prototype to fly later on operations. W4051 flew on 10 June 1941 to

become the third Mosquito to fly. (W4052, the night fighter prototype, flew on 15 May 1941). W4051 became the first of three PR versions (the other two were W4054 and W4055) used by the PRU at Benson, Oxfordshire, although it was W4055 which made the first operational Mosquito flight, on 17 September 1941. Meanwhile, what of the fighter version? De Havillands had received a contract for 150 Mosquitoes on 30 December 1940, although it was not specified how many would be fighters and how many would be bombers; indeed, no firm figure was given on the number required as photo-reconnaissance versions. This indecision would cause problems in production because wings for the bomber and fighter versions were different (the fighter version needed

strengthened wing spars for stronger manoeuvre load factors) and bomber noses too were not the same as fighter noses since accommodation had to be provided in the fighters for four machine guns and four 20mm Hispano cannon. Fortunately, de Havillands recognized this and had arranged space under the floor to house these weapons if and when required. Even so, twenty-eight completed bomber fuselages later had to have the nose replaced. While the Ministry deliberated, W4052, which was built to Specification F.21/40, was also completed at Salisbury Hall. It differed from the bomber prototype in having uprated Merlin 21s, each capable of producing 1,460hp (1,088kW), a flat bullet-proof windscreen, and the then secret AI Mk IV radar. Entry was by a door

W4051 PR.I prototype, which flew on 10 June 1941. The fuselage originally intended for this aircraft was used to replace W5040's fuselage, which had been fractured in a tail wheel incident, and so W4051 received a production fuselage instead, a factor which enabled this prototype to fly operational sorties with the PRU, starting that summer. via Philip Birtles

W4052, the fighter prototype, differed from the bomber prototype in having two uprated Merlin 21s of 1,460hp (1,088kW), and a flat bullet-proof windscreen. Constructed at Salisbury Hall, it was flown out of a field adjacent to the assembly hangar on 15 May 1941 by Geoffrey de Havilland Jr. W4052 completed handling trials at Boscombe Down by the end of July 1941 and from 1942 onwards was used to test various modifications, such as 40mm cannon, underwing bomb racks and drop tanks, barrage balloon cable cutters in the wing leading edges, Hamilton Standard airscrews and braking propellers, drooping aileron systems for steeper approaches, and a larger rudder tab. W4052 joined the FIU at Ford and was eventually scrapped on 28 January 1946.

(Right) W4050 was used in a long and varied testing programme. In June 1942 it was fitted with two-stage Merlin 61s. Standing on the left is John de Havilland. Mosquito Museum via Ian Thirsk

in the starboard side of the cockpit instead of through a trapdoor in the floor as on the bomber version. To save a month of dismantling, transport and reassembly, W4052 was flown out of a field adjacent to the assembly hangar on 15 May 1941 by Geoffrey de Havilland Jr. W4050 was used to help eliminate problems on W4052, not least of which concerned armament and exhaust systems. (Flash eliminators later had to be fitted to the machine guns on the NF.II to prevent the crew being dazzled when they were fired at night.) The cooling intake shrouds for the 'Saxophone' type exhausts tended to overheat and even burn through after prolonged use. Flame-dampers prevented the giveaway exhaust-glow at night but they inhibited performance. The problems became so great that Frank B. Halford, head of de Havilland Engine Division, felt moved to say that 'next time it would be better to design the aircraft around the exhaust system!' Multiple ejector, open-ended exhaust stubs solved the problem and were fitted to PR.VIII, B.IX and B.XVI models with a resulting quantum leap in performance, the B.IV, for instance, gaining an additional 10–13mph (16–21kph) as a result.

On 21 June 1941, the Air Ministry finally decided on the composition of the Mosquitoes they had contracted de Havillands to build. Apart from five prototypes (one bomber, one PR and three fighter), nineteen aircraft were to be PR models and 176 fighters. At this time the further fifty Mosquitoes ordered were unspecified. In July the Air Ministry finally confirmed that these would be unarmed bombers. The irony was that in the same month the Mosquito became the world's fastest operational

1   Rudder Mass Balance.
2   Rudder Upper Hinge.
3   Rudder Trim Tab.
4   Rudder Trim Tab Linkage.
5   Pitot Head.
6   Aerial.
7   Fin Structure.
8   Rudder Structure.
9   Starboard Elevator.
10 Elevator Mass Balance.
11 Elevator Internal Mass
    Balance.
12 Tailcone.

13 Rear Navigation Light.
14 Elevator Trim Tab.
15 Port Elevator.
16 Tailwheel retraction
    Mechanism.
17 Tailwheel Leg.
18 Anti-shimmy Sunderstrand
    Tailwheel
19 Bulkhead No. 7.
20 Bulkhead No. 6.
21 Fin Attachment.
22 Rudder Control Linkage.
23 Control Cables.

24 Green/Amber ventral
    Identification Lamps.
25 Bulkhead No. 5.
26 Flare Chute.
27 Aft Camera Mounting Boxes.
28 Williamson F.24 Camera.
29 Fuselage Longerons.
30 Aft Access Door.
31 Bulkhead No.4.
32 Transmitter/Receiver.
33 De-Icing Reservoir.
34 Bulkhead No. 3.
35 Hydraulic Fluid Reservoir.

De Havilland DH98 Mosquito B.Mk.IV.

36 Dingy Stowage.
37 H.T. Power Unit.
38 Aerial Mast.
39 Forward Spar Wing Attachment.
40 Bulkhead No.2.
41 T.1154 Transmitter.
42 Flap Jack Inspection/Access
    Panel.
43 Pilots Seat and Harness.
44 Rear Vision Blister.
45 Control Column.
46 Folding Navigation Table.
47 Instrument Panel.
48 Outboard Flap.
49 Aileron Trim Tab.
50 Aileron.
51 Formation Light.
52 Navigation Light.

53 Removable Wingtip.
54 De Havilland Three-blade
    Hydromatic Propeller.
55 Engine Nacelle.
56 Exhaust Flame Damping
    Shroud.
57 Spinner
58 Bomb Aimer's Side Window.
59 Bomb Aimer's Optically Flat
    Aiming Windscreen.
60 Bomb Aimer's Kneeling
    Cushion.
61 Hand-Held Fire Extinguisher.

62 Oil and Coolant Radiators.
63 Coolant Header Tank.
64 12 Cylinder, 27 Litre Rolls
    Royce Merlin Engine.
65 Engine Exhaust Stubs.
66 Engine Bearers.
67 Air Intake.
68 Undercarriage Oleo Fairing.
69 Wheel Axle.
70 Mainwheel Tyre.

71 Wheel Hub and Brake Unit.
72 Mudguard.
73 Undercarriage Doors.
74 Wing Leading Edge.
75 Front Spar.
76 Wing Ribs.
77 Rear Spar.
78 Aileron Control Linkage.
79 Fuel Tank.
80 Inboard Flap.

KB471, Canadian built B.XXV fitted with Merlin 225s. via Philip Birtles

aircraft, a distinction it would enjoy for the next 2½ years. On 18–19 July during further speed trials, W4050, fitted with Merlin 61 engines, reached 433mph (697kph) at 28,500ft (8,690m)! Multiple ejector exhausts were a contributory factor. On 20 October W4050 achieved a speed of 437mph (703kph) in level flight! Using two-stage Merlin 77s, W4050 – which made its last flight around December 1943 – shaded this with a maximum speed of 439mph (706kph) in level flight.

In addition to the construction totals agreed on 21 June the Air Ministry further specified that the last ten aircraft (W4064–72) from the nineteen originally ordered in Contract 69990 on 1 March 1940 as PR versions, could be converted to unarmed bombers also. These ten aircraft came to be known as the B.IV Series I.

Prime Minister Winston Churchill, flanked by Sir Geoffrey de Havilland to his right, and company chairman, Mr Alan S. Butler to his left, tours the Hatfield factory on 19 April 1943. BAe

(Middle) HX956, a Mk VI built at Hatfield in 1943. via Shuttleworth Collection

(Bottom) FB.VIs of 82 Squadron in Burma, 1945. Mosquitoes suffered badly in the Far East climate and several aircraft crashed after shedding wings because of structural failures. On 13 September 1944, HP886 of 82 Squadron crashed whilst making dummy attacks on another aircraft and the crew were killed. Further structural failures led to the grounding of all Mosquitoes in India in 1944, and again in 1945. via Ron Mackay

W4072, the prototype B.IV bomber, flew for the first time on 8 September 1941. The fifty B.IV Series II bombers differed from the Series I in having a larger bomb bay to increase the payload to four 500lb (230kg) bombs instead of the Series I's four 250 pounders (115kg).

This was made possible by C. Tim Wilkins, R.E. Bishop's Assistant Chief Designer, who shortened the tail stabilizer of the 500lb (230kg) bomb so that four of these larger weapons could be carried. Twenty-seven B.IV Series II (W4066 was the only PR.IV Series I) were later converted to PR.IV reconnaissance aircraft, with three additional fuel tanks in the bomb bay, while twenty B.IVs were modified by DH, Vickers-Armstrong and Marshalls to carry a 4,000lb (1,810kg) bomb.

Canadian-built FB.26s fresh off the production lines at Downsview. Altogether, 191 FB.26s were built, the most numerous of the 1,076 Mosquitoes that were built in the Dominion. via Graham M. Simons

FB.40 A52-1, the first FB.40 (identical to the British FB.VI) built at Bankstown, NSW, for the RAAF. A52-1 is fitted with two Packard Merlin 31s and first flew on 23 July 1943. Deliveries of the first Mk 40s to the RAAF began on 4 March 1944 and 209 were built before de Havilland Aircraft Pty ended production in June 1948 with A52-212. A52-1 was lost on 14 June 1944 at RAAF Laverton when an air bottle burst while being refilled. via Shuttleworth Collection

output would be badly needed because in July the Air Ministry confirmed that it was looking to de Havillands to produce 150 Mosquitoes a month. Eighty would have to be built at Hatfield, while thirty would be built by Second Aircraft Group (SAG), a widely dispersed shadow scheme first conceived in 1940 (when de Havillands had considered building Armstrong Whitworth Albemarles), and forty in Canada.

By September 1941 it was anticipated that by 1942 Mosquitoes would be coming off the production lines at the rate of 200 (ninety fighters and, with Canadian production included, 110 bombers) a month. Canadian production though, was to suffer as a result of the climate. The wooden jigs used to make the fuselage varied considerably. Heating the glue used in the half shells of the fuselage to make it set fast, and the humidity of Toronto, which is on the Great Lakes, caused the 40ft (12m) long wooden moulds to vary so much that concrete moulds finally had to be used.

By the end of January 1942 contracts awarded to de Havillands totalled 1,378 Mosquitoes of all variants, including twenty T.III trainer versions and 334 FB.VI bombers by the SAG at Leavesden. Additionally, 400 more were planned to be built by de Havilland Canada. From now on, there was no looking back.

The Mosquito's place in history was assured.

Fortunately, as plans for Mosquito production materialized at Hatfield, Tiger Moth production had moved out to Morris Motors at Cowley near Oxford, and Dominie production had moved to Brush at Loughborough. While Hatfield geared up for mass production of Mosquito aircraft, a second Mosquito line was planned for a new factory at Leavesden. To take a leaf out of Henry Ford's book, in May, Standard Motors had been approached with the idea of producing more Mosquitoes there. Their

Mosquito Specifications

	Span ft (m)	Length ft (m)	Height ft (m)	Wing Area sq.ft (sq.m)	All-up Weight lb (kg)	Max Speed mph (kph)	Cruise Speed mph (kph)	Initial Climb ft/min (m/min)	Ceiling ft (m)	Range miles (km)	Armament/ Max Bomb-load lb (kg)
PR.I	54ft 2in (16.5)	40ft 6in (12.3)	12ft 6in (3.81)	454 (42)	19,670 (8,920)	382 (615)	255 (410)	2,850 (869)	35,000 (10,670)	2,180 (3,510)	
F.II/NF.II	"	"	"	"	18,547 (8,411)	370 (595)	255 (410)	3,000 (914)	36,000 (10,970)	1,705 (2,740)	4 × mg/4 × 20mm
T.III	"	"	"	"	16,883 (7,656)	384 (618)	260 (418)	2,500 (762)	37,500 (11,430)	1,560 (2,510)	
B.IV	"	40ft 9½in (12.4)	"	435 (40)	21,462 (9,733)	380 (611)	265 (426)	2,500 (762)	34,000 (10,360)	2,040 (3,280)	2,000 (910)
B.IV (4,000lb conv)	"	"	"	"	22,570 (10,235)	380 (611)	265 (426)	"	25,000 (7,620)	1,430 (2,300)	4,000 (1,810)
FB.VI	"	40ft 6in (12.3)	"	"	22,258 (10,094)	378 (603)	255 (410)	2,850 (869)	33,000 (10,060)	1,855 (2,980)	4 × mg/4 × 20mm, 8 × RP
PR.VIII	"	"	"	"	21,395 (9,702)	436 (700)	258 (415)	2,500 (762)	38,000 (11,580)	2,550 (4,100)	
B.IX	"	44ft 6in (13.6)	"	454 (42)	22,850* (10,362)	408 (656)	250 (402)	2,850 (869)	36,000 (10,970)	2,450 (3,940)	2*–4,000 (910–1,810)
PR.IX	"	"	"	"	22,000 (9,977)	408 (656)	250 (402)	2,850 (869)	38,000 (11,580)	2,450 (3,940)	
NF.XII	"	40ft 6in (12.3)	"	"	19,700 (8,934)	370 (595)	255 (410)	3,000 (914)	36,000 (10,970)	1,705 (2,740)	4 × 20mm
NF.XIII	"	"	"	"	20,000 (9,070)	370 (595)	255 (410)	3,000 (914)	34,500 (10,520)	1,860 (2,990)	4 × 20mm
NF.XV	62ft 6in (19.1)	44ft 6in (13.6)	"	"	17,600 (7,982)	412 (412)	230 (370)	3,500 (1,067)	43,000 (13,110)	1,030 (1,660)	4 × mg
B.XVI	54ft 2in (16.5)	"	"	"	23,000 (10,431)	408 (656)	245 (394)	2,800 (853)	37,000 (11,280)	1,485 (2,390)	4,000 (1,810)
PR.XVI	"	"	"	"	22,350 (10,136)	415 (668)	250 (402)	2,900 (884)	38,500 (11,730)	2,450 (3,942)	
NF.XVII	"	40ft 6in (12.3)	"	"	19,200 (8,707)	370 (595)	255 (410)	3,000 (914)	36,000 (10,970)	1,705 (2,740)	4 × 20mm/4 × mg
FB.XVIII	"	40ft 9½in (12.4)	"	"	23,274 (10,555)	"	"	"	"	"	1 × 57mm
NF.XXX	"	44ft 6in (13.6)	"	"	21,600 (9,796)	407 (655)	250 (402)	2,850 (869)	38,000 (11,580)	1,300 (2,090)	4 × 20mm

continued overleaf

	Span ft (m)	Length ft (m)	Height ft (m)	Wing Area sq.ft (sq.m)	All-up Weight lb (kg)	Max Speed mph (kph)	Cruise Speed mph(kph)	Initial Climb ft/min (m/min)	Ceiling ft (m)	Range miles (km)	Armament/ Max Bomb-load lb (kg)
TR.33	"	40ft 6in (12.3)	"	"	23,850 (10,816)	376 (605)	262 (422)	1,820 (555)	30,100 (9,170)	1,265 (2,040)	
PR.34	"	"	"	"	22,100 (10,022)	425 (684)	300 (483)	2,000 (610)	43,000 (13,110)	3,340 (5,370)	
B.35	"	"	"	"	23,000 (10,430)	422 (679)	276 (444)	2,700 (823)	42,000 (12,800)	1,750 (2,820)	4,000 (1,810)
NF.38	"	41ft 2in (12.5)	"	"	21,400 (9,705)	404 (650)	"	"	36,000 (10,970)	"	4 × 20mm
TT.39	"	43ft 4in (13.2)	"	"	23,000 (10,431)	299 (481)	"	"	"	"	
FB.40	"	40ft 6in (12.3)	"	"	22,258 (10,094)	378 (608)	255 (410)	2,400 (732)	33,000 (10,058)	1,855 (2,980)	4 × mg/4 × 20mm, 8 × RP

FB.VIs on the production line at the Standard Motor Co. works at Coventry. Standard Motors built 1,066 Mosquitoes, all of them FB.VIs. via Air Research Publications

CHAPTER TWO

Photo-Recce

Reconnaissance in Europe and the Far East

On 10 June 1941 Mosquito I W4051 flew for the first time. The following month, on 13 July, W4051 was handed over to No 1 Photographic Reconnaissance Unit (PRU) at Benson, Oxfordshire. W4054 and W4055 followed, on 22 July, and 8 August respectively, and the three aircraft became the first Mosquitoes to be taken on charge by the RAF. These unarmed PR.I Mosquitoes made their operational debut on 17 September 1941 when W4055, crewed by S/L Rupert Clerke and Sgt Sowerbutts, made a daylight photo-reconnaissance (PR) of Brest, La Pallice and Bordeaux. They were pursued by three Bf 109s but the PR.I easily outpaced them at 23,000ft (7,000m) and returned safely. A second photo-reconnaissance was made in W4055 three days later, when F/L Taylor DFC and Sgt Horsfall flew to Sylt-Heligoland. In October the three Mosquitoes carried out sixteen successful sorties, all of them to Norway.

By spring 1942 the PRU at Benson was in need of additional PR.Is, only nine having been built. During April to June 1942 four NF.IIs – DD615, 620, 659, and W4089, all without long-range tanks – were diverted to the PRU, and in December, two B.IV bomber variants – DZ411 and DZ419 – arrived. Ground crew at Benson installed the three vertical and one oblique cameras aboard each of the machines and they were pressed into service. On 7 May F/L Victor Ricketts flew the furthest flight over enemy territory so far when he used DK284, a modified Mk IV, to photograph Dresden, Pilsen and Regensburg, returning after six hours. On 10 June a 7¾-hour sortie was flown from Benson to La Spezia, Lyons and Marseilles. Ricketts was killed on 11 July when he and his navigator, Boris Lukhmanoff, failed to return from a sortie in W4089 to Strasbourg and Ingolstadt.

On 14 May, meanwhile, W/C Ring used DD615, the first of the modified NF.IIs, to photograph Alderney. On 25 May F/L

Ricketts used it to photograph targets in France and on the 27th, F/L Gerry R. Wooll RCAF used DD615 to successfully photograph Saarbrucken and Amiens. Wooll was not so fortunate on 24 August, when he and Sgt John Fielden were dispatched on a PR sortie in DK310 to confirm a report that Italian warships were putting to sea. They were to obtain photos of Venice, Trieste, Fiume, and perhaps Pola, if conditions were right. DK310 took off from Benson and stopped at Ford to top off its tanks before proceeding uneventfully to Venice. However, as Wooll departed the area the glycol pump on the starboard engine began malfunctioning. The shaft had become slightly elliptical and fluid began escaping. Within a few seconds, the engine seized. Wooll found the aircraft too heavy and unbalanced to attempt to continue on one engine and his problems were compounded a few minutes later when the port engine began overheating. Wooll headed for Switzerland and managed to put down safely at Belp airfield near Berne. After landing, Fielden tried unsuccessfully to set the aircraft on fire before the two men were marched off to a small village camp at Yen. After four months Wooll and Fielden were repatriated as part of an exchange deal which allowed two interned Bf 109 pilots to leave for Germany. (The Mosquito was retained by the Swiss, who later used it as a turbine test bed aircraft). Wooll returned to flying, as a test pilot for de Havilland in Canada.

On 19 October 1942 'H' and 'L' Flights of the Photographic Reconnaissance Unit at Leuchars were merged to form 540 Squadron. That same day, 544 Squadron formed at Benson, equipped with Ansons, Wellington IVs and Spitfire PR.IVs. In the main, 540 Squadron were used to photograph German capital ships in Baltic waters and North Germany, later the Mediterranean also. On 8 March 1943 the Commanding Officer (CO), W/C M.J.B.

Young DFC, in Mk VIII DZ364, became the first Mosquito pilot to photograph Berlin. 540 Squadron also carried out battle-damage assessment and target reconnaissance at such places as the German rocket research site at Peenemünde on the Baltic coast. It was on 12 June 1943, when F/L R.A. Lenton in a Mosquito took photos of a V-2 rocket lying horizontally on a trailer at Peenemünde that the attention of RAF intelligence at Medmenham was aroused. On 23 June F/Sgt E.P.H. Peek brought back such clear photos of rockets on road vehicles that news was relayed immediately to Prime Minister Winston Churchill. In all, six Mosquito pilots of 540 Squadron at Leuchars photographed Peenemünde and in August 1943 Peenemünde was bombed by the RAF and USAAF. In November, 540 Squadron became the first to take photographs of V-1 flying bombs.

544 Squadron, meanwhile, continued to use Ansons, Wellingtons and Spitfire PR.IVs in the PR and night photography roles over Europe, until in April 1943 Mosquito PR.IVs replaced the Wellingtons. In October, PR.IXs completed 544 Squadron's re-equipment. One of the crews who joined 544 in November 1943, was P/O John R. Myles DFC RCAF and his navigator, F/O Hugh R. Cawker, a fellow Canadian. The RCAF had interrupted Myles' tour with 541 Squadron and posted him to 410 Squadron RCAF at Colby Grange where the Canadians wanted him to form another PRU for them, but it fell through. He recalls:

PRU was a very interesting job, and we knew in advance of many occurrences such as the Dams raid, V-2 rockets and the like. It was also one of the few jobs where one had the opportunity for independent action. We operated singly, and although we were briefed for definite targets, how and when we got there was largely up to us. We also had authority to divert to photograph any convoys, or other unusual targets spotted.

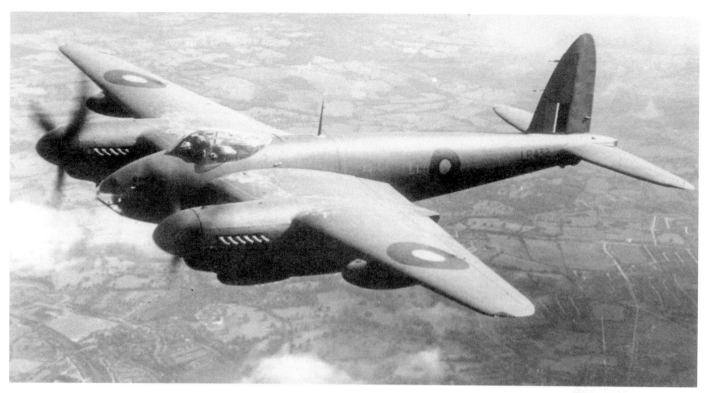

PR.IX LR432 in flight. Ninety PR.IX models were built, the first two production aircraft being delivered to 540 Squadron at Benson on 29 May 1943. With underwing tanks the PR.IX could cover 2,450 miles (3,940km) at a cruising speed of 250mph (400kph), ideal for photographing Nazi rocket research centres and test sites. via RAF Marham

(Right) **PR.IX LR412 in flight. A small blister on the cabin roof was a standard feature of the Mk IX although this aircraft and LR432** *(above)* **have not had them fitted.** via Shuttleworth Collection

We covered the whole of Europe in daylight from Norway to Gibraltar, and inland as far as Danzig and Vienna. On one trip we landed at a detachment at San Severo just north of the Foggia Plain in Italy. From there we did a sortie over Yugoslavia.

While covering targets in the south of France on 20 January 1944 in MM242, over Toulouse we had to feather the prop on the port engine due to low oil pressure caused by a split in the 'banjo' union [oil pipe]. We first thought of going to Corsica but we decided there was too much

water to fly over and we were not sure where the aerodromes were, anyway. We next considered returning to base, but I knew there was a lot of activity on the north French coast that day and I did not like the idea of coming out through it at 10,000ft [3,050m] on one engine. Besides, if anything did happen on the way it would mean walking all the way back again.

Finally we decided to set course for Gibraltar. I did not know what our petrol consumption would be on one engine and I did not think we had enough to reach Gib, but we figured we

Long range fuel tanks installed in the bomb bay of late version PR Mosquitoes permitted 9-hour sorties over Europe. Graham M. Simons

would fly as far as possible, then bail out and walk the rest of the way. After two hours on one engine we were getting a bit tired, but we had computed our petrol consumption again and it proved to be less than the first estimate. If only that engine would hold out! After three hours we found ourselves over the Pyrenees mountains at 14,000ft [4,270m] with about one hour left. We flew over the mountains full of expectancy, and we pin-pointed ourselves on the coast at Malaga. There, silhouetted against the sinking sun was the Rock of Gibraltar. We circled the Rock at 10,000ft [3,050m], descended to 2,000ft [610m] over the runway, and fired off the colours of the day. I then made my first single engined landing in a Mosquito after spending 6½ hours in the air, 3½ hours of which were on one engine over the Pyrenees and it did not even heat up.

F/L Peter Farlow and F/L E.E.G. 'Dicky' Boyd of 540 Squadron were not as fortunate, on 15 May, during a similar operation (their twenty-fifth), to the south of France, to cover about ten airfields as part of the preparations for the southern invasion. Dicky Boyd explains:

Whilst over the fourth target we were 'jumped' by a dozen Me's. We turned tail and headed off north going flat out, and although we were able gradually to pull away from them, it was not

before they had holed a fuel tank. Fortunately, there was no fire but on checking the gauge we found that we had very little juice left – it was streaming out like white smoke behind us. We had to find a suitable spot to put down on. Peter put her down [near Chateauroux], wheels up of course – a superb landing. The props were a tangled mess, there were a few splinters of wood, and the perspex nose was shattered, otherwise we were intact! As usual, the special detonator canister would not work, but I was able to open a 'chute' in the nose and fire a Verey light into it to 'get it going'. We were caught by a German motorcycle and sidecar while crossing a road and a week later we were in Stalag Luft III.

In March 1944 544 Squadron received PR.XVI aircraft, while 540 had to wait until July 1944. G.W.E. 'Bill' Newby, a navigator in 544 Squadron, flew in the prototype PR.XVI (MM258, a converted B.XVI), the first aircraft in the world (apart from the pre-war Bristol Type 138A) to be fitted with a pressurized cabin. He recalls:

I had the privilege of flying on cabin tests with my squadron commander, W/C D.W. Steventon DSO DFC, and Geoffrey de Havilland. We were having trouble with 'misting up' of windows and I was the smallest navigator on the two squadrons, so we flew '3-up' for short periods to carry out tests. Crews from Benson covered the

DD744, seen here with four machine guns fitted like the all-black NF.II behind, was converted from Mk II to PR.II standard and was used by 60 Squadron SAAF on the Squadron's first sortie from Castel Benito, Tripoli, on 15 February 1943. DH via Philip Birtles

PR.XVI NS502 'M' which was delivered to 544 Squadron on 23 May 1944 and operated over Europe until 21 February 1945 when it crashed. After repair this aircraft served with the Royal Navy at Fleetlands from 7 November 1947. *via Ron Mackay*

Dams project, keeping an eye on how full they were in readiness for the raid, May 1943, and photographing the after-damage and the chaos the Dambusters caused locally. Our job in 544 Squadron was to take photographs before and after air attacks, by both RAF night- and USAAF day-bombers (high-tailing it back and overtaking the USAAF on the way home) – we photographed Wiener Neustadt, north of Vienna before the USAAF arrived, then we cleared off to Lake Constance to take the Zeppelin sheds at Friedrichshafen, before returning to take the after-damage shots. We also took strategic photos of the coastal defences prior to the invasion of Europe; U-boat pens; pocket-battleships holed up in various French, German and Danish ports; oil-plants and aircraft factories deep in Germany; V-1 launching sites in the Pas de Calais; and even secret underground manufacturing sites in the Hartz mountains; and fields etc, which were to be used for dropping zones in France for SOE agents. For all of this, the Mosquito was ideal.

Most PR flights, in cinematograph terms, were very routine. Occasionally, they were spiced up with 'one-offs', like rushing to Copenhagen late on Whit Sunday afternoon, 1944, because one of our 'informers', sitting on a hillside in Sweden, was sure that the pocket-battleship *Deutschland* [renamed *Lutzow*], had disappeared from its moorings overnight and was thought to be free in the North Sea. We did a square search up the Kattegat and Skagerrak but could find no trace. So with light fading, we swept low over the Tivoli gardens and Hans Christian Andersen's Mermaid to the dockyard, only to find that the ship had been moved to a new berth and was disguised overnight to look like a tanker.

Other flights were more exciting: long hauls up the Baltic as far as Gydnia, equally long trips to Austria, and on over the Alps, to Venice and Yugoslavia, stopping overnight at Foggia (San Severo), after the landings in Italy; returning via Ajaccio, Corsica, or Gibraltar, to refuel, on one occasion taking photographs of Vesuvius in eruption. Another operation which took pride of place in the national press was a visit to the Gnome-Rhône aircraft engine works at Limoges on the morning of 9 February 1944 after it had been a special target of Bomber Command the night before. The place had been utterly devastated and we could easily see the damage from 30,000+ [9,140m] but we had been authorized to 'go low-level', so we could not pass up the chance to scream across at tree-top height to take really close 'close-ups', which later appeared in the press. My operational life on Mossies came to an abrupt end on 18 July, when we met four 'squirts' and they blew our nose off, hit both engines, put cannon shells in the cabin behind the pilot's armour-plate and we had to evacuate in quick time. We became guests of the Luftwaffe.

F/L Alan Morgan and Sgt Frank Baylis completed forty-six successful PR sorties in 544 Squadron, January–October 1944. Morgan recalls:

They were nearly always high level jobs, mostly without untoward incidents apart from the usual flak and occasional pursuit by fighters, which we could outpace if they were spotted in time for us to apply full power and accelerate to full speed. The Me 262 jet and the He 163 did not appear until about the end of our tour and we did not encounter either. The main threat arose during the actual photo runs when the navigator would be prone in the nose compartment, operating the cameras and directing the pilot, who would be concerned mainly with accurate flying, concentrating on the flying instruments. The rearward visibility from the pilot's station was not adequate, even from the perspex port window adjacent to his seat.

When we were en route in hostile skies, Frank would kneel on his seat, facing aft. He did not care for this but it proved a wise precaution. Although the Mosquito had the legs of the opposition, we could not afford the fuel to cruise on full power and thought that good look-out astern was imperative for the early sighting of any pursuer. The aircraft was at its most vulnerable when making photo-runs, especially on the 'railway recces' in which the navigator was constrained to remain in the nose compartment for perhaps 28 minutes at a time. The normal complement was two massive 36in [91cm] focal length cameras, one 6in [15cm] focal length camera for vertical photography at 6,000ft [1,830m] or below, and forward and side-facing cameras for really low-level work. With all the film magazines and control gear, this was a really significant load.

toppled. I felt dazed and ill and put out a mayday call on VHF. Manston gave me a course to steer and I landed shakily. But after a couple of hours on oxygen I was able to fly back to Benson. All our oxygen masks were modified the next day so some good came of it.

We had two further jousts with oxygen! One was on our seventh trip when I began to feel 'woozy' again while we were being 'flakked' when photographing naval units in Oslo Fjord. Sure enough, the supply indicator was in the red sector. Having finished our task, we dived away out to sea and returned at low level. The third

and wind up to maximum power. Meantime, our pursuers were diving on us and gaining rapidly and opening fire. I put the nose hard down with full power and tried to jink to disturb their aim while we made for some scanty cloud cover far below. I feared for the integrity of the aircraft structure, but we reached the cloud unscathed. After some hide-and-seek our pursuers gave up and we sneaked off home, duly chastened! I have since thought these were US fighters as there was a bombing raid in the area at about this time. I believe that a Mosquito of 540 Squadron went missing in this area at the time.

In 1944 540 Squadron went over totally to reconnaissance of the German rail transportation system in preparation for D-Day. Mosquitoes in 4, 140 and 400 Squadrons in 2nd TAF were also used to carry out reconnaissance over the continent for a limited period. 'B' Flight in 4 Squadron and 'A' Flight in 400 Squadron (their other flights were equipped with Spitfires) operated Mosquitoes from January until mid-May 1944 when both converted to the Spitfire XI. 140 Squadron, at Northolt, however, continued to operate its Mosquito PR.IXs on long-range photo reconnaissance from France after the invasion, and in 1945 PR.XVIs equipped with *Gee* and *Rebecca* were used on blind night photography operations.

Overseas, PR Mosquitoes were based in the Middle and Far East. The only Mosquito PR squadron in the Middle East theatre in 1943 was 683 Squadron, which formed at Luqa, Malta on 8 February. It was equipped initially with Spitfires before adding Mosquito IIs and VIs in May 1943 for a month of operations over Italy and Sicily. In early February 1944 680 Squadron at Matariya added Mk IXs and XVIs to its strength for photo-reconnaissance operations in the Mediterranean. Eventually, the Mosquitoes and Spitfire XIs became the standard equipment, and in August 1944 680 Squadron moved to San Severo to range over the Balkans and Hungary, finishing the war mapping Italy.

PR.XVI NS705 in flight over England with its port airscrew feathered for the benefit of the camera. via Ron MacKay

Mosquitoes in the Far East

In the Far East in 1943 the aerial reconnaissance of Burma and Malaya from bases in Ceylon and India proved one of the most difficult tasks facing South East Asia Command (SEAC). The success of the Mosquito in the PR role in Europe was viewed with envy in India where strike photographs

Our worst hazard arose from our life-preserving oxygen supply! It happened on our second trip. We were climbing outbound over the Channel when, at about 25,000ft [7,620m], I passed out. I later discovered that the oxygen supply had become disconnected from the face-piece of my mask. Frank told me later that he noticed we were flying erratically and he saw me 'hanging in the straps' as he put it. He pushed the stick forward and held the oxygen tube to my mask and I gradually came to. We were at 6,000ft [1,830m] in thick haze. The compass was swinging wildly, the engine temperatures were 'off the clock' and the gyro flying instruments had

(and thankfully last) encounter came when crossing the North Sea *en route* to Berlin. I saw Frank had passed out. The bayonet fitting of the tube which ran from his harness to the oxygen supply point had come adrift. I only had to get down from my seat and connect the pipe. He soon perked up and we completed the trip.

One of our most 'dodgy' encounters occurred on our tenth trip. We had just finished a long run in the Lyons area with Frank in the nose when we spotted a gaggle of fighters bearing down on us. We were at about 25,000ft [7,620m] with drop tanks still attached. It seemed a long time to shed these impediments

were taken from obsolescent Blenheim bombers and the only two camera-fitted B-25Cs of 681 Squadron at Dum Dum, Calcutta. These were the only aircraft that possessed the range and speed for long-range PR over the Bay of Bengal and the Rangoon area. At the beginning of April 1943 three Mosquito F.II Series 1s, and three FB.VIs, were allotted to 27 Squadron at Agartala. Three were for performance tests and familiarization and three were to be used in weathering trials during the coming rainy season under the supervision of Mr F.G. Myers, de Havilland's technical representative. However, late in the month, it was decided that the aircraft should supplement the unit's 'initial equipment' of Beaufighters for intruder operations.

It is reported that Major Hereward de Havilland, visiting 27 Squadron, was horrified to find that the Mk IIs were put to operational use and attempted to have them grounded because he considered that the casein glue with which they were bonded was unlikely to withstand insect attack and the tropical weather (the FB.VIs, still awaited, were supposedly bonded with 'waterproof' formaldehyde adhesive). It was rumoured that Major de Havilland attempted to damage the wing of one Mk II to ensure that it could not be flown. In the event, 27 Squadron flew the first Mosquito operation, a reconnaissance over Burma on 14 May, and then used the Mk IIs again on only one occasion; one crashed and the other was damaged by ground fire on 5 June.

In August, when the aircraft situation in 681 Squadron became so bad, (the two B-25Cs had been in use for over 12 months) the Air Ministry agreed that Mosquitoes could be converted to PR aircraft at No.1 CMU (Central Maintenance Unit), Kanchrapara. Two Mosquitoes and their flight crews were transferred to the twin-engined Flight of 681 Squadron, and these were followed by three newly arrived Mk VIs. All five had been fitted with a camera, but not the four cameras of the 'PRU type', nor did they have additional fuel tanks, or in the case of the Mk IIs, provision for fitting underwing fuel tanks. During September 681 Squadron flew eight PR sorties over vast areas of Burma. On 29 September 1943 684 Squadron formed at Dum Dum from the twin-engined Flights of 681 Squadron with Mk IIs, VIs and IXs and a few Mitchell IIIs and continued operations with the early aircraft until they were replaced with nine pressurized PR.XVIs in February 1944.

The feared deterioration of adhesive did not happen despite the aircraft being continually exposed to high temperature and humidity and so effective was 684 Squadron's use of the PR Mosquitoes, that the Air Ministry decided, in January 1944, to equip twenty-two bomber and strike squadrons with FB.VIs to replace Vengeances and some Beaufighters. De Havilland were to produce replacement airframe components at Karachi. (At Yelahanka, near Bangalore, 1672 MCU was established to begin a conversion programme to FB.VIs, beginning with 45 Squadron in March 1944. 82 Squadron began conversion at Kolar in July and were followed by 47 and 110 Squadrons). It seemed likely that 681 Squadron's efforts would produce record photographic coverage in November but all Mosquito operations came to an abrupt end on 12 November, when, following a series of accidents, a signal to all units required Mosquito aircraft to be grounded pending inspection.

The effects of all of this were far-reaching. The intended manufacture of components at Karachi was abandoned and the re-equipping of squadrons delayed. Early in 1945, 45, 82, 47 and 110 Squadrons received new replacement aircraft and continued operations. 84 Squadron received FB.VIs in February 1945 and 89 were given NF.XIXs in May, but the large scale re-equipping of

squadrons never took place (211 and 176 Squadrons never saw action with FB.VIs before the end of hostilities).

684 Squadron operated long-range PR sorties during the Burma campaign, regularly going to the Andaman Islands, Rangoon and the Burma–Thailand railway. Survey flying using Mk IXs and XVIs from Calcutta took place before the squadron moved to Alipore for the remainder of the war. In June 1945 the PR.34, a VLR (Very Long Range) version of the Mk XVI, entered service, and based on the recently completed airfield at Cocos Island, made reconnaissance missions to Kuala Lumpur and Port Swettenham. By the end of July some twenty five sorties had been carried out by PR.34s from Cocos, and thirteen more by VJ-Day.

In Europe, meanwhile, 540 Squadron had ended the war making a complete photo reconnaissance of the whole of France, starting in March 1945 and finishing in November that year, when the squadron returned to Benson, disbanding there on 30 September 1946. After VE-Day 400 Squadron remained in Germany with BAFO until it disbanded at Luneberg on 7 August 1945. In February 1945, 680 Squadron's PR.XVIs at San Severo finished the mapping of Italy and flew to Egypt to work solely as a survey squadron. They then moved to Palestine to survey that country.

Mosquito Reconnaissance Squadrons/Units 1941–1946

Unit	Theatre	Period	Types
1 PRU	UK	17.9.41–10.42	PR.I/II/IV
521	UK	8.42–31.3.43	PR.IV
540	UK	19.10.42–3.53[1]	PR.IV/IX/XVI/32/34/34A
683	Malta	3.43–c3.43	PR.IV
544	UK	4.43–10.45	PR.IV/IX/XVI/32/34
543	UK	6.43–10.43	PR.IV (training)
4(B Flt)	2nd TAF	8.43–5.44	PR.XVI
681	India	8.43–11.43	II/PR.IV
684	India/Burma	29.9.43–31.8.46	II/PR.VI/IX/XVI/34
140	2nd TAF	11.43–11.45	PR.IX/PR.XVI
400 RCAF	2nd TAF	12.43–7.8.45	PR.XVI
680	Middle East	16.2.44–31.8.46	PR.IX/XVI
653rd USAAF[2]	UK (WR*)	7.44–5.45	PR.XVI
654th USAAF[2]	UK (PR*)	7.44–5.45	PR.XVI

Also:
Pathfinder Navigation Training Unit (PFFNTU)
Photographic Development Unit

[1] Disbanded 30.9.46. Reformed 1.12.47
[2] 25th Bomb Group (also received 16 F.8 versions but unused)

*PR–Photo Reconnaissance. WR–Weather Reconnaissance

CHAPTER THREE

Bombs on Target
The Pioneers of 2 Group

By November 1941, 105 Blenheim Squadron had decamped to the 2 (Light Bomber) Group airfield at Swanton Morley, Norfolk, to lick its wounds after suffering high losses on low-level anti-shipping operations from Malta. W/C Peter Simmons DFC and his battered crews badly needed a morale-boost – the squadron had been decimated like almost everyone else in 2 Group in the Battle of France in 1940. It came, on 15 November 1941, when Hatfield's Chief Test Pilot, Geoffrey de Havilland Jr., treated them to a quite breathtaking performance in W4064 – 'Mk IV bomber conversion type'. Crews realised that the new Mosquito bomber was something special when Geoffrey de Havilland whipped it across the grass expanse at little more than 500ft (150m) at a speed approaching 300mph (480kph). He then put W4064 into a vertical bank at about 3,000ft (900m), before turning a circle so tight and at such a speed that vapour trails streamed from his wing tips.

Geoffrey de Havilland Jr. flew the new bomber back to Hatfield the next day, but W4066, the first Mosquito bomber to enter RAF service, arrived on 17 November watched by the AOC 2 Group, AVM d'Albiac, and his staff. Three more Mk IVs – W4064, W4068 and W4071 – were delivered at intervals to Swanton Morley by Geoffrey de Havilland and Pat Fillingham. In December the squadron moved to Horsham St Faith, near Norwich. Deliveries were held back by the need to develop the shortened-vane 500lb (230kg) bomb so that the new bomber could carry four of them instead of four 250 pounders (115kg), and by mid-May 1942 only eight Mk IVs had been taken on charge by 105 Squadron. One of the aircraft was fitted with Lorenz beam approach equipment, while DK286 was fitted with the new Mk XIV bomb sight for testing.

No 2 Group was anxious to despatch its new wonder aircraft on the first operation as soon as possible. At dawn on 31 May 1942, only a few hours after the 1,000 bomber raid on Cologne, four of the Mk IVs, armed with 500lb (230kg) bombs and cameras, harassed and photographed the devastated city. S/L A.R. Oakeshott DFC, followed later by P/O W.D. Kennard, took off from Horsham before the heavies had returned and were followed, shortly before lunchtime the following day, by P/O Costello-Bowen with W/O Tommy Broom, and F/L J.E. Houlston with F/Sgt J.L. Armitage. Oakeshott flew at 24,000ft (7,310m) over the battered and blasted city and added his four bombs to the devastation, but with smoke reaching to 14,000ft (4,270m), his F24 camera was rendered useless. Kennard failed to return, his aircraft being hit by anti-aircraft fire. Costello-Bowen and Houlston added their bombs to the conflagration from high-level to prolong the night of misery for the inhabitants and bomb disposal teams. In the late afternoon S/L P.J. Channer DFC took off and flew in thick cloud to within 60 miles (97km) of Cologne before diving down at almost 380mph (610kph) to low level to take photographs of the damage. Channer quickly realised that this highly successful approach would be particularly effective for future Mosquito bombing operations.

On the evening of 1 June two Mk IVs returned to Cologne to bomb and reconnoitre the city. One failed to return. Then, just before dawn on 2 June, 18 hours after the 1,000 bomber raid on Essen, F/L D.A.G. Parry and F/O Victor Robson flew a lone 2hr 5 minute round trip to Cologne armed with four 500lb (230kg) bombs and a camera to stoke up the fires and observe the damage. However, thick smoke made the latter task impossible. On 8 June, 139 Squadron was formed at Horsham St Faith by using crews and some Mk IVs from 105 Squadron. W/C Peter Shand DFC assumed command and 139 Squadron flew its first operation on 25/26 June with a low level raid on the airfield at Stade near Wilhelmshaven. S/L Jack Houlston returned after dark just as the RAF heavies were heading for Bremen, in the third of the 1,000 bomber raids. Two of 105 Squadron's Mk IVs flew reconnaissance over the city after the raid and four more went to reconnoitre other German cities to assess damage and bring back photographs.

On 2 July, 139 Squadron sent six Mk IVs to bomb the U-boat yards at Flensburg in the first mass low level strikes by the aircraft. Two aircraft were shot down by German fighters. G/C J.C. MacDonald was made PoW while W/C A.R. Oakeshott DFC and F/O V.F.E. Treherne DFM, were killed. S/L Houlston came off the target pursued by three Fw 190s, and F/L G.P. Hughes was chased by two more fighters after he had been hit by flak. Both pilots made their escape hugging the wave tops, and, applying extra boost, they easily outpaced their pursuers. (A perspex blister was later added to the canopy roof to permit the navigator to kneel on his seat facing aft to obtain a clearer view of pursuing fighters.)

On 11 July it was the turn of 105 Squadron to bomb the yards at Flensburg, the low-level raid serving as one of two diversions for forty-four Lancasters attacking Danzig. P/O Laston returned with part of his fin blown away by flak while F/L Hughes and F/O T.A. Gabe were killed when their Mosquito crashed, possibly as a result of flying too low. Sgt Peter W.R. Rowland flew so low that he hit a roof and returned to Horsham with pieces of chimney pot lodged in the nose.

July was significant for a number of daylight cloud-cover raids to Germany and, whenever clear skies dawned, the B.IVs flew high level 'Siren Raids' over Germany at night to cause maximum disruption to war workers and their families. The sorties, however, were not without their own casualties. On 16 July, a B.IV failed to return from a bombing sortie to Wilhelmshaven,

33

and another was lost, on 28 July. Four B.IVs were lost in August, the last failing to return on the 27th when four were dispatched to targets in Germany. One of the Mk IVs dropped three bombs on Bremen and scored a direct hit on part of the Vulkan shipyard which stopped production for several days.

On 3 August 1942 W/C Hughie I. Edwards VC DFC, who had won the VC for his courageous leadership of 105 Squadron on a raid on Bremen on 4 July 1941, returned from Malta to take command of 105 Squadron again. From the outset the

bombed Hamburg and one bombed the Berlin area through thick cloud. George Parry dropped down through the layers but did not have enough height with which to bomb. He finally turned for home and headed back across the north coast of Germany and into Holland. At 1,000ft (300m), just off the Dutch coast, two 109s attacked Parry's Mk IV but although one put some shells into the Mosquito, Parry dropped down to sea level and soon outran them. Another Mk IV was not so fortunate and failed to return, believed shot down by enemy fighters.

Mosquito operation so far. To avoid interception the Mosquitoes flew across the North Sea at heights of just 50–100ft (15–30m), using dead reckoning all the way. Near the target two Fw 190s of 3/JG5 intercepted the Mk IVs and one shot down Carter's aircraft in flames. Rowland and Reilly were chased by the second Fw 190 until their attacker struck a tree and was forced to return to base. At least four bombs entered the roof of the Gestapo HQ, one had remained inside and failed to detonate and the three others crashed through the opposite wall before exploding. On the

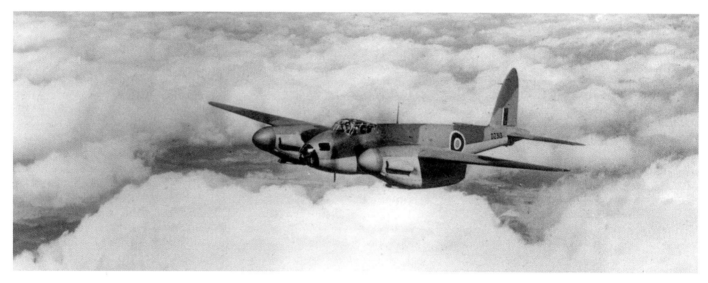

B.IV DZ313 of 105 Squadron in flight. This aircraft failed to return on 20 October 1942 following a raid on Hanover. F/Sgt L.W. Deeth and W/O F.E.M. Hicks were killed. via Shuttleworth Collection

uncompromising Australian led the Mosquitoes in the same courageous manner which had characterized his Blenheim operations. On 29 August, when two Mk IVs of 105 Squadron were dispatched to Pont-à-Vendin power station, Edwards and his navigator, F/O H.H. 'Bladder' Cairns DFC, were returning when they were attacked by about a dozen Fw 190s 40 miles (64km) inside enemy territory. The fighters approached from head-on before turning to give stern chase. Edwards easily outpaced them but not before his port engine had been hit by enemy fire. Edwards belly landed at Lympne while the second Mk IV also bellied in, at Oakington.

On 19 September six crews from 105 Squadron flew the first daylight Mosquito raid to Berlin. Two returned early with mechanical problems, while two more

On 25 September, four 105 Squadron crews, George Parry and 'Robbie' Robson, Pete Rowland and Dick Reilly, F/O Bristow and P/O Bernard Marshall, and F/Sgt G.K. Carter and Sgt W.S. Young, flew from Horsham St Faith to Leuchars, Scotland and refuelled and bombed up with four 11-second delayed action 500lb (230kg) bombs for a strike on the Gestapo Headquarters in Oslo. The raid had been requested by the Norwegian Government in Exile in London in response to reports received from the Norwegian Underground that morale in Norway needed a boost. A rally of *Hirdsmen* (Norwegian Fascists) and Quislings taking place in Oslo, between 25–27 September provided an extra impetus. The operation, led by Parry, meant a round trip of 1,100 miles (1,770km), and an air time of 4hr 45 minutes; the longest

night of 26 September listeners to the BBC Home Service heard that a new aircraft, the Mosquito, had been revealed officially for the first time by the RAF and that four had made a daring roof top raid on Oslo. Next day, when the first photo of a Mosquito was published, the caption said that 'armament may consist of four 20mm cannon and four .303in machine guns.'

Increase in Daylight Raids

On 29 September 1942 105 and 139 Squadrons began moving to Marham nearby. Marham had just been transferred from 3 Group to 2 Group and was destined to play a major role in Mosquito operations right up until March 1944. The first such operation from Marham was flown on

Direct hits are scored on the Gestapo HQ at Victoria Terrasse (far left) in Oslo by Mosquitoes of 105 Squadron on Friday 25 September 1942. The large white building (top left) is the university. Middle right is the central cupola on which the pilots saw the Nazi flag flying. BAe Hatfield

B.Mk.IV Series ii DK296 was flown on the Oslo Gestapo raid of 25 September 1942 by S/L D.A.G. 'George' Parry DFC and F/O Victor Robson of 105 Squadron. 'G-George' passed to S/L Bill Blessing DSO DFC RAAF, who crash-landed DK296 at Marham and broke its back. The aircraft was repaired and on 24 August 1943 was placed into store with 10 MU at Hullavington. In September 1943 it was issued to 305 Ferry Training Unit at Errol, Scotland where it was given Russian markings and trained Russian crews who were converting to Albemarles. On 20 April 1944 DK296 was ferried to the Soviet Union by a Russian crew, being officially accepted there on 31 August 1944 and subsequently going on to serve with the Red Air Force. via Graham M. Simons

1 October 1942 when three Mk IVs were dispatched. Two attacked a chemical works at Sluiskil and an oil depot at Ghent while the third returned from a sortie to Entvelde still carrying its bombs after they failed to release.

Nuisance raiding over Germany and the Low Countries remained the order of the day for the crews of 105 and 139 Squadrons, although, on 29/30 November, six Mk IVs of 105 Squadron flew the first Mosquito night operation of the war when five rail targets in Belgium were bombed without loss. In December, another milestone was reached, when, on the 6th the first all-out daylight raid was made by 2 Group, which dispatched eighty-four bombers to the Philips Stryp Group main works and the Emmasingel valve and lamp factory in Eindhoven, Holland. Ten Mosquitoes took part in 'Operation *Oyster*', as it was code-named, W/C Hughie Edwards VC DFC, leading eight Mk IVs of 105 Squadron and two of 139 Squadron to the Stryp works, while S/L J.E. Houlston AFC DFC of 139 Squadron carried out post-bomb damage assessment. The much faster Mosquitoes should have rendezvoused with the Bostons and Venturas at the target but they caught up with them at the Scheldt Estuary. Edwards had to slow the Mosquitoes to just 150mph (240kph) and fly at 50ft (15m) in order to stay behind them when they should have been flying to the Stryp Works at 270mph (435kph), before climbing to 1,500ft (460m), diving and releasing their bombs from 500ft (150m). F/O J.E. O'Grady and Sgt G.W. Lewis' Mosquito in 139 Squadron was hit in the engine, and trailing smoke and flames, crashed into the sea 30 miles (48km) off Den Helder. Both crew perished. Two other Mk IVs were forced to abort. In all, more than 60 tons of bombs hit the factories, which were very badly damaged, but fourteen aircraft were lost.

On 27 January 1943 Hughie Edwards led nine Mk IVs of 105 and 139 Squadrons in another daring low-level raid, this time on the Burmeister and Wain Diesel engine works at Copenhagen. Light flak from ships near the coast bracketed the formation on the way in. F/L J. Gordon DFC and F/O R.G. Hayes DFC aborted the operation when Gordon thought their aircraft had been hit. When the trailing edge of the starboard wing became enveloped in blue smoke Gordon decided to carry out evasive action, but in so doing, he hit a telegraph line and headed back to Norfolk with a damaged port

A precision bombing raid on the Stork Engineering and Diesel Works at Hengelo, Holland on 10 October 1942. via Graham M. Simons

(Right) **The navigator of a B.IV demonstrates how the Mk IV bomb sight was used, just as in heavy bombers.** Shuttleworth Collection

aileron. (Both men were killed on 5 November, returning from a raid on Leverkusen on one engine. In the circuit at Hardwick USAAF base they were reportedly refused clearance to land because of a truck on the runway. The aircraft struck the top of an oak tree and cartwheeled across a field before

leaving the target Sgt J.G. Dawson's Mosquito was seen to explode on the ground. He and Sgt R.H. Cox, navigator, died instantly.

Three days later, on 30 January, Mosquitoes bombed Berlin for the first time. Two attacks, one in the morning by three Mk IVs of 105 Squadron, led by S/L 'Reggie' W.

and their bombs rained down, disrupting the Reichsmarschall's speech for over an hour. The afternoon raid was not as successful and one Mosquito was shot down. S/L D.F.W. Darling DFC was killed.

In February Hughie Edwards left to take up a post at HQ Bomber Command, but

B.IV DZ353 'E' of 105 Squadron in formation with DZ367 'J'. DZ353 later served with 139 and 627 Squadrons in 8 Group (PFF), and failed to return from a raid on the marshalling yards at Rennes on 8 June 1944. F/L Bill Steere DFM and F/O 'Windy' Gale DFC RAAF, were killed. DZ367 failed to return from Berlin, 30 January 1943 when it was crewed by S/L D.F.W. Darling DFC and F/O W. Wright (both KIA). RAF Marham

bursting into flames.) Edwards and Cairns found the target only at the last moment and were on the point of returning, but made their attack then broke for the sea and home. Light flak at the target was intense and Edwards' Mosquito received two holes in the starboard nacelle. Five minutes after

Reynolds and P/O E.B. 'Ted' Sismore, and one in the afternoon, by three Mosquitoes of 139 Squadron, were timed to disrupt speeches in the main broadcasting station in Berlin by Hermann Göring and Dr. Joseph Goebbels, respectively. 105 Squadron arrived over Berlin at exactly 1100 hours

his successor, W/C G.P. Longfield remained only a short time, being killed in a mid-air collision. W/C John de Lacy Wooldridge DFC DFM assumed command of 105 Squadron in March. (Wooldridge, who added a DSO and a bar to his DFC, was one of the leading low-level Mosquito

B.IV DK338 of 105 Squadron in flight. On 1 May 1943 DK338 was launching for an operation to Eindhoven when an engine failed just after take off and the aircraft crashed near Marham, killing F/O O.W. Thompson DFC **RNZAF and F/O W.J. Horne** DFC.
via Shuttleworth Collection

(Right) **B.IV DZ464 'C-Charlie' of 139 Squadron, the only one of four to escape unharmed after a chase by two Fw 190s following an attack on Malines on 11 April 1943. This aircraft later failed to return on 21 May 1943 during an operation to the locomotive sheds at Orleans, its 17th 'op'. S/L R.G. Harcourt** DFC, **the CO, and W/O J. Friendly** DFM **SAAF were killed.**
RAF Marham

raiders and in 1944 he wrote a superb account of these raids, called *Low Attack*).

The final large-scale daylight Mk IV raid in 2 Group was on 27 May 1943, when fourteen Mosquitoes led by W/C Reggie Reynolds DSO DFC, and F/L Ted Sismore, set out to attack the Zeiss Optical Factory, and the Schott Glass Works, at Jena. Eight Mk IVs of 105 Squadron were to hit the Zeiss Works, while six of 139 would bomb the Schott Works. Eleven machines bombed the two targets with great accuracy, but the operation cost five aircraft. En route, two Mk IVs of 139 Squadron, crewed by F/L Sutton and F/O Morris, and F/O Openshaw and Sgt Stonestreet, collided west of Kassel and crashed. DZ467 'P' of 105 Squadron was lost in the attack while F/O Dixon and P/O Bush died when they crashed at Marham on the return while trying to land on one engine.

F/L W.S. 'Jock' Sutherland and P/O G.E. Dean of 139 Squadron were also killed when they crashed after hitting power cables while trying to land at Coltishall.

Morale in some bomber squadrons in 2 Group was low and it was certainly not helped by the news that 105 and 139 Squadrons were now to be transferred to 8 Group (Pathfinder) Bomber Command for a complete change of role.

CHAPTER FOUR

Night Fighting

Nocturnal Defensive and Offensive Operations

On 13 December 1941, 157 Squadron, commanded by W/C Gordon Slade, became the first Mosquito fighter squadron in Fighter Command when it reformed at Debden, Essex. It took delivery of its first T.III on 17 January 1942 when the Squadron had moved to Castle Camps to begin work up on the new fighter. Unfortunately, deliveries of the NF.II were slow to arrive and only fourteen were on strength by the end of March. Six others arrived during mid-April but three were minus complete AI (Airborne Interception) radar sets and only seven crews were trained to fly the aircraft. A similar situation persisted at Wittering where 151 Squadron, commanded by W/C Irving Stanley Smith DFC RNZAF, awaited NF.IIs to replace its Defiants. 'A' Flight received its first Mosquito (DD608) on 6 April but 'B' Flight would have to wait. Radar equipped night-fighters were desperately needed at this time because the Luftwaffe had launched a series of terror (known as *Baedeker*) raids against British cities of historic or aesthetic importance, as retribution for an attack by RAF Bomber Command on the historic city of Lübeck on 28/29 March. (The phrase originated from a press briefing given in Berlin on 24 April 1942 by Baron Gustav von Stumm, Deputy of the German Foreign Office Press Department who announced, 'We shall go all out to bomb every building in Britain marked with three stars in the *Baedeker* Guide'.) Exeter and Bath were the first to suffer Baedeker raids, with resultant heavy loss of life.

157 Squadron flew its first patrol on the night of 27/28 April when three NF.IIs (equipped with AI Mk V radar) joined just nineteen Beaufighters and Spitfires in opposing the twenty-six Luftwaffe aircraft that made the first *Baedeker* raid on Norwich. Although radar contacts were made, none of the attackers were intercepted, and cannon flash, exhaust manifold, and

cowling burning problems were manifest. (Worse, on 19 May, in the first of three NF.II crashes that month, a 157 Squadron aircraft suffered an engine failure and crashed at Castle Camps, killing both crew). On 28/29 April the Luftwaffe struck at York, killing eighty-three people.

F/L Pennington flew the first 151 Squadron Mosquito operation, in DD613, on 29/30 April, when about seventy-five German raiders operated over Britain. A Do 217 was chased by a 157 Squadron NF.II, but the fighter was spotted in the moonlight and contact was lost. On 3/4 May Exeter was again bombed, and on 4/5 May a two-wave attack on Cowes on the Isle of Wight resulted in the deaths of sixty-six people, with seventy more injured. On 8/9 May Norwich was again bombed, and although thirty-seven night-fighters rose to meet the raiders, they were powerless to stop them. Hull, and Poole were bombed and then, on the night of 29/30, it was the turn of Grimsby. But now the Mosquitoes began to bite back. F/L Pennington of 151 Squadron intercepted a damaged Heinkel 111H-6 and put several cannon shells into it from 400yd (370m). As Pennington closed for a second attack from 80yd (73m), the enemy returned fire, hitting the Mosquito in the starboard wing, tail and the port engine. Pennington's quarry was seen to be hit in the port wing and engine. It dived away on fire into the haze above the sea and contact was lost. Pennington flew 140 miles (225km) home on one engine. Well out over the North Sea P/O John Wain and F/Sgt Thomas S.G. Grieve in DD608 closed in on a Do 217E-4 of KG2. Wain opened fire and the enemy machine immediately burst into flames and started to fall towards the sea. They claimed it as a 'probable'. Another Do 217E-4 was probably destroyed south of Dover by S/L G. Ashfield of 157 Squadron.

On 24/25 June, when the Luftwaffe mounted an unsuccessful raid on

Nuneaton, five bombers were claimed destroyed by British defences. W/C Smith and his navigator F/L Kernon-Sheppard, scored 151 Squadron's first NF.II victories after intercepting three enemy aircraft within 30 minutes. At 23.30 an He 111 was intercepted at 8,000ft (2,440m). Smith closed to 300yd (275m) before opening fire, but the Heinkel dived away trailing fuel from its port tanks as a second approach was made. (That night an He 111H-6 of Erprp.u.Lehr. Kdo 17 was badly damaged by a Mosquito when flares on board exploded. Radio-operator Ofw Paul Wilhelm Krause, baled out, prematurely as it turned out, because the Heinkel limped back to Holland and landed safely. Krause's body was washed ashore at Pakefield on 5 July.) Ten minutes later, Smith was vectored on to Do 217E-4 F8+AC of II/KG40. This time he approached unseen to 100yd (90m) before opening fire. The Dornier dived abruptly into the sea and exploded. At 23.48 radar contact was made with another Do 217E-4 (U5+AB of I/KG2, flown by Lt Karl Von Manowarda). Smith closed and opened fire from 200yd (185m). Both the Dornier's wing tanks exploded and the aircraft was engulfed in flames. The New Zealander closed still further and fired a short burst to finish it off. U5+AB fell into the Wash.

The following night, 25/26 June, P/O John Wain and F/Sgt Tom Grieve of 151 Squadron shot down an He 111H-6 in the North Sea and on 26/27 F/L Moody and P/O Marsh destroyed a Do 217E-4 of 3/KG2 flown by Fw Hans Schrodel, when He 111 pathfinders and Ju 88s of KGr 506 and Do 217s of I, II, and III/KG2 raided Norwich. 151 Squadron went on the rampage in July shooting down four Dorniers. Wain and Grieve failed to return in DD623 on 10/11 August.

Despite the need for more Mosquito night-fighters over Britain, moves were set afoot to use the NF.IIs in offensive night-fighting, or intruder operations, on the continent. RAF bombers had begun to suffer increasing losses from Luftwaffe night-fighters and it was decided that RAF intruder aircraft roving over enemy airfields in France and the Low Countries could reduce the attacks on bomber streams. The first major support of bombers by night-fighter squadrons was on 30/31 May during the 1,000 bomber raid on Cologne when Hurricane IICs, Havocs and Bostons intruded over the continent. No radar-equipped aircraft were used as its operation over enemy territory was still banned. The much faster Mosquito ,was ideal for intruder operations, and converted NF.IIs, stripped of their Mk IV radar, and with increased fuel capacity, were used for intruding until 1943 when the FB.VI could be made available in numbers.

NF.II DZ230 YP-A of 23 Squadron flown by the CO, W/C Peter G. Wykeham-Barnes DSO DFC **over Valetta, in January 1943. The Squadron operated from Malta (Luqa), December 1942–September 1943.** Air Research Publications

MP469, the prototype NF.XV, at Hatfield, 16 September 1942. This aircraft was converted from a high-altitude bomber configuration and was intended for use against high-altitude Ju 86 reconnaissance bombers, but the threat evaporated before the NF.XVs, equipped with AI Mk VIII radar, could be used. via Graham M. Simons

Mosquito Intruders

First of the Mosquito intruder units was 264 Squadron at Colerne, which, since early 1942, had operated Defiant night-fighters. On 3 May it received its first Mosquito, a T.III, and on 13 June, the Squadron flew its first operational sorties

using NF.IIs. On 27/28 June a Do 217 was claimed as 'damaged' and on the 28/29th, F/O Hodgkinson forced down Uffz Rudolf Blankenburg over Creil as he made for home in a KG2 Do217E-2 after a raid on Weston-Super-Mare. Their first air-to-air victory occurred on 30/31 July when a Ju 88A-4 was destroyed. Late in 1942 *Night*

Rangers to airfields in France were flown. *Rangers* were low level operations on moonlight nights, mainly against railway rolling stock and road transport, although one could shoot down enemy aircraft if they were encountered.

23 Squadron at Ford meanwhile, had received a T.III for training on 7 June 1942.

Eventually, twenty-five of the modified NF.IIs would be issued to the squadron (which was destined for Malta before the end of the year) but for a time the only one available for intruding was 'S-Sugar'. The first intruder sortie was flown in this aircraft on 6/7 July by W/C Bertie Rex 'Sammy' O'Bryen Hoare, one of the leading intruder pilots of his generation, and W/O J.F. Potter. Sammy's first successful intruder kill was in a Havoc, on 3/4 May, when he got an He 111 for certain and a Ju 88 as a probable. The 6/7 July sortie proved uneventful but the following night Sammy dispatched a Do 217 16 miles (26km) east of Chartres with three short bursts of cannon fire. On 8/9 July S/L K.H. Salisbury-Hughes, in 'S-Sugar' again, destroyed a Do 217 over Etampes and an He 111 at Evreux.

In August, 85 Squadron at Hunsdon started intruder patrols with the NF.II.

Britain, as well as launching several small-scale night raids. On 22/23 August, 157 Squadron scored its first victory when the CO, W/C Gordon Slade, and P/O P.V. Truscott, shot down a Do 217E-4 of 6/KG2, flown by twenty-nine-year-old ex-Lufthansa pilot Oblt Hans Walter Wolff, 20 miles (32km) from Castle Camps. In September, 151 Squadron destroyed two more Dornier Do 217E-4s. On 30 September 157 scored its first day combat victory, when W/C R.F.H. Clerke shot down a Ju 88A-4, 30 miles (48km) off the Dutch coast. By October 157 Squadron had added three more victories to its rising total. One of them, 3E+CM, a Ju 88A-4 of KG6, flown by Lt Dr Willy Blackert, was brought down near Southwold and was credited to F/Sgt N. Munro and W/O A. Eastwood without a shot being fired! Munro closed to about 600yd (550m),

7/KG2 piloted by Lt Günther Wolf, during a raid on Lincoln. On 17/18 January the 85 Squadron CO, W/C G.L. Raphael DFC, with W/O Addison DFM, shot down a Ju 88A-14 of I/KG6. On 22 January a Mosquito of 410 Squadron, the third RCAF night fighter squadron to be formed, and which had fully converted from Beaufighters to NF.IIs in January 1943, claimed a 'probable' Do 217E. In February all of 25 Squadron's Beaufighters were finally phased out (25 Squadron had received its first NF.II on 21 October 1942); 605 Squadron at Ford began equipping with NF.IIs; and on 16 February 151 Squadron at Wittering began night intruder operations over France using NF.IIs fitted with the *Monica* tail-mounted radar. The squadron continued to fly *Night Ranger* operations over the continent, attacking all kinds of targets. They also carried out high level patrols at night defending the bomber stream. Also during February 1943, 410 Squadron moved south from Acklington for moonlight *Night Ranger* operations from Coleby Grange. The first 410 Squadron intruder operation was flown on 26 February 1943. In June a detachment was sent to Predannack (for Coastal Command operations) and another intruder detachment was temporarily established at Hunsdon.

Night Defences

In March, 85 Squadron, which a month earlier had tested the *Turbinlight* Mosquito (an aircraft-mounted searchlight system for night-fighting), went over to night intruder patrols with five NF.XVs (each capable of reaching altitudes of 43,000ft/13,100m), and NF.XIIs. On 23 March 1943, 157 Squadron carried out its first *Night Ranger* operations over enemy airfields and in February–March, 456 RAAF Squadron, which was largely equipped with Beaufighter VIfs, had begun to include some Mosquito *Ranger* operations in addition to their day fighting role, first from Middle Wallop and then from Colerne. From late May they were successfully employed on sorties over France attacking railway rolling stock and intruding on French airfields. Also in May, 418 'City of Edmonton' Squadron RCAF received its first Mosquito, its first such sorties being dispatched on the night of the 7/8th.

At home, the danger from German raiders persisted. After a lull in night

NF.II DD607, which W/C R.F.H. Clerke used to shoot down a Ju 88 on 30 September 1942.
via Graham M. Simons

However, they had to wait until October that year before getting their first scent of a kill, a Ju 88 damaged and a Do 217 probably destroyed. (In December 1942 23 Squadron transferred to Malta. They would not return until late June 1944, when they joined 100 Group.)

Mosquito fighters were meanwhile still needed to repulse attacks at home. During August 1942, III/KG2 sent single aircraft on daylight low level or cloud cover 'pirate' sorties against selected targets in

sighted the enemy aircraft and cried, 'Tally Ho', when the enemy aircraft turned on its back and dived straight down. AA fire and ships in Lowestoft harbour had succeeded in bringing down the bomber.

307 Polish Squadron began re-equipping with NF.IIs in December 1942 and flew its first patrol on 14 January 1943. On 15/16 January 151 Squadron scored the first Mosquito kill of the New Year when F/Sgt E.A. Knight RCAF and Sgt W.I.L. Roberts shot down Do 217E-4 U5+KR of

fighting kills, on 18/19 March 1943 the Luftwaffe's IX Fliegerkorps directed its entire strength of fifty-four aircraft in an attack on Norwich. F/O G. Deakin and P/O de Costa of 157 Squadron at Bradwell Bay shot down a Ju 88 which fell into the sea about 4 miles (6.4km) off Southwold. (That same month 157 Squadron began training for intruder operations and the first *Night Ranger* was flown on 23 March). Over Norfolk, F/O D. Williams and P/O P. Dalton of 410 Squadron RCAF from Coleby Grange stalked Dornier 217E-4 5523 U5+AH of 1/KG2, flown by Uffz Horst Toifel. Toifel, it seems, aware that a fighter was looming up on him, carried out a too violent manoeuvre, and hit the ground before Williams could open fire. The Dornier crashed near Terrington St Clements.

On 28/29 March 1943, forty-seven bombers of IX Fliegerkorps bombed Norwich again. An NF.II of 157 Squadron flown by F/O John R. Beckett RAAF and F/Sgt Phillips took off from Bradwell Bay at 1940 hours and patrolled some 30 miles (48km) off Orfordness before they were vectored by HCI Trimley Heath on to an enemy aircraft approaching Lowestoft. Beckett had got contacts before on two of his previous twelve patrols, but so far had made no kills. After two momentary contacts, on a fighter crossing rapidly from starboard to port, another contact was obtained dead ahead on an aircraft flying west at 12,000ft (3,660m). It was changing course and height as it approached the coast. With some difficulty the NF.II closed in to 1,000ft (300m), where a visual sighting was obtained. Evasive tactics became more violent which made the target difficult to identify, but from its exhaust system, which glowed orange-red, it appeared to be a Dornier 217 (it was Do 217E-4 U5+NM 4375 of IV/KG2 flown by Fw Paul Huth). Beckett wrote:

The searchlights and ack-ack made identification difficult as we were also hit a few times. After we closed up to our firing position to identify the plane positively as an enemy one, their rear gunner fired at us, but missed, firing too high. I returned the fire at once with two bursts of cannon fire at 300–400ft [90–120m] range lasting about two seconds each. After that I saw hits and sparks on the rear of the aircraft and as a result, the enemy fire stopped and the plane dived into the clouds a few hundred feet below us. Visual contact was lost, but AI contact was held by Phillips from 10,000ft [3,050m] down to 5,000ft [1,520m] with the Dornier turning hard

to port. During that time we were constantly turning in left circles. Contact was lost when the enemy plane turned hard to port and left our screen.

The Do 217 crashed a few minutes later in the sea off Horsey, just north of Yarmouth. All the crew were killed. The victory was shared with a 68 Squadron Czech Beaufighter crew.

April and May provided rich pickings for the Mosquito night fighters, both over England and the continent. On 13 May 85 Squadron moved from Hunsdon to West Malling in Kent to help counter the new menace of Focke Wulf 190A-4/U8 fighter-bombers of Schnelles Kampfgeschwader (I/10SKG/10) based in France. John Cunningham recalls: 'To our great joy and satisfaction we found that using max. continuous power from the Merlin throughout the whole climb – from take-off to interception, and with skilful use of the radar by one's radar operator – it was just possible to intercept and close in, identify, and then shoot down a Focke-Wulf 190 carrying a bomb. It really was quite remarkable how the Merlin stood up to such harsh treatment.' 85 Squadron shot down seven Fw 190 fighter-bombers in May, plus on 29/30 May, the first Ju 88S-1 to fall over England.

Also in May, 60 OTU (Operational Training Unit) at High Ercall was expanded and made responsible for all intruder training. Meanwhile, on 7/8 May 418 RCAF Squadron, still mainly equipped with Bostons and Havocs, flew its first FB.VI sortie, when P/O Tony Croft claimed a Ju 88 destroyed in the Melun–Britigny area. On 27/28 June S/L C.C. Moran and F/Sgt Rogers claimed a Ju 88 and an He 111 destroyed at Avord. Moran also blasted a train and bombed a radio mast. By the end of the summer Moran had earned something of a deserved reputation as a trainbuster, his technique usually consisting of a strafing run to stop the locomotive and then finishing off the halted train with bombs. Rogers was killed on 22 September when both men baled out into the sea while trying to reach Manston, following an intruder mission to Hopsten airfield.

96 and 29 Squadron's Beaufighters were replaced by NF.XIIs in June 1943, the first 29 Squadron Mosquito victory occurring on 5 June when a Ju 88A-14 was shot down off Ostend. In June–July four NF.IIs of 410 Squadron began *Instep* anti-air and anti-shipping patrols from Predannack. 307

Polish Squadron also used Predannack for *Night Rangers* with NF.IIs while the station was used also by a flight of six 25 Squadron NF.IIs detached to 264 Squadron. (25 Squadron had received Mk IIs in October 1942 and had started freelance *Ranger* sweeps over the continent). On 11 June 25 Squadron scored its first NF.II victory when six Mosquitoes took off from Predannack at 1430 hours for an *Instep* patrol in the Bay of Biscay.

'Blue' Section was led by F/L Joe Singleton whose navigator was F/O W.G. Haslam, while 'Green' Section was led by F/L G. Panitz. At about 1617 hours F/O Wootton reported sighting a formation of five enemy aircraft identified as Ju 88s flying at about 6,000ft (1,830m). Singleton ordered the formation to close (one Mosquito had returned to base with engine trouble), and to commence climbing in order to position themselves between the sun and the enemy. The three NF.IIs soared to a gap in the cloud, climbing at 2,000ft (610m) per minute, keeping the Ju 88s in sight. The enemy aircraft saw them and altered course, commencing a climbing orbit to port in loose line astern. 'Blue' Section broke and went into the attack. Singleton's aircraft was bracketed by a series of two second bursts fired simultaneously from three or four of the Ju 88s' dorsal turrets. The tracer passed well above the Mosquito.

Singleton selected the rearmost Ju 88 in the formation, which was nearest to him, performed a climbing turn to port inside the enemy aircraft at about 170mph (270kph), and closed to about 200ft (60m) below him. From about 800yd (730m) range he opened fire with a full deflection shot of 70 degrees, giving a short burst of less than one second with cannon only, as his machine guns failed to fire because of an electrical fault. The Ju 88's port engine emitted considerable volumes of thick black smoke, and the aircraft peeled off to starboard in a dive. Singleton followed on his tail and gave him another one second burst from dead astern and slightly above, with cannon only, from about 300yd (275m) range. Sheets of flame were emitted from the port engine. The dorsal gunner continued to fire at the oncoming Mosquito but his tracer failed to find its target. The Ju 88 pulled out of its dive and the dogged Singleton followed. He gained on the Ju 88 and closed to within 25yd (m) before giving his victim a 3 second burst from dead astern whilst closing right in.

Mk II DZ716 UP-L of 605 Squadron in flight in 1943. The squadron scored its first NF.II 'kills' on the night of 4/5 May when two Do 217s were shot down near Eindhoven by F/O Brian Williams with P/O D. Moore. Two more Do 217M-1s were shot down by NF.IIs of 605 on 13/14 and 25/26 July 1943. via Ron Mackay

Flames appeared inboard of the port engine, followed by black smoke from the starboard engine. Singleton and Haslam's windscreen became covered in oil from the Ju 88, making sighting difficult, and Singleton was compelled to peel off suddenly to starboard to avoid a collision, Singleton overtook the Ju 88, which was now in a steep dive, and turned into the attack again, following and then overtaking the burning aircraft, before administering the *coup de grace*. From slightly above the enemy aircraft at a range of 500ft (150m) and from the starboard quarter, he gave the Ju 88 a one second burst of cannon. Pieces of cowling from the starboard engine, and pieces of the Ju 88's mainplane flew off as the cannon shells hit home. Immediately afterwards, as Singleton and Haslam passed above and behind the Ju 88, two of the crew were seen to bale out. One made his exit through the top hatch and was struck a glancing blow by the port tailplane of the Ju 88, which then turned over and in a vertical dive, and entered the sea. Singleton orbited at about 2,000ft (610m), then climbed through a gap in the cloud to search for more 'game' but none were seen and he called the section to return to Predannack. They landed just after 1800 hours.

(On the night of 14/15 March 1944 F/L Joe Singleton DFC and F/O Geoff Haslam of 25 Squadron at Coltishall destroyed a Ju 188, which crashed in the sea 5 miles (8km) east of Southwold. On 19/20 March they shot down three Ju 188s in the space of just 13 minutes. Singleton finished the war with seven aircraft kills.)

In June 1943 NF.IIs of 456 and 605 Squadrons also began successful, albeit small scale, Bomber Support *Flower* attacks on German night-fighter airfields during raids by Main Force bombers. *Flowers* supported bombers by disrupting the enemy flying control organizations. Long range intruder aircraft fitted with limited radar equipment were used, and these proceeded to the target at high altitude, diving down whenever they saw airfields illuminated. This type of operation if correctly timed, prevented the enemy night-fighters, often already short of fuel, from landing at their bases.

During June–July 1943 there occurred some notable victories by 85 Squadron crews. On 13/14 June W/C John Cunningham DSO* DFC*, the squadron CO (who had shot down sixteen enemy aircraft flying Beaufighters), and F/L C.F. Rawnsley DFC DFM*, shot down Fw 190A-5 CO+LT of 3/SKG 10 over West Malling. It was Cunningham's seventeenth victory and his

first on the Mosquito. A month later, on 13/14 July, F/L Edward Nigel Bunting and Freddie French in an 85 Squadron NF.XII downed the first Me 410 'Hornisse' (Hornet) to be shot down over Britain when they destroyed U5+KG crewed by Fw Franz Zwissler and Ofw Leo Raida of 16/KG2. The Me 410 burst into flames and fell into the sea off Felixstowe. One of the worst disasters to befall the Luftwaffe raiders of KG2 in 1943 occurred on the night of 15/16 August, when it lost ten aircraft; six of them to Mosquitoes of 256 and 410 Squadrons, in a raid on Portsmouth.

Meanwhile, in July 1943, 456 and 605 Squadrons had re-equipped with the FB.VI for intruding while 418 Squadron gave up its Bostons to fly *Flower* operations using the Mk VI. By September 605 were flying intruder sorties over Denmark and Germany. That same month W/C Sammy Hoare DSO DFC* assumed command of 605 Squadron, having left 23 Squadron prior to its departure overseas, to set up a specialized Intruder training 'school' at No. 51 OTU at Cranfield, Bedfordshire. Sammy Hoare returned to combat operations on 27/28 September and with W/O J.F. Potter, his radar navigator, promptly dispatched a Do 217 at Dedelsdorf; his seventh confirmed air-to-air victory.

Sammy Hoare was to write later of intruder pilots:

I should like to tell you not to measure the value of this night fighter work over German aerodromes by the number of enemy aircraft destroyed. This is considerable, but our mere presence over the enemy's bases has caused the loss of German bombers without a shot being fired at them. Night-fighter pilots chosen for this work are generally of a different type to the ordinary fighter pilot. They must like night-fighting to begin with, which is not everybody's meat. They must also have the technique for blind flying, and when it comes to fighting, must use their own initiative and judgement, since they are cut off from all communications with their base and are left as freelances entirely to their own resources.

Personally I love it. Once up, setting a course in the dark for enemy-occupied country, one gets a tremendous feeling of detachment from the world. And when the enemy's air base is reached there is no thrill – even in big game shooting – quite the same. One short burst from the guns is usually sufficient. The bomber's glide turns to a dive – the last dive it is likely to make. Whether you get the Hun or miss him, he frequently piles up on the ground through making his landing in fright.

Included in the non-radar *Flower* force for a short time during August–September 1943 were 264 Squadron, which had taken delivery of FB.VIs in August, 410 RCAF at Coleby Grange, and 25 Squadron at Church Fenton, which was equipped with NF.IIs (although 'C' Flight had FB.VIs). On 20 October, 410 Squadron moved to West Malling to fly fighter patrols in 11 Group, destroying a Bf 110 on 5 November. In September–October also, the Mosquitoes, fitted with AI Mk IV, and *Monica*, switched to *Mahmoud* sorties.

Fighter-bait

Mahmoud was the code-name for a special kind of operation which was devised after it was realized that the Luftwaffe were operating radar equipped night-fighters against the 'heavies' of Bomber Command. In August 1943, this had led to a decision to release some Beaufighters with AI Mk IV radar over enemy territory as bait for enemy night-fighters in their known assembly areas. The British fighters flew individually over the continent to try and induce German night fighters to intercept them. (Mosquito night fighters also flew *Mahmoud* operations, but were less successful at pretending to be bombers, as the Germans soon recognized the speed difference.) AI Mk IV had an all round scan, so it was possible for the radar observer to detect on his CRT (Cathode Ray Tube) an enemy night-fighter trying to intercept

DZ659/G, a modified NF.II, fitted with two Merlin 21s and AI Mk X (US SCR.720/729 Eleanora) **radar in the universal nose.** 'Dutch' Holland via Basil McRae

them from astern. The British pilot would then carry out a 360 degree turn to try and get on the tail of the enemy and shoot him down. With the more powerful centimetric AI being used in Mosquitoes it was necessary to add *Monica* tail warning devices, as these later Mks of AI did not scan to the rear. (Later in the war when the RAF received details of the Luftwaffe night-fighter assembly point beacons from the Resistance, *Mahmoud* sorties by single aircraft were also made against them.)

On 15 October 1943 W/C C.M. Wight-Boycott DSO replaced W/C S.N.L. Maude DFC as CO of 25 Squadron at Church Fenton. (Wight-Boycott had shot down an He 111 on 20/21 September 1941 in 219 Squadron flying a Beaufighter 1f. Then, posted to 29 Squadron, on one remarkable night, 17/18 January 1943, he had destroyed two Do 217s and a Ju 88 and damaged three other Dorniers. The following night the W/C shot down two more Dornier 217s, and a Ju 88.) Wight-Boycott recalls:

25 Squadron had been given the role of Intruder operations over Western Europe using bombs, for which crews, trained for night defence of the UK using AI Mk IV, had no previous training or experience. Morale was not high. They had had a number of casualties. 'A' Flight Commander, S/L Brind RNZAF, had been intercepted returning from a low level sortie and ditched. He and his navigator were taken prisoner. Just before I arrived a flight commander and his crew attempting a single-engined landing in bad weather had been killed. A few days later another flight commander, S/L Matthews and crew, failed to return from a sortie over the Low Countries and a month later, the most experienced squadron pilot, F/L Baillie and F/O Simpson, on their last flight before going on rest, also failed to return from a night sortie. It was not surprising that morale among aircrew was not high, especially as intelligence could not give any clue as to how these experienced crews had got into trouble.

The *Mahmoud* Mosquitoes were only with us for a month before 25 Squadron moved to Acklington to re-equip with NF.XVIIs which were fitted with Mk X AI. During that time I flew two *Mahmoud* sorties. On the first one we were briefed to fly over the Low Countries and wait for a German night-fighter to get on our tail, and then turn 360 degrees to get ourselves in position to get behind the German night-fighter. This manoeuvre was quite unsuccessful. Although I tried it three times in all, the German night-fighter remained on my tail, and I

NF.II DD739 RX-X of 456 Squadron RAAF in June 1943 during a flight from Middle Wallop. Below the cockpit is a small roundel with an Australian marsupial in red in the centre. *'Dutch' Holland via Basil McRae*

had to take some pretty drastic evasion tactics to avoid being shot down myself. Our intelligence were quite unaware of the very efficient German ground control in the Low Countries.

My next sortie was to fly a pin-point near Bonn at 20,000ft [6,100m] where I was told I would find a narrow vertical beam, around which there would be a German night-fighter orbiting waiting to be ordered by ground control into a heavy bomber stream. Nobody explained how a defensive night-fighter crew could possibly find the vertical beam navigating by dead reckoning, no means of checking wind speed and direction, and unable to see the ground. Moreover, the crew had only experience of positioning by ground control – the navigator was Navigator Radar on board just to work a radar set. If this wasn't enough, no information was in the briefing on our own bomber routes and heights, and we arrived in the midst of our own

bomber stream and were lucky not to be shot down by unfriendly 'friendly' rear gunners. In our efforts to avoid the stream, we became more and more lost and could never have got closer to our target than 50 miles [80km]. We decided optimistically to assume we were reasonably close to our target and set course for home (Coltishall) and with relief, recognized that we had reached the North Sea and would soon sight the Norfolk coast. We seemed to fly for hours and couldn't understand why we didn't reach the coast unless there was a 90mph [145kph] head wind. We eventually had to break R/T silence and get a 'steer' from Coltishall which showed that we were so far south we were flying west down the English Channel, any moment about to start a trans-Atlantic crossing! We had had no fix for over three hours. I was very relieved that shortly afterwards we left our *Mahmoud* operations behind.

Fighter Command Mosquito Squadron Movements (WWII)

Sqdn	
23	To 100 Group 5.44; to Fighter Cmd 1945
25	
29	To 148 Wing, 85 (Base) Group, 2nd TAF, 1.5.44; to 147 Wing, 6.44; to ADGB 26.8.44
68	
85	To 100 Group, 1.5.44; to Fighter Cmd 1945
96	
108	Mediterranean
125	
141	To 100 Group, 11.43
151	
157	To 100 Group, 1.5.44
169	To 100 Group, 7.12.43
219	To 147 Wing, 85 (Base) Group, 2 TAF, 28.8.44–7.5.45
239	To 100 Group, December 1943
255	Italy
256	Mediterranean
264	To 141 Wing, 85 (Base) Group 2nd TAF, 19.12.43 (Administered as such from 10.3.44); to 148 Wing, 26.6.44; to UK on rest, 23.9.44; 148 Wing, 8.1.45–7.5.45.
307	
406	
409	To 148 Wing, 85 (Base) Group, 2nd TAF, 30.3.44
410	To 141 Wing, 85 Group, 2nd TAF, 12.5.44; to 147 Wing, 85 Group, 8.6.44–7.5.45
418	To 136 Wing, 2nd TAF, 21.11.44–7.5.45
456	10 Group/11 Group
488	To 147 Wing, 85 (Base) Group, 2nd TAF, 12.5.44; disbanded, 26.4.45
515	To 100 Group, 15.12.43
600	Italy
604	To 141 Wing, 2nd TAF, 26.4.44–2.5.44; to 147 Wing, 85 (Base) Group, 2nd TAF, until 23.9.44; to UK for rest; to 148 Wing, 85 Group, 31.12.44; non-operational from 15.4.45 (disbanded 18.4.45)
605	To 136 Wing, 2nd TAF, 21.11.44–7.5.45

In November 1943, a 307 Squadron detachment at Sumburgh, Scotland, carried out *Rhubarbs* over Norway, destroying two He 177s and a Ju 88. When they returned south they continued intruding and also flew Bomber Support operations until March 1945. On 19 December 1943

264 Squadron joined 141 Wing, 85 (Base) Group 2nd TAF. November–December 1943 in fact brought many more changes for the Mosquito fighter squadrons. Escalating bomber losses over Germany had made it necessary for a command to be formed to integrate all forms of countermeasures operations and offensive night-fighter operations with those of the Bomber force. 100 Group (Special Duties, later Bomber Support) was therefore formed in Bomber Command on 23 November 1943, under Air Commodore (later AVM) E.B. Addison. Addison's Mosquito squadrons were to be used on loose escort duties for the Main Force as well as on night intruder operations, while his heavy bomber squadrons were to be used on radio countermeasures (RCM) and 'spoofing'.

Fighters in Bomber Command

The first NF.II squadron to join 100 Group, on 4 December, was 141 Squadron. In June they had been the first in Fighter Command to use Beaufighter VIfs fitted with the *Serrate* airborne homer. In the hands of a good operator, *Serrate* could track enemy night-fighter *Lichtenstein* (FuG202/212) AI radar emissions. *Serrate* had an effective range of up to 50 miles (80km), or 10 miles (16km) when the enemy radar was facing away from the receiver. It could not give range or altitude, merely direction, so it was only used until final closure, when AI Mk IV radar took over. (AI Mk IV was also needed to obtain contacts on enemy night-fighters that were not using their radar). In September *Serrate* was installed in 141 Squadron's first Mosquito NF.IIs and early in December, 239 and 169 Squadrons were similarly equipped. Meanwhile, 192 Squadron, which was equipped with Mosquito IV, Halifax and Wellington X aircraft, was destined for an ELINT (Electronic Intelligence) role, monitoring German radio and radar frequencies and jamming enemy VHF transmissions.

Crews selected for Mosquito operations in 100 Group were all volunteers from night-fighter squadrons with at least one tour of operations plus experience of intruding into enemy territory on *Ranger* sorties. The first 100 Group operation was flown on 16/17 December 1943 when two Beaufighters and two NF.IIs of 141 Squadron supported the Main Force raiding Berlin. The

first victories occurred on the night of 28/29 January. F/O Harry White DFC and F/O Mike Allen DFC of 141 Squadron shot down a Bf 109 and F/O N. Munro and F/O A.R. Hurley of 239 Squadron destroyed a Bf 110. On the night of the 30/31st, S/L Joe Cooper and F/L Ralph Connolly scored 169 Squadron's first Mosquito victory when they shot down a Bf 110. In February 1944, three more enemy night-fighters were shot down by 141, 169, and 239 Squadrons.

Most of the Mk IIs supplied to 100 Group were war-weary, whose well-used Merlin 21 engines often proved unreliable, while maintenance and radar problems were all too frequent. The FB.VI would have been an ideal solution but not enough were available until late in 1944, and 141, 239 and 169 Squadrons would have to retain their NF.IIs until then! Beginning on 29 February 1944, 515 Squadron's Beaufighters and Blenheims were replaced by NF.IIs for training on the type, but the squadron's role was intruding, and when they began operations in March, it was equipped with FB.VIs. At first, 515 Squadron's Mosquitoes operated on detachment with 605 Squadron's Mosquitoes at Bradwell Bay. An He 177 was destroyed by a 515 Squadron NF.II flown by the CO, W/C Freddie Lambert with F/L E. Morgan, in the first squadron sortie, on 5 March.

1943 had ended with the Luftwaffe desperately trying to wage war over the British mainland. With RAF fighter pilots and radar-navigators determined as ever to stop them, the technological war literally reached new heights in 1944. In April the Special Duty Radar Development Unit was formed in 100 Group for trials and development work on radar and other equipment carried by the group's aircraft. On 1 May it became the Bomber Support Development Unit (BSDU). Apart from the B.IV and B.XVI, the BSDU operated a mix of aircraft, including the Beaufighter, Stirling, and Halifax. Following the disastrous raid on Nürnberg on 30/31 March 1944, when Bomber Command lost ninety-six aircraft, it was decided to release the latest AI Mk X centimetric radar over Germany. In April–May, 85 and 157 night-fighter squadrons, equipped with NF.XII and XVII, and XIX, respectively, were transferred from Fighter Command to 100 Group. AI Mk X, unlike Mk IV, gave no backward coverage, so *Monica IIIE* tail warning equipment had to be fitted before operations could commence.

100 Group Mosquito Units HQ Bylaugh Hall, Norfolk

Sqdn	Aircraft	1st Mosquito Op.	Station
141	II/VI/XXX	16/17.12.43	West Raynham
239	II/VI/XXX	20/21.1.44	West Raynham
515	II/VI	3.3.44	Little Snoring
192	IV/XVI (C Flt)	12.43	Foulsham
169	II/VI/XIX	20/21.1.44	Little Snoring
157	XIX/XXX	5/6.6.44	Swannington
85	XII/XVII	5/6.6.44	Swannington
23	VI	5/6.7.44	Little Snoring

Also:
1473 Flt; 1692 Flt (BSTU); 1694 Flt; 1699 Flight; Special Duty Radar Development Unit / Bomber Support Development Unit (BSDU)

NF.IIs first equipped 157 Squadron on 13 December 1941. DD750, which served with 157, 25, 239 and 264 Squadrons, is fitted with AI Mk IV 'arrowhead', and wing mounted azimuth aerials. The matt all-black scheme could slow the aircraft by up to 23mph (37kph). When NF.IIs began equipping 100 Group in December 1943, the extended operational service had begun to tell and the Merlin 21s were well used. All four machine guns were deleted to make room for Serrate apparatus. via Philip Birtles

(Right) NF.II DZ716 UP-L of 605 Squadron ready for a dusk sortie at Castle Camps, May 1943. This aircraft stalled and crashed at Castle Camps, 7 July 1943.
via Philip Birtles

Mosquito night-fighters at sunset awaiting the start of an operation over occupied Europe. Richard Doleman

In June 1944 the FB.VI intruders of 23 Squadron joined 100 Group following a stint in the Mediterranean, beginning operations in July. Meanwhile, on the eve of D-Day, 5/6 June, 85 and 157 Squadrons flew their first 100 Group operations. 85 Squadron dispatched twelve aircraft over the Normandy invasion beaches. Four NF.XIXs of 157 (and ten from 515 Squadron) made intruder raids on enemy airfields while twenty-one *Serrate* Mosquitoes were dispatched to northern France. During July, 85 and 157 squadrons transferred to West Malling for a month of anti-*Diver* operations against V-1 flying bombs over southern England.

Serrate's effectiveness had been rendered almost useless from May 1944 onwards by the German introduction of SN-2 radar, because the homer was still calibrated to the frequencies of the old *Lichtenstein* AI sets. Eventually, the *Serrate* squadrons began to receive AI Mk X equipped Mosquitoes but these too were of doubtful vintage, as John Beeching explains:

On 14 January 1945 myself and my navigator, F/Sgt Fred Herbert, flew over to Swannington to pick up the first of the Mk XIXs as 85

Other squadrons in 100 Group had to soldier on with old equipment. Pilot, F/Sgt John B. Beeching RNZAF, of 169 Squadron, which in June moved to Great Massingham with Mk VIs, recounts:

On a hot summer's evening, the No.2 runway at Great Massingham, which was 2,000 yards [1,830m] long, was barely long enough to get some of our old boilers (the 'poorer' squadrons used to inherit the cast-offs from other squadrons) off the ground. They used to unstick at around 110mph [177kph]. By now night-fighter Mosquitoes had reached the stage of development where they were like race-horses filled with lead-filled pannier bags. Half a ton of radar, plus *Serrate* equipment, G Box, IFF, infra-red telescopes; two lots of transmitter-receivers, 800 rounds of cannon ammunition, and 716 gallons [3,255 litres] of fuel (100 gallon/455 litre drop tanks). There was no space for the nav. to stow anything, including the chest type parachute. Twice, Fred Herbert, my navigator, managed to get his heel hooked up in the D ring and a white cloud slowly filled the lower part of the cockpit. I don't know what would have happened if Fred had had to bail out – clutch it all to his bosom like bringing in the washing in a hurry on a wet day, I suppose.

NF.IIs and XIXs of 157 Squadron at Swannington, Norfolk. Far left is NF.II HJ911, which S/L G.J. Rice and F/O J.G. Rogerson of 141 Squadron used to destroy a Ju 88 at Cambrai on the night of 27/28 June 1944 and a Bf 110G-4 which crashed west of Chievres, Belgium, thought to be Wrk Nr 730006 D5+ of 2./NJG3. The pilot and Gefr Richard Reiff, who was wounded, both baled out safely but Ogefr Edmund Hejduck was killed. BAe

Squadron had just started to receive Mk XXXs. Both of these marks were equipped with Mk X radar, housed in a nose the size of W.C. Field's, which made taking off and landing, especially at night, something of an adventure until one got used to the arrangement. One of these which I flew had about five V-1s painted on the nose and it must have spent half its working life with the throttles through the gate. It had about as much go as an Austin Seven.

Changes were not confined to 100 Group. Some fifty NF.XIIIs in Fighter Command had earlier had their Merlins modified to use nitrous oxide (better known as 'laughing gas'), injection with petrol for added performance at altitude. W/C John Cunningham, CO, 85 Squadron, for instance, had used Mk XIII HK374 on 2/3 January to shoot down an Me 410 off Le Touquet. Over Britain RAF night-fighters were by now encountering all manner of enemy types, even the occasional Fw 190 and He 177A-3 *Greif*. These, and Do 217s and Me 410s, were used in a series of revenge raids on British cities, code-named, Operation *Steinbock*. The *Baby Blitz*, as Britons called it, had begun on 21/22 January against

NF.XXX NT585 of 157 Squadron from Swannington. NF.XXXs began to equip 157 in February 1945.
Richard Doleman

(Left) **PZ315, a 23 Squadron FB.VI at Little Snoring, which was flown by 'Kit' Cotter (arm on fuselage).**
Tom Cushing

London when nine aircraft, including the first He 177 to be destroyed over the British Isles (by a NF.XII flown by W/O H.K. Kemp and F/Sgt J.R. Maidment of 151 Squadron) were shot down by Mosquitoes. Future raids were to prove equally costly. During 20–30 April alone, Mosquitoes claimed 16 raiders during attacks on Hull, Bristol, Portsmouth and Plymouth.

In February 125 Squadron had begun replacing its Beaufighters with NF.XVIIs and in June they began flying patrols over the French invasion coast. Other Mosquito squadrons kept up the pressure on German shipping and aircraft targets over France and the Western Approaches. One of the Mosquito fighter squadrons involved on *Rangers* and *Instep* sweeps, in February

1944, was 157 Squadron, at Predannack. An example of this type of operation took place on 8/9 February 1944, when two NF.IIs flew a *Night Ranger* to Lake Biscarosse in a search for Blohm und Voss Bv 222 *'Wiking'* ('Viking') six-engined flying-boats of 1.(F)/129. (On 21/22 June 1943 a Bv 3 and Bv 5 had been strafed and sunk at their moorings by four of 264 Squadron's marauding Mosquitoes). S/L Herbert Tappin DFC and F/O I.H. Thomas were accompanied by F/L R.J. Smyth and F/L J. McAllister but the latter were forced to return almost immediately after take off because of R/T failure.

longer. At 2116 hours the fighter was 'flicked over' by four searchlights from the NNW corner of the lake. Two minutes later, navigation lights were seen for a few seconds at 1,000ft (305m), and at 1,000yd (910m) distant, flying in a westerly direction. Before the navigation lights were doused the crew obtained a visual. They closed in on the aircraft, which was now flying south. At 500yd (450m) it was identified as a Bv 222. The Mosquito was then illuminated by searchlights. Undaunted, Tappin gave a short burst from astern, but no strikes were seen, and another two short bursts were given closing to 300yd (275m)

four more Mosquito night-fighter squadrons to 2nd TAF that spring; 604 Squadron joining on 26 April, 29 Squadron transferring on 1 May 1944, and 410 and 488 Squadrons joining on the 12th. In April 406 'Lynx' Squadron RCAF, which had been formed on 10 May 1941 as the first Canadian night-fighter squadron, and which had begun night intruding over France with Beaufighter VIfs, began re-equipping with the NF.XII. Based at Winkleigh, Devon, from April 1944, the squadron helped provide fighter defence for the build up of invasion forces along the south coast. Its first Mosquito victory occurred on the night of 29/30 April

HP850, a Mk VI operated on Ranger sorties by 157 Squadron, 1943–44. via Philip Birtles

On 8/9 February 1944, an NF.II of 157 Squadron crewed by S/L Herbert Tappin DFC and F/O I.H. Thomas flew a Night Ranger from Predannack to Lake Biscarosse and shot down a Blohm und Voss Bv 222 Viking six-engined flying-boat of 1.(F)/129.

Tappin and Thomas set course at 'zero feet' for Biscarosse at 1905 hours and they soon crossed the French coast. They reached Biscarosse at 2108 hours and started to patrol north and south on the west side of the lake. No activity was seen except for two motor launches, although bars of lights were burning north-south of the western shore of the lake and on the lake itself. There were also numbers of red lights around the northern part of the lake. The Mosquito did not go unnoticed for much

range from dead astern. The centre section of the huge flying-boat burst into flames and the inboard engines caught fire. Gradually losing height, the Bv 222 then went into a diving turn to starboard and crashed off the SW point of the lake before blowing up. Thomas set course for Predannack at 2122 and they landed there at 2345 hours.

During March, 409 Squadron began replacing its Beaufighters with NF.XIIIs and on the 30th it transferred to 2nd TAF. ADGB (Air Defence of Great Britain) lost

when W/C D.J. Williams DFC and F/O Kirkpatrick shot down two Do 217s off Plymouth. On 14/15 May, 406 Squadron shot down one enemy aircraft while claiming three probables and one damaged. After a quiet lull, in August, 406 Squadron returned to the offensive equipped with the NF.XXX before training for intruder operations again in September. The first intruder victory occurred on 24 December 1944 when W/C Russ Bannock, the CO, shot down a German aircraft.

W/C M.H. Constable-Maxwell DSO DFC, seen here with his navigator, F/L John Quinton DFC, when he commanded 84 Squadron at Sourabaya, Java in 1946, gained his first confirmed Mosquito victories in May–June 1944, shooting down a Ju 188 on 15/16 May, a Ju 88 on 2/3 July, and another Ju 88 on 2/3 July. via Ron Mackay

(Below) Me 410A-1 9K+KH of I./KG51 which was shot down by W/C E.D. Crew DFC* and W/O W.R. Croysdill in a 96 Squadron Mosquito on 18/19 April 1944. It crashed at St Nicholas churchyard, Brighton. Hptmnn R. Pahl was killed and the body of his radar operator, Fw W. Schuberth, was washed up at Friston next day. via Dr Theo Boiten

(Below) On 13/14 April 1945, F/L K.D. Vaughan and F/Sgt R.D. MacKinnon of 85 Squadron, in NF.XXX NT334 'S', destroyed an He 219 near Kiel. K.D. Vaughan via Dr Theo Boiten

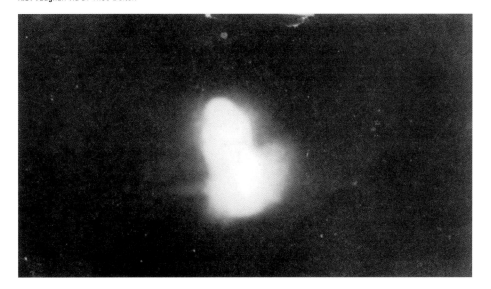

Chasing the Doodlebug

The enemy had intended to launch V-1s against Britain as part of the *Steinbock* offensive, but problems delayed the anticipated 'rocket blitz' until 13 June 1944, when ten V-1s were catapult launched at the capital from sites in north-eastern France. The *Vergeltungswaffe* 1 (Revenge Weapon No. 1), or Fieseler 103 *Kirschkern*

(Cherry Stone), was a small pilotless aircraft with a 1,870lb (850kg) high explosive warhead which detonated on impact shortly after the pulse-jet, as it was designed to do, had cut out over England. The first V-1 destroyed by a Mosquito was on 14/15 June by F/O Rayne Dennis Schultz, ex of 410 Squadron and at the time an instructor with No 54 OTU, during a freelance sortie from Manston. Schultz flew straight into

the debris of the exploding flying-bomb, returning to Manston with little skin left on his aircraft.

From June–September Tempests, Mustangs, Spitfires and Mosquitoes chased the 300–420mph (480–675kph) pilotless bombs, or *Doodlebugs*, as they became to be known. NF.XIII crews in 96 Squadron at Ford were particularly successful on anti-*Diver* patrols, as the V-1 patrols were code-

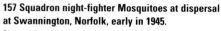

157 Squadron night-fighter Mosquitoes at dispersal at Swannington, Norfolk, early in 1945.
Richard Doleman

(Below)
NF.XXX MV529 being prepared for test flying at Leavesden in September 1944. Fitted with AI Mk X, it saw service with 25 Squadron at Castle Camps. On 23/24 January 1945, crewed by S/L J. Arnsley DFC **and F/L D.M. Reid** DFC**, MV529 was destroyed in a mid-air collision with MT494, flown by F/L D.L. Ward** DFC **and F/L E.D. Eyles, over Camps Hall, Cambridgeshire during an AI practice interception.**
BAe via Philip Birtles.

NIGHT FIGHTING – NOCTURNAL DEFENSIVE AND OFFENSIVE OPERATIONS

named. Their top scorer was S/L R.N. Chudleigh, who destroyed 152 V-1s, including six in one night. Mosquito crews in 264, 456, 219, 605 and 418 Squadrons, destroyed hundreds more at night. (418 Squadron was transferred to 2nd TAF on 21 November 1944). By the end of June 1944, 605 Squadron had shot down thirty-six *Doodlebugs*, and in July, twenty-nine V-1s were destroyed by the Squadron. (605 Squadron was also transferred to 2nd TAF, on 21 November 1944). On 25 June 1944, 85 and 157 Squadrons arrived at West Malling from 100 Group in Norfolk for anti-*Diver* patrols. More Mosquitoes were maximized for anti-*Diver* operations with the injection of nitrous oxide with petrol to give the added power needed to catch the V-1. 85 and 157 Squadrons continued flying anti-*Diver* patrols until 20 August when they returned to Norfolk.

approximately 50 miles (80km) off shore. Only AI Mk X equipped Mosquitoes, and Tempest Vs, could intercept them.

The first Heinkel He 111H-22 shot down by Mosquitoes was shared between a 409 Squadron and a 25 Squadron aircraft over the North Sea on 25 September. Two more were destroyed that month and in October three more fell to 25 and 125 Squadron. In November another four He 111H-22s were shot down, plus one 'probable'. In December 125 Squadron at Coltishall damaged an He 111H-22 and shot down another, while a 68 Squadron NF.XVII, destroyed a second over the sea. On the night of 6 January 1945 a NF.XVII of 68 Squadron crewed by W/O A. Brooking and P/O Finn, who failed to return, carried out the last shooting down of an He 111H-22.

During the remaining months of the war, 25, 68, 96, 125, 151, 307, 406 and 456

tube for any activity from below. The time spent over the target area, often without incident, could become rather tedious and I would look for targets of opportunity on the way home. Roads and autobahns showed up well in moonlight and vehicles could be seen quite distinctly from 500ft [150m].

'Operation Lure' was designed to intercept enemy fighters should they be following our bombers returning from the target. For this purpose we would join the rear of the stream and by throttling back and lowering a few degrees of flap, we could simulate the bomber's speed. Equipped with rear facing Monica, it was my navigator's function to watch for any unidentified aircraft approaching. In the event, it was 'open throttles, raise flaps, smart 180 degree turn, make contact with our Mk X radar and intercept, or perhaps I should say, 'investigate'. Sometimes, they turned out to be a crippled Lanc or a Halifax.

Our final operations were night intruding to strafe preselected airfields. Due to the rapid advance of the Allied armies designated airfields for attack had to be 'cleared' just prior to briefing. On 22 April 1945 Frank Sweet and I were disappointed to learn that the airfield allocated had not been 'cleared'. The airfields that had were being visited at hourly intervals, so I sought and got permission to attack Neuberg airfield half an hour later, when, hopefully, the element of surprise would be on our side.

We lost *Gee* en route to the target and as I recall we located the Danube and proceeded to navigate visually below the cloud base of around 1,500ft [460m]. We located what appeared to be a marshalling yard with many white wagons bearing the red cross. It was rumoured that much ammunition was transported this way and having circled the area a couple of times, I was tempted to have a 'go'! Frank was not in agreement, saying that they may have been 'legit'. At this juncture a break in the cloud allowed bright moonlight which revealed our target airfield which we had been overflying whilst circling. Many parked aircraft were plainly visible. The instant I pressed the firing button, intense fire was returned from all sides; tracer shells seemed to be everywhere. I managed to silence one gun position, but not before being hit, which caused an almighty shudder throughout the aircraft. It was then time to disengage and head rapidly for cloud cover and a worrying return to base, where, fortunately, the damage to the Mosquito was not very serious, the butts of the cannons having taken most of the impact. This proved to be our last operation of the war.

Despite the dangers Mosquito intruders faced, night-fighting was the safest part of the war. You were the aggressor.

NF.XXX of 239 Squadron flown by W/O Graham 'Chalky' White over Hamburg at the end of the war just after hostilities had ended. Graham White

68 Squadron's first NF.XVII sortie took place on 9 July 1944 and the first XIX sortie on 26 July. At the end of August, 219 Squadron transferred to 85 (Base) Group, 2nd TAF. By September the Allied advance had overrun launching sites in the Pas de Calais but the enemy mounted a new terror blitz by air-launching *Doodlebugs* from aircraft over the North Sea. By August 410 V-1s had been air-launched against London, Southampton and Gloucester, and all of them were fired from modified Heinkel 111H-22s of III/KG3 based in Holland, and later Germany, each capable of carrying a single Fieseler Fi 103. Normally, the Heinkels took off at night, flew low over the North Sea to evade radar and climbed to about 1,475ft (450m) before firing their missiles from

Squadrons, Fighter Command, and 141, 239, 515, 169, 157, 85 and 23 Squadrons in 100 Group, flew Bomber Support, 'lure', and intruder operations to pre-selected airfields on the other side of the 'bomb line'. F/O Basil McRae, a 25 Squadron Mk XXX pilot, explains:

On Bomber Support operations, the objective was to protect our bombers from attack by enemy fighters from airfields adjacent to the target area. By timing our arrival some 10 minutes prior to the coloured TIs [Target Indicators] being dropped by the pathfinders, and the subsequent arrival of the main bomber force, we would orbit allocated airfields. During the bombing we would continue to orbit the designated airfields, my navigator, F/O Frank Sweet, keeping a watchful eye on the AI Mk X radar

Armourers, 20mm belts around their necks at the request of the cameraman, attend to a Mosquito Intruder at Little Snoring. Both 23 and 515 Squadrons flew day and night intruder operations 1944–45 from the airfield, where, over 500 years earlier, longbowmen practised their archery skills in firing butts nearby. Tom Cushing

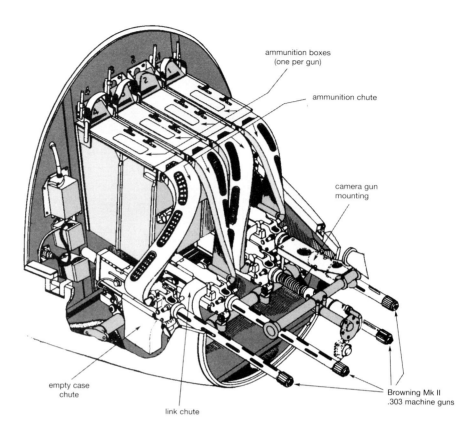

ammunition boxes
(one per gun)

ammunition chute

camera gun
mounting

empty case
chute

link chute

Browning Mk II
.303 machine guns

Mosquito .303in machine gun installation.
Graham M. Simons

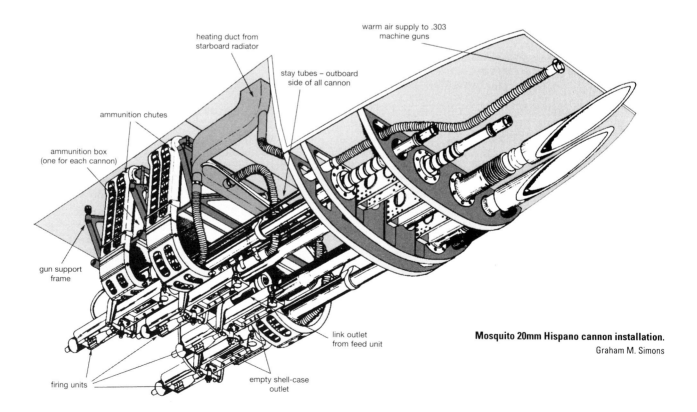

heating duct from
starboard radiator

warm air supply to .303
machine guns

stay tubes – outboard
side of all cannon

ammunition chutes

ammunition box
(one for each cannon)

gun support
frame

link outlet
from feed unit

firing units

empty shell-case
outlet

Mosquito 20mm Hispano cannon installation.
Graham M. Simons

CHAPTER FIVE

Find, Mark and Strike

8 Group PFF Operations

When in June 1943, 105 and 139 Squadrons were transferred to 8 Group (PFF) they were joining a force unique in Bomber Command. Donald C.T. Bennett, the C-in-C, an Australian ex-Imperial Airways and Atlantic Ferry pilot, was determined to get more Mosquitoes for pathfinding and target-marking duties. Formed originally from 3 Group, using volunteer crews, his organization had started as a specialist Pathfinder Force on 15 August 1942, until on 13 January 1943 it became 8 Group (PFF). Don Bennett was promoted Air Commodore (later AVM) to command it. PFF's task, simply, was to 'find' the target (using *Gee*, *Oboe*, and later *H2S*), then 'illuminate' and 'mark' with coloured TIs (Target Indicators) for the Main Force.

Oboe was the code-name for a high-level blind bombing aid, which took its name from a radar-type pulse which sounded rather like the musical instrument. (All non-*Oboe* equipped squadrons in 8 Group were termed 'non-musical'!) Mainly because of this device, Bennett's force was able to conduct *eine kleine nacht musik* almost every night over Germany. Pulses were transmitted by two Type 9000 ground stations, at Walmer, Kent, ('cat'), and Trimingham near Cromer, Norfolk ('mouse'). They could be received by a high-flying *Oboe*-equipped aircraft up to 280 miles (450km) distant. The 'cat' station sent the pilot and navigator a steady sequence of signals describing an arc passing through the target, with dots to port and dashes to starboard. If inside the correct line, dots were heard; if outside the line, dashes. A steady note indicated that the aircraft was on track. The 'mouse' station indicated distance from target, and was monitored by the navigator only.

Flying the beam made considerable demands on the *Oboe* pilot, who for 15–20 minutes had to maintain constant airspeed, altitude and rate of change of heading. The navigator monitored the aircraft's position along the arc, and only he received the release signal, from the 'mouse' station, when the aircraft reached the computed bomb-release point. Ten minutes away he received in Morse, four 'A's; four 'B's at 8 minutes; four 'C's at 6 minutes, and four 'D's at approximately 4 minutes. The bomb doors were then opened. Next was heard the release signal, which consisted of five dots and a 2½-second dash, at the end of which the navigator released the markers or bombs. The jettison bars were operated and the bomb doors closed. As the pilot could not hear the 'mouse' signals, the navigator indicated to him the stage reached by tracing with his finger on the windscreen in front of him, the 'A's, 'B's and 'C's etc. When the release signal came through, the navigator held his hand in front of the pilot's face. Permitted limits were strict – up to 200yd (183m) off aiming point, and crews were expected to be at the target within a 4-minute time span, from 2 minutes early to 2 minutes late. Sixty seconds off time on release point were acceptable. Failure to meet these criteria, and the crew were off the squadron! *Oboe* was to become the most accurate form of blind bombing used in WWII and in practice, an average error of only 30 seconds was achieved.

105 became the second *Oboe* Mosquito squadron, after 109 Squadron, which moved from Wyton to join 105 at Marham in July, and Bennett used 139, which went in the opposite direction, to Wyton, as a 'supporting squadron' to go in with the markers. 109 Squadron had begun trials using Wellington VIs in August 1942 but as the Mosquito B.IV was able to reach 30,000ft (9,140m) or more, well above the altitude a 'Wimpy' could be expected to achieve, Bennett knew that the Mosquito would be ideal for marking duties. *Oboe* was first used on 20/21 December 1942 when six B.IVs of 109 Squadron were dis-patched to bomb a power station at Lutterade in Holland. The first *Oboe*-aimed bombs were dropped by the CO, S/L H.E. 'Hal' Bufton, and his navigator, F/L E.L. Ifould, and two other crews, but the equipment in the three remaining aircraft malfunctioned and they dropped their bombs on targets of opportunity.

On 31 December 1942/1 January 1943, on a raid on Düsseldorf, sky-marking using *Oboe* was tried for the first time. 'Sky markers' were parachute flares to mark a spot in the sky if it was too cloudy to see the target. Two Mosquitoes of 109 Squadron provided the sky-markers for eight Lancasters of the Path Finder Force acting as bombers but a gale had blown down the mast at one of the *Oboe* stations, and only one Mosquito was able to bomb. Later that night, two of the three *Oboe* Mosquitoes dispatched to the night-fighter control room at Florennes airfield, Belgium, dropped their HE cargoes from 28,000ft (8,530m) through cloud. Results were unobserved. All Mosquitoes returned safely.

Marking Techniques

Three types of marking, using names selected by Bennett from the home towns of three of his staff, were later employed. *Parramatta* in New Zealand gave its name to the blind ground marking technique, which used only *H2S* in bad visibility or broken cloud. *Newhaven* was ground marking by visual methods when crews simply aimed at the TIs on the ground, and *Wanganui* in Australia lent its name to pure 'sky marking'. The TIs themselves were made in various plain colours and used vivid starbursts of the same or a different colour to prevented the enemy from copying them at their many decoy sites near major cities.

109 Squadron joined 8 Group at Wyton on 1 June 1943. The only other operational Mosquito unit in 8 Group at that time was

1409 Met Flight, which was established at Oakington on 1 April using Mk Is and crews from 521 Squadron, Coastal Command at Bircham Newton. Their Met (meteorological reconnaissance) flights were known as *Pampas* and usually they were made in daylight to determine the type of weather likely to affect that night's bombing raid. They also helped determine whether sky or ground TIs should be carried by the marking pathfinders. In July 1943 109 Squadron provided five B.IXs (modified Mk IVs with *Oboe*) and crews for 105 to speed its conversion for *Oboe* duties. 105 Squadron flew its first *Oboe* operation on 13 July when two B.IVs attempted to mark Cologne. In September 1943 the squadron began precision bombing of pinpoint targets in western Germany.

F/O J.R. 'Benny' Goodman arrived at 1655 MTU Marham in mid-September 1943, with 1,300 hours as pilot, having completed a tour of thirty-seven sorties on

Wellingtons. While on 'rest' at 15 OTU in 1942 he took part in the first thousand bomber raids, flying training Wellingtons to Cologne and Essen. By mid-1943 those in OTUs who had completed tours early in the war were due to return to squadrons for a second tour. Most veteran aircrew left for the heavy bomber squadrons, with a very small number of pilots and navigators going to Mosquito squadrons, as 'Benny' Goodman recalls:

Two of my closest friends at 15 OTU had responded to the blandishments of the '8 Group Body Snatcher' – as that splendid character, G/C Hamish Mahaddie was known. He was responsible for touring around Bomber Command, attracting the right type of aircrew members into the Pathfinder Force. I was still ruminating on the possibilities when an abrupt signal arrived at 15 OTU posting me to No 1655. So my mind was made up for me. I was to be a member of that elite force whether I liked it or not.

It was quickly made clear to all the new arrivals at 1655 MTU that they were not to interest themselves in what 105 and 109 Squadrons were doing. A wall of secrecy surrounded these high-level precision marker squadrons. So secret was *Oboe* that no one was allowed even to mention the name in the Officers', Mess. 139 at Wyton, which supported the *Oboe* squadrons, was about to be equipped with a bombing aid called 'G-H', and later, with the radar navigational aid, *H2S*. When the Mosquito force in 8 Group was expanded in 1944, 139 Squadron led up to 150 of these superlative aircraft in nightly attacks on Berlin. This was the famous 'Light Night Striking Force' of Bomber Command.

Mosquito bombers of the PFF Group had only one navigational aid – *Gee*. This employed three widely-spaced ground radar transmitters which acted in unison and transmitted pulses in a set order. A receiver in the aircraft enabled the navigator to measure the difference in time between the reception of the various pulses and

F/L A.J.L. 'Bill' Hickox DFC **(later Captain, DFC*) and F/L J.R. 'Benny' Goodman** DFC **(later G/C** DFC* AFC AE**), of 627 Squadron at Oakington, December 1943, in front of B.IV DZ484 AZ-G. They flew this aircraft for most of their time there, late November 1943–June 1944, after which Goodman flew 'G-George' back to 1655 MTU to become a flying instructor. DZ484 was honourably retired to an MU after the war before being broken up.**
G/C J.R. Goodman

by referring these to a special *Gee* map of Europe, covered with lattice lines, the position of the aircraft could be determined with considerable accuracy. Unfortunately, *Gee* could easily be jammed and the Germans did this with great gusto. This reduced the effective range of the raid to an arc running along the Dutch coast, which meant that navigators had to work very quickly to calculate an accurate wind speed and direction before heading into Germany. On long trips, to Berlin and Munich for example, we sometimes had the bonus of a route marker put down for us at a point midway to the target and possibly another closer to the target. Such markers were laid either by PFF Lancasters or 139 Squadron Mosquitoes equipped with the *H2S* air-ground radar aid. The only other aid in a Mosquito at that time was a VHF radio set, a superb piece of equipment. Many were the occasions on which I thanked the Lord for the sound of the quiet, efficient voice of the WAAF radio operator giving me a course to steer to reach home. Bomber Command Mosquitoes had no defensive armament, they relied entirely on speed to get them out of trouble.

My first flight in a dual Mosquito took place on 23 September; F/O Herbert being the instructor. For an hour we did local familiarization, single engine flying and circuits and landings. It was a flight I shall never forget. The Mosquito was small, powerful, incredibly fast, and instantly responsive to the slightest movement of the controls. Flying the Wellington had been a push and pull affair; by contrast the Mosquito had to be tickled. As the Flight Commander said: 'Treat her like your best girl friend – gently'. My first solo trip lasted 50 minutes and was sheer joy, all 1,200 horses in the Merlin engine on each side neighing with delight – or so it seemed to me. Could there be anything more perfect than this?

All pilots posted to 8 Group on Mosquitoes had to complete a laid-down syllabus of 30 hours flying at 1655 MTU – ten in the Dual Flight and twenty in the Bomber Flight; the latter complete with navigator. No pilot was allowed to touch the controls of a Mosquito until he had 1,000 hours as first pilot under his belt and had been selected to fly Mosquitoes. Having completed their prescribed time in the Dual Flight, the pilots of No 15 Course now reported to the Bomber Flight and joined the navigators. The system of crewing-up was easy – we were all assembled in the Crew Room and told to sort ourselves out. This we did fairly quickly and I sound found myself talking to a tall, rather quiet F/O named John Hickox. He was known in the RAF as 'Bill' – after Wild Bill Hickok of American West fame. He told me that he had done his first tour of ops on

'Wimpys' [Wellingtons] and that he had been shot down and walked back through the desert. He did not relish the idea of being shot down in a Mosquito and walking back from Germany. I assured him that his thoughts accorded closely with mine so we shook hands and became a Mosquito crew.

The next thing we did as crews in the Bomber Flight was to gather round a B.IV for drill in abandoning aircraft. The Chief Ground Instructor, S/L Cairns, explained that if we were hit at high level we had about 45 seconds in which to get out. We had to disconnect our oxygen tubes and radio intercom plugs, release our seat belts, switch off engines if time permitted, jettison the bottom hatch and bale out. This sounds straightforward, and indeed it was, but the Mosquito was a very small aircraft and the pilot and navigator were meant to climb in, strap in and stay put. When Bill Hickox and I tried to do it the first time there was an unholy mix-up and after 45 seconds the CGI announced, 'You're dead'.

The difficulty about getting out of a Mosquito wearing parachutes was that the navigator had to clip on his chest parachute and then manoeuvre his way through the main hatch in the floor of the aircraft. This hatch was scarcely large enough to get through without a chute. If the navigator got out safely, the pilot was supposed to follow him wearing the pilot-type parachute attached to his backside. Bill and I decided that we would stay with the aircraft if humanly possible. I resolved mentally that if all failed and we had to get out in a hurry I would wait until Bill was clear and then go out through the top hatch (which was standard drill for the pilot seated in the left hand seat of a dual Mosquito). Fortunately, our agreed plan was never put to the test but other crews had to jump out over Germany and did so successfully.

Flying the Mosquito was a pleasure, but navigating it was a completely different kettle of fish. Most navigators had come from Wellingtons but the Mosquito flew twice as fast so the poor old navigator had to work very much more quickly than before. However, it seemed to come right in the end for everyone and I am sure that by the time Bill Hickox and I rolled to a standstill for the last time in our squadron Mosquito he had become almost as blasé about navigating it to and from remote parts of the Third and last Reich.

No 15 Course ended during October 1943, after all the crews had done four cross-countries by day and two by night. We were then allocated to squadrons, a small number to 105 and 109 Squadrons and the majority to 139 Squadron at Wyton. Bill Hickox and I were posted to 139 where the squadron was so large that it comprised three flights. We did not know that we

were to become part of the expansion of the Mosquito Force in the Pathfinder Group from three squadrons to eleven.

My first operational sortie from Wyton took place on 3 November 1943, the target being Cologne. Marking was to be done by 105 and 109 Squadrons, using *Oboe*. Our bomb load was four 500lb [230kg] HE bombs and the attack was to be an all-Mosquito affair. Our first operational take-off in DK313 was only marginally longer than our take offs from Marham in Mosquitoes without bombs. The acceleration was rapid and in next to no time we were at the unstick speed of around 100 knots [185kph] and climbing smoothly away. We climbed rapidly to 28,000ft [8,530m], levelled out and settled down to an economical cruising speed of around 250 knots [463kph] (true airspeed). As we neared Cologne the first of the *Oboe*-aimed target indicators began to cascade down ahead of us. Bill took his place at the bombing panel and began the time honoured verbal directions: 'Left, left…Steady…' and ultimately, 'Bombs gone.' We then turned for home, more bacon and eggs; and bed. The post-flight interrogation was much the same as on any operational squadron in Bomber Command, with the important exception that 139's full title was 139 (Jamaica) Squadron and we were all offered a tot of rum on return from every operational sortie – the rum being provided by the good people of Jamaica. When I was on 139 we had with us a Jamaican named Ulric Cross, a flight lieutenant navigator, highly efficient and well liked. Later he became Lord Chief Justice of Jamaica.

The best *Oboe* crews could place a bomb within a few yards of the aiming point from 28,000ft [8,530m]. However, since they had to fly straight and level for several minutes in the final run to the target they were vulnerable to flak and fighters. Moreover, they could only approach a given target from two directions – in the case of Ruhr targets, almost due north or south – the Germans quickly realized this and set up searchlight cones over the aiming point which they plastered with heavy flak. Another little trick was to position Ju 88s near the searchlight cones, at a higher level than the Mosquitoes. Thus, when coned, a Mosquito might first be blasted with heavy flak and then the barrage could suddenly cease. If the pilot wasn't in a position to react instantly, the next happening would be a highly unpleasant squirt of cannon fire from the night-fighter. The average time for a trip to the Ruhr was 2½ hours, while a run to Berlin took about 4½ hours. To carry out such sorties in a Wellington had taken something like 5½ hours and 8 hours respectively. For this reason alone, Mosquitoes were greatly to be preferred to Wellingtons – it is better to be shot at for a short time than for a long time!

Mosquito Strike Force

Bennett was able to carry out an expansion of his Mosquito force and in April 1943 it began 'nuisance' raiding. This does not adequately begin to describe these activities, for the Mosquito could carry a 4,000lb (1,810kg) 'Cookie' or 'Blockbuster' to Berlin; 500lb (230kg) more than the US four-engined Flying Fortress, (whose bomb bay was too small for a blockbuster, and which needed an eleven-man crew and a much larger load of ammunition). By the summer 'nuisance raiding' had become so

ground marking which enabled 728 bombers to rain down 2,284 tons of HE and incendiaries in 50 minutes on the dockyards and city districts of Hamburg, creating a fire-storm which rose to a height of 2½ miles. RAF losses were light and this was mainly due to *Window*, which was being used for the first time. *Window* was the British code-name for strips of black paper with aluminium foil stuck to one side and cut to a length (12in/30cm by .6in/1.5cm), equivalent to half the wavelength of the *Würzburg* ground, and *Lichtenstein* AI, radar. When dropped by air-

The bundles of *Window* produced a 'clutter' of blips on German radar screens and German fighter controllers sent up their nightfighters so that when the heavies *did* arrive, the Nachtjagdgeschwaders were on the ground having to refuel. On 26 November three Mosquitoes of 139 Squadron, flying ahead of the Main Force, scattered *Window* on the approaches to Berlin and returned to drop bombs. They also made feint attacks on other targets to attract enemy night-fighters anything up to 50 miles (80km) away from the main stream during an attack.

B.IV DZ379/H of 105 Squadron at Marham. On 17 August 1943 this aircraft, now with 139 Squadron at Wyton, failed to return from Berlin, the diversion for the famous Peenemünde raid. It was shot down by a night-fighter to crash at Berge, Germany, and F/O Cook, the American pilot, from Wichita Falls, Texas, and his navigator, Sgt D.A.H. Dixon, were killed. RAF Marham

effective that the Mosquitoes in 8 Group were now referred to as the Light Night Striking Force (or, at Bennett's insistence, the Fast Night Striking Force). One of their greatest achievements came during the nine days of Operation *Gomorrah*, the 'Battle of Hamburg', 24/25 July–2 August 1943, when the PFF and LNSF flew 472 sorties, with the loss of just thirteen Mosquitoes. The first raid was led by H2S PFF aircraft and Mosquitoes using *Parramatta*

craft in bundles of a thousand at a time at one-minute intervals, *Window* reflected the radar waves and 'snowed' the tubes with thousands of spurious contacts.

On 18/19 November 1943 'spoof' raiding was first tried by 139 Squadron and *Window* was one of the main ingredients used to give the impression of a large bomber force when in fact it was a mere handful of Mosquitoes. Meanwhile, the true raid by heavies was heading elsewhere.

During the third week of November it was suddenly announced in the 139 Squadron Crew Room at Wyton that a new Mosquito squadron, 627, was to be formed at Oakington, near Cambridge, and that 'C' Flight would become the nucleus of the new squadron. (627 was apparently needed for a secret operation, the details of which are secret until 2003, but which never actually materialized). 'Bill' Hickox and 'Benny' Goodman prepared to move to their new station on 24 November.

We climbed aboard DZ615 and flew her to Oakington. It was a rule in Bomber Command that every new squadron became operational as soon as possible after it was formed, and when we arrived, Bill and I found out that we were on the Battle Order for that night.

The resident squadron at Oakington was No 7, a Lancaster squadron of the PFF force, and on the day of 627's arrival, the station was a hive of industry. A Bomber Command maximum effort was in preparation and Lancasters were being made ready for ops that night. To the Oakington effort would now be added six Mosquitoes of 627 Squadron. As the day wore on it became apparent from reports from the Station met office that operations that night had become questionable; a warm front was spreading in from the south-west more quickly that had been expected. At tea time the Lancasters were stood down, but 627 remained on standby and after tea we were briefed for an-all Mosquito attack on Berlin in company with 139 Squadron.

Early that evening Bill and I boarded DZ615 and set off for the 'Big City', a trip which turned out to be completely uneventful except that on returning to the airfield we were flying in thick cloud and pouring rain. We broke cloud at 500ft (150m), still in heavy rain, and approached and landed very carefully. On reporting to the Operations Room for debriefing, we were astounded to be told that DZ615 had been the only RAF aircraft over Germany that night. Ops had been cancelled by Bomber Command at a very late stage but two of us were already airborne and were left to get on with it. The other pilot had trouble with his aircraft and turned back, which left me on my own.

The winter of 1943–44 was famous – or infamous, depending on your point of view – because it saw the Bomber Command offensive against Berlin. Our C-in-C said that if we could lay waste the Big City the Germans would be brought to their knees. Sixteen major attacks were mounted but Berlin was not destroyed. The truth is that the target was too vast and the weather, which could often be worse than enemy action, was appalling. Bill Hickox and I took part in seven of these attacks against the German capital and also busied ourselves with spoof raids against other targets, for example Kiel and Leipzig. We knew only too well that we were engaged in a battle of attrition, as was the US 8th Air Force, and the outcome could be defeat for the bombers.

During the Battle of Berlin we lost S/L 'Dinger' Bell, our Flight Commander. However, he and his navigator managed to bale out and became

PoWs. At this time, Bill and I began to wonder if the sands were also running out for us when, on the way home from the Big City, the oil pressure on the starboard engine suddenly began to drop and the oil and coolant temperatures increased. Eventually the readings reached their permitted limits and I throttled back the engine and feathered the propeller. Now we were in the cart with a vengeance, for we had to lose height and were eventually flying along at a height and speed comparable to that of our heavy brothers, but with no means of defending ourselves if attacked. Moreover, since the only generator on the Mosquito was on the starboard engine we had to turn off our internal lights, the Gee box and our VHF set. So we drove on through the darkness with our fingers and toes slightly crossed and feeling very tense. Wouldn't you?

Eventually our ETA at the Dutch coast came and Bill switched on the Gee. We were in luck; it worked, and Bill quickly plotted a fix. So far, so good. Next we turned the Gee box off and I called up the VHF guardian angels on Channel 'C' – the distress frequency. At once there came that voice of reassurance, asking me to transmit for a little longer. She then gave us a course to steer, and shortly afterwards said, 'Friends are with you.' Bill and I took a good look round and spied a Beaufighter, which stayed with us until we reached the English coast. We motored on eventually and got down fairly expertly which drew from the imperturbable Mr Hickox the comment, 'Good Show'. Praise indeed.

Shortly after this effort came another indication that Lady Luck was on our side. We were briefed for yet another trip to Berlin, but during the afternoon the raid was cancelled and a short-range attack on a Ruhr target was substituted. This was to be an all-Mosquito affair, led by 105 and 109 Squadrons. Our CO, W/C Roy Elliott, decided that this was an opportunity for new crews to have a go and Bill Hickox and I were stood down in favour of two 'makey-learns'. We had air-tested the aircraft that morning and were satisfied that it was in all respects serviceable, yet as the Mosquito lifted off at night and entered the area of blackness just beyond the upwind end of the flare path both engines failed and there came the dreadful sound of a crash as the aircraft hit the ground. Both crew members were killed. Would this have happened if Bill and I had been on board? We shall never know.

'Block-busting'

By early 1944 suitably modified B.IVs were capable, just, of carrying a 4,000lb (1,810kg) 'Blockbuster', although it was a

tight squeeze in the bomb bay. To accommodate this large piece of ordnance the bomb bay had been strengthened and the bomb doors redesigned. 692, which became the fourth Mosquito squadron in 8 Group when it formed at Gravely on 1 January, was given the dubious honour of being the first Mosquito squadron to drop one of these 'Cookies', or 'Dangerous Dustbins' as they were also known (because of their shape) over Germany. DZ647 released one during a raid on Düsseldorf on 23/24 February. 'Cookies' continued to be carried in modified B.IVs until the B.XVI high-altitude Mosquito, which had first flown in prototype form in November 1943, became operational in the spring. B.IVs, meanwhile, proved to be not entirely suitable, as 'Benny' Goodman testifies:

Our CO announced that we were to fly the 'Cookie-carrier' as much as possible and the most experienced crews were detailed to take her on normal operations. The night arrived when Bill Hickox and I were ordered to try our hand with this new machine on a target in the Ruhr. The aircraft looked like a pregnant lady, because its belly was markedly rotund. Take off was not difficult, but quite definitely she was not a scalded cat. As soon as her tail came up I pushed the throttles quickly forward to the gate (plus 9lbs [4kg] boost, 3,000rpm) and then clenched my left hand over the gate catch releases and eased the throttles to the fully open position (plus 12lbs [5.4kg] boost, 3,000rpm). In 'G-George' this would have resulted in a glorious acceleration and a hop, skip and jump into the air. Not so with our pregnant lady; she waddled along and took most of the runway before she deigned to unstick. Moreover, the climb was a sedate affair and we took much longer to reach 25,000ft [7,620m] than with our usual steed; and when we arrived there she took a long time to settle to a steady cruise. However, we eventually sorted ourselves out and headed resolutely for the Ruhr.

In the target area I felt distinctly nervous – there we were, with the bomb doors open and Bill droning away with his 'Left, left…right…steady' and I just knew that every gunner in the Ruhr could see the enormous bomb we were carrying and was determined to explode it and blow us to smithereens. I looked at the bomb jettison handle in front of me – no delicate lever this; it was a solid bar of metal which, if moved, would manually release the massive catch holding the 'Cookie' and down the bomb would go. If the bomb doors had not been opened, that was hard luck – the 'Cookie' would still drop away and take the bomb doors with it! However, no such inglorious thing happened. Bill suddenly announced, 'Bomb gone', and as he did so the Mossie suddenly shot up like a lift. There was no delicate porpoising, as with four 500 pounders; the altimeter moved instantly through 500ft [150m] of altitude. I had never seen anything like this before. More importantly, as soon as I had closed the bomb doors our fat little lady became almost a normal Mosquito and accelerated to a fast cruising speed.

The B.XVI, with its bulged bomb bay and more powerful two-stage 1,680hp (1252kW) Merlin 72/76s or two 1,710hp (1274kW) 73/77 engines, which gave a top speed of 419mph (674kph) at 28,500ft (8,690m), was a much more acceptable 'Cookie-carrier'. No 692 Squadron first used the B.XVI operationally on 5/6 March, on a raid on Duisburg. 692 Squadron pilot, P/O J. Ralph Wood RCAF who, following a first tour of twenty-six 'ops' on heavies,

would fly fifty more from 6 July–3 November 1944, as a navigator with Andy Lockhart AFC, recalls. 'With a 4,000 pounder [1,810kg] aboard and the Mosquito tanked up for a 1,200 mile [1,930km] sortie, the worst moment for the crew was take-off. Fused or unfused, a bomb of this size might go off on heavy impact.' Even without a 4,000 pounder aboard, flying in a Mosquito had other problems. Ralph Wood again:

The pilots had a steel plate under their seats to protect them. Navigators had an extra sheet of plywood. We all had a nagging fear that our 'jewels' might be shot off. The moral seemed to be that pilots make better fathers. I wore a Mae West and a harness to which I would attach my parachute, which was kept on the floor near my feet. I sat on the dinghy, the little lifeboat all done up in a neat, square package. The rubber sucked out your piles if fear didn't. The hooks on my harness were snapped onto the dinghy clamps. If I jumped, the dinghy came with me.

With the parachute on my chest and the dinghy on my ass, I wonder if I could ever have squeezed through that small escape hatch. There we were, snug as two peas in a pod. This was no place for claustrophobia. My lap-board, maps and Dalton computer completed the picture.

On 1/2 February 1944, 139 Squadron, which had pioneered the use of Canadian-built Mosquitoes, and was now operating a mix of B.IV, IX, XVI and XXs, used H2S for the first time, for marking the target for a raid on Berlin. H2S provided a map-like image on a CRT (Cathode Ray Tube) screen, which in the Mosquito was connected to a revolving scanner antennae housed in a bulbous nose radome. Targets had to be carefully selected using H2S and city areas on coastlines or estuaries were picked because of the verifiable distinction between water and land on radar screens. From 1944, H2S-equipped B.IXs of 139 Squadron frequently led and

A 4,000 pounder (1,810kg) inscribed 'Happy Xmas Adolf', is wheeled into position to be hoisted aboard MM199 'Q-Queenie', a B.XVI 'Cookie carrier' of 128 Squadron, Christmas 1944. via Rolls-Royce

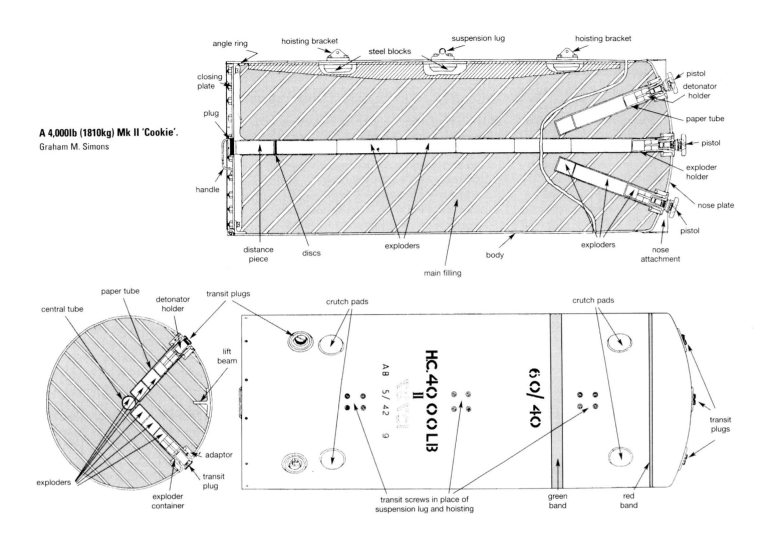

A 4,000lb (1810kg) Mk II 'Cookie'.
Graham M. Simons

**A 4,000lb (1,810kg) bomb being released by B.XVI
MM200 'X' of 128 Squadron.** Graham M. Simons

marked for other Mosquitoes, and *Oboe Mk II*-equipped B.IXs of 109 and 105 Squadrons spearheaded the main force bombing raids.

F/O Grenville Eaton, a 105 Squadron pilot, flew his first Mosquito operation on 1/2 March 1944, in 'A-Apple', an *Oboe*-equipped B.IV.

Venlo, the target, was a German fighter aerodrome on the Dutch border near Aachen. (The first few trips were usually to 'less difficult' targets, but they were certainly no less important in countering the threat of fighters). With a full load of bombs, four 500 pounders [230kg], and of petrol, it took, perhaps, one hour following carefully planned and timed 'legs' all over East Anglia until setting course from Orfordness to the Dutch coast. Then, at the operational height of 28,000ft [8,530m], we flew towards the 'waiting point [where the track to the target extended backwards for a further 5 minutes], and there, at the precise appointed time [to hear the call-in signal in Morse], we switched on *Oboe*.

The navigator worked out the flight plan and calculated the time to set course in order to reach the target at the correct time. On marking sorties it was important that TIs were dropped at the correct time in order not to compromise the Main Force. Having worked out the time to set course, navigators actually did this with 6 minutes in hand to allow for any errors in the forecast wind, etc. Having settled into the flight and arrived at the ETA for the waiting point, crews usually had to make some sort of correction. If the full 6 minutes had to be lost, the pilot did a 360 degree orbit and most pilots became expert in achieving this in the 6 minutes. Lesser times to be lost were accomplished by making a dog leg.

Grenville Eaton had to find the beam and keep on it for perhaps 10–15 minutes to the target.

Thanks to *Gee*, Jack Fox's navigation was spot on, and we had a good run to target. His signals gave him our distance to target, and finally, the bomb release signal, like the BBC time signal, five pips then the sixth, a dash, to press to release the bombs. We had a clear run. Holding steady for some seconds after bomb release to photograph the bomb explosions, we turned smartly on to the planned course home, keeping our eyes skinned for fighters, flak and searchlights, around 360 degrees above and below. A gentle, slow dive at top speed and we arrived at the Dutch coast around 20,000ft [6,100m] and

the English coast at 12,000ft [3,660m]. We landed at 0330 hours. So, Jack's 31st, and my first 'op', took 3hrs 25 minutes. A simmering feeling of incipient fear throughout, had been kept in check by being fully occupied. Now, home, we felt a tremendous feeling of relief and achievement, especially when we were told at debriefing that we had achieved a 'Nil' target error on this, our first *Oboe* trip. Finally, a heavenly operational aircrew breakfast of bacon, eggs, toast, rum and coffee. Smashing!

Our second operation was on 7/8 March. The target was Aachen, an important road and rail junction just inside Germany. I was feeling more confident. Crossing Holland at 28,000ft [8,530m], with a clear sky, we could see the distant Zuider Zee. We switched on *Oboe*, found we were early, so guided by the navigator, I wasted a precise number of minutes and seconds until finding and settling into the beam towards the target, about 15 minutes' flying time away. We noticed we were leaving long white contrails behind us – frozen water vapour crystals in the exhaust of each engine. Suddenly streams of cannon-shells and tracers enveloped us from the rear, hitting us in numerous places, but luckily missing Jack and me and the engines. I immediately dived to port, then up to starboard several times, then resumed height and regained the beam. The only protection was a sheet of steel behind my seat. Most instruments seemed to work, so we continued. Half a minute later, a second and noisier attack from the rear, so again I took evasive action, more violent and longer, and again regained height and beam. Now there was considerable damage to dashboard, hydraulics and fuselage. Shells had missed us,

truly by inches. However, engines and *Oboe* still worked, so being so near we had to continue to target, deliver the load, and turn for home, changing course and height frequently, and assessing the damage as far as we could. Certainly, hydraulics, flaps, brakes, ASI and various other instruments were smashed – but we were okay.

At Marham, landing in pitch darkness was a problem, but for safety I landed on the grass, by feel I suppose, at about 150 knots [280kph] with no brakes. We hurtled across the aerodrome, just missing two huge armament dumps, straight on through hedges and violently into a ditch. Jack was out of the emergency exit like a flash. I could not move, could not undo the safety belt. Jack leapt back, released me and we scampered away to a safe distance in case of exploding petrol tanks, and emergency services were quickly there. Debriefing was interesting, as not only was our run 'seen' on the CRT, but our bombing error was precisely calculated and we wondered whether all operations were to be like this one! Incidentally, we never saw the attacking fighter. Our aircraft was a write off.

Eaton was awarded an immediate DFC for this operation and went on to complete ninety operations by 18 March 1945. On 10 July 1944 he and Jack Fox took off on their first daylight operation when the port engine blew up as they reached the end of the runway, an event that was usually fatal. Eaton somehow flew a circuit and landed safely on one engine but when Fox dropped prematurely through the escape hatch he was killed by the propeller.

The Lyons engine factory taken from 10,700ft (3,260m) during the marking by 8 Group Mosquitoes on 25/26 March 1944. Jim Shortland

Low-level Markers

In the 12 months, January–December 1944, apart from 692 Squadron already mentioned, five more Mosquito squadrons joined 8 Group. On 7 April 571 Squadron was formed at Downham Market. A shortage of Mosquitoes meant that 571 had to operate at half-strength for a time. On the night of 13/14 April two crews from 571, and six from 692, attacked Berlin for the first time carrying two 50 gallon (230 litre) drop tanks and a 4,000lb (1,810kg) bomb. On 1 August 608 Squadron formed in 8 Group at Downham Market and on 15 September, 128 Squadron at Wyton joined the LNSF. On 25 October, 142 Squadron reformed at Gransden Lodge and that same night they flew their first operation, when their only two B.XXVs were dispatched to Cologne. On 18 December 162 Squadron reformed at Bourn with B.XXVs and soon accompanied 139 Squadron on target-marking duties. (163 Squadron, the eleventh and final Mosquito squadron in 8 Group, reformed at Wyton on 25 January 1945, also on B.XXVs, under the command of W/C (later AM)

Ivor Broom DFC and quite remarkably, flew its first LNSF operation on the night of 28/29 January when four B.XXVs dropped *Window* at Mainz ahead of the PFF force. The other eight squadrons in 8 Group were equipped with the Lancaster, two returning to 5 Group in April 1944).

Rivalries and politics being what they are, covetous eyes were cast in 8 Group's direction in the spring of 1944, as 'Benny' Goodman recalls:

A high level decision at Bomber Command HQ was about to result in 627 Squadron moving to Lincolnshire, to join 617 Squadron at Woodhall Spa in specialized marking operations for 5 Group. Since the beginning of 1944 the 'Dam Busters', led by W/C Leonard Cheshire, had been successful in marking and destroying small industrial targets at night. To do this, Cheshire had dropped flares over the target and by the light of these had marked the target with red spot fires dropped visually from his Lancaster in a shallow dive at low level. This technique was to achieve far reaching results later in the year and heralded an improvement in hitting power in Bomber Command.

F/L (later Air Marshal Sir, Ivor KCB CBE DSO DFC AFC) G. Broom, and F/L (later S/L) Tommy Broom (not related) of 128 Squadron (note the crossed broomsticks on the nose!). Ivor Broom was ordered to form 163 Squadron at Wyton in January 1945 and have it operational in 24 hours, which he did on 25 January. via Rolls-Royce

Juvisy railway marshalling yards, Paris, before (above) and after (below) the attack, 18/19 April 1944. The yards were marked at each end with red spot-fires by four Mosquitoes of 627 Squadron, 5 Group, and with three Oboe Mosquitoes of 8 Group. The 200 Lancasters bombed between the TIs so effectively that the yards were not brought back into service until 1947. G/C J.R. Goodman

The brilliant AOC of 5 Group, Air Marshal the Hon Ralph Cochrane, was quick to appreciate that if a single aircraft could mark a target accurately for a squadron then it should be possible for a squadron of properly trained crews to mark targets with similar accuracy for the whole Group. The Lancaster was a splendid aircraft but was vulnerable to light flak at low level; a more manoeuvrable aircraft was required for the operations Cochrane had in mind. Leonard Cheshire was aware of the limitations of the Lancaster and had already decided that the best aircraft for low level marking was the Mosquito. He briefed the AOC on his ideas and this led to the meeting at Bomber Command HQ which resulted in the redeployment of 627 Squadron from Oakington to Woodhall Spa and 83 and 97 Lancaster Squadrons from their respective Pathfinder bases to Coningsby. 5 Group was about to receive its own PFF Force and 8 Group was no longer to enjoy its hitherto unchallenged monopoly over pathfinder tactics.

No hint of these momentous events reached the crews of 627 Squadron 'in the trenches' at Oakington. We had, of course, heard of Leonard Cheshire, but he belonged to 5 Group – the Independent Air Force as it was known in

Bomber Command. We were too busy attending to daily grind in 8 Group to concern ourselves unduly with what the glamour boys of a rival Group were doing.

My flying Log Book reveals in its cold and unremarkable way that in early April Bill Hickox and I went to Cologne, Essen, Hanover and Osnabruck, the last three taking place on the 12th. Next day coincided with the announcement that 627 Squadron was to redeploy to Woodhall Spa, and two days later Bill Hickox and I insinuated ourselves into DZ484 'G-George' and flew to Lincolnshire with the rest of the squadron. After landing, we were formed into a single line and the Station Commander arrived with what I can best describe as a bevy of brass. It was the AOC with his principal staff officers. He moved along the line with W/C Roy Elliott, our CO, who introduced us individually to the great man. Within a few minutes I found myself looking into the cold eyes of a tall, rather ascetic man, who abruptly welcomed me to 5 Group and moved on along the line. Why had he taken the trouble to meet us? Such a thing was unheard of in bomber circles. We all felt somewhat uneasy. Obviously, something was 'up', and it promised to be bloody dangerous.

Next day the whole squadron journeyed by bus to Coningsby and were directed to the Station Cinema. Here were assembled all crew members of 83 and 97 Lancaster PFF Squadrons, our own Squadron, the AOC and his entourage, and Leonard Cheshire. The AOC opened the meeting by saying that a number of successful attacks had been made by 617 Squadron on important pinpoint targets and it was now intended to repeat these on a wider scale. The Lancaster pathfinder squadrons were to identify the target areas on H2S and were to lay a carpet of flares over a given target, under which 627 Squadron would locate and mark the precise aiming point. The target would then be destroyed by 5 Group Lancaster bombers. So that was it – we were to become low-level visual markers, and it did sound dangerous.

Cheshire now took the stand and explained carefully how the low-level marking business was done. What the Lancasters had to do was lay a concentrated carpet of hooded flares, the light from which would be directed downwards onto the target, making it as bright as day. A small number of Mosquitoes – four or possibly six – would orbit, find the aiming point, and then mark it in a shallow dive with 500lb

[230kg] spot-fires. Marker Leader would assess the position of the spot-fires in relation to the aiming point and would pass this information to a 'Master of Ceremonies' in one of the pathfinder Lancasters. The MC would then take over and direct the main force Lancasters in their attack on the target.

On returning to Woodhall, the CO called the Flight Commanders to his office and an intensive programme of dive bombing at Wainfleet Bombing Range was worked out. Although Leonard Cheshire had said we must fly low for the best results it was decided to try dropping smoke bombs from various levels. Attempts were made to dive bomb from 15,000ft [4,570m] and, when this failed, from progressively lower heights. In the end we found it was as Cheshire had said – to get a smoke marker close to the target in the Wash we had to come down to around 2,000ft [610m] and then dive directly at the blob in the sea; down, down, until it was held in the middle of the windscreen, then 'Bomb away'. This time however, it was not master Hickox who did the releasing of the bomb. I had a button on the control column and merely had to press it with my right thumb when I judged that the correct moment had arrived. It was entirely a matter of practice, and within a very short time the crews of 627 Squadron could plop their markers right alongside the Wainfleet target. The question now was – could we do this under battle conditions?

We did not know the plans for the invasion of France – Operation *Overlord* – required destruction of the French railway system leading to the landing area. The best way of doing this was by employing heavy bombers, but grave doubts existed at the highest level as to the accuracy with which this could be done. Winston Churchill was adamant that French lives must not be lost needlessly and eventually it was agreed that 5 Group should undertake a mass attack on a marshalling yard in the Paris area to prove the case one way or the other. Juvisy was selected as the target and the marshalling yard was attacked on the night of 18/19 April, by 202 Lancasters led by Leonard Cheshire and a small force of Mosquitoes – 627 Squadron participating as 'makey-learns'. One of our pilots, Jim Marshallsay, was not detailed for the trip but thumbed a ride in a 617 Squadron Lancaster.

The attack on Juvisy was a bombing classic; the railway yards were marked at each end with red spot-fires and the heavy bombers laid their cargoes between the target indicators. The bombing was concentrated, the yards were put out of action, few French lives were lost and all but one Lancaster returned safely to base. The railway yards were so badly damaged that they were not brought back into service until 1947.

The real test of the new tactics had still to be made – against targets in Germany. 5 Group was therefore unleashed against three of these targets in quick succession – Brunswick on 22/23 April; Munich two nights later; and Schweinfurt on 26/27 April.

After these attacks the Group turned exclusively to support of the bombing campaign against interdiction targets for Operation *Overlord*. So far as Brunswick and Munich were concerned, considerable damage was done; and in the case of Munich, 90 per cent of the bombs fell in the right place, doing more damage in one night that had been achieved by Bomber Command and the 8th Air Force in the preceding four years.

The flexibility and superiority of the new system was clearly revealed and, speaking for myself, I found the business of marking a German target no worse than marking anywhere else. The point was that enemy AA defences in Germany were almost exclusively of the heavy variety, for use against relatively high flying aircraft. There was not much light flak; this was concentrated in France and the Low Countries. Consequently, when the Mosquitoes of 627 Squadron circled Brunswick on 22 April, there was not much opposition from the ground. The aiming point was a large park and we plonked our four spot-fires into it with the greatest of ease. Only three of the 265 Lancasters taking part in this attack were lost.

During the week in which these early low-level marking efforts against German targets were taking place, Bill Hickox and I were suddenly called to the CO's office. We were trying desperately to fathom what we could have done wrong when we were ushered in to Roy Elliott's presence. He got up from his chair, grinned broadly, and announced that we had each been awarded the DFC. This was a proud moment for us, particularly since these were the first DFCs awarded to members of 627 Squadron.

While no award of the Victoria Cross was ever made for a Mosquito sortie, Cheshire's contribution to the success of the Munich operation on 24/25 April, when he led four Mosquitoes of the Marking Force in 5 Group, was mentioned in his VC citation on 8 September 1944. The crews who took part were: W/C Cheshire and Pat Kelly; S/L Dave Shannon DSO and Len Sumpter; F/L Terry Kearns and F/L Hone Barclay, and F/L Gerry Fawke and F/L Tom Bennett. Sir Arthur Harris had sanctioned the release of the Mosquitoes to 617 Squadron and insisted they could be retained only if Munich was hit heavily. 'Benny' Goodman continues:

1 May was another 'first' for Bill and me. The target was an engineering works outside Tours – the Usine Lictard works. We air-tested our faithful Wooden Wonder in the morning and then settled down to study maps of the Tours area and photographs of the target itself. The factory had been bombed a few days earlier by 8th Air Force B-17s, but the photographs showed that nearly all the bombs had fallen in the surrounding fields. To drop bombs a few hundred yards from the aiming point might be good enough on a large area, but on a pin-point target like a factory the bombs had to be 'on the button'.

We took off in the late evening and headed for France, climbing rapidly to 25,000ft [7,620m]. The PFF Lancasters of 83 and 97 Squadrons had taken off about an hour before us and were to drop a yellow target indicator 10 miles [16km] from Tours, from which the four low-level marker aircraft would set course accurately for the target area. Having dropped the yellow indicator for us, the Lancasters would head directly to the target, identify it on *H2S* and discharge hundreds of illuminating flares above it. As Bill and I approached the final turning point, losing height steadily, the yellow TI suddenly cascaded down ahead of us. So far, so good. We flew over the TI and headed for the target. Approaching Tours a great carpet of light suddenly spread out in front of us; we lost more height and soon we were under the carpet at 1,500ft [460m] and it was as bright as day. If a fighter appeared now, we would be dead ducks, and if there was light flak in the area we would certainly have a very rough time. Nothing happened. We circled around, and suddenly I saw the factory close by. I immediately pressed the transmit button on my VHF and called 'Pen-nib Three Seven, Tally Ho'. This was the laid-down method of informing the other marker pilots that the target had been found; they now withdrew from the illuminated area to give me room to manoeuvre and make my dive onto the factory.

I circled around the works, losing speed and positioning the Mosquito for the dive, then opened the bomb doors and pressed the control column gently forward. Our speed increased and the target leapt up towards us, filling the windscreen. At about 500ft [150m] I pressed the bomb release button and there was a slight jerk as the four spot-fires left their slips. I continued in the dive for another couple of seconds, selected bomb doors closed and turned sharply to the left in order to check our results. There was a red glow among the factory buildings and in fact the spots had fallen through the glass roof of a machine shop. This was splendid from my point of view – I had marked the target accurately – but as the spot fires were inside the machine shop they could not be seen clearly by the Main

Force crews, now trundling towards Tours.

Marker Leader (Roy Elliott) flew over the works and called in the next marker pilot to lay his red indicators in the yard alongside the machine shop. This was done. Marker Leader then called the Controller and told him that the target had been marked successfully; the Controller broadcast to the Main Force on W/T and VHF to bomb the clump of red spots, and this was done. The marking had taken less than 5 minutes, from my 'Tally Ho' to Roy Elliott's confirmation to the Controller that the target was ready for Main Force action. The low-level marking technique had been vindicated once more, and the target was flattened.

Two nights later I made a grave tactical miscalculation which might easily have killed us – or alternatively might have set Bill Hickox on another long hike home from an enemy target,

with me in tow. The target was Mailly-le-Camp, a German tank depot near Epernay. Cheshire was to lead the low-level marker aircraft and eight Mosquitoes of 627 Squadron were to be at a slightly higher level and were to dive bomb the light flak positions which were known to be around this depot. The raid was timed to begin at 0001 hours, when all good troops should be in bed, and the Mosquito force arrived over Mailly 5 minutes before zero hour as briefed. Although the target was marked accurately and Cheshire passed the order to bomb, confusion occurred. The first wave did not receive instructions and began to orbit the target. This was fatal and the German night-fighters moved in and began to shoot down the Lancasters. Eventually the situation was sorted out and bombs began to crash down onto the depot; but the cost was high – forty-two of the 362 attackers were lost.

From our worm's eye view, Bill and I could see bomber after bomber coming down in flames towards us; and we had a scary time as we dived on the light flak batteries, dropped our bombs singly on them, avoided light flak and burning Lancasters and contrived to keep ourselves out of harm's way. When our fourth bomb had gone I called Marker Leader and was told to go home. Bill gave me a course to steer for the French coast and I should have climbed to 25,000ft [7,620m], but because of the mayhem in the target area I stayed at low level. All went well for a few minutes and then a searchlight shone directly on us, followed immediately by two or three more. Light flak batteries opened up and the pretty blue, red, green and white tracery associated with light AA fire came shooting up the beams and exploded all around us.

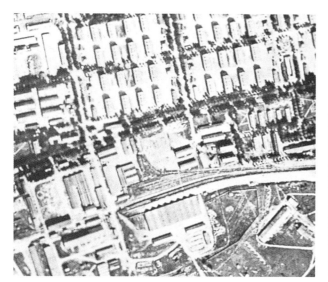

Mailly-le-Camp, before (above), **during** (above right) **and after** (right) **the raid by 346 Lancasters, fourteen Mosquitoes and two PFF Mosquitoes on the night of 3/4 May 1944. Despite good marking the main force delayed its attack and paid dearly, losing 42 Lancasters, or 11.6 per cent of the force. 1,500 tons of bombs were dropped with great accuracy and hundreds of buildings and vehicles, including 37 tanks, were destroyed.**
G/C J.R. Goodman

We were at 500ft [150m] and I did not dare to lose height, nor could I climb because this would have been a 'gift' to the German gunners. With Bill's exhortation 'watch your instruments' ringing in my ears I turned steeply to port through 30 degrees, levelled out for a few seconds, then rolled into a steep turn to starboard and repeated the performance. Although we were in searchlights and flak for quite a long time, we were not being held by any one light or being shot at by any one gun for very long; and we zig-zagged our way steadily towards the coast. It was a tense time for us and we did not speak; we could hear the explosions around us from light AA shells, but incredibly, were not hit. Deliverance came eventually as we breasted a low hill and ahead of us lay the sea. Now we were treated to a rare sight. The final group of searchlights were shining through the trees on top of the hill we had just passed, and the beams were actually above us and lighting us on our way. We roared along a river estuary, below the level of the lighthouse at Le Treport and then were away over the 'drink' and climbing to safety, home and bed.

More trips to railway yards followed, and then, on 28 May, we were briefed for something entirely different. We were to attack a heavy German gun on the coast of the Cherbourg Peninsula, at a place called St Martin de Varreville, which covered the approach to Utah Beach, which would be assaulted by American troops on D-Day. This sortie took just under 3 hours – it would have been shorter still, but we had great difficulty in finding the gun which was well camouflaged. However, it was found, marked and bombed, and a captured German report said that after several direct hits by armour-piercing bombs the casemate burst open and collapsed. This particular gun certainly did not impede the Americans on D-Day; the area was a heap of rubble.

1 June 1944 was the same as any other day at Woodhall Spa. Bill and I walked to the Flights after breakfast, found that we were on the Battle Order and went to the dispersal and tested 'G-George'. We then strolled to the Operations Room and were told that the target was to be the marshalling yard at Saumur. The day proceeded normally, with detailed briefing about the target and a close examination of maps and photographs. At the end of the afternoon we attended the AOC's broadcast link-up with the COs of all squadrons participating, then made ready to go.

The operation was a copy-book 5 Group attack, with no alarms and excursions. After landing, we switched off everything and climbed out as we had done so often before. 'G-George' stood black and silent; the ground crew moved forward to ask if all was well; it was a lovely summer night. After debriefing we ate the usual bacon and eggs and went to bed. Maybe tomorrow there would be a stand-down for us. We did not know it, but in fact our tour was over. We had flown together against Fortress Europe thirty-eight times; soon we would be instructors again; and soon our work in 5 Group would be recognised by the award of a Bar to the DFC to each of us. Paradoxically, however, Bill and I would never fly together again.

B.IX ML897 of 1409 Met Flight landing at Wyton in November 1944 after its 153rd sortie. via Philip Birtles

Jewish Times! It is doubtful whether the Germans had time to read it before two Fw 190s jumped them but their Mosquito sustained further damage. Joe turned into one of the Focke Wulfs, prepared if nothing else to take one with him, but at the last moment the night-fighter veered away. Joe finally broke off the engagement by going down to 200ft [60m] and flying back to Manston. Manston was blacked out so the Verey recognition signal was fired. With the

An 8 Group weather report by P/O Joe Patient and P/O Norry Gilroy a 1409 Met Flight crew, delayed the Normandy invasion by one day and D-Day finally went ahead on 6 June. *Pampa* flights such as this were sometimes equally as memorable. P/O Edwin R. Perry, a navigator in the Met Flight, recalls that Patient and Gilroy had a 'particularly unenviable encounter' during a 'special' *Pampa* to Berlin, carrying bombs.

They were disabled at 27,000ft [8,230m] by AA fire. They went on to Berlin and released their bombs, together with a brick which Norry let out through the Window chute wrapped in the

runway lit up they touched down, when a returning Typhoon also making an emergency landing, skidded round and sliced the Mosquito in half. Our two scrambled out and managed to extricate the fighter pilot, who was trapped and fearful that fire would develop.

Edwin Perry and his pilot, P/O V.J.C. 'Ginger' Miles, had been flight sergeants in 139 Squadron, like Patient and Gilroy, before joining 1409 Met Flight after nineteen 'ops'. Perry recalls:

Commissioning involved interviews with the OC, S/L Mike Birkin, the Wyton station

Oblt Fritz Krause, a staffel-kapitan **in I./NJGr.10, (later Kommandeur III./NJG11) stands beside his Fw 190A-5 of the** Wilde Sau **staffel, one of the** Luftwaffe **Nachtjagd units used mainly to hunt Mosquitoes at night at high altitude. The Fw is fitted with FuG 217** Neptun J **radar and a long-range belly tank. Near Berlin on the night of 7/8 July 1944 Krause shot down a 692 Squadron Mosquito crewed by F/L Burley** DFC **(KIA) and F/L E.V. Saunders** DFC **(PoW) in this fighter.**
via Hans Peter Debrowski

commander, G/C O.R. Donaldson, and the AOC, AVM Don Bennett at Group HQ. The great Don only asked one elementary navigation question. He pointed to two adjoining parallels of latitude on a wall map in his office and asked, 'If your aircraft is travelling at 240 knots, how long to cover the distance?' On being answered '15 minutes' he wished me good fortune and the interview, taking all of 3 minutes, was over.

P/O Perry had completed exactly 100 sorties by the war's end. Not all crewmen were as fortunate. On the night of 19/20 September 1944, luck finally ran out for another hitherto charmed airman, W/C Guy Gibson VC DSO DFC. The designated Master Bomber for the raid on Rheydt was unavailable and the famous dams raid leader, at this time attached to the Master Bomber Team at No 54 Base, Coningsby, took his place, with S/L J.B. Warwick DFC as navigator. They used KB267 'E', a 627 Squadron B.XX, for the operation. Everything appears to have gone according to plan over the target, but while returning over Walcheren both of his engines cut and the Mosquito crashed near the sea wall. Both Gibson and Warwick were buried at Steenbergenen-Kruisland, 21 miles (13km) north of Bergen-op-Zoom. The pilot and navigator had only flown Mosquitoes on one or two occasions prior to this and the most likely theory for the accident is that the fuel transfer cocks were not operated in the correct sequence and the engines ran out of fuel.

Accuracy and Devastation

On the night of 5/6 October six Mosquitoes from 692 Squadron, five carrying a 1,000lb (450kg) mine and one a 1,500lb (680kg) mine, together with four of 571 Squadron, mined the Kiel Canal for a second time. P/O J. Ralph Wood RCAF of 692 Squadron says that this, his sixty-first operation, 'proved to be one of our more interesting ops – the 'Daddy' of them all.' He explains:

After practising for six weeks, diving and low flying over the River Ouse in East Anglia, we were ready for the actual attack. Defences were stronger now, amounting to ninety-seven guns and twenty-five searchlights. We had to mine the canal at a specific location in order to avoid the hills and balloon cables. We crossed the North Sea at around 1,000ft [300m] in order to avoid radar detection, climbing to 10,000ft [3,050m] upon reaching the enemy coast. We then flew inland a short distance and when over the canal, dove to between 150 and 250 ft [45 and 80m] into patches of ground fog, shot at by tracers that looked like oranges, and hoping we wouldn't collide with the other bombers. The flak had the appearance of being spewed from a huge garden hose. The red, orange, and yellow cataracts streamed towards us and seemed to pass along my belly as I lay prone over the bombsight with my heart in my mouth. We dropped our 'vegetable' from a height of 100ft [30m].

After sewing our mine, the order of the day was 'Pass the beads' and 'Let's get the hell out of here!' We sure had the twitch this night but it was a wizard operation. This was a parachute mine we dropped – magnetic – to blow up ships at different times as they went through the canal. Our Mosquitoes had tied up 5,000,000 tons of shipping waiting to go through. About a dozen of us were on the job and all got back, although one pilot flew back with a dead navigator beside him, for company (gulp). We certainly enjoyed ourselves, but we certainly had the 'twitch' before reaching the target. For our part in this operation, Andy and I received an immediate award of the DFC.

On 3 November, Ralph Wood's seventy-seventh 'op', he and Andy Lockhart flew their last mission together, and their seventeenth to Berlin, or the 'Snake's home' as the Canadian navigator described the 'Big City'.

A typical trip to Berlin would be a feint attack on a couple of cities on the way to our target and throwing out *Window* to foul up the radar. Once over Berlin we were usually caught in a huge cone of searchlights, so blinding [that] Andy couldn't read the instruments. 'Are we upside down or not?' he'd ask. I'd look down at the bombs exploding below and assure him that we were right side up. As the AA crap seemed to surround us, Andy would throw our *Moncton Express* around the skies trying desperately to get out of the searchlights. On three occasions we lost an engine about now and had to limp home, as one set of searchlights passed us on to another set, and so on until they ran out of lights. When over the target, we'd bomb and get out as fast as we could. This is when I'd sit in my seat, the blood draining out of my face

F/L Andy Lockhart DFC **RCAF and F/O Ralph Wood** DFC **RCAF of 692 Squadron.** Mrs Phylis E. Wood

(Below) **B.XVI P3-A MM138, one of three to bear the name** The Moncton Express, **flown by F/L Andy Lockhart and F/O Ralph Wood of 692 Squadron.**
Mrs Phylis E. Wood

F/L D.W. Allen DFC, **navigator, and F/L T.P. Lawrenson, pilot, stand in front of B.IX LR503 GB-F of 105 Squadron on the occasion of its 203rd operation. LR503 eventually set a Bomber Command record of 213 sorties, but was lost on 10 May 1945 along with the crew, F/L Maurice Briggs and John Baker, when it crashed at Calgary during a goodwill tour of Canada.** via Norman Booth

and my stomach in tight knots. Jesus, this could be it, I thought. And after tight moments like this I'd say, 'Andy, pass the beads.' I hope my eighteen visits to Berlin accomplished something. On our return trip we faced the terrors of murderous flak concentrations and the new formidable adversary in the form of the first jet fighters rising into the skies over Germany.

Berlin was the most frequent target for the LNSF. The Mosquitoes flew there so often (170 times, thirty-six of these on consecutive nights) that the raids were called the 'milk run', or alternatively, the 'Berlin Express', and the different routes there and back were known as 'Platform one, two and three.'

On 6/7 November, Bomber Command sent 235 Lancasters to attack the Mittelland Canal at Gravenhorst, the marking carried out by seven Mosquitoes of 627 Squadron.

The Mosquitoes eventually found the canal after great difficulty whereupon S/L F.W. Boyle RAAF and F/L L.C.E. De Vigne dropped their marker with such a degree of accuracy that it fell into the water and was extinguished. Only thirty-one Lancasters bombed before the Master Bomber called for the raid to be abandoned. The forty-eight Mosquitoes dispatched to Gelsen-kirchen on a 'spoof' raid to draw German night fighters away from the Mittelland attack and a 3 Group raid on Koblenz, had better luck. The Gelsenkirchen raid began as planned, five minutes ahead of .the two other attacks, at 1925 hours. The city was still burning as a result of that afternoon's raid by 738 RAF heavies. From an altitude of 25,000ft (7,620m) the Mosquitoes added their red and green TIs and HE to the fires. A few searchlights and only very light flak greeted the crews over the devastated city.

F/L John D.S. Garratt, a navigator in 109 Squadron at Little Staughton recalls:

From time to time many enterprising COs devised schemes (some cracked-brained) for improving bombing accuracy and results, or for meeting emergency calls. One such scheme which involved 109 Squadron in December 1944, was the 'Formation Daylight'. The idea was for an *Oboe* equipped aircraft to act as 'Lead Ship' (to borrow the American term) for a small force of Light Night Striker Mosquitoes, each carrying 4,000 pounders [1,810kg] to attack small, vital targets in daylight, thus achieving, it was hoped, great precision. For some odd reason, two 582 Squadron Lancaster B.VIs, specially adapted for the leadership role, were at first allocated. The Lanc VI was good for 28,000ft [8,530m], but its cruising speed was incompatible with the Mosquito IX or XVI. It was to carry an extra *Oboe* pilot and navigator

128 Squadron Mosquitoes taxi out at Wyton fitted with 50 gallon (230 litre) underwing drop tanks for a night operation. via Rolls-Royce

of 109 Squadron to fly the specialized bombing run. This arrangement was not popular with the *Oboe* Mossie crews.

One of these was F/L Bob Jordan and Ronnie Plunkett, of 105 Squadron at Bourn. Plunkett heard about the scheme on 9 December:

My pilot and myself were asked to operate the *Oboe* on the operation which took place on 23 December. [To disrupt enemy reinforcements for the Battle of the Bulge, an attack on the Cologne/Gremburg railway marshalling yards would be made by twenty-seven Lancasters and three Mosquitoes, while fifty-two Mosquitoes went to the rail yards at Limburg, and forty more to Siegburg]. We were to lead the second formation of ten, while S/L R.A.M. Palmer DFC [from 109 Squadron] and his crew, would lead the first formation [in an *Oboe*-equipped Lancaster borrowed from 582 Squadron]. Having flown a couple of experimental exercises with S/L Hildyard on a Lancaster for the purpose of familiarization, we were considered to be capable of carrying out this duty.

At Graveley (35 Squadron Lancasters) we were detailed to fly on PB272 'X for X-Ray' flown by F/O E.J. Rigby and his usual crew. Bob Jordan and I were to take over the aircraft 60 miles [100km] out from the target to operate the *Oboe*. We were airborne at 1038 with eleven 1,000lb [450kg] MC on the racks. Our outward run was normal except that two Lancs touched wings and went down. When we took over, our aircraft came under predicted heavy flak and caught fire which the crew were able to extinguish. Since we were not on the beam we did not get a release signal and had to jettison the load from 17,000ft [5,180m].

We had a clear view of S/L Palmer leading the first formation just ahead and his aircraft came under intense AA fire. Smoke billowed from the Lanc and I wondered why he did not bale out there and then because there seemed to be no hope for them. They were then attacked by a German fighter, but carried on and completed their bombing run. The Lanc then went over on the port side and went down. I cannot think what, other than sheer determination, kept him on the bombing run. He carried out his duty in text book fashion. After this we went down to

6,000ft [1,830m] and Rigby did a good job getting us all back to Manston.

Palmer was later awarded a posthumous Victoria Cross. The attacks on Siegburg and Limburg, meanwhile, were, after a change of heart, finally led by *Oboe* Mosquitoes, not Lancasters, as F/L John Garratt recalls:

After some bright spark suggested using an *Oboe* Mosquito as 'Lead Ship' – the obvious choice in the first place, my pilot, F/L C.M. Rostron DFC, and I, were detailed as 'Lead Ship' crew! The target was a small installation at Siegburg in western Germany. Our bomb load was four 500lb [230kg] MC (surprisingly!) and our kite, XVI MM123. We were to take twelve Night Light Strikers carrying 4,000 pounders [1,810kg]. Most of East Anglia was fog-bound and the heavies were stood down, but we could land on FIDO [a system of using flaming fuel along the edge of the runway to burn off fog and enable landings to be made] at Gravely if we had to. We were to rendezvous with the strikers off Orfordness and proceed in a loose gaggle to the

'Turning-on-Point' for the bombing run where the strikers would close in to a tight formation of Vics astern of the lead ship, with bomb bay doors to open 2 minutes before release point. (The bomb doors on the Mosquito were notoriously prone to creep and if not fully open when the 'Cookie' went, they went with it!) The strikers' navigators were to release on visual cue from the lead ship, which I thought was the weak link in the scheme.

We took off at 1455. Just enough time to reach the target in daylight. To my surprise we met the strikers on time and in position as planned and flew across Holland into Germany to the 'Turning-on-Point' where the *Oboe* ground stations called us in and we began to transmit, creating the beam. The run down the beam went OK. There was little opposition, and the striker pilots' station keeping I thought, remarkable, particularly since we had had no formation practice. Our timing was bang-on and the release signal came loud and clear. Immediately after bomb release we broke formation in an orderly manner (bearing in mind it was now getting dark, even at 30-odd thousand feet), and flew back to base singly. All kites returned safely. At debriefing we were told our error off AP was small and the timing spot on. Despite enquiries, I never learned

F/L Alfred J. Cork DFM **of 109 Squadron, pictured in January 1945, a month after being shot down, on 27 December 1944 during an** Oboe **marking operation to Rheydt.** A.J. Cork DFM

whether the operation was considered a success. The intelligence bods never told us much, safe in their ivory towers. However, we never flew another 'Formation Daylight'.

Efforts to relieve the pressure on the Bulge continued. On a foggy, very cold, 27 December, 200 Lancasters and eleven Mosquitoes attacked railway marshalling yards at Rheydt. F/L Hodgson and F/L Alfred J. Cork DFM of 109 Squadron, one of the *Oboe* force, took off from Little Staughton at about 1300 hours in ML961 'T-Tommy'. Cork, who was on his forty-first *Oboe* sortie, recalls:

After take off it soon became apparent that the cabin heating was not working properly, if at all. Soon after crossing the coast the windows became completely frosted over and visibility was virtually nil but we pressed on. We completed the release run and I believe that I had already received the release signal and released the first TI, when a burst of machine gun (or cannon) fire hit us. I could still see nothing through the iced up perspex. 'Hodge' signalled to me that we were out of control and pointed to the escape hatch. At that moment, a second burst of gunfire hit us and the aircraft went into a dive. I got out. Sadly,

B.XVI 'K-King' ML963 on a test flight from Hatfield on 30 September 1944. Major repair work on the aircraft had recently been carried out following damage sustained on operations. ML963 flew 571 Squadron's first sortie, 12/13 April 1944, and on 1 January 1945 was used by F/L N.J. Griffiths and F/O W.R. Ball for the raid on railway tunnels in the Eiffel region during the Battle of the Bulge. ML963 failed to return from Berlin on 10/11 April 1945 following an engine fire. The 4,000lb (1,810kg) bomb was jettisoned and F/O Richard Oliver and F/Sgt Max Young, who baled out near the Elbe, returned safely. Charles E. Brown

Hodge didn't. My parachute opened and one of my highly prized pre-war fleece lined all-leather flying boots fell off. I was angry – those boots were a mark of seniority! (Late comers had to make do with canvas legged boots!)

Cork was picked up and transported back to England. On New Year's Day 1945, with the Battle of the Bulge still raging in the Ardennes, 8 Group Mosquitoes were asked to fly one of the most remarkable daylight operations of the war. Bomber Command had to cut the railway supply lines through the Eifel region between the Rhine and the Ardennes. So, while the heavies bombed marshalling yards near Koblenz and Cologne, precision attacks on fourteen railway tunnels in the region were carried out by seventeen Mosquitoes, each carrying a 4,000lb (1,810kg) delayed-action bomb, which they would use to skip-bomb the mouths of the tunnels from 100–200ft [30–60m]. The only loss was PF411, a 128 Squadron B.XVI, which crashed on take off, killing the crew. Four crews in 128 Squadron who bombed achieved mixed results. Six out of seven B.XVIs of 692 Squadron bombed tunnels near Mayen, losing PF414 to light flak, while five crews of 571 Squadron were more successful. One bomb, dropped by B.XVI ML963 'K-King' crewed by F/L Norman J. Griffiths and F/O W.R. Ball, totally destroyed a tunnel at Bitburg.

Bill Ball wrote:

At 100ft [30m] the ground simply raced beneath us like lightning. From the big railway junction, dead on ETA the tunnel came up in a flash and we could just not position ourselves in time. We undershot the target and went around again and this time ran up, dead in line, astonished that the ack-ack batteries had not yet been alerted. We rapidly reached the target, dropped the 4,000lb [1,810kg] bomb and soared almost vertically to get away from the blast, and when we had gained height, we looked back and saw a great column of brown black smoke and sizeable debris rumbling upwards. A mixture of bricks and shattered masonry rising, falling and scattering wide. Norman and I agreed that it would be some time before trains ran again on that line.

With the war in Europe reaching a conclusion, the Mosquitoes were repeatedly called upon to mark for the bombers in day-light. One of the most dramatic marking operations of the war occurred on 14 March when a Mosquito of 5 Group and eight *Oboe* Mosquitoes of 105 and 109 Squadrons set out to mark for 5 Group Lancasters in attacks on the Bielefeld and Arnsburg viaducts. Although the four Mosquitoes attempting to mark the Arnsburg viaduct for 9 Squadron failed in the attempt (with no damage to the viaduct), and three of the *Oboe* Mosquitoes were unable to mark the Bielefeld viaduct for 617 Squadron, B.XVI MM191, flown by F/O G.W. Edwards of 105 Squadron, succeeded in getting his markers on target, and more than 100yd (90m) of the Bielefeld viaduct collapsed under the explosions. (Twenty-eight of the thirty-two Lancasters dispatched carried *Tallboy* bombs and one from 617 Squadron dropped the first 22,000lb (4,520kg) *Grand Slam* bomb.

The biggest 8 Group Mosquito operation to Berlin took place on 21/22 March when 142 Mosquitoes carried out two attacks and only one aircraft was lost. 8 Group had made their last daylight raid on 6 March when forty-eight Mosquitoes led by *Oboe* leaders in 109 Squadron bombed Wesel. The last

Oboe-**equipped B.IX LR504 of 109 Squadron at Little Staughton on 1 March 1945 after its 190th sortie. Note the 'grim reaper' motif and the painted-over plexiglas nose, the area being filled with the radar equipment with no room for a bomb sight or bomb aimer. Markers or bombs were dropped by the navigator when he heard the release signal from the 'Mouse' station. Each Oboe Mosquito had a special call-sign for use by the ground stations to call it onto the release run, at which point the navigator switched on his pulse repeater transmitter. On the run the 'Mouse' releasing station monitored the aircraft's progress, measured its ground speed, and sent warning signals to the navigator at set points. It also gave the release signal when the release point was reached.** via Philip Birtles

In the period January to May 1945, LNSF Mosquitoes flew almost 4,000 sorties. 8 Group's Mosquito squadrons finished the war with the lowest losses in Bomber Command. via Jerry Scutts

attack on Berlin by Mosquitoes took place on the night of 20/21 April when seventy-six carried out six separate raids on the long-suffering capital. Five days later, on Sunday 25 April, 359 Lancasters and sixteen Mosquitoes set out to bomb Hitler's 'Eagle's Nest' chalet and SS barracks at Berchtesgaden, deep in the Austrian Alps. Eight of the Mosquitoes were *Oboe* markers. One was crewed by F/L Derek James DFC and F/L John C. Sampson of 105 Squadron. Sampson recalls:

We took off at 0725 and the flight was 4hrs 15 minutes. We carried four red TIs to mark for the heavies. We flew at 36,000ft [11,000m] because of the Alps and, since *Oboe* signals went line of sight and did not follow the curvature of the earth, the further the target, the higher one needed to be. (Following the Normandy invasion, *Oboe* ground stations were located on the continent thus increasing the effective range of the system). I heard the first two dots of the release signal and then nothing more. We were unable to drop and brought the markers back to base. On investigation, it was established that a mountain peak between the ground station and

the aircraft had blocked out the signal. No *Oboe* Mosquito was successful this day.

To all intents and purposes, the war in Europe was over, and on 25/26 April twelve Mosquitoes dropped leaflets over PoW camps in Germany telling Allied prisoners so. On 29 April flights to deliver food to the starving Dutch population in German-occupied Holland began. The operation, called *Manna*, took place using RAF and USAAF heavy bombers, their bomb bays filled with provisions instead of bombs, the food dropping areas being marked by the *Oboe* Mosquitoes. Meanwhile, it was feared that the enemy might stage a last stand in Norway when ships laden with troops began assembling at Kiel. Therefore, on the night of 2/3 May three final raids by 142 Mosquitoes from eight squadrons in 8 Group and thirty-seven Mosquitoes of 100 Group, were organized. In the first raid, a record 126 aircraft from 100 Group, including thirty-seven *Firebash* Mosquitoes led by sixteen *Oboe* Mosquitoes, attacked airfields in the Kiel area with Napalm and incendiaries.

In the second and third attacks, one hour apart, 126 Mosquitoes of 8 Group bombed through thick cloud using *H2X* (the US development of *H2S*) and *Oboe*. One Mosquito, in 100 Group, and two Halifaxes, which collided, were lost this night.

In the period January–May 1945, LNSF Mosquitoes had flown almost 4,000 sorties. Altogether, 8 Group's Mosquito squadrons flew 28,215 sorties, yet they had the lowest losses in Bomber Command; just 108 (about one per 2,800 sorties), while eighty-eight more were written off on their return because of battle damage. This is an incredible achievement, even more remarkable when one considers that well over two-thirds of operations were flown on nights when the heavies were not operating. The Mosquito crews were never slow to point out this fact to their brethren in the heavies. To paraphrase 692 Squadron's delightful ditty; 'We fly alone', they sang: 'When all the heavies are grounded and dining, the Mosquitoes will be climbing. It's every night, but though they never can give us a French route, to the honour of 8 Group, we still press on.'

CHAPTER SIX

The Gestapo Hunters
2 Group, 2nd Tactical Air Force

On 27 May 1943 AVM Basil Embry replaced AVM J.H. d'Albiac at 2 Group HQ, Bylaugh Hall, and on 1 June, the Group's eleven Boston, Ventura and Mitchell squadrons transferred, first, to Fighter Command, then, when this divided to form Air Defence of Great Britain (ADGB), to 2nd Tactical Air Force. 2nd TAF would be in the vanguard of pre-invasion operations for destroying tactical rather than strategic targets as and when D-Day arrived. Embry coveted Mosquito FB.VIs for his new command but they were in short supply. Priority though was given to the re-equipment of the three Ventura squadrons that had suffered so unmercifully at the hands of the Luftwaffe and which were badly in need of re-equipment. 464 Squadron RAAF and 487 Squadron RNZAF received their first Mk VIs at Sculthorpe in August, and 21 Squadron

received theirs in September, but it was not until October that this first Mosquito Wing ('140 Airfield') in 2nd TAF was operational. The eight Boston and Mitchell squadrons meanwhile, were now located at bases in Hampshire, to be near the invasion front, while Embry's HQ had relocated to Mongewell Park in Berkshire.

On Sunday 3 October 1943 every bomber squadron in 2 Group was allocated one of a series of transformer stations between Paris and Brittany, all of which were to be attacked from low level. For the first time 464 and 487 Mosquito Squadrons took part, 487 Squadron being led by the station commander, G/C Percy Pickard and 464 Squadron by W/C H.J. Meakin. Their targets were power stations at Pont Chateau and Mur de Bretange and to reach them they had to fly to Exeter before crossing the Channel. The series of attacks caused

maximum disruption to the French electrical system and the railways which were electrified from Paris to Brittany.

On 15 October, 138 Wing at Lasham near Alton, Hampshire, began re-equipping with the FB.VI when 613 Squadron joined 2 Group. On 18 November 305 Polish Squadron transferred from Swanton Morley and joined 107 and 613 Mosquito Squadrons at Lasham, Hampshire. (In December, 305 Squadron converted to FB.VIs after just five operations with Mitchells). On 31 December 21, 464 and 487 Squadrons took off from Sculthorpe for the last time, bombed Le Ploy, France, and landed at their new base at Hunsdon.

On 1 February 1944 107 Squadron discarded its Bostons for the FB.VI, and moved to Lasham. On 14 February, 226 Squadron did likewise, moving to Hartford Bridge. 88 Squadron (equipped with

In the summer of 1943, 2nd TAF was formed from 2 Group whose three Ventura squadrons, 21, 464 RAAF and 487 RNZAF, were quickly converted to Mosquito FB.VIs. HX917 EG-E joined 487 Squadron in July 1943 and was lost on 5 July 1944. Mosquito night-fighters and Mk VI fighter-bombers were used throughout 2nd TAF's auspicious career, both from the UK and on the Continent where the targets of the low-flying FB.VIs were lines of communication, tank columns and, when the occasion demanded, pin-point bombing of Nazi barracks and HQ buildings. RAF Swanton Morley

75

Mitchells) and 342 (equipped with Bostons), joined 305 at Hartford Bridge to form 137 Wing. 139 Wing, comprising 98, 180 and 320 Squadrons, all of whom were equipped with Mitchells, based themselves at Dunsfold. During January–February their targets were nominally the V-1 flying-bomb sites in the Pas de Calais. Mosquitoes tried various techniques in attacking the *Noball* or *Crossbow* sites, as they were called. The normal method was to go low-level all the way but this could result in aircraft sustaining damage by 20mm flak, or small arms fire, when crossing the coast. A. 'Baron' Humphrey of 613 Squadron recalls one such outcome:

I suppose few people will have had the sight I had of a bullet hanging in mid-air in front of my face, fortunately stopped dead (but thankfully I wasn't) by, and partly buried in, my laminated windscreen. It happened on 4 February 1944. I was piloting a FB.VI. My observer was F/Sgt Joe Carroll. We were just climbing over the cliffs of northern France on a low-level *Noball* attack in the Pas de Calais. The snag was that the whole windscreen was starred so that we had no forward visibility – not very nice at 260mph [420kph] and just above the ground. Luckily, I was the last plane in a starboard echelon, so could watch the others through the port window. I moved a bit further out and a little higher to be on the safe side. Near the target the routine was to climb, split into pairs, then spread out before the dive. Each pair would then drop their bombs, with 11-second delays to let us get clear, and as they exploded the next pair would be on their approach. I stayed with my pair leader, dived and bombed as he did and stayed in formation all the way back to Lasham where we landed safely. The bullet had my name on it, or at least the number of my Mossie, and it was coming directly towards my head, but stopped in time. Incidentally, on the way back it gave up the attempt and finally fell away from the screen.

A few days later, we were returning from another *Noball* attack and were again at the end of a starboard echelon. Just before we reached the French coast I saw, to my right, a radar aerial on a small hillock and near it a German soldier frantically swinging a light AA cannon towards us. I turned towards it, raked the aerial and then the gun with my own fire on the turn, but immediately afterwards felt a shudder somewhere at the rear. The aircraft then did its best to turn my right bank into a flick roll. As we were barely 10 feet [3m] above the ground, I didn't like that idea. I had to use both hands and all my strength on the 'stick' to prevent it. We turned a full circle and

headed north again, out over the sea, miles behind the rest of the squadron, but the leader called me on the radio to find out why I had left them. I replied that I was well back, so they slowed until I caught up, to escort me home.

The fight with the control column prevented me from getting into proper formation again; oddly enough, I found that the extra speed made things easier for me, The next snag was that we were still at low level and our route home took us straight over Beachy Head, but when I eased back on the stick to climb, the violent jerk over to starboard was repeated, so I had to leave the others, turn west and hope to get down along the lower part of the coast. The nearest aerodrome was Ford, and luckily I found that when I dropped the wheels and flaps I could hold her more easily. Nevertheless, It was still a 'dicey' do. As I touched down, still wrestling with the controls, the cuff edge of my chamois gloves caught and pulled the gun trigger and, although the firing switch was on 'safe', a burst from four cannons and four machine guns flew ahead of us. Presumably something had caused a short in the system. There were no repercussions afterwards, so I presume the bullets did no harm. When we examined the aircraft after my knees had stopped trembling, we found that the tailplane on the left and the elevator on the right had caught the brunt of the enemy fire, and the end of the starboard wing was flapping because the main spar was cracked.

Sometimes, 2nd TAF Mosquitoes operated against the V-1 sites led by two PFF Mosquitoes fitted with *Oboe*, and escorted by Spitfires. However, this technique meant that they had to fly in tight formation, straight and level for 10 minutes until bomb release, and a sitting duck for the AA gunners! Mosquito squadrons on average destroyed one *Crossbow* site for each 39.8 tons of bombs dropped compared with an average of 165.4 tons for the B-17, 182 tons for the Mitchell and 219 tons for the Marauder.

The main work for 2nd TAF remained the *Ranger* operations over France, and early in 1944, 418 Squadron was very much to the fore. On 27 January F/L James Johnson RCAF, and P/O John Caine RCAF and P/O Earl Boal RCAF, in FB.VIs, attacked Clermont-Farrand airfield. Johnson shot down a Ju 88, damaged a Ju 86 and shared in the downing of two Ju W34s with Caine, who also destroyed a Ju 88. By 8 May, Caine had destroyed twelve aircraft on the ground or water, with five more damaged on the ground or water. (In April–May 1945, Caine, now

2nd TAF Mosquito Squadrons 15.11.43–7.5.45	
21 (FB)	140 Wing, 2 Group, 15.11.43–7.5.45
29 (NF)	ADGB to 148 Wing, 85 (Base) Group, 1.5.44; to 147 Wing, 6.44, back to ADGB 26.8.44
107 (FB)	138 Wing, 2 Group, 1.2.44–7.5.45
140 (PR)	HQ, 34th Reconnaissance Wing, 11.43–7.5.45
219 (NF)	147 Wing, 85 (Base) Group, 28.8.44–7.5.45
264 (NF)	ADGB to 141 Wing, 85 (Base) Group, 19.12.43 (Administered as such from 10.3.44); left 141 Wing 19.6.44; to 148 Wing, 26.6.44; to UK on rest, 23.9.44; 148 Wing, 8.1.45–7.5.45
305 (FB)	138 Wing, 18.11.43–7.5.45
400 (PR)	83 Group, 39 Reconnaissance Wing
409 (NF)	148 Wing, 85 (Base) Group, 30.3.44
410 (NF)	141 Wing, 85 Group, 12.5.44. To 147 Wing, 85 Group, 18.6.44–7.5.45
418 (NF)	136 Wing, 2 Group, 21.11.44–7.5.45
464 (FB)	140 Wing, 2 Group, 15.11.43–7.5.45
487 (FB)	140 Wing, 2 Group, 15.11.43–7.5.45
488 (NF)	147 Wing, 85 (Base) Group, 12.5.44–26.4.45
604 (NF)	141 Wing, 26.4.44–2.5.44; to 147 Wing, 85 (Base) Group, until 23.9.44; to UK for rest; 148 Wing, 85 Group, 31.12.44; non–operational from 15.4.45 (disbanded 18.4.45)
605 (NF)	136 Wing, 2 Group, 21.11.44–7.5.45
613 (FB)	138 Wing, 2 Group, 18.11.43–7.5.45

(FB) Fighter–Bomber,
(PR) Photo–Reconnaissance,
(NF) Night-fighter

with 406 Squadron, and flying NF.XXXs, destroyed a Ju 88 on the ground and damaged four other aircraft on the ground).

On 21 March Lt. James F. Luma and F/O Colin Finlayson and F/L Donald MacFadyen and 'Pinky' Wright, all in 418 Squadron, flew a long-range *Ranger* over France. Luma and Finlayson attacked Luxeuil airfield, where they shot down a Ju W34 liaison aircraft, a Ju 52/3m transport and damaged two Gotha Go 242 glider transports and two Bf 109s on the ground, while MacFadyen and Wright shot down a Bv 141 which was coming into land. Moving on to Hagenau airfield, MacFadyen proceeded to destroy nine Go 242s and a Do 217 on the ground. MacFadyen later operated in 406 Squadron where he flew the NF.XXX on night intruders, finishing the war with seven aircraft and five V-1s

418 'City of Edmonton' Squadron RCAF crews pose for the camera in front of a FB.VI. The Canadians used NF.IIs for their first night-fighter patrol on 7/8 May 1943, when a Ju 88 was destroyed near Nantes. Note the camera port above the machine guns. Lt James F. Luma is seventh from the left. Tom Cushing

(Below) **FB.VI TH-Y of 418 Squadron RCAF taxies out for an intruder raid. The Canadians converted fully from NF.IIs to FB.VIs during spring and summer 1943.** Tom Cushing

destroyed, and five aircraft destroyed and seventeen damaged on the ground. Luma finished his tour in April 1944 and was awarded both a British and US DFC. On 14 April S/L Robert Kipp and F/L Pete Huletsky, also of 418 Squadron, shot down two Ju 52/3ms minesweepers fitted with degaussing rings, and two Do 217s on the ground, plus damaging two more. Kipp finished the war with a large bag of victories which included ten aircraft shot down, and seven and eight destroyed and damaged on the ground. Meanwhile, Stan Cotterill and 'Pop' McKenna destroyed four in a night sortie, and Charlie Scherf in three months from January to 16 May 1944, racked up twenty-three destroyed, thirteen of them in the air.

Targetting the Gestapo

Two notable pin-point raids were carried out in the spring of 1944. Amiens prison was known to be holding 700 French prisoners, among them Monsieur Vivant, a key resistance leader in Abbeville. A dozen prisoners were due to be executed on 19 February, so Operation *Jericho* was carried out on 18 February, in terrible weather, using 140 Wing at Hunsdon to breach its

20ft (6m) high and 3ft (1m) thick walls with 11-second bombs in the hope that most of the prisoners could escape. The concussion from the bombs should also open the cell doors. The sixteen-ship formation was led by G/C Percy Pickard, with navigator F/L 'Pete' Broadley, in 'F-Freddie'. If 487 and 464 Squadrons failed in their mission, the four FB.VIs of 21 Squadron led by W/C I.G. 'Daddy' Dale, had orders to destroy the target.

It was snowing heavily and by the time the formation crossed the French coast, seven FB.VIs and one of three Typhoon escort squadrons had aborted. At 1201 precisely, with the guards eating lunch, bombs from eleven Mosquitoes of 487 and 464 Squadrons hit the prison. The first bomb blew in almost all the doors and the wall was breached. F/L Tony Wickham in a specially equipped Film Photographic Unit (FPU) FB.VI made three passes over the burning prison, and P/O Leigh Howard filmed the flight of some 255 prisoners. 182 prisoners were later recaptured and some of the thirty-seven prisoners who died were machine gunned by the sentries. Fifty Germans also died. 'F-Freddie' was shot down by a Fw 190 of II/JG26 and Pickard and Broadley were killed. S/L Ian McRitchie RAAF of 464 Squadron, was

hit by flak. Despite being wounded in 26 places, he managed to crash land, but navigator, F/L R.W. 'Sammy' Sampson, died.

Another precision raid, to be carried out by 613 Squadron, was scheduled early in April. The target was the five-storey, 95ft (30m) high, Huize Kleykamp in The Hague, which housed the Dutch Central Population Registry and contained duplicates of all legally-issued Dutch personal identity papers. This was a big problem for the Dutch Resistance, because falsified identity papers could easily be identified by the Gestapo. The Resistance could not attack the Kleykamp themselves, it was heavily guarded, so they requested a pin-point bombing raid by the RAF. The large white building was tightly wedged among other houses in the Schevengsche Weg, close to the Peace Palace and was strongly defended by light anti-aircraft guns. In 1943 Jaap van der Kamp, a Dutch Resistance fighter, who worked under cover in Huize Kleykamp, had drawn sketches of the building and the exact location of the heavy metal cupboards where the identity papers were kept. These were smuggled to Britain by D'Aulnis de Bourrouill, a Dutch agent. The drawings were used to construct a scale model of the building, perfect in every detail right down to the thickness

A photographic still taken from W/C Bob Iredale's FB.VI, MM412 SB-F during the precision attack on Amiens Prison, 18 February 1944, one of the most famous operations of the war, when 12 FB.VIs of 464 RAAF and 487 RNZAF breached the walls of the prison, which was holding 700 French prisoners. The aircraft following is SB-A MM402, flown by S/L W.R.C. Sugden and his navigator, F/O A.H. Bridger. via John Rayner

Result of the Operation Jericho **precision attack on Amiens Prison on 18 February 1944. Both the northern and southern perimeter walls were breached. The attack came in from the north so it must be assumed that the southern breach, left of the main gate, was caused by a bomb that skidded through the prison after being dropped from east or north. Two pilots, P/O D.R. Fowler of 487 Squadron RNZAF, who flew EG-J HX974, and S/L Ian McRitchie, of 464 Squadron RAAF, who flew MM404 SB-T claim the same hole! SB-T was shot down on this raid, McRitchie was made PoW but Sampson, his navigator, was killed.** via Philip Birtles

and the composition of the walls. Scientists worked hard to develop a new type of 500lb (230kg) bomb, a mixture of incendiary and high explosive, which was designed to have the maximum effect on the mass of Gestapo files and records.

In the early morning of 11 April W/C R.N. Bateson DFC led six FB.VIs from Lasham for Swanton Morley where they took off again at 1305 for Holland. Twenty miles from the Dutch coast the FB.VIs climbed to 4,000ft (1,220m), crossing Overflakee, then descending to very low level. They made their way to Gouda then to Delft. Bateson and his navigator, F/O B.J. Standish, noticed there were no recognizable landmarks, just a vast expanse of water, dotted with islands where no islands should have been. Unknown to the air-

crews, the Germans had opened the sluice gates on the River Scheldt, inundating a large area of the flat Dutch countryside. After flying on for a few more minutes, crews finally got their bearings and continued on track for The Hague.

As they approached, the FB.VIs split up into pairs, following in line astern, sweeping across the rooftops, the narrow streets shuddering to the din of their engines. The first two FB.VIs lined up to attack while the other four circled Lake Gouda, allowing time for the 30-second delayed action bombs carried by the first two aircraft to explode. The third and fourth aircraft carried incendiaries and the fifth and sixth aircraft each had two HE bombs and two incendiaries. At the approach of the first Mosquitoes, soldiers drilling in the

courtyard fled in all directions. Bateson streaked towards the target, bomb doors open, his port wing missing the tall spire on top of the Peace Palace by inches. F/L Peter Cobley DFC, following Bateson, saw his leader's bombs drop. Cobley had a hazy impression of a German sentry throwing away his rifle and running for his life, then he saw Bateson's bombs quite literally skip through the front door of the headquarters.

Cobley dropped his bombs in turn, pulling up sharply over the roof of the Kleykamp. Two minutes later, with dense clouds of smoke already pouring from the shattered building, the second pair, flown by S/L Charles W.M. Newman and F/L F.G. 'Trev' Trevers, and F/L R.W. Smith and F/O J. Hepworth, made their attacks. Then the third pair, F/L Vic Hester and

FB.VIs 'T', 'V' and 'D' of 487 Squadron RNZAF, photographed on 29 February 1944 each carrying two 500 pounders (230kg) beneath their wings. None of these aircraft was used in the Amiens prison raid earlier that month when six VIs from 487 participated. via Graham M. Simons

B.VI EG-T MM417 on 29 February 1944, 11 days after the Amiens Prison raid. The crew, P/O M.N. Sparks and P/O A.C. Dunlop actually flew EG-T HX982 on that raid. Tom Cushing

Bombs from six FB.VIs of 613 Squadron destroy the Central Registry in The Hague, 11 April 1944.
via Graham M. Simons

F/O R. Birkett, and F/O Rob Cohen, a Dutchman, with F/Sgt P.G. Deave, sped in. (Cohen, a former student of the Delft Technical University, had escaped to England by paddling a canoe across the North Sea.) Hester got his bombs away but they hit the old Alexander barracks. Although he made a number of attacks, Cohen's bombs hung up and he was unable to release them. Instead he photographed the burning target. He was almost weeping with rage when he returned. (Cohen was killed attacking a target in France in August.) Spitfires escorted the FB.VIs home.

The Gestapo building had been completely destroyed, together with the majority of the identity papers, but sixty-one civilians, including van der Kamp, were killed, twenty-four seriously injured and forty-three slightly injured. Only Newman's and Trevers' aircraft, which was hit in the outer starboard tank union by light flak, was damaged. Bateson was awarded the DSO. An Air Ministry bulletin later described the raid as 'probably the most brilliant feat of low-level precision bombing of the war'.

During a later raid on 30 December 1944 a dozen Mosquitoes of 627 Squadron flew from Woodhall Spa to Peterhead and dive bombed the Oslo Gestapo HQ the next day. Seven aircraft released their bombs from dives of 1,700ft–1,300ft (520–400m).

Supporting the Invasion

In the spring of 1944, 29, 264, 409, 410, 488 RNZAF and 604 Squadrons (equipped with NF.XIIs and XIIIs) formed 85 (Base) Group for the purpose of providing fighter cover leading up to, and after, D-Day. On 5/6 June, the evening of D-Day, 2nd TAF's Mosquito fighter squadrons performed defensive operations (264 Squadron flew jamming patrols before they went looking for enemy fighters) over the invasion coast. Less than fifty plots on 5/6 June were made and only F/O Pearce of 409 Squadron claimed a kill. Then things hotted up. 604 Squadron alone destroyed ten aircraft on 7 and 8 June. On 7 June, 456 Squadron destroyed four He 177s and three more on the 8th. (On 5 July, 456 claimed three enemy aircraft to bring its score to thirty victories since 1 March.)

In night operations on 7/8 June 1944, seventy FB.VIs of 107, 305 and 613 Squadrons operating to the west on rail targets at Argentan, Domfort and Lisieux, sealed approaches to the Normandy bridgehead. On 11 June six FB.VIs of 464 and 487 Squadrons, led by W/C Bob Iredale and F/L McCaul, attacked petrol tankers in a railway marshalling yard at Chatellrault at the request of the Army. W/C Mike Pollard and his six FB.VIs in 107 Squadron following, arrived at 2244 hours to find fires burning in an area 300 by 200 yards (270 by 180m) with smoke rising to 4,000ft (1,220m). Attacks continued on railway targets on the night of 11/12 June when fifty Mk VIs from 88, 98, 107, 180, 226 and 320 Squadrons bombed the railway junction at Le Haye west of Carentan. Two nights later forty-two FB.VIs of 107, 305, 464 and 613 Squadrons strafed and bombed troop movements between Tours and Angers-Vire, Dreux and Falaise, and Evereux and Lisieux.

With the breakout from the beachhead, events moved very quickly and the Mosquitoes harried the German armies in retreat. Once suitable airstrips could be made ready, the heavier components of 2nd TAF, including 2 Group's Mosquito wings, were expected to move to the continent. In the meantime, they flew from airfields such as Thorney Island on the south coast of England, and Lasham. Most of 2 Group's flying, for the Mosquito anyway, took the form of 'night interdiction'; in other words bombing and strafing the enemy's communications by night. Some of the 2 Group squadrons also interfered with German night flying. These would join the circuit of Luftwaffe airfields and shoot German aircraft down as they came into land or just as they took off.

In addition to these night expeditions, there were occasional daylight operations. These included spectacular pinpoint attacks on specific buildings. On 14 July

A night-intruder at a base 'somewhere in England' is prepared for D-Day operations.
via Harry Wilson

(Left) **FB.VI** Hairless Joe **of 418 Squadron RCAF and crew, S/L Russ Bannock** DFC **(later W/C and CO,** DSO DFC*) **and his navigator, F/O Bobbie Bruce** DFC, **pictured at Middle Wallop, August 1944.** Bernard M. Job

Mosquito Squadrons at D-Day – 5 June 1944

Sqdn	Location	Aircraft	Command
25	Coltishall	VI/XVII	ADGB
96	West Malling	XIII	ADGB
125	Hurn	XVII	ADGB
151	Predannack	XIII	ADGB
307	Church Fenton	II/XII	ADGB
4	Gatwick	XVI/ Spitfire XI	2nd TAF
21	Gravesend	VI	2nd TAF
29	West Malling	XIII	2nd TAF
107	Lasham	VI	2nd TAF
219	Bradwell Bay	XVII	2nd TAF
264	Hartfordbridge	XIII	2nd TAF
305	Lasham	VI	2nd TAF
605	Manston	VI	2nd TAF
613	Lasham	VI	2nd TAF
604	Hurn	XII/XIII	2nd TAF
617	Coningsby	FB.VI	5 Group
627	Woodhall Spa	IV	5 Group
105	Bourn	IX/XVI	8 (PFF)
109	Little Staughton	IV/IX/XVI	8 (PFF)
139	Upwood	IV/IX/ XVI/XX	8 (PFF)
571	Oakington	XVI	8 (PFF)
692	Graveley	IV/XVI	8 (PFF)
235	Portreath	NF.II/FB.VI	19 Coastal Grp
248	Portreath	VI/XVIII	19 Coastal Grp
333	Leuchars	FB.VI	18 Coastal Grp
618	Skitten	IV	18 Coastal Grp
540	Benson	IX/XVI	106 PR Group
544	Benson	IX/XVI	106 PR Group
80TU	Dyce	PR.I/NF.II/ IV/VI/PR.VIII	106 PR Group
23	Little Snoring	VI	100 Group
85	Swannington	XII	100 Group
169	Gt Massingham	II	100 Group
140	Northolt	II	100 Group
141	West Raynham	II	100 Group
157	Swannington	II/XIX	100 Group
192	Foulsham	FB.IV/ Wellington X	100 Group
239	West Raynham	II	100 Group
515	Little Snoring	VI	100 Group
1692 Flt	Gt Massingham	NF.II	100 Group

1944, Bastille Day, a large barracks at Bonneuil Matours near Poitiers was attacked by eighteen FB.VIs of 21, 487 and 464 Squadrons. In six buildings inside a rectangle just 170 by 100ft (50 by 30m), close to the village, which had to be avoided, were soldiers of the 158th Security Regiment, who were held accountable for the recent murder of an SAS unit in France. G/C Peter Wykeham Barnes, DSO DFC, and F/O Chaplin, led 487 Squadron and W/C R.H. Reynolds, DSO DFC, led four FB.VIs of 464 Squadron off in the late afternoon. They skirted the Cherbourg Peninsula at about 2,000ft (610m) and passed Alderney, in the Channel Islands, whereupon a heavy shore battery opened up on the formation. The FB.VIs scattered in a relatively disciplined way and reformed as soon as they were out of range. They made landfall near St Malo and dropped to about 50ft (15m) and stayed at this height until just short of the target, where they climbed to bombing height. The raid, timed to be made at last light, when the occupants of the barracks were eating dinner, went quite smoothly. Nine tons of bombs, fused for 25-seconds' delay, were dropped in shallow dives on the target, which was left burning fiercely. At least 150 soldiers were killed. Three trains were attacked on the return flight for good measure and two were set on fire.

Late in July, 2,000–3,000 Germans, the majority of which were billeted in the Caserne des Dunes barracks at Potiers, began massing for an anti-Maquis/SAS sweep, so the FB.VIs were once again called in to flatten the target. On 1 August, twenty-four FB.VIs of 487 and 21 Squadrons, escorted by RAF Mustangs, carried out a low-level attack on the barracks and destroyed it. Meanwhile, the SAS had learned that the survivors of the 158th Regiment were now in the Chateau de Fou, an SS police HQ south of Chatellerault. This, and Chateau Maulny, a saboteur school, was attacked by twenty-three FB.VIs of 107 and 305 Squadrons on 2 August. That same day 613 Squadron attacked a chateau in Normandy which was used as a rest home for German submariners. It appeared that Sunday was chosen because on Saturday nights the Germans had a dance which went on late.

The FB.VIs attacked, quite early in the morning, with rather devastating results. AVM Basil Embry, under the alias of 'W/C Smith' (there was a price on his head after his escape from the Germans in 1940),

and the Station Commander, G/C Bower, took part.

On 6 August, 604 became the first Mosquito fighter squadron to move to France. Others, like 138 Wing at Lasham remained in England. On 18 August, 138 Wing were granted a 24-hour stand-down by Group to celebrate the 1,000th sortie since D-Day, and crews did not expect to fly again until 19 August at the earliest. A station party was organized and crews had quite a heavy night, many getting to bed at about 0200! About 1000 hours, Black Section in 613 Squadron were rudely awakened from their slumbers by a tannoy announcement ordering them to report to the crew room. The 'Doc' did a good trade dispensing 'Hangover pills'. Fifteen FB.VI crews led by S/L Charles Newman, were to take off at 1600 hours for Egletons, 50 miles (80km) SE of Limoges where their target was a school building believed to be in use as an SS barracks. Basil Embry and G/C Bower, as usual, went along.

H. Mears, who flew as navigator for S/L Bell-Syer, known as the 'Count', recalls:

Drop tanks had been fitted to the aircraft, so we knew that it was going to be a long ride. However, we eventually started off in formation, low level, across the Channel and on the deck down to the target.

Of the fifteen FB.VIs of 613 Squadron detailed, fourteen located and bombed the target, scoring at least twenty direct hits almost completely destroying it. F/L Roy House and F/O Savill's FB.VI was hit in the starboard engine over the target area and had to crash-land in France but they returned to the squadron only five days later after being liberated by the US Army's advance.

219 Squadron joined 147 Wing on 26 August. 138 Wing, meanwhile, received incoming reports on 25/26 August of a concentration of troops and vehicles in the Rouen area and of attempts to retreat across the Seine. This now seemed to be a critical area and could well be a pivot to the successful advance of Allied troops into Belgium and Germany. An all-out attack in this zone was set for the night of the 26/27th. One who took part was F/L Eric 'Tommy' Atkins DFC* KW*, a pilot in 305 Polish Squadron based at Lasham, with his navigator, F/L Jurek Majer. They were, at this time, veterans of twenty-five night intruder 'ops'. The night before they had been searching the railways between

Belgium and Germany for trains carrying V-1s or V-2s and had attacked one in the darkness but could not determine the extent of the damage. As they were searching the scene, they were suddenly attacked by a German aircraft. Luckily, their attacker missed and Atkins was able to do a tight turn and give a burst of gunfire in return before returning to Lasham 'in a state of some excitement'. Atkins recalls:

We were told on returning to Lasham and our tent that we would be needed again that night, 26/27 August for the all-out attack at Rouen. We tried to get some sleep during the day but we were pretty tense still after the NFT of our aircraft and as we entered the briefing tent in the late afternoon. The briefing was fairly simple – we had to tour the Rouen–Gisors–Dieppe area and bomb and strafe anything that moved, and in particular, the mass of vehicles trying to retreat across the Seine. A second operation that night was also expected of us!

It was a good night for flying, not much cloud and with our 'cats eyes' we could pick out shapes on the ground. We flew quite low, at 800ft (240m) in the darkness and picked out roads and railways. We had flares and cannon and we had been told that there might also be illumination from pathfinders, but not to depend on it as the battle looked like being prolonged. My worry was that with so many Mosquitoes in the same area we had the further concern of avoiding each other! We soon picked out the convoy and some of the vehicles were already on fire. We bombed by the light of our flares and then turned around to gun the area again – the smoke rising up seemed to fill the cockpit and warned us that we were too low in the darkness. Our deed done, we turned for home. At that moment, a dark shape dived in front of us, missing us by inches. 'Another damned Mosquito!' said Jurek.

When we got back to Lasham the ground crew was standing ready to reload tanks, guns etc, proud to be taking their part in the operation. We were quickly debriefed and then into our Mosquito and away again. This time we attacked a road junction clogged full of enemy transport, just outside Rouen. They were a 'sitting target', although the light flak coming up at us did hinder a straight bombing run and we had to come round again. We had scored some serious hits and once again our ammunition and bombs were expended and we started for Lasham and our cold, dank tents.

On the ground Jurek looked at me and grinning, said, 'What about doing what you English call a 'hat trick'? I said it was OK by me if we could get turned around in time. The ground crew were magnificent and it was almost like a

professional 'pit stop'. This time there were many aircraft in the area. We decided to bomb a goods train which we found in the Rouen–Rheims–Givet area. We obtained a 'near miss', but damage had been done and on our way back we expended all our remaining ammunition on the conflagration around Rouen and the Seine. It was, indeed, the 'Rout of Rouen'. We congratulated ourselves and the ground crew and after debriefing, flung ourselves on our bunk beds in the tent and slept and slept! Our next operation was to be on the railways at night around Saarbourg and Strasbourg on 30 August, which indicated how successful our Army advance had become and our far from unsuccessful efforts to support them!

2nd TAF received the highest possible commendation for these attacks, and this support continued. On 31 August a huge petrol dump at Nomency near Nancy was destroyed, and twelve FB.VIs of 464 Squadron attacked a dozen petrol trains near Chagney from between 20 and 200ft (6 and 60m) and caused widespread destruction. W/C G. Panitz, the CO, failed to return but the panzer divisions in the Battle of Normandy were deprived of millions of gallons of much needed fuel.

Then, in September came the biggest test of all. On the 17th 138 Wing (thirty-two FB.VIs of 107 and 613 Squadron) were detailed to attack the barracks at Arnhem ahead of the *Market Garden* airborne invasion, and 21 Squadron were to do the same to three school buildings in the centre of Nijmegen which were being used by the German garrison. Both raids, timed for perhaps half an hour before the big Arnhem airborne attack began, were to eliminate the opposition before the airborne forces of *Market Garden* landed. Vic Hester, a pilot in 613 Squadron, had first learned of the operation on 4 September:

Ted Moore, my navigator, and I, were detailed to attend a briefing at RAF Netheravon which was filled to over-capacity with tugs, gliders and their crews. We were briefed by most senior Army officers on operation *Market Garden* and thereafter confined to camp. After two days of bad weather we were allowed to return to our base on no more than normal war time security, believing, at that time, the operation to be cancelled. Imagine our surprise when, roughly two weeks later, we were briefed locally for the same operation. The date was different, but the dropping zone was the same and the drop time was similar. I still have doubts that our security was not jeopardized in those two weeks.

We were briefed to film the 613 Squadron raid, then photograph the airborne drop at Arnhem. We took our usual four bombs in case we found an opportune target. Then, just prior to 'engine start time', the Wing Intelligence Officer appeared and gave us an extra brief. 'Can you take off at once and attack an undefended telephone exchange in a disused barracks in Arnhem?' He handed us a map of the town and the position of the barracks, adding that they had just found out that the German land-line communications would need to go via that exchange when the para drop began. What could be more simple? We loved undefended targets and were used to hitting small buildings.

We took off about five minutes ahead of 613 Squadron. I think they probably thought my watch was wrong. Upon arrival over Arnhem we found the target. Good boy, Good boy. We made live one bomb only. The target was a haystack-size building just inside the main gate of the barracks. Why not treat this attack as a practice bombing exercise and make four runs? We slowly descended for the first, and when we were established in a shallow dive, Ted Moore in the nose said, 'Jesus Christ! Look at that!' Now Ted was a very cool, quiet South African who seldom got excited about anything, so I realized that something was afoot. Taking my eye off the target, I saw that we were gently approaching some twenty Tiger tanks – all manned and firing at us!

We dropped our one bomb from an approach pattern we would not have used had we known the target was defended. As a result our aircraft was hit, and I got three bullets in my left leg, which stopped my left foot from working. Ted kindly fastened a field dressing around the outside of my trousers and we continued the exercise. Fusing the other three bombs, we made a further attack on the telephone exchange, but did not wait to see if we had hit the target. We were now too late to film the attack by 613 Squadron, so with regret, we continued to the para dropping zone, found, and filmed considerable German armour etc., surrounding the dropping area, and decided to head for home. There was no way I could break radio silence, and even if I had, no single aircraft transmission could have put a stop to such a large operation as *Market Garden*.

On arrival back at Lasham, AVM Basil Embry was on base. With no food for several hours, I hobbled into de-briefing. Noting my state, Embry handed me a half-pint glass full of issue rum, and proceeded to take our report. Ted Moore went off to process the films, which were flown to Monty within hours. I was put in an ambulance to take me to the military hospital at Aldershot. The driver, a young WAAF who had just passed her driving course on a

Hillman Minx and had never driven anything like a big ambulance, was having trouble, so I took over the driving and left her to go shopping in Aldershot, whilst I went to hospital for, what I thought, was an X-ray. The hospital however, had different ideas and I was soon under an anaesthetic to remove the bullets. What with the rum and the anaesthetic, I think it was about 40 hours before I sobered up! I never did find out how the WAAF driver got back to Lasham.

The Move to France

Altogether, nine Mosquito squadrons now equipped 2nd TAF. In September 1944, following the outbreak from the Normandy beach-head, plans were in progress to move them to airfields in France. In November 1944, 107, 305 (Polish), and 613 Squadrons of 138 Wing were based at Epinoy near Cambrai, France. FB.VIs of 21, 464 and 487 Squadrons remained behind at Thorney Island but in December 1944 the Australian and New Zealand squadrons both sent advance detachments to Rosières-en-Santerre. In February 1945 21, 464, and 487 Squadrons of 140 Wing left southern England and landed at Amiens-Rosières-en-Santerre. Their arrival coincided with the first anniversary of the Amiens raid by 140 Wing in February 1944 when the walls of 'Jericho' had come tumbling down.

Mosquito squadrons in 2nd TAF now made daylight *Rangers* from France and intruder sorties over the continent. On 2 October, F/O R. Lelong of 605 Squadron took off from his forward base at St. Dizier and over the Baltic claimed six enemy aircraft destroyed plus one probable and five damaged. Lelong returned to base on one engine. Five days later, on 7 October two FB.VIs of 605 Squadron destroyed ten enemy aircraft near Vienna and damaged six more. On 31 October, twenty-five FB.VIs of 21, 464 and 487 Squadrons, each carrying 11-second delayed action bombs, and escorted by eight Mustang IIIs of 315 Polish Squadron, made a daring low level attack on the Gestapo HQ building at Aarhus University in Jutland, Denmark. The operation was led by G/C Peter Wykeham-Barnes, and AVM Basil Embry, with his navigator Peter Clapham, flew the operation in a FB.VI of 2 GSU. The attack was carried out at such a low altitude that S/L F.H. Denton of 487 Squadron, hit the roof of the building, losing his tail wheel and the port half of the tail plane. Denton nursed

his Mosquito across the North Sea and managed to land safely. The following signal was received later in the day from Air Ministry: 'Gestapo HQ completely destroyed. Only one bomb failed. Barracks burning. Congratulations to all concerned.' Among the dead was SS Obersturmführer Lonechun, Head of the Security Services.

By November 1944, 107, 305 (Polish), and 613 Squadrons of 138 Wing finally arrived in France, to be based at Epinoy near Cambrai. 137 Wing, with the two Boston squadrons, 88 and 342, and 226

Squadron Mitchells and 107 Squadron FB.VIs, were now stationed at Vitry-en-Artois between Douai and Arras in northern France. On 21 November 136 Wing was created within 2nd Tactical Air Force by the arrival, from Fighter Command, of 418 and 605 Squadrons which transferred to Hartfordbridge. 418 had scored their 100th victory in May 1944 and in June had flown anti-*Diver* patrols at night, before reverting, in September, to *Rangers* and abortive *Big Ben* patrols, the latter against V-2 rockets. 139 Wing, comprising 98, 180

P/O Harry Randall-Cutler and P/O Hubert Cohen of 305 Polish Squadron beside LR303 A-Apple at Hartfordbridge, October 1944. 305 Squadron carried out night intruding over the continent from Hartfordbridge and Lasham that October, before moving to Epinoy near Cambrai, in November 1944. Harry Randall-Cutler

On 31 October 1944, 25 FB.VIs of 21, 464 and 487 Squadrons, each carrying 11-second delayed-action bombs, and led by G/C Peter Wykeham-Barnes, destroyed the Gestapo HQ at Aarhus University, Denmark (foreground) and its incriminating records. Derek Carter

(Above) This famous photo, taken on 19 December 1944 by James Jarche of Illustrated London News of a 21 Squadron FB.VI jacked up and firing into the butts, was set up especially for Jarche by F/L Good, Armaments Officer at Thorney Island. via Les Bulmer

464 and 487 Squadrons remained at Thorney Island until December 1944 while 21 Squadron did not join them at Rosières-en-Santerre, France, until February 1945. Pictured with ground crew are 21 Squadron pilot and navigator, Sid Moulds, 2nd from left, and pilot, Ted Bellis. via Les Bulmer

and 320 (Mitchell) Squadrons, were based at Brussels (Melsbroek). 21, 464 and 487 Squadrons remained behind at Thorney Island but in December 1944 the Australian and New Zealand squadrons both sent advance detachments to Rosières-en-Santerre, France, although 21 Squadron would not join them until February 1945.

By this stage of the war panzer units and other German troops were being bombed daily by Mitchells and Bostons of 2nd TAF and at night, by FB.VIs. On Christmas Eve 1944 eighteen German aircraft were shot down, five of them by four Mosquito crews in 100 Group. The rest were shot down by Mosquitoes of 2nd TAF, which dispatched 139 Mosquitoes this night to targets in south west Germany. 613 Squadron dispatched some thirty FB.VIs, LR374 crewed by W/O Baird, pilot and Sgt Whateley-Knight, navigator, failing to return from a sortie to harass German movement behind the enemy thrust in the Ardennes. Also, thirty-seven Mosquitoes of 2nd TAF patrolled the areas of Aachen, Arnhem and the Dutch Frisian Islands, and flew close support sorties over the front lines. None of these were lost and they destroyed fifty vehicles and six trains. 410 Squadron RCAF dispatched nine NF.XXXs on front-line patrols between 1750 hours on Christmas Eve and 0530 hours on Christmas Day and three crews claimed two Ju 87s and a Ju 88 destroyed.

The Luftwaffe night fighters, although deprived of fuel and experienced pilots, were far from finished and in January 1945 the Luftwaffe attempted one last major air offensive against the Allied air forces on the continent. Since 20 December 1944 many Jagdgeschwader had been transferred to airfields in the west for Operation *Bodenplatte*. About 850 fighters took off at 0745 hours on Sunday morning 1 January and attacked twenty-seven airfields in northern France, Belgium and southern Holland. The four hour operation succeeded in destroying about 100 Allied aircraft but it cost the Luftwaffe 300 aircraft, most of which were shot down by Allied anti-aircraft guns.

On 29 January 1945, crews in 21 Squadron flew from Thorney Island to Fersfield, Suffolk for a secret briefing on what they discovered was to be an attack on the Gestapo HQ in Copenhagen to destroy their records of the Danish Resistance movement. Some Resistance members were held prisoner in the building and would probably die in the attack but the Danes feared that if the records were not

destroyed the whole Danish Resistance network would be at risk. A pilot from 21 squadron recalls:

We were presented with the usual model of the target area, together with photographs of the building and the approach path to be used in the attack. Some of the photographs had been taken by the Danes themselves and smuggled out. A Danish naval officer was also present. He had been brought out of Denmark to give us up-to-date information and had left his wife and family behind in Copenhagen.

The next morning we arrived at the briefing room for final instructions and found the

weather had deteriorated and was unsuitable for low flying over the sea so the operation was postponed for 24 hours. On 31 January the raid was again postponed for a further 24 hours and next morning, 1 February, Embry announced that he could not afford to have his aircraft hanging around doing nothing for any longer. The operation would have take place at a later date and we were to return to Thorney Island that day.

On 2 February W/C 'Daddy' Dale and F/O Hackett, his navigator, went missing on a night patrol. Four days later, on 6 February, the squadron transferred to Rosières-en-

F/L Jack H. Phillips DFC **RCAF and navigator, F/O Bernard M. Job RAFVR (behind) of 418 Squadron RCAF, pose for the picture on FB.VI, NT137 TH-T, Lady Luck, at Hartfordbridge, February 1945. The Canadian squadron moved to Coxyde in March 1945 for operations from the continent.**
Bernard M. Job

(Below) **Crews in 305 Polish Squadron congregate in front of NS844 'N-Nan', which P/O Harry Randall-Cutler and Hubert Cohen flew on the daylight Operation Clarion on 22 February 1945 and which almost ended in disaster for them.** Harry Randall-Cutler

Santerre and shortly afterwards W/C V.R. Oates took command.

On 6 February 1945 21, 464, and 487 Squadrons of 140 Wing had left southern England and moved to Amiens-Rosières-en-Santerre.

Patrols were carried out on most nights with attacks on German road and rail transport when possible, and bombing rail junctions using *Gee* when bad weather prevented visual sightings. On 13 February the Mosquito squadrons took a break from night operations to practice for a daylight maximum effort operation code-named *Clarion*. On 22 February all crews and serviceable aircraft were pressed into action. *Clarion* was intended to be the *coup de grâce* for the German transport system with 9,000 Allied aircraft taking part in attacks on enemy railway stations, trains and engines, crossroads, bridges, ships and barges on canals and rivers, stores and other targets. The operations began at 1300 hours. 2nd TAF put up every available aircraft, flying 215 sorties, 176 from the continent, and the remainder by 136 Wing in England. It was to be the last time that the Mosquitoes operated in daylight in such numbers.

305 Squadron, which set off with nineteen FB.VIs at 1130 hours, was led by W/C S. Grodzicki DFC, and S/L P. Hanburg led the British Flight. P/O Harry Randall-Cutler and P/O Hubert Cohen in NS844 'N-Nan', chanced upon a train in a small station. Randall-Cutler recalls:

We flew thirty-five operations – all at night – so it was marvellous to see this train in all its glory in daylight. When we arrived the engine quickly left the train in the station and steamed off around to a bend in the track where it stopped and the driver jumped out. We and another Mosquito crew strafed the train with cannon and machine gun fire, destroying eight wagons, and then went after the engine, taking two or three runs on it from all directions and hitting it until all of our ammunition was gone. We cruised back at 250ft (80m), coming out just west of Nijmegen, where the area had been flooded by the Germans. I saw this haystack north of the river (our troops were on the other side). As we approached, I was astonished to see the sides of the haystack fall apart to reveal a 20mm gun emplacement! The gun crew held their fire as we flew right over the top of them and then they began firing at us. I gave a chunk of rudder to skid the aircraft and pulled the spade grip up and down, to put them off, but we could hear the shells hitting the left nacelle like

hail. The whole engine was soon black with oil. I throttled back and told Hugh to get ready to bale out. He replied, 'You must be joking!' I nursed 'N-Nan' in a cruise quite comfortably back to base but we landed with a burst tyre and ground looped onto the grass. The aircraft was full of holes and so badly damaged I was told to get a new aircraft.

In all, 305 Squadron had ten FB.VIs damaged and one with a British crew was lost. The pilot was killed and the navigator taken prisoner. 21 Squadron lost just one aircraft, 464 Squadron lost two and 487 Squadron lost five, mainly because they chose to take the long route around the coast and got caught by flak and fighters. 2nd TAF lost twenty-one Mosquitoes on *Clarion* with forty damaged.

The Shellhaus Raid

In March, SOE in London received intelligence that twenty-six resistance and political prisoners held captive in the Gestapo HQ Shellhaus building in Copenhagen were to be shot on 21 March. The Free Danish Resistance movement had made repeated requests that the RAF should attack the building, even though most of the prisoners were being held in the top storey to thwart any attempt to bomb the HQ. Their possible death by bombing, as far as the Resistance was concerned, was not even a consideration as the situation was desperate. A message sent by Svend Truelsen, the Danish Resistance leader, confirmed the worst: 'Military leaders arrested and plans in German hands. Situation never before so desperate. Remaining leaders known by Hun. We are regrouping, but need help. Bombing of S.D. Copenhagen will give us breathing space. If any importance at all to Danish Resistance you must help us irrespective of cost. We will never forget RAF if you come.' The Resistance members held in the attic would prefer to die by RAF bombs rather than be shot by the Gestapo.

Once resolved, Operation *Carthage*, as it was code-named, was a job for the low level experts in 140 Wing. To minimize the risks of flying over enemy territory, on 20 March Basil Embry detached eighteen FB.VIs of 140 Wing from Rosières-en-Santerre, to Fersfield, Suffolk, about 500 miles (800km) from the target. They would be escorted on the raid by thirty-one Mustang IIIs from 64, 126, and 234 Squadrons at Bentwaters,

which joined the FB.VIs at Fersfield. The attack would be made at minimum height in three waves of seven, six, and seven, led by G/C R.N. 'Bob' Bateson DSO DFC AFC and S/L Ted Sismore DSO DFC, the leading tactical navigator.

Crews studied a model of the Shellhaus and were thoroughly briefed by Bateson and Svend Truelsen. At 0855 on 21 March, the eighteen FB.VIs, each loaded with 11-second delayed action bombs, and two Film Photographic Unit Mosquitoes, took off from Fersfield, followed a little later by the Mustangs. The weather was stormy with surface winds at 50 knots (90kph). Salt spray reduced visibility on the windshields. Landfall was made at Hvide Sand at 1020, and over Jutland the formation began to attract the attention of the German fighter controllers. They flew on, across the Great Belt and to the circular lake at Tisso on the island of Zealand where the formation split into their three waves. Sismore set course and Bateson led his wave of seven FB.VIs to Copenhagen with Embry and Clapham flying on his left. The FPU Mosquito and four FB.VIs of 21 Squadron followed. The leading aircraft in the second flight being flown by the CO, W/C Peter Kleboe, DSO DFC AFC, who had succeeded W/C V.R. Oates after he failed to return from a raid on 12 March. The other waves circled to give 9 miles (14km) distance between them. The second wave of six 464 Squadron FB.VIs was being led by W/C Bob Iredale DFC with his navigator, F/O B.J. Standish, and the third wave, comprising six FB.VIs of 487 Squadron (and a FPU Mosquito), was being led by their CO, W/C F.H. Denton DFC, who had flown the Aarhus raid.

The first wave began their run-in as the flak guns opened up and one Mustang immediately went down. Peter Kleboe hit a 130ft (40m) high floodlight pylon in the marshalling yards 800yd (730m) from the target and went into a vertical dive. Three of his bombs struck a building and eight civilians were killed. The FB.VI finally crashed near the Jeanne d'Arc school in a pall of black smoke killing Kleboe and his Canadian navigator, F/O Reg Hall instantly. At 1114 Bateson's bombs hit the first and second floors of the Shellhaus. Embry and Clapham, and then S/L Tony Carlisle, the deputy leader, got their bombs away. The last two FB.VIs, flown by S/L A.C. Henderson and F/L T.M. 'Mac' Hetherington, put their bombs through the roof of the Shellhaus before they scattered and

The Shellhaus raiders low over the rooftops of the Vesterbro district of Copenhagen during the raid.
Derek Carter

(Below) F/L W.K. Shrimpton and F/O P.R. Lake of 464 Squadron RAAF in SB-G low over Søborg, Copenhagen. They made two orbits of the target area but, unable to line up for the target, flew back with their bomb load intact. Toxvaerd Foto via Derek Carter

exited the city at roof top height. Henderson was so low that Embry, below him, was forced down into the streets and they missed collision by only a few feet.

The leading three crews in the second wave were attracted by the smoke from Kleboe's wrecked aircraft. The other three FB.VIs, led by F/L Archie Smith DFC, realized the mistake and located the Shellhaus to the right of their track. Confusion reigned. Iredale decided not to attack and circled to come in again with Smith and they got their bombs away. One aircraft accidentally bombed the school area and only a few of the remaining aircraft were close enough to the Shellhaus to bomb the target. F/L W.K. Shrimpton and F/O P.R. Lake RAAF had to orbit the area twice but the third wave was now coming in and they had to abandon their final run to avoid collision. They took their bombs home. Two other FB.VIs, crewed by F/O 'Shorty' Dawson and F/O F.T. Murray, and F/O J.H. 'Spike' Palmer and his Norwegian navigator, S/L H.H. Becker, were hit by flak and were forced to ditch in the sea. There were no survivors.

The third wave had navigation problems and approached the target area from the wrong direction. All but one of the FB.VIs bombed the Jeanne d'Arc school by mistake. W/C Denton located the target, but saw so much damage already that he aborted his attack and jettisoned his bombs in the sea. F/L D.V. Pattison and F/Sgt F. Pygram's Mosquito was hit and badly damaged and they ditched in the sea

close to the Swedish island of Hveen. They were seen standing on a wing, but they later drowned, as no bodies were recovered. W/C Denton nursed his flak damaged FB.VI back and belly landed in England. F/L R.J. Dempsey flew home on one engine and the second FPU aircraft, flown by American, F/O R.E. 'Bob' Kirkpatrick with Sgt R. Hearne, of 21 Squadron, badly flak damaged, crash-landed at Rackheath, Norfolk.

When the results of the raid were known it made chilling reading. The Jeanne d'Arc school had been destroyed and eighty-six of the 482 children were dead, sixty-seven wounded, and sixteen adults too were killed, another thirty-five wounded. Several others died around the target. Of the twenty-six prisoners in the Shellhaus, eighteen escaped, the remainder being killed in the building. If all of the aircraft had bombed the target, it is unlikely any of the

(Right) **On 21 March 1945 FB.VIs of 140 Wing attacked and destroyed the Shellhaus Gestapo building in Copenhagen which contained twenty-six Danish resistance prisoners on the top floor, releasing eighteen of them. Two of the prisoners, one of whom fell to his death, can just be seen climbing from a window far right during the attack.** Derek Carter

prisoners would have survived. Four Mosquitoes and two Mustangs were lost for the loss of nine aircrew. The raid was deemed a success, not just by the RAF, but by the Danish Freedom Council who that night radioed SOE headquarters in Baker Street that the Shellhaus had been completely destroyed. The Gestapo records were destroyed and twenty-six Nazis and thirty Danish collaborators and sixteen civilians were killed. After the war a memorial was raised to the children and adults killed and to the Resistance.

140 Wing had one more low level pin-point raid to fly. On 17 April six FB.VIs of 140 Wing, led by Bateson and Sismore, taxied out for a daylight strike on a school building on the outskirts of Odense, which was being used by the Gestapo as an HQ. Basil Embry went along, as usual. The six Mosquitoes destroyed the Gestapo HQ and 18 days later Denmark was free. At 0800 hours on 8 May the cease-fire in Germany came into effect and VE-Day was declared.

Three FB.VIs hit by flak had to ditch and all three crews perished. F/L Pattison and F/Sgt Pygram's FB.VI in 487 Squadron was hit by fire from the cruiser Nürnberg, at anchor in Copenhagen harbour. F/O Palmer and S/L Becker of 487 Squadron, and F/O R.G. 'Shorty' Dawson RAAF and F/O Fergus Murray of 464 Squadron were the other two Mosquito crews lost. Dawson (left) and Murray (right) are seen here in Malta in 1943, when they were serving with 23 Squadron. Tom Cushing

CHAPTER SEVEN

Star and Bar

USAAF PR and Spying Operations

On 21 November 1944, an American Lt Cmdr, laying uncomfortably in the bomb bay of a medium bomber, recorded a transmission at 30,000ft (9,100m) over Germany with an agent on the ground. This feat was made possible by a combination of American know-how and an all-British invention, the de Havilland Mosquito. In the summer of 1942, Col Elliot Roosevelt brought two squadrons of F-5 photo reconnaissance Lightnings and a squadron of B-17F 'mapping Fortresses' to Britain. The President's son was preparing his group for the invasion of North Africa and was to work with the RAF until ready. On a visit to the PRU he saw the Mosquito and, recognizing its true

value, was given a B.IV for combat evaluation. Roosevelt discovered that the British machine both outperformed his F-5s and had five times the range.

Mosquitoes were being produced in Canada and the first of these aircraft had already given demonstrations at Wright Field. It was so good that Gen Arnold ordered that no US aircraft were to be raced against the Mosquito to avoid embarrassing American pilots! Arnold asked that Mosquitoes be obtained to equip all US PR squadrons in the European Theater of Operations (ETO) and Mediterranean Theater of Operations (MTO) – almost 200 aircraft for 1943 alone! Unfortunately, requests for

the 'wooden wonder' outstripped supply and the USAAF had to persist with F-5 mapping Lightnings and F-6s (modified P-51 Mustangs). Canadian Mosquito F-8 production never did keep pace with American demands, but in 1944 thirty-three F-8s were delivered to the USAAF. And in the 12th Air Force deliveries of the P-61A Black Widow night-fighter were so slow that the 416th Night Fighter Squadron instead operated the Mosquito. By March 1944, when American production lines were producing enough photo reconnaissance aircraft for the USAAF, the MTO cancelled its requirement for the Mosquito, choosing to standardize on the F-5 instead.

PR.XVI NS590 'B' of the 25th BG showing the newly applied stars and bars although the overall PRU blue paint scheme has failed to totally cover the old RAF roundels. Ken Godfrey

All US Mosquitoes were now sent to the 8th and 9th Air Forces. The 425th Night Fighter Squadron, 9th Air Force, used some NF.XIIIs but it was the 8th AF that operated the majority of these aircraft. The 8th had one reconnaissance group equipped with F-5s and Spitfires while the 9th Air Force had three groups. Rather than replace any of the aircraft, the decision was taken to organize a group within the 8th using Mosquitoes, and the 802nd Reconnaissance

the 653rd Light Reconnaissance, or Light Weather Squadron, and the 654th, a heavy, Special, unit, were equipped with the Mosquito T.III and PR.XVI. The 653rd flew 1,531 varied missions between 28 March 1944 and April 1945, including 1,332 missions known as *Blue Stocking*, which were associated with weather observation and forecasting. The balance of its missions was made up of command flights, target scouting missions, and chaff dispensing sorties.

They then followed the bombers, taking still photographs to allow analysis of bombardment effectiveness.

The 654th, or the 'Special Squadron', flew 700 varied types of missions, including 161 night photography flights, code-named *Joker* using B-25s, B-26s and PR.XVIs. The Mosquito was much more versatile than the two medium bombers and was employed on medium and high altitude night photography missions at an

PR.XVI NS519 of the 25th BG used for chaff (Window) missions. via Ken Godfrey

Group was formed on 22 April 1944 at Watton, Norfolk. On 9 August the 802nd was reactivated as the 25th BG (Bombardment Group), which, together with the 7th Photo Group, became part of the 325th Photographic Wing, commanded by Col Elliot Roosevelt.

Three squadrons were operated from Watton (and, during the last 50 days of the war, from Harrington, Northamptonshire). B-17s and B-24s served in the 652nd Heavy Weather Squadron, while the other two –

Chaff was the American name for *Window* and was dropped over a wide area to 'snow' German fighter control radar and radar equipped AA guns, and was dropped using an electric dispensing mechanism in the Mosquito's bomb bays. On occasion, the 654th Squadron PR.XVIs performed two duties. Their first and primary objective was to drop chaff over the defence perimeter just before oncoming bombers arrived. Turning and climbing over the bombers the PR.XVIs then filmed the bomb drop itself.

average speed of 270mph (430kph). Each PR.XVI would carry twelve Type M-46 Photo Flash bombs of one million candle-power. These were normally dropped from around 12,000ft (3,660m) at 8-second intervals to obtain a 60 per cent running overlap. They were fused to burst at 4,000ft (1,220m) to illuminate the target below. The first *Joker* mission flown by a Mosquito took place on 28 July 1944, to Lille, from the 392nd BG B-24 base at Wendling. Not many were anxious to be the guinea pigs

PR.XVI MM388 of the 25th BG. Jack Green via George Sesler

and the Mosquito was crewed by two volunteer airmen, Richard Geary, pilot, and Bill Miskho, navigator. The RAF had had some bad experiences when attempting night photography with the Mosquito. They had tried three missions, each carrying three photo flash bombs. On each occasion the aircraft exploded in the air. Only one navigator survived and when Geary talked to him he stated that he just found himself in space and pulled his ripcord. But on this occasion Geary and Miskho returned safely after 2½ hours, their mission a complete success.

Extensive high altitude photographic missions deep into enemy territory were carried out at around 22,000ft (6,700m) with the M-46 Photo Flash bombs fused to burst at 6,000ft (1,830m). Two Type K-19B cameras were installed at a 27 degree split vertical angle directly over the port holes in the front section of the forward bomb bay. A third K-19B camera was mounted in the rear of the aircraft. These cameras were mounted to tilt to port, starboard and aft.

Radar Mapping

Another fifty-five missions were still photography flights conducted in daylight to determine the effectiveness of bombing missions and to observe selected positions, conditions and events. Twenty missions were daylight motion-picture photography flights. Daylight photography flights, both still and motion picture, were code-named PRU. The other 132 missions were made up of chaff dispensing sorties, command flights, secret OSS operations, and *Mickey* radar photo mapping sorties. These last used modified B-17 *H2X* sets to create photographs of the radar display a bomber navigator would expect to see while approaching a target. By this method the 25th BG prepared photographic records of radar bombing approaches to a number of high-priority targets lying deep inside Germany. These *Mickey* bomb-approach strips, or target run-ups, were distributed to the bomb groups after proper annotation and identification, and with the exact position of the strategic target pinpointed.

The *H2X* radar scanner was placed in a bulbous nose, the amplifiers and related equipment in the nose and bomb bay, and the radar scope in the rear fuselage. Before the mission, the observer climbed in through the rear door with a camera (sometimes a motion-picture camera) to photograph the details on the radar screen. The observer's only means of escape in an emergency was to crawl over the set and jump through the bomb bay – provided that the pilot opened the bomb doors! There was a tendency for the *Mickey* set to arc or even explode when first turned on. The radar drew a heavier current than the Mosquito's electrical system could safely handle, and the aircraft were grounded several times in attempts to overcome the problem.

Much of the effort by the 654th Squadron was directed to improving the strategic value of *H2X* bombing and to alleviate civilian casualties. *Mickey* sorties suffered the highest loss rate, highest abort rate and greatest number of failures of any mission involving American PR.XVIs.

H2X Mickey **PR.XVI NS538/F of the 25th BG pictured at RAF Watton, Norfolk with Photo Laboratory personnel, Carl Wanka and John Ripley.**
via George Sesler

Three *H2X* missions flown at night did not return. There were no losses after December 1944, the month that *Mickey* switched to daylight missions with fighter escort, but the radar sets continued to malfunction. Of thirty-six missions flown in January, only four were successful, and in February, the programme was finally cancelled. To protect the vulnerable radar-equipped PR.XVIs, four P-38s were assigned to escort an *H2X* mission, going in at high altitudes. Lucien F. Peters, who had flown a tour on B-17s, was a radar-navigator/bombardier on Mosquitoes, preparing radar bombing-approach strips:

For the P-38s to escort the Mosquito at high altitude, the Mosquito had to throttle back. Crews were selected according to the Group's needs and the training, qualifications and talents of volunteers. From the constancy and tolerance essential for 13–15-hour missions over the Atlantic to the orientation talents needed by *H2X* navigators, rigid requirements were established and met. Of the crewmen volunteers who arrived for training in the specialities of the organization, one out of five failed, either in aptitude, or in resolution.

Initially, potential Mosquito pilots were drafted in from the 50th Fighter Group,

which flew P-38s in Iceland, and also from bomb groups in England and ferry squadrons in Scotland. Accidents occurred as the US pilots learned to cope with its high landing speed and tendency to swing on take-off; a new problem for them because they had been used to the P-38's contra-rotating propellers. The Mosquito pilot also had to remember to open the radiator shutters just prior to take off to prevent the engines overheating. PR.XVIs used a two-stage, two speed supercharger that would cut in automatically at high altitude. The superchargers were independent on each engine and a small difference in adjustment caused one to change gears hundreds of feet before the other. The resulting 'bang' and surge of power to one engine could wrest control from the unwary pilot and give the impression that the aircraft had been hit by Flak. Fortunately, some pilots had gained earlier experience on the Mosquito in RAF and Canadian service.

In May 1944 the Light Reconnaissance Squadron began *Blue Stocking* weather operations and immediately prior to D-Day, 6 June, gave weather predictions for the invasion. The 654th (Heavy Special) Squadron aided in the search for V-1 sites in Northern France that summer, performing *Dilly* daylight reconnaissance missions over the Pas de Calais in search of *Noball* sites. The 654th flew night *Joker* and daylight *H2X* 'Mickey' (radar mapping flights) photo missions as well as scouting sorties just ahead of the main bombing force, transmitting up-to-the-minute weather reports back to the task force commander to prevent him leading his bombers into heavy weather fronts.

PR.XVI NS590 'B', now wearing D-Day invasion stripes.
Ken Godfrey via George Sesler

PR.XVI of the 25th BG over Norfolk.
Ken Godfrey via George Sesler

Remarkable Night Joker **photo of the canal cities of Nippes and Essen, Germany, taken on 4/5 October 1944 using M46 photo flash bombs of 700,000 candlepower, twelve of which could be carried in the bomb bay of a PR.XVI. The system was perfected in 1943 by the RAF using two PR.IXs to test the American flash bombs, which were three times brighter than the British equivalents, once the cameras and the flash bombs had been harmonized.** Wright Booth via George Sesler

The D-Day invasion was prepared by intelligence gathered on *Dilly* missions of coastal defences in the Pas de Calais. Capt Walter D. Gernand, a 654th Squadron pilot, and his cameraman, Sgt Ebbet C. Lynch, 8th Combat Camera Unit (CCU), who carried out a photo reconnaissance of the beachhead, were killed when their Mosquito crashed in England on the return flight.

One of the more exotic missions of the 654th Squadron was the photographic reconnaissance of pilotless drone bombing of U-boat pens and V-weapon concrete structures in the Pas de Calais in the summer of 1944. USAAF *Aphrodite* and US Navy *Anvil* war-weary B-17s and Liberators respectively, packed with 18,000lbs (8,200kg) of TORPEX, a nitroglycerine compound, were flown by a pilot to a point over the English coast or North Sea. The crew then baled out, leaving the pilotless drone or 'Baby', to be 'flown' towards its target, and would eventually be crashed onto it, all controlled remotely from a Ventura mother ship. Both the 653rd and the 654th Squadrons were used to support these missions, the 653rd flying a *Blue Stocking* weather reconnaissance flight over the target to report to Fersfield (the drone base), and the 654th with an 8th CCU photographer, to record the flight of the drone and its effects so that strike analysis could be used to improve methods and equipment.

The missions were fraught with danger. On 4 August one *Aphrodite* crashed in England, killing its pilot, and a second refused to dive over the target and was destroyed by flak. Two days later two Aphrodite drones crashed and exploded. On the first *Anvil* mission, on 12 August, the PB4Y-1 Liberator drone flown by Lt Joseph P. Kennedy Jr, eldest son of Joseph Kennedy, the former US Ambassador to Britain, and his co-pilot, 'Bud' Willy, was blown to smithereens before either man had a chance to evacuate the aircraft. A PR.XVI, flown by Lt Robert A. Tunnel, with photographer, Lt David J. McCarthy in the nose, and which was following behind two Ventura motherships, was sent upwards a few hundred feet by the explosion, which knocked out one of the PR.XVI's engines, and peppered the aircraft with flying debris. McCarthy, who was 'knocked half way back to the cockpit', managed to crawl back and lower the wheels. Tunnel made a good landing just before the other engine cut.

Next day, 13 August, 1/Lt Dean H. Sanner and 8th CCU cameraman S/Sgt Augie

On 12 August 1944, NS569, a 654th Squadron PR.XVI, flown by Lt Robert A. Tunnel (left), with photographer, Lt David J. McCarthy (right), was sent upwards a few hundred feet when the PB4Y-1 Anvil mission drone flown by Lt Joseph P. Kennedy Jr and 'Bud' Willy, exploded, putting out the Mosquito's port engine and peppering the aircraft with flying debris. McCarthy managed to lower the wheels and Tunnel landed at Halesworth just before the starboard engine cut. via George Sesler

On 13 August 1944, 1/Lt Dean H. Sanner and cameraman S/Sgt Augie Kurjack filmed a GB-4 *Batty* 2,600lb (1,180kg) glide bombing mission to Le Havre. Sanner, in MM370, followed the launched bombs down and was knocked out of the sky by the explosion of the second *Batty* as he overflew at low level. The blast threw Sanner out and he survived. Kurjack was killed. The top photo shows Sanner closing in on B-17G 42-400043 and the bottom is of Sanner on the steps of MM370 in happier times. USAF

Kurjack flew to Fersfield to film the flight of a GB-4 *Batty* glide bombing mission to Le Havre. Experimental GB-1 glide bombs were developed by fitting small wings and empennage to a 2,000lb (900kg) GP M34 bomb which were then launched from the external wing racks of B-17s. The 2,600lb (1,200kg) GB-4 bomb, which was produced using a GB-1 with the AZON tail unit, had a TV camera installed under the nose and could be guided onto a target from 15 miles (24km) distant. Sanner recalls:

Our mission was to film the flight paths of the two glide bombs and photograph any damage to the port area. I was warned not to get between the robot glide bombs and the mother ship after release. On the way to the IP [Initial Point] I had Augie take pictures of the stubby-winged glide bombs hung under the wings of the B-17. When the first bomb was released I followed it down until it neared the ground. I found it difficult to follow and keep in sight. It seemed to be erratic in horizontal and vertical flight. After either losing sight of the bomb or seeing that it wasn't going to hit anything I broke off the

pursuit and climbed back to follow the second glide bomb. I zig-zagged back and forth considerably to hold the faster Mosquito behind the slower glide bomb. I had a difficult time keeping within photographic range because of the final steep dive of the bomb. At low altitude I once again broke away to escape the range of the explosion. It had fallen in a marsh.

Upon breaking off I remained low to the ground. Any effort to climb to altitude would slow the Mosquito and leave it vulnerable to enemy activity. My intention was to head for open water between the banks of the Seine then climb back to altitude over the English Channel. As fate would have it, I flew over the bomb as it exploded. The immense blast threw me out of the Mosquito. We were too low to have had time to crawl through the escape hatch. My cameraman was not so fortunate. Only one parachute was seen to open following the explosion.

The Special Squadron supported *Aphrodite* until January 1945. Several attempts were made to convert Mosquitoes into mother ships but they were not used operationally.

Supporting the Bombers

Meanwhile, the LORAN (LOng-RANge) HF radio navigational positioning system, had been developed by the US Navy for the Pacific Theatre, and in Europe 25th BG PR.XVIs were to be fitted with the device for scouting missions ahead of the American bomber streams. The US Navy had installed transmitting stations ('chains') in Britain and Italy. A pair of stations each sequentially transmitted a pulse at precisely timed intervals on the same frequency. At the receiver, the navigator adjusted precision time delay to overlay the pulse on a cathode-ray tube and read the time off the calibrated time delay, relay control. This in turn gave the aircraft's location, which was marked on maps overlaid with lines identified by delay times and colour coded for each individual chain.

The Navy needed data on the range, reception and accuracy of the overlay. In the summer of 1944 the opportunity came, when Light Weather Squadron PR.XVIs, fitted with LORAN, accompanied the two 8th AF shuttle bombing missions to the Ukraine. The first was flown on 21 June by 114 B-17s which bombed an oil refinery near Berlin before flying on to landing fields at Poltava and Mirgorod in the Ukraine. On 21/22 June, forty-seven B-17s were lost and twenty-nine were damaged in a German air raid on Poltava. On 26 June, seventy-two Fortresses flew home, bombing a target in Poland and staging through Italy, then bombing a target in France en route to England on 5 July. The entire tour covered 6,000 miles (9,650km), ten countries and 29¼ hours of operational flying.

Shortly before 6 August, when seventy-six Fortresses and sixty-four P-51s were due to fly the second 8th AF *Frantic* shuttle mission to the Ukraine, Lt Ralph Fish-

er, who flew a 653rd Squadron Mosquito on the first shuttle mission, briefed Lt Ron M. Nichols, pilot, and Lt Elbert F. Harris, navigator, who would fly scout on the second. B-17s would bomb the Focke Wulf plant at Rahmel in Poland en route to the Ukraine and later fly home via Italy and France. A Navy team arrived at Watton prior to departure and installed the LORAN receiver in their PR.XVI and checked Harris out on the equipment. He recalls:

We took off on schedule, flew parallel to the bomber stream going to Berlin, caught up with our task force and proceeded to the target area. The weather was clear over Germany and Poland – no problems. We spotted four fighters slightly above and some distance to the right, but they didn't come after us. We waited in the area for the bomb drop and were pleased to report an excellent pattern on the target. Shortly after, we left and passed the bombers and fighters on our SSE course which took us 75–100 miles [120–160km] to the west of Warsaw. The Polish underground uprising was being suppressed by the Germans and the city was being destroyed while the Soviets sat idly by on the outskirts of the city. Most of the city seemed to be in flames. There was a huge plume of smoke rising to about 30,000ft [9,100m] which could be seen from 200 miles [320km] away on our course.

Our orders were to drop to 6,000ft [1,830m] at Kiev and to remain at this altitude to Poltava. Lt Fisher told us about the tendency of the Soviets to fire AA and the Soviet fighters to attack American planes, and since we believed we were the lead plane contingent, we were most apprehensive during our descent. As it turned out, the other Mosquito arrived slightly ahead of us, and there were no incidents. We received good reception on the LORAN from Britain till we let down to 6,000ft [1,830m] at Kiev. The Italian chain signal was good at first, then became intermittent until we lost it over Poland. Since the weather was good, I could check against both *Gee* and pilotage, finding good agreement between the fixes. We landed at Poltava and were guided to a parking spot. Our fuel was low but not critical when we arrived.

The B-17s arrived and flew a bombing mission later against a Polish synthetic oil refinery. Nicholls and Harris flew scout for the mission, which was uneventful and the bombing pattern excellent. Then, on 8 August, the shuttle force took off for San Severo, one of many B-17 bases in the Foggia area of Italy, bombing two Rumanian

airfields en route. On 12 August the force flew back to Britain on the last stage of their shuttle, bombing the French aircraft complex, Avion Sud, and the adjacent Francazal airfield at Toulouse, en route. Nicholls and Harris flew ahead scouting the weather, reporting back to the bomber leader. At about 1145 hours, north of the target area, their PR.XVI was attacked by P-51s of the 357th FG who mistook the Mosquito for a Ju 88. Harris recalls:

Tracers passed above us. Nick began evasive action but too late. The next burst was in and around the right engine and we were on fire. The tracers kept coming around and into the Mosquito. I was wearing a chest chute harness. As I leaned down to pick up my chute pack, the Mosquito tilted and I was thrown violently against the floor. I strained to push myself up but couldn't move. The Mosquito had gone into a high-speed stall and followed with a tight spin.

Lt Elbert F. Harris (left), navigator, and Lt Ron M. Nicholls, pilot, were the weather scout crew on the second 8th AF *Frantic* shuttle mission, August 1944, and were shot down by a P-51D Mustang of the 357th FG while returning over France on 8 August. Harris baled out and with the help of the French Resistance, returned on 6 September. Nicholls was killed in the encounter. via George Sesler

Nick was fighting the controls but the Mosquito wasn't responding. A sheet of flames extended from and along the trailing edge of the right wing, caused from gasoline pouring from the right wing tank. As I shoved my escape kit into my shirt front I was considering my alternatives; bale out the top hatch and be killed by the tail stabilizer, or go out the bottom, catch fire and be burned to death. Judging that there was little time left before the aircraft exploded, I decided to take my chances on the tail. I pulled the release for the top hatch and it flew off. I climbed out, and pushed out and down. Before closing my eyes I glimpsed fierce flames under the fuselage. There was a roaring sheet of flame from under the right wing with streamers of fire. I was hit by the horizontal stabilizer, bounced off of it and fell away spinning …

Harris survived but Nicholls was killed when the Mosquito exploded. With the help of the French Resistance, Harris was returned to England, on 6 September.

Late in September LORAN Station A in Scotland and Station B in southern England became operational and the European Synchronized Chain entered service. Calibration flights, called *Skywave*, were flown over the continent, usually non-stop to San Severo, Italy, the Mosquito returning the next day after refuelling. Major John Larkin and Lt Claude Moore, 654th Squadron, flew the first mission to prove the feasibility of reading lines of position (LOP) in the air, on 28 September 1944. The missions proved LORAN's capabilities where all other navigational aids failed.

Complete coverage of the continent at all altitudes and in all types of weather was now available.

Chaff-dispensing missions proved equally effective. These were code-named, *Gray-Pea* in honour of its originators, Col Leon Gray – who assumed command of the 25th BG on 23 September 1944 – and Col (later Gen) Budd Peaslee. A formation of three (later four) PR.XVIs zig-zagged ahead of the bomber stream, dropped chaff over the target and then re-crossed it to photograph the strike. The Mosquitoes were still able to land before the bombers were over the Channel. On 20 March 1945, 2/Lt Joseph A. Polovick and 1/Lt Bernard M. Blaum, were hit by enemy fire on a *Gray-Pea* mission over Germany and were captured. On

Capt Lionel A. Proulx, navigator, and Lt Earl L. Muchway, pilot, walk to their waiting Mosquito at Watton. This crew were leading a flight of four Mosquitoes on a Gray-Pea mission over Kiel on 3 April 1945 when they were attacked by German fighters, forcing them to land in Sweden. Ken Godfrey

3 April 1945, Lt Col Alvin E. Podwojski and Captain Lionel A. Proulux, were leading a flight of four Mosquitoes on a *Gray-Pea* mission over Kiel when they were attacked by German fighters on leaving the target area. Their Mosquito was damaged, but they managed to reach Sweden safely.

Another function of the 25th BG PR.XVIs was to provide *Red Tail* missions, where they carried the Command Pilot on 8th AF bombing raids. By accelerating around his formation in a fast Mosquito bomber the Command Pilot was provided with an observation platform for greater oversight. He could better monitor the formation and advise key pilots of defects in the assembly pattern. In addition, he was not as vulnerable to enemy fighters as he might be in a lead bomber. However, enemy fighters were sometimes the least concern, for, despite red tail markings and US stars, the PR.XVIs were often mistaken for Me 262s and Me 410s. Crews were sent to bomber and fighter group bases to display their distinctive aircraft and help prevent identification problems but the confusion persisted. On 4 April 1945, a command flight piloted by 1/Lt T.B. Smith of the 653rd Squadron was carrying Colonel Troy Crawford of the 446th BG. As the colonel was overseeing his formation it was attacked by Me 262s. As the Mosquito moved in close to the B-24s for protection, it was shot down by gunners from Crawford's group. Smith and Crawford parachuted to safety and were taken prisoner. Altogether, seventy-four *Red Tail* flights were made.

On 18 September 1944, during Operation *Market Garden*, a PR.XVI piloted by 1/Lt Robert A. Tunnel with 19-year-old S/Sgt John G. Cunney, a cameraman, failed to return from a PR mission to the Nijmegen–Eindhoven area where a supply drop was to be made by Liberators to the US paratroopers. Tunnel was blinded by a 60cm searchlight, lost control and crashed on Plantlunne airfield. Both he and Cunney were killed. Bad weather during the *Market Garden* operation made regular air reconnaissance impossible so 654th Squadron PR.XVIs were instructed to fly over the Arnhem bridge 'every hour on the hour.' On 22 September a PR.XVI piloted by Lt Pat Walker flew over the northern end of the bridge at under 500ft (150m). Navigator Roy C. Conyers recalls:

We were to dip as low as possible to try to establish by visual observation who controlled the

bridge. I thought this was crazy and mentioned it to Edwin R. Cerrutti, a 654th navigator. His only comment was that the German Command wouldn't believe we were that stupid.

We could see the Germans running for the anti-aircraft guns and we were put into tracer bullet paths from at least two guns. This action lasted maybe 3–5 seconds. They hit the 'plane many times. The right engine was completely in flames. Pat turned off the fuel to the engine and the flames went out. The engine was, of course, useless. Thank goodness we were still airborne, and managed to fly back to Bournemouth.

Signalling to Spies

The most secret missions flown by the US Mosquitoes were code-named, *Red Stocking* which were so-named to help disguise the true nature of their mission and perhaps persuade the German intelligence services that this was a weather mission similar to *Blue Stocking*. However, their true purpose

cumbersome 'S-Phone' device which had to be carried in a suitcase by agents in France. (*Joan-Eleanor* took its name from a major in the WACs and Goddard's wife, respectively). *Joan* weighed only 4lb (1.8kg), and was therefore easily transportable. The agent in the field could use it to beam UHF transmissions on a radio beam so narrow, that it was practically immune to detection. As much information could be passed clearly in one 15–20 minute contact as could be passed in days by conventional radio. On board the PR.XVI the *Eleanor* airborne radio receiver in the modified bomb bay was connected to a wire recorder which the operator, who entered through a small hatch on the starboard side of the fuselage just aft of the wing, used to capture the ground-to-air conversations. When ground crews and pilots of the other squadrons asked about the drop seat and oxygen system in the bomb bay they were told of a secret radar installation.

PR.XVI Greex **attached to the 492nd Bomb Group pictured at Harrington in May 1945 for a clandestine** Red Stocking **operation over Germany.** André Pecquet

was to make radio contact with OSS agents in Germany and record transmissions using a new and highly secret device called *Joan-Eleanor* which was installed in three, later five, PR.XVIs for these missions. This very compact equipment had been developed by Lt Cmdr Steve Simpson, a Texan scientist, and DeWitt R. Goddard to replace the

The first successful contact was made by Simpson in a Mosquito on 22 November 1944 when, circling at 30,000ft (9,100m) he recorded the first of eight transmissions with agent 'Bobbie' in Holland. All told, the 654th Squadron flew thirty-two *Red Stocking* missions for OSS over Germany, Austria and enemy occupied territory.

Lt John M. Carter, 654th Squadron pilot, and Lt John L. Swingen, 652nd Squadron navigator, pictured on 22 March 1945. via George Sesler

One of the most daring was flown on 12 March 1945 when a *Red Stocking* PR.XVI flying at 30,000ft (9,100m) over Berlin successfully established radio contact with agents who had earlier been dropped by A-26C Invaders. On 13 March the briefing for OSS missions was ordered to Harrington, Northamptonshire, the 492nd BG Liberator base. The transfer took place on the 15th. The PR.XVIs (and A-26s) in which the missions were flown were, for a while, stationed and maintained at Watton because of problems maintaining them at Harrington. Crews flew from Watton to Harrington for briefing and after each mission occasionally returned to Watton. One crew, 1/Lt Kingdon R. Knapp, pilot, and 1/Lt John K. Jackson, navigator, had flown thirty *Joan-Eleanor* operational missions by 4 May 1945. Six of their missions were flown from Watton and twenty-four from

Harrington. Nine of these missions were flown within one week.

On the 9 April, mission they and OSS *Joan-Eleanor* operator, Lt Calhoun Ancrum, landed at Lunelle, France in PR.XVI NS740 and waited until it got dark. Then they took off again and headed for Munich, where they successfully made contact with 'Pickaxe', an OSS agent. During the rendezvous another agent, code-named 'Luxe' interrupted and passed on some vital information which led to the successful bombing of a railway junction at Weilheim. (Knapp and Jackson flew Lt Ancrum on the night of 17/18 April and again contact was made with agent 'Luxe' who confirmed the successful bombing of the rail junction at Weilheim. A photographic reconnaissance later brought back photos of the destruction.) Knapp then turned the Mosquito around and headed

north to the Berlin area where Ancrum tried to raise OSS agent 'Hammer', but without success because of a heavy bomber raid on the capital.

Altogether, the 25th BG flew 3,246 missions, the 653rd Squadron losing twenty-four PR.XVIs, including thirteen on operations, and the 654th losing twenty-seven PR.XVIs, sixteen of them on operations. Throughout their tenure, the two Mosquito squadrons together provided a minimum each month of thirty-four crews on hand and a maximum of forty-one and a monthly average of forty PR.XVIs and a maximum of forty-eight. With the end of the war in Europe, the 25th BG was expected to be sent to the Pacific, but their PR.XVIs were returned to the RAF and in August the Group returned to the USA, where, on 8 September 1945, it was inactivated at Drew Field, Florida.

CHAPTER EIGHT

Dive! Dive! Dive!

The Banff Strike Wing

Mosquitoes featured significantly in the dangerous low level daylight campaign of attacks on the German Kriegsmarine in WWII. Mainly, the Strike Wings in Coastal Command targeted German ships in the Baltic, which sailed between Germany and Norway, often laden with iron-ore, and the U-boat wolfpacks in the Bay of Biscay and the Western Approaches. U-boats were quite often protected by numbers of Ju 88s and Ju 188s, and they could also put up a fearsome defence of their own. Not surprisingly, the German *Unterseeboote* were highly respected adversaries. A U-boat for example, could be armed with an 88mm gun and two 20mm guns

forward, or four 20mm cannon, or a 37mm gun. Either way, when they cornered one, the Mosquito crews knew they were in for a fight, especially when Karl Doenitz, the U-boat Commander-in-Chief, ordered that U-boats, when attacked, were to remain on the surface and 'slug' it out with their low level attackers.

In 1943, to help Coastal Command in their onerous task, Mosquito fighters were detached to Scotland, and to Predannack at the southern tip of Cornwall, for sorties far out to sea. It will be remembered that from 1943 to early 1944, a few NF.II squadrons in Fighter Command assisted Coastal Command with *Instep* anti-air and

anti-shipping patrols in the Bay of Biscay and the Western Approaches. One of them, 307 (City of Lwów) Squadron, flew its first such patrol on detachment from Predannack on 13 June. Bad weather, however, caused the Poles to abort the operation. Next day four more Polish-crewed NF.IIs, led by S/L Szablowski, took off and headed for the Bay, accompanied by a 410 Squadron RCAF NF.II. Szablowski and his navigator, Sgt Gajewski, spotted five U-boats on the surface and went in to attack from line astern. Szablowski fired and hit the second U-boat before hitting the third submarine. The U-boats returned heavy fire and Szablowski's port engine was hit

During 1943–early 1944, a few NF.II squadrons in Fighter Command assisted Coastal Command with Instep **anti-air and anti-shipping patrols in the Bay of Biscay and the Western Approaches. Here, a Ju 290 burns on the sea on 19 February 1944 after falling to the guns of NF.IIs of 157 Squadron, who flew** Insteps **until April 1944.** Richard Doleman

and put out of action. F/O Pelka, the No. 2, attacked but found that his cannon would not fire, while the third and fourth Mosquitoes did not attack because by now the flak was intense. Szablowski nursed his ailing Mosquito back 500 miles (800km) to Predannack, while the others completed their patrol, and he belly-landed successfully. Five days later, on 19 June, Szablowski's three Mosquitoes and a 410 Squadron NF.II destroyed a Blohm und Voss Bv 138 three-engined reconnaissance flying boat in the Bay.

Another of Coastal Command's tasks was to attack German capital ships which lurked in the Norwegian fjords ready to

break out for raids on the rich shipping lanes of the North Atlantic. One of the capital ships that posed the greatest threat to Allied shipping in 1943 was the *Tirpitz*, but sinking it with conventional weapons was out of the question. 618 Squadron therefore, was formed at Skitten, a satellite airfield for Wick in Coastal Command, under strict secrecy, on 1 April 1943, and just one month before 617 Squadron's attack on the German dams on 16/17 May, for the sole purpose of using Dr Barnes Wallis' *Highball* weapons against the *Tirpitz* and other capital ships at sea. *Highball* weighed 950lbs (430kg) with a charge weight of about 600lbs (270kg) and a

diameter of 35in (89cm). Based on the *Upkeep* 'bouncing bomb' which 617's Lancasters had dropped on the German dams, *Highball* was significantly smaller and lighter (about 10 per cent of the weight of the larger weapon). Each modified Mosquito B.IV could carry two *Highballs*, launching them at low level with a back spin of approximately 500rpm from about ¼ mile (1.2km). On 28 February 1943 an Air Staff paper called for two squadrons of Mosquitoes and 250 *Highball* bombs and two squadrons of Lancasters and 100 *Upkeep* bombs.

Using a nucleus of nineteen crews, including, from Marham, eleven crews late

Loading an inert Highball **store into the modified bomb bay of a Mosquito during trials from RAF Manston.**
Brooklands Museum via Des Curtis

Two Highball **stores, the first released (left) about to overtake the second one, released three seconds later.** Brooklands Museum via Des Curtis

of 105 and 139 Squadrons, and their aircraft (the other eight crews, including the CO, W/C G.H.B. Hutchinson DFC and his navigator, came from Coastal Command Beaufighter squadrons), 618 spent much of 1943 perfecting the weapon and flying assimilation sorties. However, by 14 May, the day before Operation *Servant*, the intended strike on the *Tirpitz*, only six suitably-modified B.IVs were available at Skitten and the strike was called off. (Twelve other Mk IVs were at Hatfield for long-range tanks to be installed.) *Highball* trials continued but by September the Squadron had been reduced to a cadre at Benson.

618 Squadron was retasked for reassignment to the Pacific so, in July 1944, it was brought up to full strength. Its mission now was to attack, with *Highball*, the Japanese fleet at Truk, which, because of the distance involved, meant that the Mosquitoes would have to operate from a carrier! Ten crews arrived from 143, 144, 235, 236, 248 and 254 Squadrons, while from 540 and 544 PR Squadrons there arrived ten pilots and navigators whose task it would be to find the Japanese ships. P/O John R. Myles, who with F/O H.R. Cawker, formed one of the five PR crews, recalls:

We were attached to the Naval Air Torpedo School for carrier training using Barracuda II aircraft. After seventy-two aerodrome dummy deck landings (ADDLs), we five PR crews made more ADDLs during August, September and October, in Mosquito VIs, VIIIs and XVIs. Then we had to make a real deck landing and take-off from a carrier using Mosquito IVs modified with arrester hooks and four paddle-bladed props. On 10 October I made my first ever deck landing and take off, from HMS *Implacable*. Quite an experience!

On 31 October we [and twenty-four Mk IVs and three PR.XVIs] were ferried out to the Pacific on two escort carriers, HMS *Fencer* and HMS *Striker*. We berthed at Gibraltar on 4 November, and went through the Mediterranean and the Suez Canal. Unfortunately, I was quarantined with measles so I didn't see much. We spent two weeks at the Naval Base at Trincomalee in Ceylon and then proceeded to Melbourne, where we arrived on 23 December. (Fortunately, the Yanks sunk the ships before we reached Australia, otherwise it would have been a fiasco.) In January the aircraft were unloaded and on 7 February we proceeded to Narromine in NSW. I organized a trip to Alice Springs where we were conveniently grounded with engine trouble and I was able to do some sight-seeing out in the desert. We then proceeded to Darwin where a PR unit was stationed. We were scheduled to do a trip to New Guinea, but it had to be abandoned due to bad weather. On ANZAC Day, 25 April, nine of us flew a formation flypast of Mosquito IVs over Narromine and surrounding towns. We finally left Australia on VE Day on board the *Nieuw Amsterdam* and returned to England via Durban and Capetown.

Big-gun Mosquitoes

Not all of 618 Squadron's crews went to the Pacific. By December 1943, 248 Squadron based at Predannack flying Beaufighter Xs, had received a detachment of five crews from 618 Squadron. They flew Mk XVIII *Tsetse* Mosquitoes, so named because of their fearsome 57mm Molins automatic weapon for use against U-boats on the surface, which was installed in the nose in place of the four 20mm cannon. An arc-shaped magazine, holding twenty-four rounds of 57mm armour-piercing HE shells capped with tracer, was positioned vertically about midships, feeding into the breech block. The breech block was behind the crew, and the barrel extended below the floor of the cockpit, the muzzle protruding below the fairing of the nose. Two, sometimes four .303in machine guns were retained, however, for strafing and air combat. All these guns were sighted through one reflector sight, the firing buttons being on the control column. The Molins gun had a muzzle velocity of 2,950ft/s (900m/s) and the ideal range to open fire was 1,800–1,500yd (1,650–1,370m). The gun and its feed system were sensitive to sideways movement, and attacking in a XVIII required a dive from about 5,000ft (1,520m) at a 30 degree angle with the turn-and-bank indicator dead central. The slightest drift would cause the gun to jam.

On 22 October 1943 the first two Mk XVIIIs arrived at Predannack for anti-shipping operations in the Atlantic. 248 Squadron was equipped mainly with Beaufighters but earlier that month, five Mosquito crews and thirty-four ground crew from Skitten were transferred in as the 618 Squadron Special Detachment, to fly and service the new *Tsetses*. Amid great secrecy three Mk XVIIIs – HX902, 903 and 904 – were prepared for action. Operations commenced on 24 October with two XVIIIs flown by S/L Charlie Rose DFC DFM, who had been 'A' Flight commander at Skitten, and Sgt Cowley, and F/O Al Bonnett

RCAF and P/O McD 'Pickles' McNicol but they returned empty-handed. After some modifications to the aircraft, on 4 November Charlie Rose and F/Sgt Cowley in HX902, and F/O Doug Turner and F/O Des Curtis in HX903, headed south to the Bay of Biscay. Rose and Cowley failed to return when they crashed into the sea during a diving attack on an enemy trawler. Rose got off two shells and was either hit by return fire or knocked out of the sky by a ricochet from one of his own shells.

Three days later, on 7 November, F/O Al Bonnett scored hits on U-123, a Type IXB of 1,051 tons, which was returning on the surface to Brest at the end of her thirteenth war cruise. (The mine-swept channels off the French Atlantic coast leading to the U-boat bases at Brest, Lorient, St Nazaire, La Rochelle and Bordeaux, were ideal killing grounds because the water depth was too shallow to permit the U-boats to crash-dive if attacked). After the first dive Bonnett's cannon jammed and he was forced to strafe the U-boat with machine gun fire. As a result of this attack the Kriegsmarine was forced to provide escort vessels for its U-boats from now on.

By 1 January 1944 248 Squadron Mosquito Conversion Flight had mustered sixteen *Tsetses* and four FB.VIs available for anti-shipping operations. On 16 February, 248 and 618 Squadrons were moved to Portreath and the former would now provide fighter cover for the *Tsetses* for 618. On 20 February 248 Squadron flew its first interceptor and anti-shipping patrols in the Bay of Biscay. On 10 March four Mk VIs which escorted two XVIIIs to an area about 30 miles (50km) north of Gijon on the Spanish coast, got into a vicious dogfight with eight to ten Ju 88s flying top cover for a German convoy of four destroyers and a U-boat. One of the Ju 88s immediately fell to a head-on attack by the four VIs and a second was shot down into the sea in flames shortly afterwards. The XVIIIs, meanwhile, went after the convoy. S/L Tony Phillips carried out four attacks on the U-boat and F/O Doug Turner, two. They damaged a destroyer and Phillips blasted a Ju 88 out of the sky with four shots from his Molins gun. One of the shells literally tore an engine from the Ju 88 and it spiralled down into the sea.

On 25 March two *Tsetses* crewed by F/O Doug Turner and F/O Des Curtis, and F/O A.H. 'Hilly' Hilliard and W/O Jimmy Hoyle, escorted by four Mk VIs of 248 Squadron, came upon a formation of two

An FB.XVIII Tsetse **of 248 Squadron, used on anti-submarine, ground attack and anti-shipping strikes 1943–44, showing the muzzle of the 57mm Molins gun and the four Browning .303in machine guns, later reduced to just two to save weight and allow more fuel to be carried.** via Des Curtis

armed minesweepers and a destroyer. In the middle of these escorts was U-976, a Type VIIC of 769 tons, commanded by Oberleutnant zur see Raimund Tiesler, which was returning to St Nazaire after being recalled from her second war cruise. The two pairs of escorting Mk VIs dived on the escorting ships down sun and opened fire with cannon and machine guns. A heavy fusilade of fire from the ships came up to meet them. Doug Turner opened the attack on U-976 and got off five rounds with the Molins. Every burst was accompanied by a recoil which whipped the needle of the airspeed indicator back to zero. Turner made four attacks

in all, and fired off all his twenty-four rounds. One of the shells in the first diving attack destroyed one of the guns on the U-boat. Hilliard attacked U-976 on the waterline below the conning tower before breaking off. About ten hits were seen on the conning tower and on the forward deck near and below the waterline. After the attacks U-976 sank and Jimmy Hoyle saw an oil patch which he estimated to be 100yd (90m) long and 30yd (27m) wide. Survivors from the U-boat were picked up by the minesweepers.

On 27 March the same *Tsetse* crews, but with six FB.VI escorts of 248 Squadron (which had begun conversion from Beau-

fighters in December), set out for the same area again. Intelligence had monitored the course taken by two Type VIIC U-boats, U-769 and U-960, which were due to arrive at La Pallice escorted by four 'M' Class minesweepers and two *Sperrbrechers* (merchantmen converted to flak ships). RAF anti-shipping aircrews regarded these vessels, which were bristling with AA guns, as their most dangerous enemy. U-960 was commanded by Oberleutnant z.S.u. Gunther 'Heini' Heinrich, who had enlisted in the Kriegsmarine in October 1938 and had taken charge of U-960 on 26 January 1943.

Hilliard's intercom and VHF set in HX903 went u/s, but he decided to

On 25 March 1944, two Tsetses **crewed by F/O Doug Turner and F/O Des Curtis, and F/O A.H. 'Hilly' Hilliard and W/O Jimmy Hoyle sank U-976, a Type VIIC of 769 tons, commanded by Oberleutnant zur see Raimund Tiesler, which was returning to St Nazaire after being recalled from her second war cruise. This photo shows U-976 hit by a 57mm shell while returning fire. Minesweeper V604 to the right picked up some of the survivors from the U-boat.**
Des Curtis

continue. Rounding the north west peninsular of France the formation was spotted just over two hours after take-off. When they reached 2,000ft (1,830m) heavy flak began bursting all around them. Hilliard banked to port and his Mosquito escort did the same, so the pair broke from the formation for an attack, while the rest climbed. The escort went for a *Sperrbrecher* while Turner and Hilliard dived on U-960, firing off seven shells during their run-in, 'five of which I claimed as hits,' recalls Hilliard. (One of the shells hit the armoured conning tower.) He goes on:

We screamed over the U-boat at zero feet and I noticed the gunners stripped to the waist pulling their 37mm gun into a vertical position. Then I heard and felt a thud, seconds later followed by the machine gun inspection panels in front of my windscreen splitting open. I thought that the nose section had split from the shell I had collected, but looking around there was no apparent damage. [The 37mm shell had hit the Mosquito right on the nose cone but fortunately, the armour plating under the instrument panel cushioned the impact of the flying shrapnel]. Flak by this time had opened up from coastal batteries.

Altogether, the four mine-sweepers fired forty-five 88mm shells and 1,550 20mm shells and claimed one Mosquito 'definitely' shot down. Hilliard and Hoyle however reached Portreath safely despite the ruptured nose cone protruding into the slipstream and they landed almost out of fuel. Turner had started his dive as Hilliard cleared the target, and in all, four shells were seen to hit the metalwork. Five other Mosquitoes were hit in the attack. F/Sgt

C.R. Tomalin managed to put his VI down at Portreath despite a large hole in the starboard mainplane. F/Sgt L.A. Compton and Sgt Peters crashlanded also, with the hydraulics shot out. Aboard U-960 the conning tower, periscope and control room were badly damaged by Hilliard's 57mm shells. Ten men, including Heinrich, who was hit above the left knee, were wounded, some of them badly. U-960 managed to put into La Pallice for repairs. A year later she put to sea again and was sunk in the Mediterranean on 19 May by the combined efforts of four US destroyers and two squadrons of Venturas.

The first ten days of April produced no results, then on the 11th, two Mk XVIIIs of 618 Detachment escorted by five FB.VIs from 248 Squadron, and six from 151 Squadron at Predannack, took off on another coastal patrol from Portreath. One Mosquito crashed into a hill on take-off and one of the *Tsetses* returned early with mechanical problems. The others pressed on to St Nazaire where they came upon a U-boat with a four ship escort and an air umbrella of about a dozen Ju 88s. The FB.VIs attacked the escort ships and then turned their attention to the Ju 88s while F/L B. C. Roberts went after the U-boat. He saw spouts of water near the hull of the U-boat as he fired his Molins but could claim no definite hits. Flak was extremely heavy and W/C O.J.M. Barron DFC, CO of 248 Squadron, and another Mosquito, were shot down. Two of the Ju 88s were claimed destroyed. A third Mosquito was lost in a crash landing at Portreath.

At the end of April 248 Squadron began attacks on land targets and in May the 618

Squadron Special Detachment joined 248, the *Tsetses* now making attacks on surface vessels as well as U-boats. Their technique was to fire the armour-piercing shells through the wooden deck planking of the ships while rocket-firing Beaufighters went in at 500ft (150m) in a shallow dive. On D-Day, 6 June, 248 Squadron flew anti-shipping, escort and blockading sorties off the Normandy, Brittany and Biscay coasts, including one operation as escort for seventeen anti-flak Beaufighters of 144 Squadron and fourteen rocket-armed Beaufighters of 404 Squadron. During one of these sorties, a 248 Squadron Mosquito shot down a Ju 188. On 7 June two *Tsetses*, flown by Doug Turner and Des Curtis, and Al Bonnett and 'Pickles' McNicol, each made a run on a surfacing U-boat. A dozen 57mm shells were fired at U-212 but on his second run, Bonnett's cannon jammed and he only made a series of dummy runs on the U-boat which crash-dived, leaving a pool of oil and a crewman on the surface. (U-212 limped into St Nazaire for repairs and when she put to sea again, was sunk by frigates in July). Turner's *Tsetse* was hit by flak in the port wing and engine nacelle but he and Bonnett made it back to Cornwall safely. Bonnett and McNicol were killed two days later, following a search for survivors of a German destroyer in the Channel, when W/C Tony Phillips DSO DFC, now CO of 248 Squadron, collided with his Mosquito while approaching the airfield. Phillips lost 6ft (2m) of his outer wing but landed safely.

On 10 June four 248 Squadron Mosquitoes attacked U-821 near Ushant with such ferocity that the crew abandoned ship, which was then sunk by a Liberator of 206 Squadron. That afternoon F/L E.H. Jeffreys DFC and F/O D.A. Burden of 248 Squadron were shot down by a motor launch carrying the survivors of U-821. The launch was promptly sunk by the other Mosquitoes. On 22 June, wing-mounted 25lb (11kg) Mk XI depth charges and A.VIII mines were used operationally by Mosquitoes for the first time and 235 Squadron at Portreath, which had been equipped with Beaufighters, flew their first Mk VI sortie (the last Beaufighter sortie was flown on 27 June). The Mosquitoes now flew escort for the Beaufighters and they were also used to intercept Dornier 217s which carried Henschel 293 glider bombs for attacks on Allied shipping.

On 4 July W/C Tony Phillips with F/O R.W. 'Tommy' Thomson DFC, and S/L Jean Maurice (pseudonym for Max Guedj DSO DFC CdeG) with S/L Randall, flew a costly 248 Squadron operation to the Brest

survived, but Yvonne died 12 hours later. For two days the airmen were left where they lay before a German officer gave the order to bury them.

On 11 July, two *Tsetses*, flown by Doug Turner and Des Curtis, and F/O Bill Cosman and F/O Freedman, escorted by sixteen FB.VIs, made an evening raid on the approach to Brest harbour where a surfaced U-boat was proceeding slowly, with no wake, along the Goulet de Brest, escorted by three minesweepers and a *Sperrbrecher*. The shore batteries combined with the ships to put up an intense flak barrage. Undeterred, Cosman made a diving attack on the U-boat, breaking off at 50yd (or 45m), and claiming two possible hits out of four shots fired. Doug Turner scored five hits on the *Sperrbrecher* and Cosman's parting shot was a salvo of two 57mm shells at the leading minesweeper, as the Mosquitoes weaved their way through the flak to the mouth of the harbour.

Squadrons, and nineteen Beaufighters, attacked shipping between Egero and Stors Toreungen light. A flak ship and a merchantman were sunk.

On 28 September, the Banff Wing Mosquitoes were at last modified to carry eight rocket-projectiles (RP) on Mk IIIA projector rails beneath their wings just like the Beaufighters. The rails had to be set so that they were parallel with the airflow at correct diving speed, otherwise the RPs would weathercock, and either under- or overshoot the target. They would also miss if the pilot dived at the wrong airspeed. At first the RPs were armed with 60lb (27kg) semi-armour-piercing heads of the type used in the desert for tank-busting. These did not however, penetrate shipping and caused little structural damage, so were soon replaced with 25lb (11kg) solid armour-piercing warheads. Sometimes rockets would 'hang up' on the rails and fail to fire. If this happened, crews had to bale out because if they tried to land, the RPs were liable to explode.

When making an attack on shipping, the Mosquitoes normally commenced their dive of approximately 45 degrees at about 2,000ft (610m) and then opened up with machine gun fire at 1,500–1,000ft (460–300m), before using the cannons, and lastly, at about 500ft (150m), the RPs. The RPs were arranged to form a pattern spread on impact, so that if fired at the correct range and airspeed and angle of dive, four would hit the ship above the waterline and the other four would undershoot slightly to hit below the waterline. In the Norwegian fjords pilots usually had once chance, so they fired all eight rockets at once. After entering the ship's hull each would punch an 18in (46cm) hole in the far side of the hull for the sea to flood in, while the remains of the cordite motor burned inside the hull to ignite fuel and ammunition in the ship. The Mosquitoes used the RPs for the first time on 26 October.

Only a few isolated vessels were found and sunk in early October because the enemy operated at night in the knowledge that the strike wing could not fly in tight formation at night. On 9 October the Banff Wing tried out a system that had been tried at North Coates during early August 1944. A Warwick laden with flame floats and markers took off at 0415 and 2 hours later, dropped them to form a circle 19ft (6m) in diameter some 100yd (90m) from Stavanger. Half an hour later,

Mosquito Strike Wing Squadrons 1943–1945			
Squadron	Command	Period	Types
618	No.18 Coastal Group	1.4.43–8.45	IV/VI/XVIII
333(Nor)	Banff Strike Wing¹	27.5.43–20.11.45	VI
248	Banff Strike Wing¹	2.43–21.12.45	VI/XVIII
235	Banff Strike Wing¹	6.44–10.7.45	II/VI
143	Banff Strike Wing¹	10.44–25.5.45	II/VI
404	Banff Strike Wing¹	22.4.45–25.5.45	VI
334(Nor)	Banff Strike Wing¹	30.5.45–22.6.45	VI/III
489 RNZAF		6.45–1.8.45	FB.VI

(¹Formed, September 1944)

Peninsula. They found a group of minesweepers anchored in Penfoul Cove and the Kercréven docks. For greater accuracy the two Mosquitoes closed right in on their targets, skimmed over the masts of the enemy ships and dropped their bombs. AA guns were firing from Creach-Conarch heights and the ships. It is unclear if the Mosquito crewed by Phillips and Thomson was hit by flak. A witness claims that they hit the top of the mast of one of the ships. The Mosquito crashed near the Keranguyon Farm, and the crew were ejected in the explosion. Phillips was found near the aircraft, Thompson falling a hundred yards away, in front of the doorstep of Mne Berrou's farm, which caught fire after being hit by flying debris. Two farm workers, Yves Glémarec, and Yvonne Laurent, a young girl, had their clothes set alight. Glémarec badly burned,

Forming the Banff Wing

Germany's seaborne traffic travelling daily along the Norwegian coast with large quantities of supplies now assumed a much higher priority, and early in September Coastal Command ordered 235 and 248 Squadrons to Scotland. The last operation from Portreath was flown on 7 September by four Mosquitoes of 248 Squadron, in poor visibility near Gironde, while searching for U-boats. 235 and 248 joined 333 Norwegian Squadron and 144 and 404 RCAF Beaufighter Squadrons to form the Banff Strike Wing under G/C Max Aitken DSO DFC. 333 Squadron had formed at Leuchars on 10 May 1943 from 1477 (Norwegian) Flight, and commenced its first Mk VI operations on 27 May. The Banff Wing carried out their first strike on 14 September, when 22 FB.VIs and four *Tsetses* from 235 and 248

On 28 September 1944 the Banff Wing Mosquitoes were at last modified to carry, beneath their wings, eight RPs on Mk IIIA tapered type rails, which were made of lengths of tubular steel welded together. Here, YZ446 of 235 Squadron has RPs fitted, the electrical arming 'pigtails' with Niphan plugs dangling from the rear of each 25lb (11kg) rocket awaiting the armourers' attention. The rails had to be set so that they were parallel with the airflow at correct diving speed, otherwise the RPs would weathercock and miss the target. The same happened if the pilot dived at the wrong airspeed. G.A.B. Lord

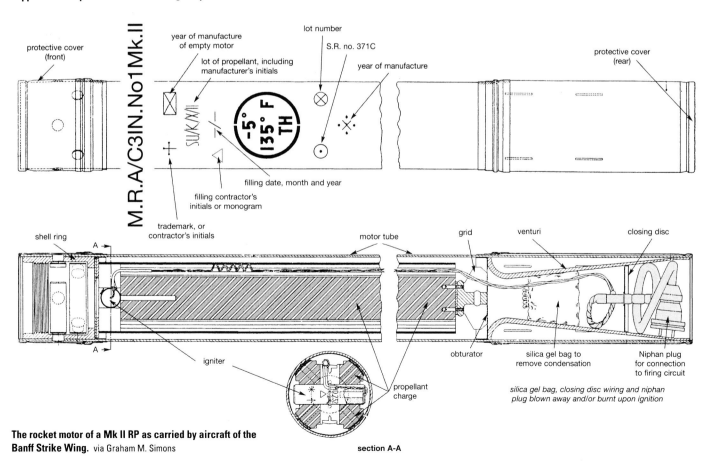

The rocket motor of a Mk II RP as carried by aircraft of the Banff Strike Wing. via Graham M. Simons

eight Mosquitoes of 235 Squadron followed by eighteen Beaufighters, traced the same course. At 0620 the first aircraft arrived and began to circle. As dawn appeared, the formation set off heading for Egrsund. Led by W/C Tony Gadd of 144 Squadron, at 0710 they sank a German merchantman and a submarine chaser, while a Norwegian vessel was badly damaged. When they had recovered from the surprise the enemy gunners put up a fierce flak barrage but this was smothered by cannon fire. Three aircraft were damaged but all returned.

their 57mm shells. Seven crew were injured. One said later that:

> ... they had been attacked by an aircraft carrying a big gun, emitting a long flame.

One 235 Squadron Mosquito was lost.

With the departure of the two Beaufighter squadrons on 22 October to Dallachy to form a wing with 455 and 489 Squadrons from Langham, 143 Beaufighter Squadron at North Coates moved north to join the Banff Strike Wing and convert to the Mosquito Mk VI. On 24 October

On 7 November 143 Squadron flew its first FB.VI operation when two aircraft carried out a search for enemy aircraft between Obrestad and Lindesnes. Frequent snow and hail were a feature of operations on 8 and 9 November when the Mosquitoes looked for shipping off Ytterîene, Marstein and Askvoll. The Banff Wing now began to operate in increasingly larger formations, including for the first time, on 13 November, a combined 'op' with the Dallachy Wing. The largest strike so far occurred on 21 November when New Zealander W/C Bill Sise

PZ405 NE-A of 143 Squadron, with 25lb (11kg) RPs on rocket rails, flown by S/L David Pritchard DFC**. At first, RPs with 60lb (27kg) semi-armour-piercing heads of the type used in the desert for tank-busting were used on anti-shipping strikes. These did not penetrate shipping and caused little structural damage so were soon replaced with the solid armour-piercing rockets shown.** via Andrew D. Bird

On 19 October the flak alarm was raised by lookouts on three vessels at anchor at Askvoy at 1330 as nineteen Mosquitoes streaked towards them. Flashes erupted from the nose of each Mosquito and spouts of water erupted in a line towards V-5116. Rounds struck the bridge and more triggered a fire which the *Tsetses* fanned with

two Mosquitoes of 235 Squadron attacked three enemy aircraft, the first seen by the strike wing. W/O Cogswell dispatched one Bf 110, while F/L Jacques finished off the second Bf 110 hit by Cogswell, who had set an engine on fire. Jacques then destroyed the third aircraft, a Ju 88C. By the end of the month, five strikes had been made.

DSO DFC, who had taken over 248 Squadron on the death of W/C Phillips, led a formation of thirty-three Mosquitoes, accompanied by forty-two Beaufighters, and twelve Mustang escorts, in a shipping strike at Ålesund.

On 29 November in a diving attack on a U-boat off Lista, F/O Woodcock in a

An FB.VI dramatically test-fires 25lb (11kg) RPs and
cannon on a sea range at night. G.A.B. Lord

(Right) **Mosquitoes used RPs for the first time on 21
October 1944, when six FB.VIs of 235 and 248
Squadrons, led by S/L Max Guedj** DSO DFC **of 248
Squadron, accompanied by a 333 Squadron outrider
and fifteen Beaufighters, sank the 1,923 ton**
Eckenheim, **and the 1,432 ton** Vestra, **off Haugesund.
FB.VI 'V' of 235 Squadron is seen here opening fire on
one of the ships. Flak brought down PZ251 of 248
Squadron.** G.A.B. Lord

Tsetse fired off eight 57mm shells, scoring two hits, while other XVIIIs attacked with depth charges and cannon. *Tsetses* were again in action on 5 December when Bill Sise led thirty-four Mosquitoes in an attack on merchantmen in Nord Gullen. On the 7th, twenty-one Mosquitoes and forty Beaufighters, escorted by twelve Mustangs, set out to attack a convoy in Ålesund harbour. Landfall was made as briefed but S/L Barnes DFC led them further up the coast, towards Gossen airfield, whereupon they were jumped by approximately twenty-five Fw 190s and Bf 109Gs. They dived through the middle of the Mosquitoes and attacked singly and in pairs. Mustangs shot down four fighters and two more collided but two FB.VIs (flown by Bill Cosman, and K.C. Wing), a Mustang and a Beaufighter, were lost. Seven enemy fighters were shot down.

On 12 December the Mosquitoes returned to Gossen but this time no fighters were seen. The following day W/C R.A. Atkinson DSO DFC CO, 235 Squadron, and his navigator, F/O Val Upton, were killed when a cable across a fjord cut off the Australian's starboard wing during their attack on merchantmen at Ejdsfjord. On the 16th the Mosquitoes came upon a merchantman and its escort between the steep cliffs of a fjord at Kraakhellesund. Despite intense flak from the escort and surrounding cliff sides, the Mosquitoes dived into the attack in line astern, because there was no space to manoeuvre. Two of the FB.VIs were shot down. On 19 December Mustangs escorted the Mosquitoes to Sulen, Norway but no fighters appeared.

On 26 December, twelve FB.VIs of 235 Squadron led by S/L Norman 'Jacko' Jackson-Smith, with two outriders from 333 Squadron, attacked two merchant ships at Leirvik harbour, about 70 miles (110km) up Sogne Fjord, with machine guns and cannon. A Mosquito crewed by F/O Bill Clayton-Graham and F/O 'Ginger' Webster, was hit in the port engine during the second attack. Clayton-Graham climbed to 1,000ft (300m) and tried to make his escape but twenty-four fighters high above sent about half their number to attack the wounded and badly smoking Mosquito. His cannons were empty but Clayton-Graham turned to meet them, and fired his machine guns as the fighters raced towards and then past him. Incredibly, the Mosquito was not hit but several of the fighters were, one of them severely. Clayton-Graham was a sitting duck but they roared off and turned

their attention on another aircraft, piloted by F/O Jim Fletcher, which they shot down. Clayton-Graham and Webster came home hugging the wave tops escorted by an ASR Warwick and reached Scotland safely. One Mosquito crash-landed.

On 9 January 1945, eighteen FB.VIs of 235 Squadron returned to Leirvik with an escort of a dozen Mustangs and attacked eight merchant ships in the harbour. They left three ships burning and the Norwegian Underground later reported one ship sunk at its moorings. Two days later there was more success when F/L N. Russell DFC and another Mosquito pilot shot down a Bf 109 during an anti-shipping strike in Flekke fjord by fourteen Mosquitoes and eighteen Beaufighters. The Mosquitoes though, did not have it all their own way when a formation of thirteen strike Mosquitoes, one *Tsetse*, and two 333 Squadron outriders, led by W/C Guedj, now CO of 143 Squadron, returned to Leirvik again on 15 January. They completely surprised two merchantmen and an armed trawler and left them burning and sinking before they were jumped by about thirty Fw 190s of III./JG5. *Tsetse* 'Z' fired four shells at a Fw 190. Five enemy fighters were shot down but five Mosquitoes, including the one piloted by 'Maury' Guedj, were also lost. The rest fought their way back across

the North Sea pursued for a time by nine fighters. This sudden rise in Banff Wing losses caused concern at Northwood and after this attack 248 Squadron's *Tsetses* were transferred south to North Coates.

On 11 February delayed action bombs were dropped in a narrow fjord off Midgulen to roll down the 3,000ft (1,050m) cliffs to explode among the ships in the harbour below. On 21 February 235 Squadron carried RPs for the first time when a 5,000 ton ship in Askevold Fjord was attacked. Taking part for the first time were spare aircrew from 603 Squadron who had flown Beaufighters in the Middle East, led by W/C C.N. Foxley-Norris DSO. Nearly all had joined 235 Squadron. In March, Mosquitoes began operating independently of the Beaufighters, seeking out specific targets in Norway. Over the first few days the installation of new, Mk IB

FB.VIs of 235 Squadron en route to their target. LA-V, its tailwheel unretracted, is flown by G.A.B. Lord at about 50ft (15m) above the waves. G.A.B. Lord

tiered RP projector rails, enabled long range drop tanks to be carried in addition to the RPs. 235 and 248 Squadrons were now able to operate at an increased range, but with a 50 or 100 gallon (230 or 460 litre) drop-tank and four RPs under each wing, the Mosquitoes tended to stagger on take-off!

On 7 March, forty-four Mosquitoes led by W/C R.K. Orrock DFC, CO, 248 Squadron, and escorted by twelve Mustangs, destroyed

(Top) **Striking view of NE-Y of 143 Squadron flown low over the sea by the CO, W/C Foxley-Norris.**
'Dutch' Holland via Basil McRae

(Above) **FB.VI PZ202 with the Mk IB double-tiered RP projector rail system introduced early in March 1945, which allowed enough space for 100-gallon (454-litre) underwing drop tanks to be carried.** 'Dutch' Holland via Philip Birtles

143 Squadron FB.VIs, led by W/C C.N. Foxley-Norris DSO**, attacking the** Lysaker, **a 910-ton motor vessel, at Tetgenaes on 23 March 1945 with RPs.** via Alan Sanderson

143 Squadron FB.VIs, led by W/C C.N. Foxley-Norris DSO**, pulls up over the** Lysaker **at Tetgenaes on 23 March 1945. Two Mosquitoes were shot down.** via Alan Sanderson/Graham M. Simons

eight self-propelled barges in the Kattegat with machine guns, cannon and rocket fire. Two Mosquitoes collided shortly after the attack. No enemy fighters showed but a similar raid on 12 March by forty-four Mosquitoes and twelve Mustangs over the Skagerrak and Kattegat was met by a formation of Bf 109s. Two enemy fighters were shot down. On 17 March six ships at Ålesund harbour were repeatedly strafed by thirty-one FB.VIs of 235 Squadron after they had been led in by two Norwegian crews in 333 Squadron. Flak was heavy and two aircraft were lost but the Mosquitoes fired their cannon and RPs to deadly effect, leaving three of the ships sinking and the other three crippled. One ship was holed thirty-two times and another thirty-seven times. All except twenty-four of the RPs hit below the waterline.

On 21 March, 235 and 143 Squadrons made short work of another ship at Sandshavn and two days later a troopship, the 7,800-ton *Rothenfels*, at anchor in Dalsfjord, was attacked by nine Mosquitoes. The strike leader, S/L Robbie Read, and one other, was shot down. In the afternoon,

W/C Foxley-Norris led another strike, attacking a motor vessel at Tetgenaes. On 24 March some crews in 404 Squadron arrived to convert to Mosquitoes while the remainder attacked merchantmen at Egersund using Beaufighters. On 30 March W/C A.H. Simmonds, CO of 235 Squadron, led thirty-two rocket-firing FB.VIs, with eight more as escorts, in an attack on Porsgrunn-Skein harbour. No fighters troubled the formation and the eight FB.VIs detailed as escorts were able to fire against gun positions in the sides of the fjord. The attackers flew so low against the four merchantmen that they crested the wave tops. Two, Mosquitoes, one crewed by F/L Bill Knowles and F/Sgt L. Thomas, which struck an overhead electric cable and crashed, failed to return. Three of the four merchantman were sunk and the fourth was badly damaged while a warehouse on Menstad quay full of chemicals was also destroyed.

On 5 April, thirty-seven Mosquitoes escorted by Mustangs flew across Denmark to attack a widely-spread out and heavily-

armed convoy in the Kattegat. Every ship in the convoy was left on fire and sinking and an estimated 900 German soldiers were lost. One *Sperrbrecher* sank with all hands, 200 bodies being recovered by Swedish vessels. An escorting Mustang was shot down over Denmark and a Mosquito crashlanded with the crew picked up by the Danish Underground. Four days later, on 9 April, thirty-one rocket-projectile FB.VIs of 248, 143, and 235 Squadrons with five others as fighter cover, and DZ592, a 2nd TAF photo-Mosquito, returned to the area on the look out for enemy shipping. Three U-boats – 804, 843 and 1065 – were spotted in line astern on the surface of the Kattegat coming from Denmark and heading for Norway. S/L Bert Gunnis DFC, who was leading the strike, ordered the nine FB.VIs of 143 Squadron near the rear of the formation being led by S/L David Pritchard, to attack. The U-boats had not seen the Mosquitoes. Then they did, but it was too late. With the rest of the wing wheeling in behind, 143 Squadron attacked, their cannons blazing as they fired seventy RPs into the U-boats,

235 Squadron attack on a motor vessel in Dalsfjord on 23 March 1945. via Alan Sanderson

115

On 30 March W/C A.H. Simmonds, CO of 235 Squadron, led thirty-two rocket-firing FB.VIs, with eight more as escorts, in an attack on four merchantmen at Borgestad (Porsgrunn-Skein harbour). Three FB.VIs of 248 Squadron are seen pulling off the target leaving a merchantman on fire (bottom) while the pall of smoke (centre) is F/L Bill Knowles and F/Sgt L. Thomas' Mosquito which struck an overhead electric cable and crashed. Three merchantmen were sunk and the fourth was badly damaged while a warehouse on Menstad quay full of chemicals was also destroyed.
via Alan Sanderson

(Right) W/C C.N. Foxley-Norris, 143 Squadron CO, in 'A-Apple', (right) and his wingman (left), make their runs on shipping moored at Sandefjord, 2 April 1945, letting fly with salvoes of RPs.
via Alan Sanderson

now frantically trying to escape beneath the waves. All three were sunk, one of them taking the photo-Mosquito with it in an explosion. In fact the Mosquitoes were so low,

three more suffered damaged engines when they were hit by flying debris and were forced to land in Sweden.

On 11 April another attack was made

on Porsgrunn, by thirty-five Mosquitoes. Bf 109G-14s shot down two, although the remainder left four merchantmen sinking. Next day a FB.XVIII of 248 Squadron, one of five *Tsetses* sent on detachment to 254 Beaufighter Squadron at North Coates, attacked a U-boat in the North Sea. The *Tsetse* detachment was used primarily for operations against midget submarines and U-boats, with Spitfire XXIs for cover. Two *Tsetses* found five U-boats on the surface on 18 April. The XVIIIs got off just one round each before the submarines crash-dived. On 19 April the FB.VIs at Banff sank U-251 in the Kattegat. 150 miles (240km) off the Scottish coast on 21 April, forty-two FB.VIs of 235, 248, 143 and 333 Squadrons, led by W/C Foxley-Norris, CO, 143 Squadron, shot down five Ju 88A-17 and four Ju 188A-3 torpedo carrying aircraft of KG26, The German strike mission was inbound from Gardermoen, Denmark to attack convoy JW66 which had left the Clyde three days before. Twenty-four Mustang escorts missed the mêlée, having

404 Squadron RCAF going out on a strike. W/C E.W. Pierce, the CO, is flying 'P-Peter' RF856.
via Andrew D. Bird

(Right) **A minesweeper escorting U-boats in the Kattegat on 2 May 1945 burns furiously after an attack by FB.VIs of 248 Squadron.** via Alan Sanderson

U-boat under attack in the Kattegat, 2 May 1945, by FB.VI 'A-Apple' of 235 Squadron. G.A.B. Lord

FB.VIs of 143 Squadron attack U-boats in the Kattegat, 2 May 1945. G.A.B. Lord

sought and gained permission to return early for a party at Peterhead!

On 22 April, 404 'Buffalo' Squadron flew its first operation from Banff since replacing its Beaufighter Xs with Mosquito VIs in March. They sank a Bv 138 flying boat at her moorings but the Squadron had little time left to make an impression as the war in Europe was now drawing to a close. However, on 2 May, a strike by twenty-seven Mosquitoes in the Kattegat resulted in the sinking of U-2359. On 4 May, forty-eight Mosquitoes, from 143, 235, 248, 333 and 404 Squadrons, escorted by eighteen Mustangs, with three ASR Warwicks with airborne lifeboats along, carried out the last large-scale shipping strike of the war. The wing had its last loss when F/L Thorburn DFC failed to return and there was a close call when F/L Gerry Yeates of 248 Squadron returned with the top of a masthead complete with German flag embedded under his Mosquito's nose! This final, massive, battle was the end of the shooting war for the strike wing but patrols for U-boat crews who might be inclined to continue the fight, went on until 21 May, when four Mosquitoes of 143 and 248 Squadrons found only passive E-boats.

The Banff Wing provided escorts for the King of Norway as he sailed back to his country under heavy naval escort. Days later a schnorkel was seen and attacked by a single Mosquito from 404 Squadron. By 25 May the rapid run down of the anti-shipping wing had begun.

U–Boat Sinkings by Mosquitoes		
618	25.3.44	U-976
143, 235, 248	9.4.45	U-843/U-804/U-1065
143, 235, 248, 333	19.4.45	U-251
143, 235, 248, 333, 404	2.5.45	U-2359

On 4 May 1945 F/L Gerry Yeates of 248 Squadron returned from an operation which sent four U-boats to the bottom of Kiel Bay, with the top of a masthead complete with German flag embedded under his Mosquito's nose! via Graham M. Simons

'Flying on one engine was almost like flying on two but with a bit less power. Once, when I had many
more hours under my belt, I flew formation, with one feathered, on another aircraft flying on two ... In all
the Mosquito flying which I was privileged to enjoy, I never had an engine failure. Another feature which
we appreciated was the flat bullet-proof windscreen which not only gave a sense of security, but provided
a fine field of view and a good surface for the windscreen wiper ...' 'Dutch' Holland

CHAPTER NINE

What Was It Like to Fly?

by Leslie 'Dutch' Holland

In September 1942 I had enjoyed a brief flirtation with this amazing aircraft, and when I renewed the acquaintance almost exactly two years later, the twelve blissful hours I logged on it seemed like a distant dream. 85 Squadron received the first of its Mosquito IIs that month and they were only the second to be re-equipped with the first of the night-fighter variants. So I suppose it was an impossible dream that a lowly sergeant pilot on Havocs like myself should long enjoy this privilege.

My first flight was as passenger to F/O McClusky, a large bluff Canadian whose friendship I much enjoyed during my short stay with 85. The sortie was an afternoon air firing outing in VY-T. We had temporary issue of a Mk III dual control aircraft for conversion. I had two dual rides in this with F/L Bunting, which I flew from the left hand seat. It was immediately apparent that this was an entirely new sort of aircraft, right from the moment of entry. The T.III and all the night-fighters were entered through a rather small door in the starboard side of the fuselage just behind the propeller, by climbing a very flimsy telescopic ladder which was then stowed on the inside of the door. One pushed one's parachute up first and shoved it in the seat. This was OK on night-fighters with only one control column, but a bit awkward with two on the dual version. These aircraft were almost brand new and had a pungent smell of dope and their own special glue. There was also an ever present aroma of 100 Octane fuel. These scents persist so exactly in the memory that just looking at a photo of the inside of any aircraft evokes the smell unmistakably. I had occasion many times after the war to sit in Mosquitoes at de Havilland's factories, but not fly them. All of them were new, not having yet flown, and they had that same smell.

The first thing that struck me as strange was the offset hand-grip on the top of the control column. This gave a splendid unobstructed view of the standard blind-flying instrument panel but trying to fly level for the first few minutes called for a bit of concentration. The layout of other instruments was a bit higgledy-piggledy. Those for the engines were well grouped but mostly below the level of one's knees with ignition switches, fire extinguishers and feathering buttons over at the top of the right hand facia – more of these later. On the right wall above the door, the fuel gauges with ridiculously small dials and above them a row of half a dozen switches for nav lights, ultra-violet cockpit lights and a few other odd services. Anyone who thought they presented a confusing array would have been somewhat bewildered by future generations of the industry's offerings. In amongst all this lot was a *Lorenz* Beam Indicator. I never heard of anyone actually using one – I certainly did not and could not understand why they continued to occupy space in a crowded cockpit.

The engines started very easily, firing straight away on all twelve cylinders, settling into a sort of growling purr, and taxying was simplicity itself. I could not say that it was like driving a car because at that time I had never driven one; in fact I had flown 1,000 hours before I ever sat behind a steering wheel, but it was easier than the first few miles in a car. The landing gear struts contained squabs of rubber, which without the shock-absorbing action of the usual hydraulic struts made for rhythmic bounciness – not at all unpleasant.

On my first take off I did have to make a conscious effort to keep straight, which is the surest way to start a Mosquito swinging. Anyway, I stayed on the runway and Bunting didn't have to grab the controls. I had not used flap, so there were no trim changes to worry about and only the gear to get up. This involved taking the stick hand grip which was over to the right, with the left hand in order to lift the U/C lever with the right. Naturally, this causes a bit of lateral wavering the first time, but the aircraft is nice and stable on the climb. Speeds at this stage were not so very different from the Boston so things did not happen quicker than one was used to. A trial stall proved to be an untraumatic event and the slight wing drop was corrected with aileron as the nose had already dropped and speed increased slightly. At cruising speed of 240mph (386kph) IAS, the aircraft had the feeling of being nicely balanced on top of a pole, unlike some I had known which seemed to slide around as if they were at the bottom of a bowl. The roll rate was not exciting but whatever attitude it was put into, it seemed quite happy as if just waiting for the next word of command.

Flying on one engine was almost like flying on two but with a bit less power. Once, when I had many more hours under my belt, I flew formation, with one feathered, on another aircraft flying on two, but he did keep his speed down; in fact deliberately dropped it until I nearly fell out of the sky – a good thing we didn't because we were just above the tree tops over woods near Little Snoring. On those first training sorties it was strange to look out of the window at the stationary prop just outside. Restarting was no problem, but I will tell shortly of an incident which occurred two years later when I was re-introduced to the Mossie on my second time through night-fighter OTU. After that interval of time, I find that, although I had only done 12 hours in 1942, my check ride took ten minutes. One could hardly claim on that evidence that it was a difficult aeroplane in any respect. The occasion referred to was again on a Mk II, which Bob Young, my navigator, and I were flying on a cross-country including a low level leg to Filey. What a splendid idea it would be to beat up the beach with one engine feathered, what great guys the girls would think we were.

'… The first thing that struck me as strange was the offset handgrip on the top of the control column (right). This gave a splendid unobstructed view of the standard blind flying instrument panel but … the layout of other instruments was a bit higgledy-piggledy. Those for the engines (top right, lower) were well grouped but mostly below the level of one's knees with ignition switches, fire extinguishers and feathering buttons over at the top of the right hand facia.' BAe Hatfield

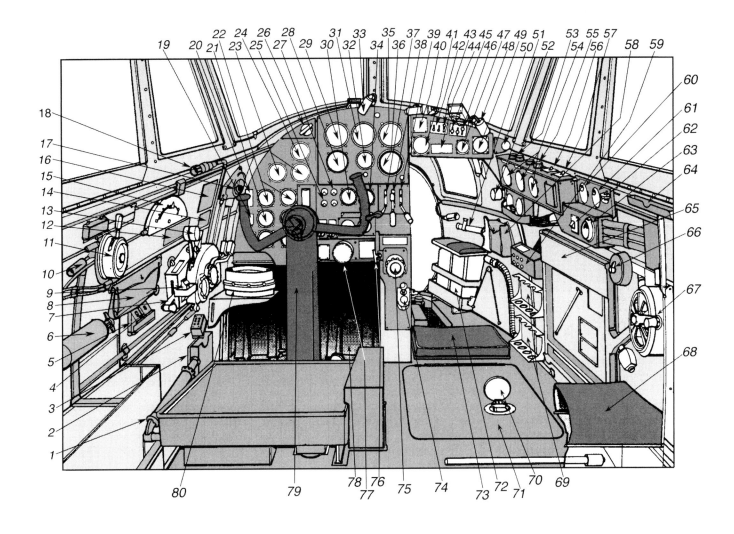

1	Pilot's Seat Adjustment Lever.	28	Altimeter.
2	Map Pocket.	29	Airspeed Indicator.
3	Radio Push-button Unit.	30	Undercarriage Position Indicator.
4	I.F.F. 'Distress' Switch.	31	Artificial Horizon.
5	Beam Approach Switch.	32	Directional Gyro.
6	Fire Extinguisher.	33	Panel Light and Dimmer Switch.
7	Mixture Control Lever.	34	Flap Position Indicator.
8	Bag for Pilot's Personal Effects.	35	Rate of Climb/Descent Indicator.
9	Supercharger Gear Change Switch.	36	Turn and Bank Indicator.
10	Interphone/Radio Socket.	37	Bomb Doors Selector Lever.
11	Radio Controller.	38	Undercarriage Selector Lever.
12	Undercarriage – Emergency Instructions.	39	Flaps Selector Lever.
13	Throttle Levers.	40	Clock.
14	Compass Deviation Card.	41	Beam Approach Indicator.
15	Elevator Trim Tab Indicator.	42	Radiator Flap Switches.
16	Engine Limitations Data Plate.	43	Navigation Lights Switch.
17	Cabin Cool Air Control.	44	Propeller Feathering Buttons.
18	Pilot's Bomb Release Button.	45	Pitot Head Heater Switch.
19	Oil Pressure Gauges – Obscured by Control Yoke.	46	Immersed Fuel Pump Switch.
20	Fuel Pressure Warning Lights.	47	Air Temperature Gauge.
21	Port Oil Temperature Gauge.	48	Panel Light and Dimmer Switch.
22	Boost Pressure Gauges.	49	Voltmeter.
23	RPM Indicators.	50	Fireman's Axe.
24	Steering Indicator.	51	Generator Warning Light.
25	Port/Starboard Booster Coil Buttons.	52	High-pressure Oxygen Master Valve.
26	Boost Control Cut-out.	53	Fire Extinguisher Buttons.
27	Port/Starboard Engine Electric Starter Buttons.	54	Fuel Tank Gauges.

55	IFF Detonator Buttons.
56	IFF Switch.
57	Navigation Headlamp Switch.
58	Camera Lead Stowage.
59	Camera Distributor Box.
60	Identification Switchbox and Key.
61	Air Recognition Lights Switchbox.
62	Identification Lights Selector Switch.
63	Watch Holder.
64	Pencil Tray.
65	Folding Navigator's Table.
66	GP/VHF Changeover Switch.
67	Trailing Aerial Winch.
68	Navigator's Seat.
69	Signal Cartridge Stowage.
70	Drift Sight Mounting.
71	Crew Entry Door.
72	Emergency Oxygen Bottles.
73	Observer's Kneeling Cusion.
74	Windscreen De-icing Pump.
75	Aileron Trim Tab Control and Indicator.
76	Bomb Jettison Control Handle.
77	Triple Pressure Gauge.
78	Rudder Pedal.
79	Control Column.
80	Compass.

Mosquito cockpit.

Cockpit of B.35 RS709, the former G-MOSI, which was flown from the UK to Wright-Patterson AFB in October 1984 and subsequently painted to represent NS519/P, a 653rd BS, 25th BG PR.XVI for permanent display at the Air Force Museum. The instrument panels are coated in either plain matt black paint or a baked-on 'crackle' black, to reduce reflections. Graham M. Simons

So, along the beach, heading south and climb round heading west, to unfeather when we got to 300 or 400ft (90 or 120m).

Now this aircraft had Mk IV AI, and the feathering buttons in their normal position would have been covered, so they were extended over the top of the AI indicator on snail's eye extensions. Unfeathering required the buttons to be pressed, then when the revs got up to about 1,500, the buttons would be pulled out so that the engine could warm up a bit. Imagine our embarrassment when the inaccessible snail's eye pulled out of its socket. The prop went on unfeathering until it got to a sort of superfine with the revs still climbing to way above the normal 3,000 maximum. The braking effect of a prop in this configuration is pretty severe, so it was necessary to *do something*. As luck would have it, we were not only in the vicinity of Carnaby, one of the three emergency runways in the UK with 3,000yd (2,740m) runways, but actually on the runway QDM. A quick call on the emergency frequency got an immediate response. Lowering the landing gear and a bit of flap was going to further increase the drag, so some power was used on the overspeeding engine – might as well have a bit of work out of it. The landing was uneventful and took up very little of their 3,000yd (2,740m) which also had 500yd (460m) each of undershoot and overshoot. We could have got down comfortably in either of these.

All this digression and we haven't even done our first landing in 1942. The one

odd thing about the Mosquito was that lowering the flaps caused a nose up change of trim, quite unlike any other aircraft I knew. This feature for me gave an even greater impression of being balanced on a pole, which by no means made the final stages of the approach difficult because control was so positive right down to touch down, which was three-point. I would never have dreamed of landing in other than three-point attitude for the simple reason that the aircraft touched down slower and required far less braking. Only people who have been accustomed to having 2,000yd (1,830m) or more do wheelies. All the talk of landing tail up to prevent swinging is absolute nonsense. The aircraft is going to have its greatest tendency to swing when the tail comes down because of the change of the plane of rotation of the propellers. This causes a gyroscopic precession which converts the vertical torque of the props into a horizontal one. Mind you, I didn't know this at the time. The truth is that we landed tail down because that was the proper way to land an aeroplane, especially if you didn't have a long run. Most airfields had one runway which was only 1,100yd (1,000m). Also, one needed to have a lot more speed to make the tail stay up, another reason for not adopting that practice. I only swung that one time on landing from my first flight and also quite fortuitously discovered a simple way of avoiding the dreaded swing on take-off, by letting my first and

second fingers adopt their natural curve round the rather small throttle knobs, pushing them forward with the left leading slightly, and taking both to full power once the tail was up. This very satisfactorily compensated for any tendency to drift off onto the grass and I never had any trouble from that particular bogey. A lot of it is in the mind.

One soon got used to the off-set handle and its very short radius. It did not increase the effort needed to roll and was very smooth. The ailerons did become a bit heavy at speeds above 300 but the short stick gave quite adequate leverage. The elevator was powerful, but the nose up trim in a high speed dive required a lot of push force which could, however, be easily trimmed out. Personally, I never liked putting on a lot of trim for a temporary manoeuvre on any aircraft because it could cause difficulty in resuming normal equilibrium. Different variants had different ranges of centre of gravity (CG). After the war when I worked at de Havillands aerodynamics department, I was responsible for the weight and CG of later marks. The only one which caused any problems was the PR.34 with two fuel tanks in the bomb-bay. On the climb, in its original configuration, the tanks were directly interconnected, and the situation arose where the rear tank was full and the front one empty, sending the aircraft CG down towards the wing trailing edge. A simple arrangement of valves sorted this out.

Learning the Trade

The halcyon days of flying Mosquito IIs for gaining enjoyable experience were now past, and in future it would have to be used as a tool for more serious work. But the learning curve had not quite levelled out. The Mk VI fighter-bomber to which I was introduced at Little Snoring on 515 Squadron was the first I had flown with drop-tanks. For type familiarization, Bob and I were sent on a cross country exercise to Newquay and back. The Mk II did not carry wing drop tanks and for this flight we carried them for the first time. The drill was supposed to be that we took off on internal tanks then switched to drop tanks. The control was behind my seat where I could not see it. Bob said, 'It says jettison tanks. Does that mean jettison *tanks* or *jettison* tanks?' Quandary. We worked out that it was possible to get round the tour prescribed on internal tanks, and if we had to divert, then we would be forced to experiment with the said control, but did not want to risk dropping 100 gallons (460 litres) of 100 octane somewhere on middle England. We did this trip and landed back with full drop tanks, only to discover that the switch for jettisoning the tanks was buried amongst a clutter of bomb selector switches next to the U/C lever. So we continued to live and learn but had a bit of explaining to do. I have a copy of Pilot's Notes for the Mk VI before me. The control for transferring fuel is not illustrated and the ambiguity of the bomb/container switch is all too evident.

Now we come to the all important consideration of the qualities of the Mosquito as a fighting vehicle from the pilot's point of view. I'm speaking here of night operations. I was never called upon to face the enemy in daylight although plenty of 100 Group crews did a number of *Day Rangers* and long range daylight escorts. The Mosquito would cope easily with the Ju 88, Me 410 and Me 110, but I think anyone who

Leslie Holland of 515 Squadron at Little Snoring, 1944, in front of his FB.VI, 'D-Dog', which is equipped with AI Mk XV ASH (Air-Surface-H) radar. ASH was normally a wing mounted radar but could not be fitted to the Mosquito wing, so was installed in a 'thimble' radome in the nose.

'Dutch' Holland

tangled with a Me 109 (of any of the later series) or a Fw 190, would have been asking for trouble in a big way. It could not be expected to out-turn, out-climb or out-dive those opponents and certainly could not roll as fast as the 190. I once did some mock combat with US 8th Air Force Fortresses and the verdict of the waist gunners was:

We'd 'a had you guys, but those Fw 190s – they rooooll on their backs and shoot hell outa ya.

Occasionally, a '109 or '190 would fall to a *Ranger*, but without in any way trying to detract from their achievements, I think they probably caught trainees in the areas where they thought they were safe. What 190 pilot near the Austrian border would expect to find a Mosquito on his tail in the daytime just when he was thinking about his schnapps and fraulein? For all that one required of it in the night-fighter/bomber role, it had everything. Range and duration: 100 gallons (460 litres) per hour at 240mph (386kph) IAS with the fuselage tank (63 gallon/286 litres) and 50 gallon (230 litre) drop tanks, total 616 gallons (2,800 litres) would give 6 hours and a 1,500 mile (2,410km) round trip. The sortie on which I carried various sorts of flare and bomb internally, (for which the fuselage tank was removed) I was airborne 5 hours and 50 minutes on 553 gallons (2,514 litres).

Manoeuvrability: I had occasion to dance a few measures with a Heinkel 219 by night and very nearly collided with it. Looking back, I recall that it was so natural to perform steep turns without any loss of height that I found myself executing perfect turns when that was the last thing I should have been doing. My opponent was probably doing the same which is probably why we nearly collided in a crossing interception in the dark. Most of our work was near the ground at night, and that meant anything down to 50ft (15m) across an airfield which was completely

blacked out until one had illuminated it. All sorts of attacks were carried out on trains, transport, aircraft on the ground, buildings, flak positions, boats etc, during which it seemed one only had to think the line of attack and the aircraft turned itself onto the best line. And always one could have confidence that steep turns, climbing turns and pull outs entailed no risk of having anything less than complete control, so much so that one did not even have to think about it.

In all the Mosquito flying which I was privileged to enjoy, I never had an engine failure. This included twenty-six intruder operations, in fact the only malfunction of any sort was the unfeathering problem mentioned and that could hardly be blamed on the basic design. Another feature which we appreciated was the flat bullet-proof windscreen which not only gave a sense of security, but provided a fine field of view and a good surface for the windscreen wiper. Something that we tried to hide at the back of our minds was that the chances of successful exit were very slender indeed, especially as our normal operating height was below 2,000ft (610m). The two methods of egress offered were through the side door or out through the roof hatch. The first method we did practise, but not very seriously, as it meant diving head first onto gym mats with a parachute strapped to your backside. The second we could not effectively practise and leaving by that route would have involved a high risk of collision with the fin or tailplane (horizontal stabilizer), and/or various aerials.

As an illustration of how forgiving this aircraft could be, I was taking off one night on our 1,100 yard (1,000m) runway with wing bombs and fuselage tank. Having gone a fair way down the runway, I reckoned I ought to have been airborne but wasn't. I didn't have any flap down. Quick as a flash I grabbed the lever and gave it a

twitch down and back to neutral. With a lively little skip, 'D-Dog' cleared the obstruction lights and no-one was any the wiser, except perhaps Bob, but he never complained so long as we came back in one piece. I have seen photos of aircraft which got back with plenty of battle damage, indeed at Little Snoring we saw one with no nose in front of the instrument panel, and another with all the fabric burnt off the fuselage and rudder, leaving it with no effective surface. The only damage we sustained was to have the spar of the starboard elevator shot through which caused severe vibration and considerably limited our performance, but it brought us home without shedding any more bits.

The variants I flew had Mk IV AI with its arrowhead aerials, the Mk V with a somewhat similar array, the Mk VI with the AN/APS4 (ASH), none of which obstructed the forward view, and finally, the Mk X (SCR 720) which required the bulbous nose which became familiar on the Mk 19, 30, 36 and 38 Mosquitoes. This nose was only objectionable to us because we had been used to a very good view forwards and downwards. Can you believe that in 1949 the Mk 38 was still in production as our first line of defence? We had had Vampires and Meteors already in service for four years, but up to that time, there was no sign of a night-fighter version. The old Mossie had done such sterling work, it was a pity that it ended its days as a definitely outclassed anachronism. By this time the same basic airframe was labouring under all-up weights way in excess of the original 18,000lb (8,160kg) for the Mk II, late marks gave appreciably more power, but only improved the performance at altitude. And the TT.39 target tower was the final indignity. But the Mosquito was not the only one to suffer this fate. Looking back to the Mk II, I can only feel glad that I was able to have my hands on the breed when it was still a lively colt.

CHAPTER TEN

Swan Song

The Mosquito Post-war, in RAF, RN and Foreign Service

In the immediate aftermath of WWII the Mosquito continued to serve the RAF at both home and overseas, and new models were even introduced, at a time when other wartime aircraft had already ended their development. The Royal Navy had wanted to have Mosquitoes for carrier operations in WWII, but it did not begin to operate Mosquitoes until 1946, long after the Pacific War had ended. Admiralty Specification N 15/44 had been issued in 1944 for a twin-engined aircraft that was capable of operating from carriers and de Havillands had responded with the Sea Mosquito. The first prototype was actually a converted Mk VI – LR359 in fact – with an arrester hook added, the rear fuselage strengthened on either side by reinforced longeron ribs, Merlin 25s boosted up to +18lbs (8kg) boost and non-feathering four-bladed de Havilland airscrews.

Boscombe Down test pilot, Lt Cmdr Eric 'Winkle' Brown OBE DSC, was asked in January 1944, 'Do you think you could land a Mosquito on an aircraft carrier?' With all the 'brash arrogance of youth', he said 'Yes!' As he later confessed;

When I reconsidered it I wasn't so sure, but I'd burnt my boats by this time, because as a form of entertainment, deck landing is probably on a parallel with Russian roulette.

In the immediate aftermath of WWII, Mosquitoes saw action in the Far East where, based in Java, they were used against Indonesian extremists. Here, 60lb (27kg) RPs are fitted to an FB.VI of 47 Squadron by Leading Aircraftsmen Harry Coulson and H. Simkins of 3210 Servicing Commando in preparation for attacks on two radio stations at Soerakarta Jogjakarta in December 1945. via Ron Mackay

(Top) **LACs of 3210 Servicing Commando Unit prepare an FB.VI for operations over Java. Nos 47, 82, 84 and 110 Squadrons all provided detachments for attacks on Indonesian separatists in the Netherlands East Indies until more faulty wing-structures were discovered in some FB.VIs.** via Ron Mackay

(Above) **F/L A.J. Jacomb-Hood** DFC **(wearing life preserver) has just returned from the strike on two radio stations at Soerakarta Jogjakarta in December 1945.** via Ron Mackay

(Top) **By early 1946 the RAF in the Far East had begun to return to peacetime establishment and surplus Mosquitoes were flown to Maintenance units in India. This PR.XVI is pictured at 322 MU, Cawnpore in 1946.**
Author's Collection

(Above) **NF.XIX TA272 of 89 Squadron pictured at Dum Dum, Calcutta 1945–46.** Author's Collection

PR.XVI NS688 in India, 1945–46. Author's Collection

Early in March 1944 deck landing trials with LR359 were ready to take place aboard the 766ft (233m) long flight-deck of HMS *Indefatigable*. The deck was 95ft (30m) wide but this diminished to 80ft (24m) at the island, and the Mosquito had a span of 54ft (16.5m) – not much margin for error! Lt Cmdr Brown recalls:

The first landing occurred on 25 March, so we hadn't really had much time between getting the aircraft to making the actual first landing. In 1944 the arrester gear on an aircraft carrier had limitations in that it could only absorb an entry speed of about 65 knots [120kph], and that for an aircraft of some 10,000lbs [4,530kg] weight or so. Here we were talking about an aircraft that, in the pilots' notes, said the approach speed was 125mph [201kph], and the weight for the first landings we were going to make was 16,000lbs [7,260kg]. Another problem was would the undercarriage, which had not been modified, take the vertical velocities which are normally extremely high in deck landing? or would it collapse under the strain? The aircraft, strangely enough, behaved extremely well on the approach and the actual touchdown speed was believe it or not, 78mph [125kph]. There were about 8–10 wires on HMS *Indefatigable* and I caught the second wire.

Then we carried on the landings mounting up the weight. All went well until the eighth landing, which was at the weight of 18,000lbs [8,160kg] and when at touch down I felt the deceleration start, which is normal when you catch a wire, then suddenly it stopped, and the aircraft began to move forward again. Well, I had to make a lightning assessment – one of two

Mosquitoes were stationed in Germany with BAFO (British Air Forces of Occupation) post war. These FB.VIs belong to 305 Polish Squadron at Wahn. Harry Randall Cutler

things could have happened: either the hook had broken, in which case we had to go on (there was no crash barrier) and take off again. If the wire had broken however, then if I opened up again too early I might cause another disaster and pull the hook out, because I had to give it sufficient time to get to at least one more wire. We did get to this position, when I realized that something had gone wrong that was not going to arrest us. So I had to give it the full gun, irrespective of the swing and the torque caused. What actually happened was that the claw of the arrester hook had rotated and the wire thrown clear of the claw because the forward bolt, one of two which held the frame of the hook to the claw, had sheared off. Hatfield very rapidly modified it for the second series of landings, and all told, the whole thing was a very successful exercise.

Production of the TR.33 Sea Mosquito began at Leavesden late in 1945. Their Lordships had specified folding-wings but the first thirteen TR.33 Sea Mosquitoes built had non-folding wings. When folding

wings were introduced from the fourteenth Sea Mosquito on, the folded width, at 27ft 3in (8.3m), was greater than the 20ft (6.1m) folded width for the lifts of the Navy's new carriers then coming into service! Manual folding was used too as power folding would have meant a complete redesign of the hydraulic system. The original undercarriage using rubber blocks in compression though, was later changed, from the fourteenth Sea Mosquito TR.33 by the installation of a Lockheed oleo-pneumatic undercarriage with slightly smaller wheels. The TR.33 could carry an 18in (46cm) MK XV or XVII torpedo, or a mine, or a 2,000lb (910kg) bomb under the fuselage, plus two 500lb (230kg) bombs in the bomb bay and either two 50 gallon (230 litre) fuel tanks beneath the wings, or two 30 gallon (136 litre) tanks and four rocket-projectiles, while the four 20mm cannon were retained. One of the main distinguishing features was a thimble nose, which housed ASH radar. Two detachable RATO (Rocket Assisted Take Off) bottles either

Two views of LR359, the modified FB.VI, which, in the hands of Lt Cmdr Eric 'Winkle' Brown, was the first twin-engined aircraft to land and take off from a carrier. He flew from the 766ft (233m) long flight-deck of HMS Indefatigable **on 25 March 1944.** BAe Hatfield

The first of fifty Sea Mosquito TR.33s began equipping No 811 Squadron at HMS Peregrine at Ford in August 1946. Pictured is LR387, which was converted from a B.VI in 1945. BAe Hatfield

FAA and Coastal Command Mosquito Squadrons/Units 1945–1950

Unit	Period	Types
811 RN Training Squadron	9.45–7.47	VI/TR.33
790 RN Squadron	10.45–11.49	TR.33
771 RN Training Squadron	11.45–1950	VI/TR.33/III
762 RN Squadron	2.46–11.49	TT.39
703 RN Squadron	1946–1947	TR.37
772 RN Training Squadron	1946–1947	T.III/PRXVI/TR.33
728 Fleet Requirements Unit	1948–1950	TT.39
14 Coastal Command	6.45–3.46	VI
36 Coastal Command	10.46–10.47	VI
254 Coastal Command	3.45–9.45	XVIII

side of the fuselage, which fell away after firing, could also be fitted. The first production TR.33, TW227, flew for the first time at Leavesden on 10 November 1945.

The first of fifty Sea Mosquito TR.33s began equipping No. 811 Squadron at HMS *Peregrine* at Ford in August 1946, replacing the Mk VIs which had arrived in September 1945. Nos 771 and 772 Training Squadrons also used TR.33s. No 811 Squadron disbanded at RNAS Brawdy in July 1947. Only fourteen Chester-built TR.37 models which followed the TR.33, were built, and just six saw service with No. 703 Squadron. The TR.37 differed from the TR.33 only in having British ASV Mk XIII

radar in a larger nose radome. These were followed into production by twenty-four TT.39 high-speed shore-based naval target tugs, which entered service with Fleet Requirements Units in 1948 and served with No. 728 FRU at Hal Far, Malta. All of these, and the two prototypes, were converted from B.XVIs by General Aircraft Ltd at Hanworth. TT.39s were replaced by Short Sturgeon TT.2s from 1950.

Civil Mosquitoes also operated throughout the world and RAF record-breaking attempts saw many more Mosquito achievements in the late 1940s. On 6 September 1945 W/C J.R.H. Merrifield DSO DFC and F/L J.H. Spires DFC DFM made the east-west

crossing of the Atlantic from St Mawgan to Gander in a PR.34 in 7 hours, returning on 23 October in 5 hours 10 minutes. In April 1947 two PR.34As (one a reserve) were prepared by RAF Transport Command for an attempt on the London to Cape Town record, set in 1947 by a de Havilland DH.88 Comet. On 30 April S/L H.B. 'Micky' Martin DSO DFC and S/L Ted Sismore DSO DFC, took off from Heathrow Airport for the 6,717 miles (10,807km) flight with stops at El Adem, in Libya, and Kisumu in Kenya. They easily broke the record, landing at Cape Town's Brooklyn Airport on 1 May after 21 hours 31 minutes at an average speed of 279mph (449kph).

TF.37 Sea Mosquito VT724, the first of the torpedo fighters, which differed from the TR.33 only in having
British ASV Mk XIII radar in a larger nose radome. BAe Hatfield

Some twenty-four TT.39 high-speed shore-based naval target tugs, and the two prototypes, were converted
from B.XVIs by General Aircraft Ltd at Hanworth. TT.39 PF606, seen here in September 1948, was used by
RAE Farnborough and by Boscombe Down for radio trials, before being struck off at Lossiemouth on 27
November 1952. The protruding dorsal cupola accommodated the observer and drogue operator, and the
extended and bulged glazed nose contained the camera operator. TT.39s entered service with Fleet
Requirements Units in 1948 and were replaced by Short Sturgeon TT.2s from 1950. BAe Hatfield

Leaving Odiham on 1 July 1948, three PR.34s PF620/621/ 623 of No.1 Transport Command Ferry Unit, equipped with LORAN (APN-9), provided navigation and advance information on wind strengths and weather data for the six Vampire F.3s of 54 Squadron on the first-ever jet crossing of the Atlantic. Pictured at Odiham before departure are the three PR.34 crews (left to right): F/L 'Curly' Waterer and F/L Ron Bartley; F/L Anderson and F/L Sims (both crews remaining at RCAF Trenton near Toronto); and W/O Simpson and S/L H.B. 'Micky' Martin DSO DFC (wearing KDs for their onward trip to the USA). After a very successful tour, the jets were shepherded back to Britain on 17 August. Ron Bartley

Post-war Mosquitoes

PR.34s were operated for a number of years by RAF home and overseas commands. 540 Squadron, which had disbanded at Benson on 30 September 1946, reformed there on 1 December 1947 with PR.34 aircraft. Frank Baylis, a wartime 544 Squadron PR navigator, who had just finished an overseas tour in 13 Squadron, joined 540 in June 1949:

Early one Saturday evening in September, I was 'mooching' around the parade ground at Benson, when I was accosted by W/C Bufton. He ordered me to collect my overnight gear and report to the briefing room. Much mystified, I did. F/O Mike Whitworth-Jones and I were briefed for a flight to Leuchars. We were told that some 'boffins' from Harwell were fixing a

filter to the belly of a PR.34. It meant nothing to us. Off we went to bonny Scotland. Next day we had to fly along a pre-arranged bearing to PLE (Prudent Limit of Endurance). It was a long and boring flight over the sea all the way. Next day we did another trip to PLE, this time around the eastern coast of Iceland, and back. Each time we landed, the filter was removed and flown immediately to Harwell. A few days later, the Government announced that the Russians had exploded their own atomic bomb. The New Year's Honours List showed Mike Whitworth-Jones and myself with King's Commendations – for two straightforward flights!

540's PR.34s were used on PR and survey duties until December 1952 when Canberra PR.3s took over. Meanwhile, 58 Squadron had reformed at Benson on 1

October 1946 in the PR role and its first task was involvement in the Ordnance Survey of Great Britain, using Ansons and PR.34s. In 1953 both types were replaced by English Electric Canberras. At Wyton that winter, 58 Squadron's PR.34, and PR.35 aircraft (including four in 'B' Flight converted for night photo reconnaissance using flashlights), and 540 Squadron's PR.34s at Benson, were used to photograph the terrible floods which hit Britain's east coast in February 1953. For eight days they photographed the devastation, taking over 100,000 photographs which were used to help aid the rescue and repair efforts. In mid-1953 58 Squadron's PR.34s were replaced by Canberra PR.3s, 540 having begun re-equipment with the jet in December 1952.

In the Far and Middle East, Mosquitoes still had a role to play. After VJ-Day 684 Squadron had used its PR.34s as a high-speed courier service throughout the Far East, before moving to Bangkok in January 1946 to take up survey duties. This continued until 1 September when 684 disbanded at Seletar, Malaya by renumbering as 81 Squadron. On 1 August 1947 Spitfires from 34 Squadron were added to the strength and 81 Squadron became the only PR unit in FEAF (Far Eastern Air Forces), responsible for long-range PR and survey over the East Indian area. 13 Squadron had disbanded as a Boston squadron in Greece on 19 April 1946 but reformed on 13 September that year vice 680 Squadron, which disbanded at Ein Shemer. Using PR.IXs and XVIs 13 Squadron carried out PR and photo-survey work in Palestine and the Canal Zone April 1946–February 1952, when they were replaced by Meteor PR.10s.

NF.36s, fitted with AI Mk X radar, provided night defence for the Canal Zone from bases at Fayid and Kabrit, 1949–53, while forty NF.36s also equipped 23, 25, 29, 85, 141 and 264 Squadrons at home. (In fact, they represented Fighter Command's only all-weather fighters until replacement by Vampire NF.10s and Meteor F.11s in 1951–52). 39 and 219 Squadrons, both of which reformed at Kabrit, in May 1949 and early in 1951 respectively, were the last two squadrons to be re-equipped with NF.36s. Peter Verney, navigator, who was posted to 39 Squadron in February 1952, recalls:

All told, I did some 230 hours on the Mosquito and feel privileged to have done so. We had a few alarms and excursions but low level during the Egyptian summer was not enjoyable with cockpit temperatures reaching 160°F [70°C]. It was also very easy to boil an engine while waiting to take off and Kabrit was one of the few

stations where piston-engined aircraft had precedence over jets, 13 Squadron, who we shared the airfield with having exchanged their PR.34s for the Meteor PR.10 early in 1952. By the time we relinquished our Mosquitoes in March 1953 they were becoming tired but they were allowed a certain tolerance at a 'glue joint' and if this tolerance was exceeded, the aircraft was scrapped. While waiting for the Meteors to arrive the MU ran short of replacements due to this rule and so a 'technical conference' was held at which it was decided that this tolerance could be increased. All was well until they again ran short and another 'technical conference' decided that this 'glue joint' was not a problem after all and could be ignored! When we received our Meteors the ferry pilots took the Mosquitoes back to the UK but a few were left under repair at the MU and I had the honour, with my CO, S/L 'Fungus' (or 'Coggers') Cogill, to ferry the last one home to RAF Benson on 24/25 July 1953. This was the last time that the night-fighter was flown by a squadron crew.

PR.34 RG190 and Spitfire PR.XIX of the PR Flight at Benson, 1948. D.J. Mannion via Jerry Scutts

PR.34 VL618 in overall PRU Blue in flight showing the five underbelly circular windows for vertical and oblique cameras. BAe via Jerry Scutts

(Above) **PR.34A RG176, the first PR.34 built before conversion by Marshalls, May 1950,
was operated by 540 Squadron at Benson July 1951–June 1952, when after an
accident it was reduced to spares by 58 MU. It is pictured here with 200-gallon
(910-litre) wing drop tanks during trials at the A&AEE.** 'Dutch' Holland via Philip Birtles

(Right) **NF.XXXs of 264 Squadron, which at this time were stationed at Church Fenton,
pictured at Tangmere at the end of March 1946 when the squadron began to convert
to the NF.36.** Richard Doleman

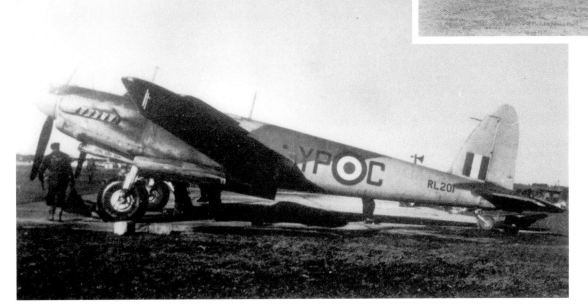

Leavseden-built NF.36 RL201 YP-C of 23 Squadron at RAF Coltishall, Norfolk, 1947. Tom Cushing

NF.36 RL261 'A' of 23 Squadron at RAF Coltishall, 1947. Tom Cushing

NF.36s of 39 Squadron based at RAF Fayid, Egypt, late 1949, pass HMS Amethyst
(*bottom left*) **on the frigate's passage through the Suez Canal following the Yangtse**
incident. She had been damaged by gunfire between the Nationalist and Communist
forces in China on 20 April and held 'captive' before breaking out on 30/31 July. She
arrived in Plymouth harbour on 1 November 1949. Richard Doleman

(Above) **Percival-built PR.34 PF650 of 13 Squadron at Fayid, January 1949.**
Frank Baylis

(Left) **Two PR.34s of 13 Squadron fly up the Suez Canal in 1949.**
Richard Doleman

(Right) **Four NF.XXXs of 39 Squadron over Fayid, 1949.** Richard Doleman

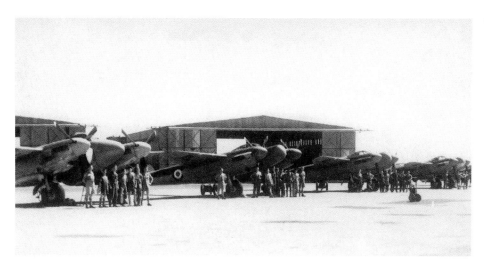

VT610, 39 Squadron's first T.III, with the squadron's NF.XXXs, at Fayid, 1949.
Richard Doleman

(Right) **NF.XXXs and an NF.36 of 39 Squadron, Kabrit, in 1949. Both 39 and 219 Squadrons began conversion from the NF.36 to Meteor night-fighters in March 1953.** Richard Doleman

(Left) **Ground crews in front of a 39 Squadron NF.36 at Fayid. Some have 'got their knees brown', while others look as if they are just 'off the boat'! The NF.36 was powered by two RR Merlin 113/114 or 113A/114A engines, armed with four 20mm cannon, and used AI Mk X radar with a centimetric scanner in the plastic nose radome, which in peacetime was normally unpainted.** Richard Doleman

A really tight formation of Mosquito night-fighters of 39 Squadron over Egypt, 1953. NF.36s of 39 and 219 Squadrons provided night defence for the Canal Zone, 1949–March 1953. Peter Verney

Mosquito fighters served in RAF Fighter Command until the early 1950s. NF.XXX NT585 of 125 Squadron is pictured on 10 December 1945 during a flight from Church Fenton. This aircraft later operated with 151 Squadron. via Philip Birtles

The last RAF Mosquitoes to see RAF service anywhere were the PR.34As of 81 Squadron at Seletar, Malaya (incidentally, also the last in the RAF to fly the Spitfire operationally, on 1 April 1954). In 1946–47, 81 Squadron had carried out an aerial survey of the country. A state of emergency in Malaya was declared on 17 June 1948 when a full-scale Communist uprising began, and 81 Squadron Mosquitoes reverted to their PR role as part of Operation *Firedog*, which began in July 1949. By the end of 1952, 81 Squadron had made over 4,000 sorties and had photographed 34,000 square miles (88,000 sq.km). 81 Squadron flew no less than 6,619 sorties during eight years of operations in Malaya. The honour of flying the very last Mosquito sortie went to RG314, when F/O A.J. 'Collie' Knox and F/O 'Tommy' Thompson returned from a *Firedog* reconnaissance sortie against two terrorist camps in Malaya on 15 December 1955. Incredibly, 14 years and 3 months had passed since the first ever Mosquito operation, 17 September 1941, when another PR machine, W5055, had photographed Brest and the Spanish-French border. In 1955–56 a number of PR.34As were converted for civil use at Hatfield and many were subsequently operated in the United States, Canada, Africa, and South America on photo-survey work.

F/O 'Collie' Knox and F/O 'Tommy' Thompson of 81 Squadron at Seletar complete their pre-flight check on PR.34A RG314 before the final operational flight *(overleaf)* of a Mosquito in the RAF, 15 December 1955. This 'op' was a Firedog sortie over Malaya. via Jerry Scutts

A dramatic low-level shot of PR34A RG177 of 81 Squadron flown by F/Sgt Anderson, beating up Seletar in May 1953. *Aeroplane Monthly*

Percival Aircraft Ltd, built its last PR.34 in July 1946. Post-war production of Mosquitoes though, was centred on the plants at Hatfield and Leavesden. Standard Motors Ltd had built the last of its 1,065 FB.VIs in December 1945, while Airspeed Ltd built its last B.35 in February 1946. Although the B.35 had first flown on 12 March 1945, only just over forty had been delivered by VE-Day. The B.35 did not enter RAF service until 1948, when 109 and 139 Pathfinder Squadrons at Hemswell began receiving the type. Both squadrons began re-equipping with the Canberra B.2 in July 1952 and November 1953 respectively. In Germany, three squadrons in BAFO (British Air Forces of Occupation) also received B.35 aircraft. 69 Squadron operated the B.35 until it disbanded on 6 November 1947 and 14 and 98 Squadrons operated them until February 1951 when they were replaced by Vampire FB.5s. From 1952, 105 B.35s were converted to TT.35 target tugs by Brooklands Aviation. In 1956

B.35s undergoing overhauls late in 1947 at Airspeed's Portsmouth factory where, in February 1946, the last of sixty-five of the 274 B.35s built were produced. The B.35 did not enter RAF service until 1948, when 109 and 139 Pathfinder Squadrons at Hemswell began receiving the type. Nos 69, 14 and 98 Squadrons in BAFO also operated the B.35. (VR794 in the foreground was later sold to Spartan Air Services of Ottawa, Canada for photographic survey work, and registered as CF-HMK). *BAe Hatfield*

G-AJZE (RG231), one of two PR.34s (the other was RG238 G-AJZF) that were used at Cranfield by the BEA Gust Research Unit 1948–49 for investigating clear-air turbulence. British Airways via Air Research Publications

FB.VIs of 4 Squadron, TA539 'B' leading, followed by RS679 'A', and RS667 'F', taxi out at Celle, Germany in 1949. via S/L I.G. Dick

a few of these aircraft were modified as Met.35s for weather reconnaissance.

Chester built Sea Mosquito TR.37s and most of the 101 NF.38s, including the 7,781st and final Mosquito to be built, NF.38 VX916, on 15 November 1950. As it turned out, the NF.38 never did enter service with Fighter Command. In May 1949, a decision was taken to abandon plans to use the fighter in its intended role because by now, the NF.38 was like an elephant fitted out for a tiger shoot. It was too heavy and too slow to reach successfully the altitudes flown by the Soviet Tupolev Tu-2 and Tu-4 bombers. Also, the NF.38 suffered from incompatibility problems with the heavy AI Mk IXb radar, which was itself far from becoming fully functional. Fighter Command's Mosquito squadrons had to make do and mend using NF.36s fitted with AI Mk X in front-line service until January 1952, when 29 Squadron became the last in Fighter Command to convert to the Meteor NF.11. The last NF.36s in front-line service were a few operated on RCM duties by 199 Squadron at Hemswell until March 1953, while that same month, at Kabrit in the Canal Zone, the last of 39 Squadron's NF.36s were replaced by Meteor NF.13s.

(Above) RL248, the NF.38 prototype, January 1947, with a Vampire in the background. Chester built most of the 101 NF.38s, including the 7,781st and final Mosquito to be built, VX916, on 15 November 1950. The NF.38 did not enter RAF service, and, surplus to requirements, fifty-seven were supplied under the terms of the Mutual Defence Aid Programme (MDAP) to the Yugoslav Air Force. 'Dutch' Holland

FB.VI TA539 'B' of 4 Squadron landing at Celle, Germany in 1949. The squadron operated in the bomber role before changing to low-level fighter attack in July 1950, changing to Vampire FB.5s at Wunsdorf. via S/L I.G. Dick

T.III Mosquitoes post-war, the nearest being HJ959. T.IIIs built 1948–49 remained in operational service with No. 204 Advanced Flying School and with the Operational Conversion Units of Bomber Command until 1953. Air Research Publications

(Below) **B.35 TA694 of 14 Squadron and B.35s of 98 Squadron, from Celle, pictured during a visit to Munich in 1949.** Jerry Scutts

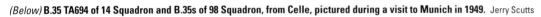

First Rocket-propelled Supersonic Robot Plane

During 1947, a Mosquito XVI from the Royal Aircraft Establishment was used as a launch vehicle for a series of tests exploring the possibilities of supersonic flight. The Miles company had been building their M52, straight-winged supersonic research aircraft to specification E.24/43. A wooden mock-up had been completed and work had started on the first complete airframe when the project was cancelled by Sir Ben Lockspeiser, the Chief Scientist to the Ministry of Supply in March 1946 amid fears for the safety of supersonic research using a piloted aircraft. He decreed that model testing would be the most economical, safe and practical way to explore supersonic flight. Accordingly, a contract was awarded to Vickers-Armstrong to build six 0.3 scale models with the same configuration as the Miles M52 and these were designed by Dr Barnes Wallis. They were powered by the R.A.E. Alpha rocket engine which should have given the models a maximum speed of 800mph (1,287kph). Signals from telemetering equipment installed in the model were expected to give two sets of figures, when entering and leaving the transonic region.

The trials were conducted from St Eval, and the Mosquito was piloted by S/L D.A. Hunt with Mr G.B. Lochee Bayne, a civilian technical observer from R.A.E. operating the launch sequence. A Meteor 4 flying alongside the Mosquito was to attempt to record the experiments visually.

A.1., the first model was lost and the initial test subsequently abandoned, but on 8 October 1947, A.2, the model shown in the photograph, painted black with yellow under surfaces was launched at 400mph (644kph) at an altitude of 36,400ft (11,095m), 1 mile (1.6km) west of St Mary's in the Scilly Isles. A brief commentary on the drop was given by Mr Lochee Bayne before the model disappeared from sight falling into the sea after its engine failed to ignite properly. The model should have flown straight and level at 35,000ft (10,668m) for 55 seconds while it accelerated and decelerated through the transonic region but it appears to have dipped its starboard wing and dived into cloud at about 10,000ft (3,050m).

On 10th October 1948, A.3, the last of the models was launched successfully at about 400mph at 36,400ft altitude, west of St Mary's, the rocket fired correctly 6 seconds after launch and the model accelerated to 930mph (1,496kph), equivalent to Mach 1.38 in level flight, 62 seconds after release. No further model tests were conducted as it was concluded that the cost did not justify the return, especially as the Americans had already achieved manned supersonic flight in the straight-winged Bell X-1 on 14th October 1947.

If nothing else, this last test proved that the M52 design incorporated sound principles and the aircraft would have achieved the specification requirements.

Information supplied by Peter Amos, Miles Aircraft Collection

A.2, the second Vickers rocket-propelled supersonic model, in position under the RAE Mosquito XVI, PF604 at St Eval in Cornwall with pilot S/L D. A. Hunt (left) and Mr G.B. Lochee Bayne before take-off on 8 October 1947. *Aeroplane Monthly*

Post-war Squadron Usage – Mosquito F/B/PR

Sqdn	Period	Types	Sqdn	Period	Types
4(F)	9.45–7.50	VI	418(F)	5.43–7.9.45	VI
8(F)	9.46–5.47	VI	500(F)	2.47–1948	XIX/NF.XXX
11(F)	10.48–8.50	VI	502(F)	8.47–1948	NF.XXX
18(F)	3.47–11.47	VI	504(F)	5.47–1948	NF.XXX
21(F)	9.43–7.11.47	VI	605(F)	4.47–7.48	XIX/NF.XXX
22(F)	5.46–15.8.46	VI	608(F)	7.47–8.48	NF.XXX
23(F)	10.46–5.52	NF.36	609(F)	4.47–3.48	XIX/NF.XXX
25(F)	10.46–7.51	NF.36	616(F)	9.47–12.48	NF.XXX
29(F)	2.45–12.50	NF.XXX/36	14(B)	4.46–2.51	XVI/B.35
39(F)	3.49–3.53	NF.XXX/36	69(B)	8.45–11.47	VI/XVI
45(F)	2.44–11.45/48	VI	98(B)	1.46–2.51	XVI/B.35
47(F)	2.45–21.1.46	VI	105(B)	4.44–1.46	IX/XVI
55(F)	6.46–11.46	XXVI	109(B)	10.45–7.52	XXV/IV/B.35
82(F)	7.44–15.3.46	VI	128(B)	10.44–4.46	XXV
84(F)	2.45–12.46	VI	139(B)	11.44–11.53	XVI/B.35
85(F)	9.44–10.51	NF.XXX/36	162(B)	12.44–7.46	XXV
89(F)	5.45–1.5.46	XIX	180(B)	9.45–4.46	XVI
107(F)	2.44–4.10.48	VI	527(B)	9.52–1.56	B.35
110(F)	1.45–15.4.46	VI	248(S)	–1.10.46	VI/XVIII
114(F)	9.45–1.9.46	VI	13(PR)	1.9.46–2.52	PR.34
141(F)	3.45–9.51	NF.XXX/36	58(PR)	10.46–1.53	PR.34/A/35
151(F)	8.44–10.46	NF.XXX	81(PR)	1.9.46–12.55	PR.XVI/PR.34
157(F)	2.45–16.8.45	NF.XXX	540(PR)	11.44–3.53¹	IX/XVI/32/
176(F)	7.45–1.6.46	VI			34/A
199(F)	12.51–3.53	NF.36	544(PR)	11.44–10.45	PR.32/PR.34
211(F)	6.45–28.2.46	VI	680(PR)	2.44–31.8.46	PR.IX/PR.XVI
219(F)	6.44/1951–53	NF.XXX/36	684(PR)	9.43–31.8.46	PR.XVI/PR.34
239(F)	1.45–1.7.45	NF.XXX			
249(F)	4.46–6.46	FB.26	*Miscellaneous*		
255(F)	2.45–31.3.46	XIX	8 OTU	204 AFS	
256(F)	9.45–12.9.46	XIX	16 OTU	CBE	
264(F)	5.45–12.51	NF.XXX/36	54 OTU	CAACUs	
268(F)	9.45–31.3.46	VI	228 OTU	CSE/RWE	
305(F)	12.43–6.1.47	VI	230 OTU	APS Sylt	
307(F)	10.44–1.47	NF.XXX	231 OCU	NFDS	
406(F)	7.44–8.45	NF.XXX	237 OCU	1668 HCU	
409(F)	3.44–6.45	XIII	204 CTU	1653 HCU	
410(F)	8.44–9.6.45	NF.XXX			

¹Disbanded 30.9.46; reformed 1.12.47

Mosquitoes in Foreign Service

In the early fifties the NF.38s, and many more Mosquitoes, simply became surplus to requirements and hundreds were refurbished for use by foreign air forces, some being supplied under the terms of the Mutual Defence Aid Programme (MDAP). In 1947 the Canadian Government sold about 205 FB.26, T.29, T.27, T.22 (1) and B.25 (1) Mosquitoes to the Chinese Nationalist Government, which were reassembled at Tazang, 40 miles (64km) north of Shanghai. In 1948 Fairey

Aviation Co. Ltd at Ringway reconditioned six FB.VIs for the Dominican El Cuerpo de Aviacion Militair (which also received a number of Canadian-built Mosquitoes), and ninety-six more for the Turkish Air Force, in addition to sixty NF.XIXs for the Swedish Air Force, where they were designated, J.30 and operated by the F1 Wing at Västeras. All of these export aircraft were re-fitted with four-bladed airscrews.

Australia received from Britain, forty-six FB.VI and twenty-nine PR.XVI aircraft; Belgium, two FB.VI, twenty-six NF.XXXs

and eight T.IIIs; Burma, some FB.VIs, while at least nineteen FB.VIs were supplied to Czechoslovakia prior to Communist take-over in 1948 and were designated B-36. New Zealand received four T.IIIs; seventy-six FB.VIs, one FB.40 and four T.43s, while Norway obtained three T.IIIs and eighteen FB.VIs for 334 Squadron (three converted to night-fighters in 1950). South Africa obtained two F.II and fourteen PR.XVIs for 60 Squadron SAAF. France received a few FB.VIs, fifty-seven FB.VIs, twenty-nine PR.XVIs and twenty-three NF.XXXs. In February 1951 the French sold fifty-nine Mk III, VI, XVI and NF.XXX Mosquitoes to the new state of Israel, which, in 1948–49, had just fought a bitter War of Independence.

The first Mosquito to reach Israel was PR.XVI NS812, an ex-US 25th BG machine converted for BOAC (G–AIRT). After the war NS812, and its sister machine, NS811 (G–AIRU), were bought by Grp Capt Leonard Cheshire and registered to VIP Association Ltd, later VIP Services Ltd. In May 1948 both aircraft were sold to dealer, H.L. White. A month later ex-RAF pilot, John Harvey, arrived at Cambridge to ferry NS812 to Exeter but he evaded Air Traffic Control and flew on to France. After being detained by French police, Harvey was released and he flew on to Corsica, then Athens and finally, Haifa, where he refuelled before flying on to Ramat David airfield, his final destination. NS811, which set out from Abingdon, crashed at Ajaccio in Corsica en route. NS812 saw action during the war, being flown by a young French-Jewish pilot with WWII experience. Harvey, who held the rank of captain in the Israeli Air Force, contributed immensely to the establishment of the fledgling IDFAF, flying all manner of aircraft to the new state, and testing many of the ex-French Mosquitoes. On one of these test flights his Mosquito went into an uncontrollable spin and Harvey was killed.

Once the British arms embargo to Israel was lifted, a number of surplus PR.XVIs and TR.33s were flown from Blackbushe to Israel, after overhaul and de-navalization by Eagle Aviation (later British Eagle International Airlines). Some T.IIIs, about sixty FB.VIs, at least five PR.XVIs, and approximately fourteen Sea Mosquito TR.33s, were ferried to Israel from England between October 1954 and August 1955, where they equipped two squadrons. Late in 1955 these were disbanded because of re-equipment with jets and in June 1956

Canadian-built FB.26 (believed to be B-M008) one of almost 180 FB.26s supplied to the Nationalist Chinese in 1947 and reassembled in Shanghai. Standing in front is flying instructor, Canadian George Stewart, a WWII Intruder pilot who completed fifty operations with 23 Squadron at Little Snoring. via Air Research Publications

NF.XIX (J.30) of the Swedish Air Force delivered from Hatfield in 1948 to Västeras and Bromma for allocation to the 1st, 2nd and 3rd Squadrons of F1 Wing at Västeras. The nearest aircraft is TA242. 'Dutch' Holland via Jerry Scutts

(Right) **HR354, one of sixty FB.VIs acquired by the Turkish Air Force post war.** Jerry Scutts

(Below)
B-36 (FB.VI) 'IY-12' of the Czech Air Force at Malacky airfield in 1947. RF838 began its career with 404 Squadron RCAF at Banff in March 1945, before being sold to Czechoslovakia on 5 June 1947. At least nineteen FB.VIs were supplied to Czechoslovakia prior to the Communist takeover in 1948. John Stride via Graham M. Simons

Post-war France received a few FB.IVs, fifty-seven FB.VIs, (including these, with RS621 nearest the camera, at Dijon Longuic), twenty-nine PR.XVIs and twenty-three NF.XXXs from Britain. In February 1951, the French Government sold fifty-nine Mk III, VI, XVI and NF.XXX Mosquitoes to the new state of Israel.
P. Gandillet Archives via Serge Blandin

151

Once the British arms embargo to Israel was lifted, a number of surplus Mosquitoes were acquired by the new state. Most, including about sixty FB.VIs like these, were ferried to Israel from England between October 1954 and August 1955, and saw action in the 1956 war against Egypt. Israeli Air Force

they were placed in storage. However, by October they were needed again, when war with Egypt broke out. The Mosquitoes were taken out of store and used in the interceptor, bomber and photo reconnaissance roles before and during the Sinai (Suez) campaign, 29 October to 2 November, fought jointly with Anglo-French forces. Although many of the Mosquitoes received combat damage and a few had to crash-land, none were lost in combat and serviceability of the elderly aircraft remained high. The Mk VI was the main variant, its rocket rails and bomb racks

the transfer of aircraft deliveries under MDAP to the Tito regime, which had been expelled from the Communist bloc in January 1948. Late in 1951 the JRV began receiving Mosquitoes and by the end of the year, thirty-three NF.38s, two FB.VIs and two T.III trainers had arrived. By the end of 1952 seventy-four FB.VIs, fifty-seven NF.38s and three T.IIIs were on strength. In 1953 as tension with its pro-Soviet neighbours intensified, the Yugoslav Mosquitoes were used to patrol the Hungarian border, and in March, some escorted Marshal Tito's ship as it returned from the UK. Yugoslav

1957, experiments were also undertaken with the Yugoslav-built Letor-2 torpedo. In addition, many Mk 38s in the 97th and 184th Aviation Regiments were fitted with RB-50 and RB-57 cameras.

Despite the introduction of jet aircraft in the JRV inventory (103 Reconnaissance Regiment) from 1955 onwards, the Mosquitoes continued operating with 184 and 97 Aviation Regiments, until 1960, when the 184th Reconnaissance Regiment ceased using its Mosquitoes. Nine FB.VIs and two T.IIIs continued in service, however, with a sea-reconnaissance

Late in 1951, the JRV (Yugoslav Air Force) began receiving Mosquitoes and by the end of 1952 seventy-four FB.VIs, fifty-seven NF.38s and three T.IIIs were on strength. These are FB.VIs of the 32nd Bomber Division at Zagreb. BAE

being used to good effect, while some escorted the two surviving Israeli B-17s on bombing missions over Egypt, but the larger-nosed NF.XXXs were difficult to master and in the heat their overall black finish contributed greatly to rapid deterioration of the airframes.

A few years earlier, in 1951, a Yugoslavian delegation from the Jugoslovensko ratno vazduhoplovstyo (JRV, or Yugoslav Air Force) arrived in Britain to negotiate

Mosquitoes were also used to reconnoitre the border with Italy in October 1953 when that country made territorial claims on Trieste. That same month, testing was undertaken with TR-45/A torpedoes filled with water-ballast mounted on FB.VIs. These bombing trails proved so successful, that in 1954 four FB.VIs of the 97th Aviation Regiment were converted to carry live TR-45/A torpedoes, and one was loaded with the 'ASAG' minelaying system. Later, in

squadron primarily as target tugs, until 1963. That same year, in Britain, the last operational Mosquitoes – of No 3 Civil Anti-Aircraft Co-Operation Unit (CAACU) at Exeter Airport – made their final bow, when that unit's seven TT.35s and two T.3s were finally retired. Shortly afterwards the Mosquitoes were used in flying and ground sequences in the film *633 Squadron*, and again, in 1968, for the filming of *Mosquito Squadron*.

De Havillands inexplicably ordered that W4050 be destroyed, but it survived, thanks to the efforts of Mr W.J.S. Baird in the PR Department at Hatfield. In 1958 W4050 returned to its birthplace at Salisbury Hall where, on 15 May 1959, it took its rightful place of honour in the Mosquito Aircraft Museum in its original all-yellow prototype scheme. This, the oldest aircraft museum in Britain, plans to move to Hatfield in the next few years. Author's collection

Also on display at the Salisbury Hall Museum is the nose section of B.35 TJ118 (written off at 3CAACU Exeter in 1961 and used in ground sequences in 633 Squadron), pictured here in front of B.35 TA634. FB.VI TA122 (with wing from TR.33 TW233) is undergoing restoration at the Museum. Author's collection

TT.35 TA634 of No.3 Civil Anti-aircraft Co-operation Unit (CAACU) at Exeter Airport pictured on 14 September 1963, the year that this unit's seven TT.35s and two T.3s were finally retired, to bring the Mosquito's RAF service to an end. Shortly afterwards, TA634, seven other TT.35s, and three T.IIIs, were used in flying and ground sequences in 633 Squadron. **Suffering for their 'art', three of these aircraft were sacrificed for crash effects in the movie but TA634 survived and in 1968 starred in the film** Mosquito Squadron. via Ian Thirsk

(Below) **A beautiful photograph of B.35 TA634 undergoing a face-lift in a hangar at Speke Airport, Liverpool in May 1968 in preparation for the film** Mosquito Squadron. Photoflex Ltd via Ian Thirsk

B.35 TA634 makes engine runs at Speke Airport, Liverpool in June 1968, prior to taking part in the filming of Mosquito Squadron.
Now, after a complete restoration, it is on display at the Salisbury Hall Museum as B.XVI ML963 'K-King' of 571 Squadron.
Photoflex Ltd via Ian Thirsk

TT.35 VR806/J of 5 CAACU photographed in 1956. This aircraft was the last of fifteen B.35s built by Airspeed Ltd and one of 105 B.35s
which were converted to TT.35 target tugs by Brooklands Aviation from 1952. Norwich Aviation Museum

TA639, photographed here in 1963, like TA634, one of eighty Hatfield-built B.35s, was operated by CFS,
3 CAACU at Aldergrove Target Tug Flight. After appearing in 633 Squadron it was later acquired by the RAF
Museum, Cosford, where it is displayed as TA639 AZ-E of 627 Squadron. via Norwich Aviation Museum

CF-IME, one of fifteen PR.35s acquired by Ottawa-based Spartan Air Services Ltd, 1954–57, pictured in 1963.
Five were cannibalized at Hurn to provide spares for ten prepared by Derby Aviation Ltd at Burnaston and used
in Kenya, North and South America and the Dominican Republic on survey work. Norwich Aviation Museum

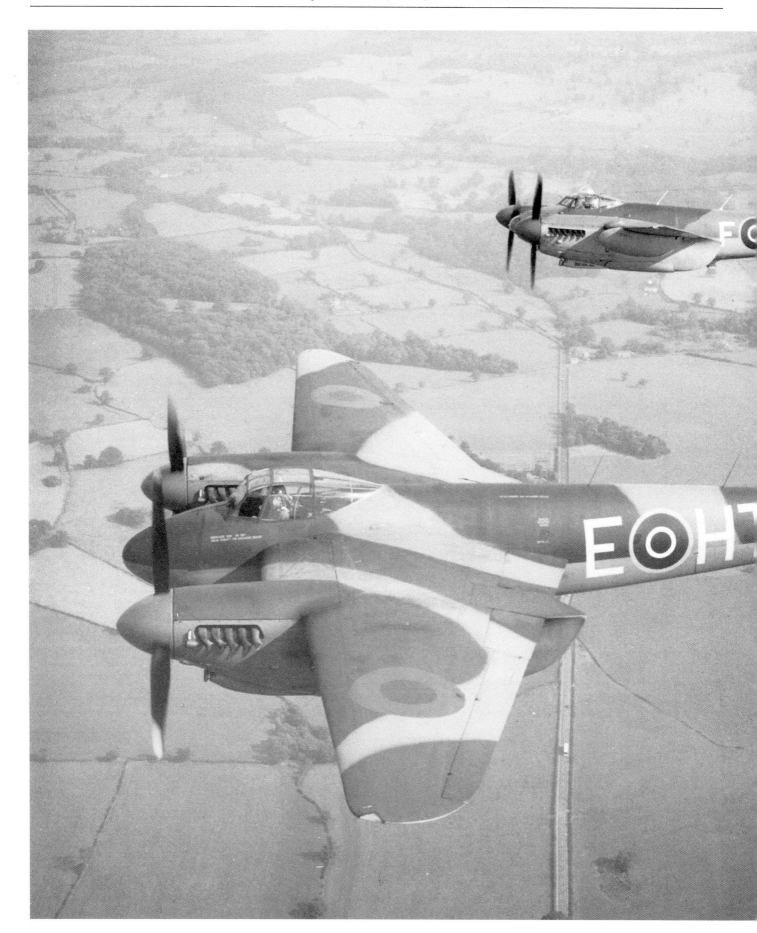

(Top) T.III TW117/Z, one of fifty Leavesden-built aircraft, pictured in 1967, four years after it appeared in 633 Squadron. It was subsequently displayed at the RAF Museum, Hendon before being loaned to the Norwegian Air Force Museum at Gardermoen and is now believed to be in California. Hendon replaced this aircraft with B.35 TJ138 in 1992. Norwich Aviation Museum

(Above) T.III RR299 in 1966. Built at Leavesden in 1945 and restored in the mid-sixties, RR299 was purchased by de Havillands in 1963 and registered as G-ASKH, 10 September 1965 by Hawker Siddeley Aviation (later BAe) at Hawarden. Restored again in 1992 by Historic Flying at Audley End, RR299 for many years was operated by BAe on the airshow circuit. Norwich Aviation Museum

(Left) T.III RR299 (G-ASKH) in formation with B.35 RS712 (G-AKSB), which was operated by Mirisch Films Ltd at Bovingdon for the 1963 film 633 Squadron before being acquired by G/C T.G. Hamish Mahaddie at Elstree, in August 1964. RS712 was purchased in 1987 by US warbird operator Kermit Weeks. On 21 July 1996 RR299 crashed at Great Barton, Manchester, killing pilot Kevin Moorhouse and flight engineer, Steve Watson. BAe via Darryl Cott

World-wide Production of Mosquito Variants

(Built at Hatfield unless otherwise stated)

SERIAL NO.	TYPE	SERIAL NO.	TYPE	SERIAL NO.	TYPE
W4050	Prototype	DD712–DD714	F.II (Special) Intruder for 23 Squadron		544/549/553/557, cvt to PR.IV. DZ540 proto- type pressure cabin XVI)
W4051	PR.I prototype				
W4052	F.II prototype	DD715	Prototype Mk XII		
W4053	Turret fighter. T.III prototype	DD716–DD758	F.II	DZ575–DZ618	B.IV Series II (DZ576/580/ 584/588/592/596/600; DZ604
W4054–W4056	PR.I	DD759	F.II cvt to XII		cvt to PR.IV) (DZ599; 606;
W4057	Bomber prototype, B.V	DD777–DD800	F.II		608; 611; 630/634;
W4058–W4059	PR.I	DK284–DK303	B.IV Series II (DK287 to Canada 9.9.42)		636/644; 646; 650,
W4060–W4061	PR.I (Long-range)	DK308–DK333	B.IV Series II (DK324 PR.VIII to B.IX)		cvt to carry 4,000lb [1,810kg] bomb)
W4062–W4063	PT.I (Long-range/ Tropicalized)	DK336–DK339	B.IV Series II		Highball Conversions:
W4064–W4072	PRU/Bomber Conversion Type, or B.IV Series I	DZ228–DZ272	F Mk II		DZ471(Proto); DZ520/ DZ524/G; DZ529;
		DZ286–DZ310	F.II (DZ302 cvtd by Marshalls to NX.XII)		DZ530/G/531/G;
W4073	Second turret fighter prototype, mod to T.III	DZ311–DZ320	B.IV Series II		DZ533; DZ534/G;
		DZ336	NF.XV		DZ535/G; DZ537/G;
		DZ340–DZ341	B.IV Series II		DZ539; DZ541/
W4074	First production F.II (single control)	DZ342	PR.VIII		DZ543; DZ546/547;
		DZ364	PR.VIII		DZ552; DZ554/55;
W4075	Production T.III (or II dual control)	DZ365	B.IV Series II		DZ559; DZ575;
		DZ366	NF.XV		DZ577/579; DZ581;
W4076	F.II	DZ367–DZ384	B.IV Series II		DZ583)
W4077	Production T.III (or II dual control)	DZ385	NF.XV	DZ630–DZ652	B.IV Series II
		DZ386–DZ388	B.IV Series II	DZ653–DZ661	F.II
W4078	F.II	DZ404	PR.VIII	DZ680–DZ727	F.II
W4079	Production T.III (or II dual control)	DZ405–DZ408	B.IV Series II	DZ739–DZ761	F.II
		DZ409	NF.XV	HJ108–HJ628	390 Canadian built aircraft reallocated
W4080	F.II	DZ410–DZ416	B.IV Series II (DZ411 cvt to PR.IV/G-AGFV BOAC)	HJ642–HJ661	F.II
W4081	Production T.III (or II dual control)	DZ417	NF.XV	HJ662–HJ682	B.VI Series I (HJ662/G FB.VI prototype (ex-DZ434)
W4082	F.II	DZ418–DZ423	B.IV Series II (DZ419 cvt to PR.IV)		(HJ680 to BOAC as G-AGGC)
W4083	Production T.III (or II dual control)	DZ424	PR.VIII		(HJ681 to BOAC as G-AGGD)
W4084	F.II	DZ425–DZ442	B.IV Series II (DZ431; DZ438, cvt to PR.IV. DZ434 cvt to prototype FB.VI Series I (HJ662/G))	HJ699–HJ715	F.II
W4085–W4099	F.II (W4089 cvt to PR.II)			HJ716–HJ743	B.VI Series I (HJ718 to BOAC as G-AGGE)
DD600–DD644	F.II (DD615; DD620; cvt to PR.II, and back again)	DZ458–DZ497	B.IV Series II (DZ459/ 466/473/480/487/ 494 cvt to PR.IV)		(HJ720 to BOAC as G-AGGF)
DD659–DD669	F.II (DD659 cvt to PR.II)				(HJ721 to BOAC as G-AGGG)
DD670–DD691	F.II (Special) Intruder for 23 Squadron	DZ515–D559	B.IV Series II (DZ517/ 523/527/532/538/		

SERIAL NO.	TYPE
	(HJ723 to BOAC as G-AGGH)
	(HJ732, FB.XVIII prototype)
HJ755–HJ792	B.VI Series I
	(HJ667 & HJ792 to BOAC as G-AGKO & G-AGKR)
HJ808–HJ833	B.VI Series I
HJ851–HJ899	T.III (Leavesden)
	(HJ898 to BOAC)
HJ911–HJ944	F.II (Leavesden)
HJ945–HJ946	F.II (Leavesden/ cvt by Marshalls to NF.XII)
HJ958–HJ999	T.III (Leavesden)
	(HJ985 to BOAC)
HK107–HK141	F.II (Leavesden/cvt by Marshalls to NF.XII)
HK159–HK185	F.II (Leavesden/cvt by Marshalls to NF.XII)
HK186	F.II (Leavesden/cvt by Southern Aircraft/ Marshalls to NF.XII)
HK187–HK194	F.II (Leavesden/cvt by Marshalls to NF.XII)
HK195	F.II (Leavesden/cvt by Marshalls to NF.XVII)
HK196–HK204	F.II (Leavesden/cvt by Marshalls to NF.XII)
HK222–HK235	F.II (Leavesden/cvt by Marshalls to NF.XII)
HK236–HK265	F.II (Leavesden/cvt by Marshalls to NF.XVII)
HK278–HK327	F.II (Leavesden/cvt by Marshalls to NF.XVII)
HK344–HK362	F.II (Leavesden/cvt by Marshalls to NF.XVII)
HK363–HK382	NF.XIII (Leavesden) (HK364 to NF.XIX prototype)
HK396–HK437	NF.XIII (Leavesden)
HK453–HK481	NF.XIII (Leavesden)
HK499–HK536	NF.XIII (Leavesden) (HK535/536 renumbered SM700/701)
HP848–HP888	FB.VI
HP904–HP942	FB.VI
HP967–HP989	FB.VI
HR113–HR162	FB.VI
HR175–HR220	FB.VI
HR236–HR262	FB.VI
HR279–HR312	FB.VI (Standard Motors)
HR331–HR375	FB.VI
HR387–HR415	FB.VI
HR432–HR465	FB.VI
HR485–HR527	FB.VI
HR539–HR580	FB.VI
HR603–HR649	FB.VI

SERIAL NO.	TYPE
HX802–HX835	FB.VI
HX849–HX869	FB.VI (HX849/850 not delvd)
HX896–HX901	FB.VI
HX902–HX904	FB.XVIII
HX905–HX922	FB.VI
HX937–HX984	FB.VI
KA100–KA102	FB.XXI (Canadian)
KA103–KA450	FB.XXVI and T.XXIX (Canadian) (37 cvt to T.29)
KA451–KA773	Cancelled (Canadian)
KA873–KA876	T.XXII (Canadian)
KA877–KA895	T.XXVII (Canadian)
KA896–KA897	T.XXII (Canadian)
KA898–KA927	T.XXVII (Canadian)
KA928–KA929	Cancelled (Canadian)
KA930–KA999	B.XXV (Canadian)
KB100–KB299	B.XX (Canadian, 9 to USAAF as F-8)
KB300–KB324	B.VII (Candian, 6 to USAAF as F-8)
KB325–KB369	B.XX (Canadian)
KB370–KB699	B.XXV (Can) (KB409/ 416/ 490/ 561/ 625 with 4,000lb [1,810kg] bay)
LR248–LR276	FB.VI
LR289–LR313	FB.VI (LR296 to BOAC as G-AGKP)
LR327–LR340	FB.VI
LR343–LR389	FB.VI (LR387 converted to Mk 33 with folding wings and arrester hook, 1945)
LR402–LR404	FB.VI
LR405–LR446	PR.IX
LR459–LR446	PR.IX
LR475–LR477	PR.IX
LR478–LR481	B.IX
LR495–LR513	B.IX
LR516–LR541	T.III (Leavesden) (LR524 to BOAC)
LR553–LR585	T.III (Leavesden)
ML896–ML920	B.IX
ML921–ML924	B.IX
ML925–ML942	B.XVI (ML935/ 956/ 974/ 980/ 995 cvt to TT.39 for RN)
ML956–ML999	B.XVI
MM112–MM156	B.XVI (MM112/117/ 142/156/177/192 cvt to TT.39 for RN
MM169–MM179	B.XVI (MM170 undelivered)
MM181–MM205	B.XVI
MM219–MM226	B.XVI
MM227–MM236	PR.IX

SERIAL NO.	TYPE
MM237–MM238	B.IX
MM239–MM240	PR.IX
MM241	B.IX
MM243–MM257	PR.IX
MM258	PR.XVI
MM271–MM314	PR.XVI
MM327–MM371	PR.XVI
MM384–MM397	PR.XVI
MM398–MM423	FB.VI
MM424–MM425	FB.VI
MM426–MM431	FB.XVIII
MM436–MM479	NF.XIII (Leavesden)
MM491–MM534	NF.XIII (Leavesden)
MM547–MM575	NF.XIII (Leavesden)
MM615–MM623	NF.XIII (Leavesden)
MM624–MM656	NF.XIX (Leavesden)
MM669–MM686	NF.XIX (Leavesden)
MM686–MM710	NF.XXX (Leavesden)
MM726–MM769	NF.XXX (Leavesden)
MM783–MM822	NF.XXX (Leavesden)
MP469	Pressure cabin prototype bomber mod to NF.XV
MT456–MT500	NF.XXX (MT480 undelivered) (Leavesden)
MV521–MV570	NF.XXX (Leavesden)
NS496–NS538	PR.XVI (NS538 H2X prototype for USAAF)
NS551–NS596	PR.XVI
NS619–NS660	PR.XVI
NS673–NS712	PR.XVI
NS725–NS758	PR.XVI (NS735/G-AOCK, NS639/G-AOCI civil conv BOAC)
NS772–NS816	PR.XVI (NS811/ G-AIRU, NS812/ G-AIRT civil conv BOAC)
NS819–NS859	FB.VI
NS873–NS914	FB.VI
NS926–NS965	FB.VI
NS977–NS999	FB.VI
NT112–NT156	FB.VI
NT169–NT199	FB.VI
NT200	FB.XVIII
NT201–NT207	FB.VI
NT219	FB.VI
NT220	FB.XVIII
NT221–NT223	FB.VI
NT224–NT225	FB.XVIII
NT226–NT238	FB.VI
NT241–NT283	NF.XXX (Leavesden)
NT295–NT336	NF.XXX (Leavesden)
NT349–NT393	NF.XXX (Leavesden)
NT415–NT458	NF.XXX (Leavesden)
NT471–NT513	NF.XXX (Leavesden)
NT526–NT568	NF.XXX (Leavesden)

SERIAL NO.	TYPE	SERIAL NO.	TYPE	SERIAL NO.	TYPE
NT582–NT591	NF.XXX (Leavesden)	RG283–RG318	PR.34	TE738–TE780	FB.VI (Standard Motors)
NT592–NT593	FB.XVIII	RK929–RK954	NF.XXX (Leavesden)		
NT594–NT621	NF.XXX (Leavesden)	RK955–RK960	NF.36 (Leavesden)	TE793–TE830	FB.VI (Standard Motors)
PF379–PF418	B.XVI (Percival)	RK972–RK999	NF.36 (Leavesden)		
PF428–PF469	B.XVI (Percival) (PF439/445/449/452; cvt to TT.39)	RL113–RL158	NF.36 (Leavesden)	TE848–TE889	FB.VI (Standard Motors)
		RL173–RL215	NF.36 (Leavesden)	TE905–TE932	FB.VI (Standard Motors)
		RL229–RL268	NF.36 (Leavesden) (RL248 NF.38 prototype)		
PF481–PF511	B.XVI (Percival) (PF481–483/489; cvt to TT.39)			TH976–TH999	Ordered as B.XVI, built as B.35/ TT.35
		RL269–RL273	Cancelled		
PF515–PF526	B.XVI (Percival)	RL288–RL329	Cancelled	TJ113–TJ158	Ordered as B.XVI, built as B.35/ TT.35
PF538–PF579	B.XVI (Percival) (PF560/569/576; cvt to TT.39)	RL345–RL390	Cancelled		
		RR270–RR319	T.III (Leavesden)	TK591–TK635	Ordered as NF.XXX, built as B.35
		RS501–RS535	FB.VI		
PF592–PF619	B.XVI (Percival) (PF599/606/609; cvt to TT.39)	RS548–RS580	FB.VI	TK648–TK656	Ordered as NF.XXX, built as B.35
		RS593–RS633	FB.VI		
		RS637–RS680	FB.VI (Airspeed)	TK657–TK679	Cancelled. (Ordered as NF Mk 30)
PF620–PF635	PR.34 (Percival)	RS693–RS698	FB.VI (Airspeed)		
PF647–PF680	PR.34 (Percival) (PF652/ 656/ 662/ 669/ 670/ 673/ 678–680 A52–1– A52–212 FB.40 (Australia) (6 as PR.40) cvt to PR.34A)	RS699–RS723	B.35 (Airspeed) (14 cvt to TT.35)	TK691–TK707	Cancelled (Ordered as NF Mk 30)
		RS724–RS725	Cancelled (Airspeed)	TN466–TN497	Cancelled (were to be built at Leavesden)
		RS739–RS779	Cancelled (Airspeed)		
		RS795–RS836	Cancelled (Airspeed)	TN510–TN530	Cancelled (were to be built at Leavesden)
		RS849–RS893	Cancelled (Airspeed)		
		RS913–RS948	Cancelled (Airspeed)	TN542–TN590	Cancelled (were to be built at Leavesden)
PZ161–PZ203	FB.VI	RS960–RS999	Cancelled (Airspeed)		
PZ217–PZ250	FB.VI	RT105–RT123	Cancelled (Airspeed)	TN608–TN640	Cancelled (were to be built at Leavesden)
PZ251–PZ252	FB.XVIII	RV295–RV326	B.XVI		
PZ253–PZ259	FB.VI	RV340–RV363	B.XVI (RV348–350 cvtd to TT.35 with Merlin 113As)	TN652–TN674	Cancelled (were to be built at Leavesden)
PZ273–PZ299	FB.VI				
PZ300–PZ301	FB.XVIII			TN690–TN736	Cancelled (were to be built at Leavesden)
PZ302–PZ316	FB.VI	RV364–RV367	B.35 (RV365–367 cvtd to TT.35 with Merlin 113As)		
PZ330–PZ345	FB.VI			TN750–TN789	Cancelled (were to be built at Leavesden)
PZ346	FB.XVIII	SZ958–SZ999	FB.VI		
PZ347–PZ466	FB.VI	TA113–TA122	FB.VI	TN802–TN838	Cancelled (were to be built at Leavesden)
PZ467–PZ470	FB.XVIII	TA123–TA156	NF.XIX		
PZ471–PZ476	FB.VI	TA169–TA198	NF.XIX	TN850–TN864	Cancelled (were to be built at Leavesden)
RF580–RF625	FB.VI (Standard Motors)	TA215–TA249	NF.XIX		
		TA263–TA308	NF.XIX	TS444	Prototype TR.33 (Leavesden)
RF639–RF681	FB.VI (Standard Motors)	TA323–TA357	NF.XIX		
		TA369–TA388	FB.VI	TS449	Prototype TR.33 (Leavesden)
RF695–RF736	FB.VI (Standard Motors)	TA389–TA413	NF.XIX		
		TA425–TA449	NF.XIX	TV954–TV984	T.III
RF749–RF793	FB.VI (Standard Motors)	TA469–TA508	FB.VI	TW101–TW109	T.III
		TA523–TA560	FB.VI	TW227–TW257	TR.33 (Leavesden) (TW240 TR.37 prototype)
RF818–RF859	FB.VI (Standard Motors)	TA575–TA603	FB.VI		
		TA614–TA616	PR.XVI		
RF873–RF915	FB.VI (Standard Motors)	TA617–TA618	B.35	TW277–TW295	TR.33 (Leavesden)
		TA633–TA670	B.35	VA871–VA876	T.3 for RAF (Leavesden)
RF928–RF966	FB.VI (Standard Motors)	TA685–TA724	B.35		
		TE587–TE628	FB.VI (Standard Motors)	VA877–VA881	T.3 for RN (Leavesden)
RF969–RF999	PR.XVI			VA882–VA894	T.3 for RAF (Leavesden)
RG113–RG158	PR.XVI	TE640–TE669	FB.VI (Standard Motors)		
RG171–RG175	PR.XVI (RG171–173 fitted with arrester hook for RN)	TE683–TE707	FB.VI (Standard Motors)	VA923–VA928	T.3 for RAF (Leavesden)
				VA929–VA948	Cancelled
RG176–RG215	PR.34R	TE708–TE725	FB.VI (Standard Motors)	VL613–VL625	PR.34 (VL625 to PR.34A)
RG228–RG269	PR.34				

SERIAL NO.	TYPE
VL626–VL725	FB.VI Cancelled (Airpseed)
VL726–VL732	FB.VI (Airspeed)
VP178–VP202	B.35/ TT.35/ PR.35 (Airspeed)
VP342–VP355	T.III
A52–300	FB.42 (Australian–converted)
A52–301–327	PR.41 (Australian–converted)
A52–1050–1071	T.43 (Australian–converted)
VR330–VR349	T.III
VR792–VR806	B.35 (Airspeed) (VR793 cvt to TT.35 prototype)
VT581–VT596	T.3
VT604–VT631	T.3
VT651–VT683	NF.38
VT691–VT707	NF.38 (Hatfield/ VT670 1st from Chester 30.9.48)
VT724–VT737	TR.37 (Chester)
VX860–VX879	NF.38 (Chester)
VX886–VX916	NF.38 (Chester) VX916 completed 11.50, 7,781st and final Mosquito built (of which 6,710 were built during WWII)

PRODUCTION TOTALS

Hatfield, Herts	3,326
Leavesden, Herts	1,476
Standard Motors, Coventry	1,066
Percival Aircraft, Luton	245
Airspeed, Portsmouth	122
Chester	96
de Havilland Canada (Toronto)	1,076
de Havilland Australia (Sydney)	212

EXPORT SALES

Australia	46 FB.VI and 29 PR.XVI
Belgium	2 FB.VI and 18 NF.30
Burma	Some FB.VIs
Nationalist China	Approx 205 FB.26, T.29, T.27, T.22 (1) and B.25 (1) reassembled in Shanghai
Czechoslovakia	19 FB.VIs supplied prior to Communist takeover in 1948
Dominica	6 FB.VI (301–306) + several from Canada
France	A few B.IVs; 57 FB.VI, 29 PR.XVIs, 23 NF.XXX
Israel	Some T.IIIs, about 60 FB.VIs, at least 5 PR.XVIs, and approximately 14 'denavalized' Sea Mosquito TR.33s
New Zealand	4 T.IIIs; 76 FB.VIs, one FB.40 and 4 T.43s
Norway	3 T.IIIs; 18 FB.VIs for No.334 Squadron (3 converted to night fighters in 1950)
South Africa	2 F.II and 14 PR.XVI/ IXs for No.60 Squadron
Sweden	46 NF.XIX (J30)
Turkey	96 FB.VI and several T.IIIs
Yugoslavia (JRV)	60 NF.38s, 80 FB.VIs, 3 T.IIIs

Mosquito Variants

PR.I: Photo-reconnaissance Mosquito which first flew (W4051) on 10 June 1941. Powered by two 1,460hp (1,088kW) Merlin 21 or 23 engines with two-speed single-stage superchargers and de Havilland Hydromatic constant speed airscrews. Each machine carried three vertical cameras and one oblique. The prototype (W4051) and nine aircraft (W4054–W4056, W4058/4059 and W4060–4063) were built, all with short engine nacelles. Four (W4060–W4063) were modified into long-range aircraft with increased all-up weight, and two (W4062/4063) were tropicalized.

PR/Bomber Conversion: Nine aircraft, a conversion of the PR.I airframe, were built, (W4064–W4072) being designated PR/Bomber Conversion Type, then, prior to operational service, B.IV Series I. These could carry a 2,000lb (910kg) bomb load and retained the short nacelles of the early models. The first flew in September 1941. One aircraft (W4066) was converted to PR.IV Series I.

F.II: Day and night long range fighter and intruder, built with long nacelles. Powered by two 1,460hp (1,088kW) Merlin 21, 22 or 23s. W4052 prototype first flew 15 May 1941. Fitted with AI Mk IV. Armed with four 20mm Hispano cannon and four .303in Browning machine guns in the nose. In turn, W4052 was fitted experimentally with a four-gun Bristol B.XI dorsal turret and a bellows-operated segmented airbrake around the mid-fuselage, and later a Mosquito II was fitted experimentally with a *Turbinlight* in the nose. 25 (Special) Intruder models were built for 23 Squadron with AI radar equipment deleted. As late as 1943–44 many surviving aircraft were refurbished, re-engined, had AI Mk IV and V radar sets installed, and were given to 100 Group. A few aircraft were converted for photo-reconnaissance duties. 494 built; 97 converted to NF.XII and 100 converted to NF.XVII; six converted to T.III.

T.III: Unarmed dual control trainer. First flew January 1942. 358 built, including six from F.II. Powered by Merlin 21, 23 or 25s.

B.IV Series I: See PR/Bomber Conversion.

B.IV Series II: Day and night unarmed bomber, powered by two Merlin 21 or 23s. The prototype Mk IV (W4072) first flew on 8 September 1941. 292 were built, 27 being converted to PR.IV Series II, one to FB.VI prototype, four being completed as PR.VIIIs, four completed as NF.XV high-altitude aircraft and one (DZ540) being converted to B.XVI prototype. The B.IV Series II could carry a 2,000lb (910kg) bomb load, normally four 500lb (230kg) GP short-tailed bombs, as well as two droppable wing tanks, each of 50 gallons (230 litres). In 8 Group 54 Mk IVs were converted to carry a 4,000lb (1,810kg) bomb. DZ531/G and 26 other B.IVs were modified to carry *Highball* mines.

PR.IV: Day/night reconnaissance aircraft. The 27 built were all conversions of existing B.IV Series II. First flew April 1942.

B.V: Projected bomber version with two 50 gallon (230 litre) droppable wing tanks or two 500lb (230kg) wing-mounted bombs beneath a new standard strengthened wing. W4057, which was originally started as a PR.I, and flew in September 1941, was the prototype for trial installations at Boscombe Down but the Mk V never went into production.

FB.VI: Day and night fighter-bomber, intruder, and long range fighter powered by two 1,460hp (1,088kW) Merlin 21 or 23, or two 1,635hp (1,218kW) Merlin 25s. First flew, 1 June 1942. Prototype HJ662/G was converted from B.IV DZ434. Production aircraft first flew in February 1943. Altogether, 2,289 (almost one-third of total Mosquito production) were built, including 1,065 by Standard Motors Ltd and 56 by Airspeed Ltd; 19 of these were completed as FB.XVIIIs, two converted to Sea Mosquito TR.33 prototypes. Armed with four 20mm cannon and four .303in machine guns and able to carry two 250lb (115kg) bombs in enclosed bomb bay plus two more (later, two 500lbs/230 kg), or eight 60lb (27kg) rocket projectiles under the wings. Alternatively, one mine or depth charge beneath each wing.

B.VII: Canadian bomber version based on the B.V. First flown 24 September 1942. 25 aircraft built, six converted to F-8DH for the USAAF. Not used outside of North America.

PR.VIII: Interim photo-reconnaissance version intended to fill the gap until deliveries of the PR.IX and PR.XVI were met. The unpressurised VIII was based on the PR.IV but with 1,565hp (1166kW) two-stage Merlin 61 engines in place of Merlin 21/22s. Prototype (DK324) first flew, 20 October 1942. The four built began as B.IVs.

B.IX: Unarmed high-altitude bomber, but not pressurized, which first flew on 24 March 1943. 54 built. Powered by two-stage 1,680hp (1,252kW) Merlin 72 (starboard)/73 (port) or 76 (starboard)/77 (port) fitted with Bendix Stromberg low pressure injection unit and reverse flow cooling. Prototype (DK324) converted from PR.VIII. A few were modified to carry a 4,000lb (1,810kg) bomb in the internal bomb bay.

PR.IX: Photo-reconnaissance version which first flew on 6 May 1943. Powered by two 1,680hp (1,252kW) Merlin 72/73s or 76/77s. Could carry either two 50 gallon (230 litre), two 100 gallon (455 litre) or two 200 gallon (910 litre) droppable fuel tanks under the wings. 90 built.

NF.X: Night-fighter powered by two-stage Merlin 61 engines. Although ordered in quantity, the NF.X never went into production.

FB.XI: Fighter-bomber version similar to the B.VI but with two-stage 1,565hp (1,166kW) Merlin 61s. Not ordered into production.

NF.XII: Prototype (DD715) and the 97 NF.XII night-fighters built were all conversions of the NF.II. Powered by two 1,460hp (1,088kW) Merlin 21 or 23 engines. Main distinguishing feature was a 'thimble-nose' containing a powerful transmitter with a parabolic reflector for the 10cm wavelength AI Mk VIII radar, which removed the need for any external aerials. First flew in August 1942. Armed with four 20mm cannon only.

NF.XIII. Night-fighter powered by Merlin 21, 23 or 25s with universal wing similar to that of the Mk VI bomber. AI Mk VIII in 'thimble' or Universal ('bull') Nose. First flew in August 1943. 260 built.

NF.XIV: Night-fighter based on the NF.XIII and intended to be powered by two-stage Merlin 67 or 72 engines, but was never put into production, being superseded by the NF.XIX and NF.XXX.

NF.XV: High-altitude fighter, capable of reaching 45,000ft (13,700m), built in response to the threat posed by the Ju 86 high altitude bomber. Prototype (MP469) was the first Mosquito with a pressurized cabin, and first flew on 8 August 1942, later being fitted with AI Mk VIII radar, as were the four NF.XVs built – all modified B.IVs with two-stage 1,680hp (1,252kW) Merlin 72/73 or 1,710hp (1,274kW) 76/77 engines driving three- or four-bladed airscrews. The NF.XVs were armed with four .303in machine guns in underbelly pack. MP469 was delivered to the newly formed High Altitude Flight at Northolt on 16 September 1942, but this, and the Fighter Interception Unit at Ford, which received DZ366, DZ385, DZ409 and DZ417, March–August 1943, never had need to use them as the Ju 86s ceased operations over Britain. All five were used by 'C' Flight of 85 Squadron at Hunsdon and later some went to Farnborough for pressure cabin research.

PR.XVI: Unarmed photo-reconnaissance aircraft powered by 72/73 or 76/77 Merlin engines and fitted with pressure cabin. Prototype (MM258) first flown in July 1943. 435 built.

B.XVI: Same as the PR.XVI and initially designed to carry 3,000lb (1,360kg) bomb load but was capable of carrying up to 4,000lbs (1,810kg) of bombs. Prototype (DZ540) was converted from B.IV and first flew on 1 January 1944. 402 were built, including 195 by Percival Aircraft Ltd. 26 were later converted to TT.39s.

NF.XVII: 100 night-fighter variants converted from NF.II and powered by 1,460hp (1,088kW) Merlin 21 or 23 engines. Fitted with SCR720/729 or AI Mk X radar. First flown, March 1943.

FB.XVIII: Ground attack and anti-shipping fighter-bomber with four cannon deleted and replaced by a Molins 57mm 6 pounder cannon weighing 1,580lb (716kg), while retaining the four .303in Browning machine guns. Twenty-four 57mm rounds for the cannon, which had a muzzle velocity of 2,950ft/s (900m/s), were carried. The eighteen *Tsetses* built started as FB.VIs, whose two 1,635hp (1,218kW) Merlin 25s, were retained. Prototype (HJ732/G) was converted from FB.VI and was first flown on 8 June 1943.

NF.XIX: Night-fighter powered by two Merlin 25s and fitted with AI VIII or X/SCR720 and 729

in 'thimble' or Universal Nose similar to the NF.XIII. First flown, April 1944. 280 built.

B.XX: Canadian bomber version of the B.IV Series II with two 1,460hp (1,088kW) Packard-built single-stage Merlin 31 or 33 engines. 245 built, of which 8 crashed on test or delivery.

F-8DH: Thirty-four Canadian B.XXs modified for the USAAF, powered by two Packard-built single-stage Merlin XXXIs or XXXIIs. Equivalent to the RAF B.IV, 16 were delivered to the 25th BG at Watton, England in July 1944 but were considered unsatisfactory above 25,000ft (7,600m). Eleven were soon transferred to the RAF and the rest were returned to the USA.

FB.21: Canadian version of the FB.VI superseded by the FB.26. Three built.

T.22: Canadian version of the T.III developed from the FB.21. Six built. Powered by two 1,460hp (1,088kW) Packard-built single-stage Merlin 33 engines.

B.23: Canadian version of the B.IX to be powered by two 1,750hp (1,304kW) Packard-built single-stage Merlin 69 engines but none built.

FB.24: Canadian high-altitude fighter-bomber version based on the FB.21, with two 1,620hp (1,207kW) Packard-built single-stage Merlin 301s, but not ordered into production.

B.25: Uprated Canadian version of the B.XX with improved Packard-built single-stage Merlin 25s. Could carry a 2,000lb (910kg) bomb load. 400 built.

FB.26: Uprated Canadian version of the FB.VI fighter-bomber, improved from the FB.21, powered by two 1,620hp (1,207kW) Packard-built single-stage Merlin 225s. 300 built, plus a further 37 were converted to T.29 standard.

T.27: Dual control trainer version developed from the T.22 with more powerful (two 1,620hp/1,207kW) Packard-built single-stage Merlin 225 engines. 49 built.

Mk 28: Canadian allocated model not used.

T.29: Thirty-seven dual control trainers converted from the FB.26, powered by two Packard-built single-stage Merlin 225s.

NF.XXX: Night-fighter development of the NF.XIX which appeared in March 1944. Powered by two-stage 1,680hp (1,251kW) Merlin 72s, 1,710hp (1,274kW) Merlin 76 or 1,690hp (1,259kW) Merlin 113s. Fitted with AI Mk X. 529 built.

NF.31: NF 30 with two 1,750hp (1,304kW) Packard-built single-stage Merlin 69s but never put into production.

PR.32: High-altitude unarmed photo-reconnaissance aircraft based on the PR.XVI with two-stage 1,690hp (1,259kW) Merlin 113 (starboard)/114 (port). Pressure cabin and specially lightened and lengthened wing tips. First flown, August 1944. Five built, all of which started as PR.XVIs.

TR.33: Torpedo-reconnaissance/fighter-bomber for Royal Navy carrier-borne operations. Two prototypes (LR359 and LR387) were converted from Mk VIs to meet Specification 15/44, with arrester hook and reinforced fuselage for deck landing and 1,635hp (1,218kW) Merlin 25s driving four-bladed airscrews, but the wings were non-folding. Two more (TS444 and TS449), fitted with upward folding wings and arrester hook (and extra bulkhead over the arrester hook attachment point), were built for handling trials. The first production TR.33, TW227, flew for the first time on 10 November 1945. From the 14th TR.33 onwards, manual folding wings were introduced and the rubber blocks in compression undercarriage were replaced by Lockheed oleo-pneumatic shock absorbers to reduce the rebound in deck landings. Slightly smaller wheels were also fitted. The TR.33 could carry an 18in (46cm) Mk XV or XVII torpedo, or a mine, or a 2,000lb (910kg) bomb under the fuselage, plus two 500lb (230kg) bombs in the bomb bay and either two 50 gallon (230 litre) fuel-tanks beneath the wings, or two 30 gallon (140 litre) tanks and four RPs. A thimble nose housed ASH radar, while the four 20mm cannon were retained. Two detachable RATO (Rocket Assisted Take Off) bottles either side of the fuselage, which fell away after firing, could also be fitted. 50 TR.33s were built but an order for 47 more was cancelled.

PR.34, PR 34A: VLR (Very Long Range) unarmed high-altitude photo-reconnaissance aircraft with all armour and fuel tank bullet-proofing removed. 1,192 gallons (5,419 litres) of fuel in tanks in bulged bomb bay and two 200 gallon (910litre) drop tanks under the wings gave a still air range of 3,600 miles (5,800km) cruising at 300mph (480kph). Powered by two 1,690hp (1,259kW) Merlin 114s first used in the PR.32. The port Merlin 114 drove the Marshall cabin supercharger. 181 PR.34s were built, including 50 by Percival Aircraft at Luton. Two of these, VL621 and VL623, were fitted with *H2S*. The first PR.34 (RG176) flew on 4 December 1944. The first operational sortie was made by RG185 'Z' from a special detachment of 684 Squadron on Cocos Islands on 3 July 1945. All PR.34s carried four split F.52 vertical cameras, two forward, two aft, of the belly tank, and one F.24 oblique camera (or alternatively, a vertical K.17 camera for air survey) aft also. Seven PR.34s were used up until the end of August 1945 in 38 sorties over Malaysia, southern Sumatra and Java. 35 PR.34s were converted to PR.34A standard by Marshalls of Cambridge with the addition of 1,710hp (1,274kW) Merlin 113A and 114As, with anti-surge supercharger diffusers, and modified *Gee-H II* equipment and improved undercarriage retraction gear.

B.35: Day and night bomber with enlarged bomb bay for 4,000lb (1,810kg) bomb or four 500lb (230kg) bombs, like the B.XVI, except for two 113/114 Merlins (later 1,710hp/1,274kW 113A/114A). 274 built, including sixty-five by Airspeed Ltd. The prototype B.35 first flew on 12 March 1945 and forty had been delivered by VE-Day, although none saw service until after the war. Some B.35s were modified by Marshall's Flying Services Ltd to take new type bomb sights and *Rebecca* and *Gee-H II* radars. One B.35 was used for airscrew testing by de Havilland Propellers Ltd and TA651 (later a TT.35) had *H2S* in a ventral radome. Ten B.35s were converted to PR.35 special night photo-reconnaissance versions using flash. From 1952 105 were converted to TT.35 target tugs by Brooklands Aviation Ltd, being fitted with an ML Type-G wind-driven winch under the forward fuselage in a cylindrical fairing to trail four drogue targets stowed in the bomb bay. From 1956 a few B.35s

were converted to Met.35s. Most B.35s saw service post war with the RAF overseas.

NF.36: Night-fighter development of the NF.XXX, with improved AI radar and four 20mm cannon. Powered by two 1,690hp (1,259kW) Merlin 113 (starboard)/114 (port), or 1,710hp (1,274kW) 113A (starboard)/114A (port). 163 built, a few being converted to Met.35s. The first NF.36 (RK955) flew in May 1945. NF.36s were retired from service in 1953.

TR.37: Torpedo-fighter/bomber, of which only fourteen were built. The prototype, TW240, a modified TR.33, first flew in 1946. The TR.37 differed from the TR.33 only in having a British ASV (Air to Surface Vessel) Mk XIII in thimble nose radome slightly larger than the TR.33. 14 built at Chester. Powered by two 1,635hp (1,218kW) Merlin 25s.

NF.38: Night-fighter with Merlin 1,710hp (1,274kW) 114As. One prototype (RL248) converted from NF.36. Some models were fitted with AI Mk IX radar. Most of the 101 built were acquired by Yugoslavia.

TT.39: High-speed shore-based naval target tug. Two prototypes (ML995 and PF569), plus twenty-four more were converted from existing B.XVI aircraft by General Aircraft Ltd, under their designation GAL.59 to Royal Navy Specification Q.19/45 to replace the Miles M.33 Monitor TT.11. The B.XVIs two 1,680hp (1,252kW) Merlin

72/73 engines were retained but the extended (and glazed) nose (which housed the camera operator) resulted in the airscrew blades having to be cropped. The third crew member, a rear-facing observer/drogue operator, sat in a dorsal cupola aft of the wings. Drogue targets were streamed from a hydraulically-operated winch in the bomb bay, powered by a retractable wind-driven generator in the forward bomb bay. A radio altimeter was fitted for radar-calibration exercises. The TT.39 first entered service with Fleet Requirements Units from 1948.

FB.40: 212 Australian-built versions of the FB.VI were the product of de Havilland Australia Ltd. Six were converted to PR.40; 28 to PR.41s; one to FB.42, and twenty-two to T.43s. Powered by 1,460hp (1,088kW) Packard-built single-stage Merlin 31,33s.

PR.41: twenty-eight of these Australian reconnaissance aircraft similar to the Mk IX and FB.40 were converted from existing FB.40 airframes. Powered by Packard-built single-stage Merlin 69s.

FB.42: Single Australian fighter-bomber converted from FB.40 (A52-90) to become A52-300 (later PR.41 prototype). Powered by two 1,750hp (1,304kW) Packard-built single-stage Merlin 69s.

T.43: 22 Australian trainer versions similar to the T.III. converted from FB.40s (A52-1050 to A52-1,071). Powered by two 1,460hp (1,088kW) Packard-built single-stage Merlin 33s.

RAF/BOAC Mosquito Leuchars to Sweden Service 1943–45

The Mosquito's high speed made it ideal for use as a courier aircraft and a number were operated between Leuchars in Scotland and Stockholm. These carried diplomatic mail and personnel in a pressurized bomb bay. The initial proving flight had been made in August 1942 by an unmarked RAF Mosquito from Horsham St Faith to Stockholm with a load of mail, the aircraft returning the next day empty, and subsequent flights were made by civilian registered aircraft operated and crewed by BOAC, these continuing until the end of the war in Europe.

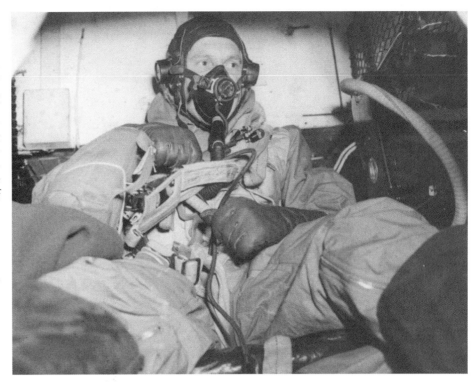

Converted bomb bay accommodation for BOAC Mosquito passengers on the Scotland–Sweden service was very cramped, cold and uncomfortable, but many VIPs and downed airmen, as well as cargoes of precious ball-bearings, were brought back successfully from Sweden during 520 round trips flown from 3 February 1943–17 May 1945. One important passenger was nuclear physicist Dr Nils Bohr, who was flown to England in a Mosquito on 7 October 1943. Brt Official

A/C	TYPE	DETAILS
DK301	IV	4.8.42 F/L (later W/C) D.A.G. Parry and F/O V. Robson, 105 Squadron, flew the 1st diplomatic flight to Sweden, returning next day.
G-AGFV (DZ411)	IV	Operated with BOAC 15.12.42–6.1.45.
G-AGGC (HJ680)	VI	Operated with BOAC 16.4.43–9.1.46.
G-AGGD (HJ681)	VI	Operated with BOAC 16/17.4.43–3.1.44. Crash-landed in Sweden.
G-AGGE (HJ718)	VI	Operated with BOAC 23.4.43–22.6.45.
G-AGGF (HJ720)	VI	Operated with BOAC 24.4.43–17.8.43. Crashed, Capt L.A. Wilkins and R/O N.H. Beaumont, killed.
G-AGGG (HJ721)	VI	Operated with BOAC 2.5.43–25.10.43. Crashed nr. Leuchars returning from Sweden. Capt M. Hamre & R/O S. Haug killed.
G-AGGH (HJ723)	VI	Operated with BOAC 2.5.43–22.6.45.
G-AGKO (HJ667)	VI	Operated with BOAC 8.3.43–22.6.45.
G-AGKR (HJ792)	VI	Operated with BOAC 11.4.44–28.8.44. Lost at sea returning from Sweden. Capt J.H. White & R/O J.C. Gaffeny killed.
G-AGKP (LR296)	VI	Operated with BOAC 22.4.44–19.8.44. Crashed in sea 9m (14.5km) from Leuchars. Capt G. Rae, R/O D.T. Roberts, Capt B.W.B. Orton killed.
HJ898	III	Crew trainer 22.4.45, ret. to RAF 12.5.45.
HJ985	III	Crew trainer 28.11.43, ret. to RAF 26.1.44.
LR524	III	Crew trainer 21.1.44, ret. to RAF 4.12.44.

G-AGFV, Mk IV DZ411, the first Mosquito to be used by BOAC, who received the aircraft on 15 December 1942. Graham M. Simons

(Right) Captain Gilbert Rae, BOAC Mosquito captain, who was killed when G-AGKP crashed in the sea 9 miles (14km) from Leuchars on 19 August 1944. His R/O D.T. Roberts, and passenger, Capt B.W.B. Orton, also perished. Brt Official

Mosquito Squadrons and Codes

No. 4 Squadron (*NC; UP*).
Command Assignments: 2nd TAF (PR), WWII;
BAFO Germany, 31.8.45–7.50
Aircraft: ('B' Flight) PR.XVI, 8.43–5.44; FB.VI,
9.45–7.50.

No. 8 Squadron (*HV*).
Command Assignments: Middle East.
Aircraft: FB.VI, 9.46–5.47.

No. 11 Squadron (*OM*).
Command Assignments: BAFO Germany.
Aircraft: FB.VI, 10.48–8.50.

No. 13 Squadron.
Command Assignments: PR, Middle East.
Aircraft: PR.IX, PR.XVI, PR.34, 8.46–2.52.

No. 14 Squadron (*CX*).
Command Assignments: Coastal Command,
6.45–31.3.46; BAFO Germany, 4.46–51.
Aircraft: FB.VI, 6.45–3.46. XVI/B.35,
4.46–10.47; B.35, 12.47–2.51.

No.18 Squadron (*EV*).
Command Assignments: Suez Canal Zone.
Aircraft: FB.VI, 3.47–11.47.

No. 21 (City Of Norwich)
Squadron (*YH*).
Command Assignments: 2nd TAF; BAFO Germany.
Aircraft: FB.VI, 9.43–10.47.

No. 22 Squadron.
Command Assignments: Far East.
Aircraft: FB.VI, 5.46–8.46.

No. 23 Squadron (*YP*).
Command Assignments: Fighter Command; 100
Group (Special Duties later Bomber Support).
Aircraft: NF.II, 7.42–8.43; B.VI, 6.43–9.45;
NF.XXX, 8.45–2.47; NF.36, 10.46–12.51.

No. 25 Squadron (*ZK*).
Command Assignments: Fighter Command.
Aircraft: NF.II, 11.42–3.44; FB.VI, 8.43–9.43;
NF.XVII, 12.43–11.44; NF.XXX,
9.44–9.46; FB.VI, 1–2.45; NF.36, 9.46–9.51.

No. 27 Squadron.
Command Assignments: India.
Aircraft: NF.II, 4.43–6.43; FB.VI, 12.43–4.44.

No. 29 Squadron (*RO*).
Command Assignments: Fighter Command.
Aircraft: NF.XII, 5.43–4.44; NF.XIII, 10.43–2.45;
NF.XXX, 2.45–1946; NF.36, 8.46–6.50; NF.XXX,
6.50–10.51.

No. 36 Squadron
(248 Squadron re–numbered).
Command Assignments: Coastal Command
1946–1947.
Aircraft: FB.VI, 10.46–10.47.

No. 39 Squadron.
Command Assignments: Canal Zone, Egypt,
1950.
Aircraft: FB.VI, 10.45–9.46; NF.36, 3.46–
3.53.

No. 45 Squadron (*OB*).
Command Assignments: India.
Aircraft: FB.VI, 2.44–5.46.

No. 46 Squadron.
Command Assignments: Mediterranean.
Aircraft: NF.XII, 8.44–11.44.

No. 47 Squadron (*KU*).
Command Assignments: India–Burma/Malaya.
Aircraft: FB.VI, 10.44–11.44, 2.45–2.46.

No. 55 Squadron.
Command Assignments: Greece.
Aircraft: FB.XXVI, 7.46–1.11.46.

No. 58 Squadron (*OT*).
Command Assignments: PRU, UK,
10.46 – mid 1953.
Aircraft: PR.34, 10.46–8.52; PR.34A,
10.51–1.54; PR.35, 11.51–4.54.

No. 60 Squadron SAAF.
Command Assignments: PR, Western Desert;
Italy.
Aircraft: Mk II, 2.43–11.43; Mk IV (1), PR IV (1),
PR.IX, 8.43–45.

No. 68 Squadron (*WM*).
Command Assignments: Fighter Command.
Aircraft: NF.XVII, 6.44–4.45; NF.XIX, 7.44–2.45;
NF.XXX, 6.44–20.4.45.

No. 69 Squadron (*WI*).
Command Assignments: BAFO Germany.
Aircraft: FB.VI, 8.45–3.46; B.XVI, 4.46–11.47.

No. 81 Squadron.
Command Assignments: Malaya,
9.46–15.12.55.
Aircraft: PR.XVI, 9.46–9.47; PR.34, 9.46–5.53;
PR.34A, 9.52–1.56.

No. 82 (United Provinces)
Squadron (*UX*).
Command Assignments: India.
Aircraft: FB.VI, 7.44–3.46.

No. 84 Squadron (*PY*).
Command Assignments: India–Malaya.
Aircraft: FB.VI, 2.45–12.46.

No. 85 Squadron (*VY*).
Command Assignments: Fighter Command; 100
Group (Special Duties later Bomber Support).
Aircraft: NF.II, 8.42–5.43; NF.XII, 2.43–2.44;
FB.VI, 8.43–9.43; NF.XV, 3.43–8.43; NF.XVII,
11.43–10.44; NF.XIX, 5.44–12.44; NF.XXX,
9.44–1.46; NF.36, 1.46–11.51.

No. 89 Squadron.
Command Assignments: India.
Aircraft: FB.VI, 2.45–4.46; NF.XIX, 5.45–4.46.

No. 96 Squadron (*ZJ*).
Command Assignments: Fighter Command.
Aircraft: NF.XII, 6–11.43; NF.XIII, 10.43–3.45.

No. 98 Squadron (*VO*).
Command Assignments: 2 Group
9.45–30.4.47; 84 Group, 1.5.47–
Aircraft: B.XVI, 9.45–1.7.48; B.35, 8.48–2.51.

No. 105 Squadron (*GB*).
Command Assignments: 2 Group, 1940–
summer 1943; 8 (PFF) Group –1945.
Aircraft: B.IV, 11.41–3.44; B.IX, 6.43–8.45;
B.XVI, 4.44–1.46.

No.107 Squadron (*OM*).
Command Assignments: 2nd TAF, BAFO Germany.
Aircraft: FB.VI, 2.44–11.48.

No.108 Squadron.
Command Assignments: Malta.
Aircraft: NF.XII, 2.44–7.44; NF.XIII, 4.44–3.7.44.

No. 109 Squadron (*HS*).
Command Assignments: 2 Group; 8 (PFF) Group.
Aircraft: B.IV, 12.42–7.44; B.IX, 4.43–12.45; B.XVI, 10.45–12.48; B.35 48–7.52.

No. 110 (Hyderabad) Squadron (*VE*).
Command Assignments: India–Burma.
Aircraft: FB.VI, 11.44; 1.45–4.46.

No. 114 (Hong Kong) Squadron (*RT*).
Command Assignments: Aden.
Aircraft: FB.VI, 9.45–9.46.

No. 125 (Newfoundland) Squadron (*VA*).
Command Assignments: Fighter Command.
Aircraft: NF.XVII, 2.44–3.45; NF.XXX, 3.45–6.46.

No. 128 (Hyderabad) Squadron (*M5*).
Command Assignments: 8 (PFF) Group, 15.9.44–19.9.45; 2 Group –1.4.46.
Aircraft: B.XX, 9.44–12.44; B.XXV/XVI, 10/11.44–3.45.

No. 139 (Jamaica) Squadron (*XD*).
Command Assignments: 2 Group; 8 (PFF) Group.
Aircraft: B.IV, 10.42–7.44; B.IX, 9.43–9.44; B.XX, 11.43–9.45; B.XVI, 11.44–10.48; B.35, 7.48–12.52.

No. 140 Squadron.
Command Assignments: 2nd TAF; autumn 1943–5.45.
Aircraft: PR.IX, 11.43–7.44; PR.XVI, 12.43–8.45.

No. 141 Squadron (*TW*).
Command Assignments: 11 Group, Fighter Command; 100 Group (Special Duties later Bomber Support), 12.43–1945; Fighter Command, 17.6.46–.
Aircraft: NF.II, 11.43–8.44; FB.VI, 8.44–4.45; NF.XXX, 3.45–9.45; 6.46–8.47; NF.36, 8.47–1.52.

No. 142 Squadron (*4H*).
Command Assignments: 8 (PFF) Group, Light Night Striking Force.
Aircraft: B.XXV, 10.44–9.45.

No. 143 Squadron (*NE*).
Command Assignments: Banff Strike Wing
Aircraft: NF.II, 10.44–11.44; FB.VI, 10.44–6.45.

No. 151 Squadron (*DZ*)
Command Assignments: Fighter Command.
Aircraft: NF.II, 4.42–7.43; XII, 5.43–4.44; FB.VI, 8.43–9.43; NF.XIII, 11.43–9.44; NF.XXX, 8.44–10.46.

No. 157 Squadron (*RS*)
Command Assignments: Fighter Command, 1942–1944; 100 Group (Special Duties later Bomber Support) 5.44–16.8.45.
Aircraft: NF.II, 1.42–6.44; FB.VI, 7.43–4.44; NF.XIX, 5.44–4.45; NF.XXX, 2.45–8.45.

No. 162 Squadron (*CR*)
Command Assignments: 8 Group (PFF).
Aircraft: B.XXV, 12.44–7.46; B.XX, 1945.

No. 163 Squadron.
Command Assignments: 8 (PFF) Group, Light Night Striking Force.
Aircraft: B.XXV/BXVI, 1.45–8.45.

No. 169 Squadron (*VI*).
Command Assignments: Fighter Command, 1.10.43–11.43; 100 Group (Special Duties later Bomber Support), 12.43–10.8.45.
Aircraft: NF.II, 1.44–7.44; FB.VI, 6.44–4.45; NF.XIX, 1.45–8.45.

No. 176 Squadron.
Command Assignments: India.
Aircraft: FB.VI, 6.45–8.45; NF.XIX, 7.45–5.46.

No. 180 Squadron (*EV*).
Command Assignments: BAFO Germany.
Aircraft: B.XVI, 9.45–4.46.

No. 192 Squadron (C Flight) (*DT*).
Command Assignments: ELINT, 100 Group (Special Duties later Bomber Support).
Aircraft: B.IV, 11.42–8.45; B.XVI (six in C Flt only), 3.45–8.45.

No. 199 Squadron.
Command Assignments: 90 Signals Group (Radio Counter Measures).
Aircraft: NF.36, 12.51–3.53.

No. 211 Squadron
Command Assignments: India–Burma–Thailand
Aircraft: FB.VI, 5.45–1.46.

No. 219 (Mysore) Squadron (*FK*).
Command Assignments: 12 Group, Fighter Command, 1944; 2nd TAF, 12.44–8.45; 12 Group, Fighter Command, 8.45–1.9.46; Egypt, 1951–3.53.

Aircraft: NF.II/NF.XVII, 2.44–11.44; NF.XXX, 6.44–9.46; NF.36, 4.51–3.53.

No. 235 Squadron (*LA*).
Command Assignments: Banff Strike Wing.
Aircraft: FB.VI, 6.44–7.45.

No. 239 Squadron (*HB*).
Command Assignments: Fighter Command, 9.43–11.43; 100 Group (Special Duties later Bomber Support), 12.43–1.7.45
Aircraft: NF.II, 12.43–9.44; FB.VI, 12.43–2.45; NF.XXX, 1.45–7.45.

No. 248 Squadron (*DM: WR*).
Command Assignments: Banff Strike Wing.
Aircraft: FB.VI, 12.43–12.45; FB.XVIII, 10.43–1.45.

No. 249 (Gold Coast) Squadron (*GN*).
Command Assignments: Mediterranean/Middle East.
Aircraft: FB.26, 4.46–12.46.

No. 254 Squadron (*QM*).
Command Assignments: North Coates Wing.
Aircraft: Five FB.XVIII *Tsetse* on det. from 618 Squadron, 3.45–11.5.45.

No. 255 Squadron (*YD*).
Command Assignments: Italy.
Aircraft: NF.19, 1.45–4.46; NF.XXX, 4.45–4.46.

No. 256 Squadron (*JT*).
Command Assignments: Italy/Mediterranean.
Aircraft: NF.XII, 4.43–8.43; NF.XIII, 11.43–8.45; NF.XII, 2.45–5.45, FB.VI 4.45–8.45; NF.XIX, 9.45–9.46.

No. 264 (Madras Presidency) Squadron (*PS*).
Command Assignments: Fighter Command. To 141 Wing, 85 (Base) Group 2nd TAF, 19.12.43 (Adminstered as such from 10.3.44); to 148 Wing, 26.6.44; to UK on rest, 23.9.44; 148 Wing, 8.1.45–7.5.45; 12 Group Fighter Command, 20.11.45–51.
Aircraft: NF.II, 5.42–3.43; FB.VI, 8.43–12.43; NF.XIII, 12.43–8.45; NF.XXX, 5.45–3.46; NF.36, 3.46–1.52.

No. 268 Squadron (*EG*).
Command Assignments: 2nd TAF; BAFO Germany, 9.45–3.46.
Aircraft: FB.VI, 9.45–3.46.

No. 305 (Ziemia Wielkopolska) (Polish) (*SM*).
Command Assignments: 138 Wing, 2 Group, 2nd TAF; BAFO Germany.
Aircraft: FB.VI, 12.43–11.46.

No. 307 (Lwow) Squadron (*EW*).
Command Assignments: Fighter Command.
Aircraft: NF.II, 1.43–3.44; FB.VI, 9.43–1.44;
NF.XII, 1.44–4.44; NF.XXX, 10.44–1.47.

No. 333 (Norwegian) Squadron ('B' Flight only) (*KK*).
Command Assignments: Banff Strike Wing.
Aircraft: NFII, 5.43–10.43; FB.VI, 9.43–11.45.

No. 334 (Norwegian) Squadron (*VB*).
Command Assignments: Banff Strike Wing.
Aircraft: FB.VI, 5.45–10.45.

No. 400 Squadron.
Command Assignments: 2nd TAF
(Photo–Reconnaissance)
Aircraft: PR.XVI, 12.43–7.44.

No. 404 ('Buffalo') Squadron RCAF (*EO*).
Command Assignments: Banff Strike Wing.
Aircraft: FB VI, 4.45–5.45.

No. 406 ('Lynx') Squadron RCAF (*HU*).
Command Assignments: Fighter Command; 2nd TAF?
Aircraft: NF.XII, 7.43–12.44; NF.XXX, 7.44–8.45.

No. 409 ('Nighthawk') Squadron RCAF (*KP*).
Command Assignments: Fighter Command; 148 Wing, 85 (Base) Group, 2nd TAF, 30.3.44–1.7.45.
Aircraft: NF.XIII, 3.44–6.45.

No. 410 ('Cougar') Squadron RCAF (*RA*).
Command Assignments: Fighter Command; 141 Wing, 85 Group, 2nd TAF, 12.5.44; 147 Wing, 85 Group, 18.6.44–7.5.45.
Aircraft: NF.II, 10.42–12.43; FB.VI, 7.43–9.43; NF.XIII, 12.43–8.44; NF.XXX, 8.44–6.45.

No. 418 (City of Edmonton) Squadron RCAF (*TH*).
Command Assignments: Fighter Command; 136 Wing, 2nd TAF; 21.11.44–7.9.45.
Aircraft: FB.VI, 5.43–9.45.

No. 456 Squadron RAAF (*RX*).
Command Assignments: 10 Group/11 Group, Fighter Command.
Aircraft: NF.II, 12.42–2.44; FB.VI, 7.43–2.44; NF.XVII, 1.44–12.44; NF.XXX, 12.44–6.45.

No. 464 Squadron RAAF (*SB*).
Command Assignments: 2nd TAF.
Aircraft: FB.VI, 8.43–9.45.

No. 487 Squadron RNZAF (*EG*).
Command Assignments: 2nd TAF.
Aircraft: FB.VI, 8.43–9.45.

No. 488 Squadron (*ME*).
Command Assignments: Fighter Command. 2nd TAF, 4.44–26.4.45; 147 Wing, 85 (Base) Group, 2nd TAF, 12.5.44.
Aircraft: NF.XII, 8.43–5.44; NF.XIII, 10.43–10.44; NF.XXX, 10.44–4.45.

No. 489 Squadron RNZAF (*P6*).
Command Assignments: Banff Strike Wing.
Aircraft: FB.VI, 6.45.

No. 500 (County of Kent) Squadron (*RAA*).
Command Assignments: RAuxAF.
Aircraft: NF.XIX, 3.47–7.48. NF.XXX, 2.47–11.49.

No. 502 (County of Ulster) Squadron (*RAC*).
Command Assignments: RAuxAF.
Aircraft: B.XXV, 7.46–early 1947; NF.XXX, 8.47–6.49.

No. 504 (County of Nottingham) Squadron (*RAD*).
Command Assignments: RAuxAF.
Aircraft: NF.XXX, 5.47–8.48 .

No. 515 Squadron (*3P*).
Command Assignments: 100 Group (Special Duties later Bomber Support), 1.44–10.6.45.
Aircraft: NF.II, 2.44–5.44; FB.VI, 3.44–6.45.

No. 521 Squadron.
Command Assignments: Meteorology.
Aircraft: Mk IV, 8.42–3.43.

No. 527 Squadron (*WN*).
Command Assignments: CSE.
Aircraft: B.35, 9.52–1.56.

No. 540 Squadron (*DH*).
Command Assignments: Reconnaissance.
Aircraft: PR.IV, 10.42–5.43; PR.XI, 6.43–5.44; PR.XVI, 6.44–9.46; PR.34, 12.47–12.52.

No. 544 Squadron.
Command Assignments: Reconnaissance.
Aircraft: PR.IV, 4.43–9.43; PR.IX, 10.43–10.45.

No. 571 Squadron (*8K*).
Command Assignments: 8 (PFF) Group, Light Night Striking Force.
Aircraft: B.XVI, 4.44–9.45; B.IX, 6.44–7.44.

No. 600 (City of London) Squadron (*BQ*).
Command Assignments: Italy.
Aircraft: NF.XIX, 12.44–8.45.

No. 604 (County of Middlesex) Squadron (*NG*).
Command Assignments: Fighter Command; 141 Wing, 2nd TAF, 26.4.44–2.5.44; 147 Wing, 85 (Base) Group, 2nd TAF, until 23.9.44; to UK for rest; 148 Wing, 85 Group, 31.12.44.
Aircraft: NF.XII/XIII, 2.44–4.45.

No. 605 (County of Warwick) Squadron (*UP: RAL*).
Command Assignments: Fighter Command; 136 Wing, 2nd TAF, 21.11.44–31.8.45. RAuxAF, 10.5.46–1948.
Aircraft: NF.II, 2.43–7.43; FB.VI, 7.43–8.45; NF.XIX, 4.47–11.48; NF.XXX, 4.47–1.49.

No. 608 (North Riding) Squadron (*6T: RAO*).
Command Assignments: 8 (PFF) Group, Light Night Striking Force; RAuxAF, 7.46–1948.
Aircraft: B.XX, 8.44–8.45; B.XVI, 3.45–8.45; T.III, 7.46–47; NF.XXX, 7.47–10.48.

No. 609 (West Riding) Squadron (*RAP*).
Command Assignments: RAuxAF.
Aircraft: NF.XXX, 7.46–4.48.

No. 613 (City of Manchester) Squadron (*SY*).
Command Assignments: 2 Group, 2nd TAF.
Aircraft: FB.VI, 10.43–8.45.

No. 616 (South Yorkshire) Squadron (*RAW*).
Command Assignments:
Aircraft: NF.XXX, 11.46–12.48.

No 617 (Dambusters) Squadron.
Command Assignments: 5 Group.
Aircraft: FB.VI/B.XVI, 8.43–1945.

No. 618 Squadron.
Command Assignments: Highball development.
Aircraft: B.IV, 4.43–11.45; B.VI, 7.44–9.44; PR.XVI, 9.44–3.45.

No. 627 Squadron (*AZ*).
Command Assignments: 8 (PFF) Group, 11.43–3.44; 5 Group, 4.44–9.45.
Aircraft: B.IV, 11.43–12.44; B.XVI, 6.44–12.44; B.XX, 8.44–8.45; B.IX, 1.45–8.45.

No. 680 Squadron.
Command Assignments: PR, Middle East/Mediterranean.
Aircraft: PR.IX, 2.44– ; PR.XVI, 2.44–9.46.

No. 681 Squadron.

Command Assignments: PR, India–Burma.
Aircraft: Mk II, 8.43–10.43; Mk VI, 8.43–12.43;
PR.IX, 8.43–12.43.

No. 683 Squadron.

Command Assignments: PR, Middle East.
Aircraft: Mk II/VI, 5.43–7.43.

No. 684 Squadron.

Command Assignments: PR.
Aircraft: Mk II, 11.43–12.43; Mk VI, 11.43–8.44;
PR.IX, 10.43–7.44; PR.XVI, 2.44–2.46; PR.34,
7.45–9.46.

No. 692 (Fellowship of the Bellows) Squadron (*P3*)

Command Assignments: 8 (PFF) Group; Light
Night Striking Force.
Aircraft: B.IV, 1.44–6.44; B.XVI, 5.3.44–9.45.

25 Bomb Group USAAF. (653rd and 654th Squadrons)

Command Assignments: 8th Air Force.
Aircraft: T.III/PR.XVI.

MISCELLANEOUS UNITS

1 PRU
1, 87 and 94 Squadrons RAAF
5 OTU RAAF
13 Squadron RCAF
6, 8, 13, 16, 51, 54, 60 and 132 OTUs
(Operational Training Units)
226, 228, 229, 231 and 237 OCUs
(Operational Conversion Units)
1655 Mosquito Training unit (MTU)
1660 Conversion Unit (CU)
1672 Mosquito Conversion Unit (MCU)
703 RN Squadron
728 Fleet Requirements Unit
762 RN Squadron
771 RN Training Squadron
772 RN Training Squadron
790 RN Squadron
811 RN Training Squadron
1, 3, 3/4, 5, 226, 229, 233, 236, and 238 Civil
Anti-aircraft Co-operation Units (CAACU)
APS Sylt
1300 Flight; 1317 Flight; 1401 Flight; 1409 Flight; 1474 Flight

1692 Bomber Support Training Flight
204 Advanced Flying School
Air Torpedo Development Unit (ATDU)
Armament Practice School (APS)
BSDU (Bomber Support Development Unit)
Bomber Development Unit
Bombing Trials Unit
Central Bomber Establishment
Central Gunnery School
Central Fighter Establishment
Central Signals Establishment
Empire Air Armament School (EAAS)
Empire Test Pilots School
Fighter Interception Unit (FIU)
Signals Flying Unit
Special Installation Unit
Night Fighter Development Wing
Photographic Development Unit
Pathfinder Navigation Training Unit (PFFNTU)
Special Installation Unit
Special Flying Unit

Mosquito Air-to-Air Victories 1942–April 1945

DATE	TYPE	SERIAL	SQN	ENEMY A/C	DETAILS	PILOT-NAVIGATOR/RADAR OP
29/30.5.42	II	W4099	157 Sqn	Do 217E-4	S of Dover	S/L C. Ashfield (Do 217E-4 of *KG2*)
29/30.5.42	II	DD608	151 Sqn	Do 217E-4	(*prob*) North Sea	P/O J. A. Wain-F/Sgt T. S. G. Grieve (Do 217E-4 of *KG2*)
28/29.6.42	II		264 Sqn	Do 217E-2	over Creil	F/O Hodgkinson (Uffz Rudolf Blankenburg, *KG2*)
24/25.6.42	II	W4097	151 Sqn	2 x Do 217E-4	The Wash	W/C I. S. Smith DFC-F/L Kernon-Sheppard (Do 217E-4 5454 of *II/KG40* and Do 217E-4 of *I/KG2*)
25/26.6.42	II	DD616	151 Sqn	He 111 H-6	N Sea	P/O J. A. Wain-F/Sgt T. S. G. Grieve
26/27.6.42	II	DD609	151 Sqn	Do 217E-4	N Sea	F/L Moody-P/O Marsh (Do 217E-4 U5+ML of *3./KG2*, flown by Fw Hans Schrödel)
6/7.7.42	II	DD670 'S'	23 Sqn	Do 217	16mls E Chartres	W/C B. R. O'B. Hoare DFC*-P/O S. J. Cornes
8/9.7.42	II	DD670 'S'	23 Sqn	Do 217	Étampes/He 111 Évreux	S/L K. H. Salisbury-Hughes
21/22.7.42	II	W4090	151 Sqn	Do 217E-4	off Spurn Head	P/O Fisher (Ofw Heinrich Wolpers and crew, Do 217E-4 U5+IH *3./KG2*)
27/28.7.42	IIs	DD629 & DD608	151 Sqn	2 x Do 217E-4	N Sea	S/L Pennington and P/O Fielding. (Fw Richard Stumpf of *I/KG2* and Lt Hans-Joachim Mohring of *3./KG2*)
27/28.7.42	II	W4099	157 Sqn	He 111	N Sea	S/L G. Ashfield
29/30.7.42	II	DD669	151 Sqn	Do 217E-4	N Sea	F/O A. I. McRitchie-F/Sgt E. S. James (Do 217E-4 U5+GV, flown by Ofw Artur Hartwig of *II/KG2*)
30/31.7.42	II	DD670 'S'	23 Sqn	UEA	Orleans	W/C B. R. O'B. Hoare DFC*-W/O J. F. Potter.
30/31.7.42	II	DD639	264 Sqn	Ju 88A-4	N Malvern Wells	S/L C. A. Cook-P/O R. E. MacPherson (Ju 88A-4 of *KüFlGr 106*)
22/23.8.42	II	DD612	157 Sqn	Do 217E-4	Worlingworth	W/C Gordon Slade-P/O P. V. Truscott (Do 217E-4 U5+LP of *6./KG2*, flown by 29-year-old ex-*Lufthansa* pilot Oblt Hans Walter Wolff, Deputy *Staffelkapitan*)
8/9.9.42	II	DD669	151 Sqn	Do 217E-4	Orwell, Cambs	F/O A. I. McRitchie-F/Sgt E. S. James (Do 217E-4 F8+AP, on loan to *3./KG2* and piloted by Fw Alfred Witting)
10/11.9.42	II	'B'	23 Sqn	UEA	12mls S Enschede	W/C B. R. O'B. Hoare DFC*-W/O J. F. Potter
17/18.9.42	II	DD610	151 Sqn	Do 217E-4	Cr Docking	F/L H. E. Bodien DFC-Sgt G. B. Brooker (U5+UR of *7./KG2* piloted by Fw Franz Elias cr at Fring. All four crew PoW)
30.9.42	II	DD607	157 Sqn	Ju 88A-4	30mls off Dutch coast	W/C R. F. H. Clerke
26.10.42	II	DD716	157 Sqn	Ju 88D-1	off Beachy Head	F/O E. H. Cave
7/8.1.43	II		23 Sqn	Ju 88 of *II/KG30*	Comiso	W/C N. J. Starr DFC
15/16.1.43	II	DD609	151 Sqn	Do 217E-4	Cr Boothby Graffoe	Sgt E. A. Knight RCAF-Sgt W. I. L. Roberts (Do 217E-4 U5+KR of *7./KG2*. Lt Günter Wolf, pilot, Uffz Helmut Knorr, Uffz Kurt Semitschka, dorsal gunner, and Ogfr Karl-Heinz Krusewitz) all KIA
17/18.1.43	II	VY-V	85 Sqn	Ju 88A-14	SE England	W/C G. L. Raphael DFC*-W/O W. N. Addison DFM (Ju 88A-14 of *IV/KG3* or *III/KG6*)
22.1.43	II	HJ929	410 Sqn	Do 2l7E-1 (*prob*) Ju 88 of *II/LG1*)		W/C P. G. Wykeham-Barnes DSO DFC*-F/O G. E. Palmer DFC
7/8.3.43	II		23 Sqn	Ju 88	Catania	W/C P. G. Wykeham-Barnes DSO DFC*-F/O G. E. Palmer DFC (Ju 88 of *II/LG1*)
18/19.3.43	II	W4099	157 Sqn	Ju 88A-14	off Harwich	F/O G. Deakin-P/O de Costa
18/19.3.43	II	HK936	410 Sqn	Do 217E8-4	King's Lynn	F/O D. Williams-P/O P. Dalton (Do 217 U5+AH Werke No 5523 of *I/KG2* flown by Uffz Horst Toifel, Uffz Heinrich Peter, gunner, Ludwig Petzold radio operator, Ogfr Georg Riedel, observer)
28/29.3.43	II	W4079	157 Sqn	Do 217E-4	off Southwold	F/O J. R. Beckett-F/Sgt Phillips (Do 217E-4 U5+NM W/Nr 4375 of *4./KG2*, flown by Fw Paul Huth. Huth, Uffz Werner Hans Burschel, dorsal gunner, Oblt Gottfried Thorley, observer, and Uffz Konrad Schuller, radio operator, all KIA. Victory shared with a 68 Squadron Beaufighter piloted by F/O Vopalecky and F/Sgt Husar; both Czech)
30.3.43	II		264 Sqn	He 111	8mls N Redon	S/L M. H. Constable-Maxwell
9/10.4.43	II		23 Sqn	Ju 88	Catania	W/C P. G. Wykeham-Barnes DSC DFC*-F/O G. E. Palmer DFC. Ju 88 of *III/KG76*
13/14.4.43	II	DZ243	157 Sqn	Do 217E-4		
14/15.4.43	XII	VY-F	85 Sqn	Do 217E-4	Clacton-on-Sea	S/L W. P. Green-F/Sgt A. R. Grimstone (Do 217E-4 F8+AM of *4./KG40*)
14/15.4 .43	XII	VY-G	85 Sqn	Do 217E-4	Clacton-on-Sea	F/L G. L. Howitt-F/O G. Irving (Do 217E-4 U5+DP of *6./KG2* flown by Uffz Franz Tannenberger)
14/15.4.43	II	DD730	157 Sqn	Do 217E-4	SW Colchester	F/L J. G. Benson DFC-F/L L. Brandon DFC (Dornier 217E-4 U5+KP of *6./KG2*. Uffz Walter Schmurr, pilot; Lt Karl-Heinrich Hertam, observer and Uffz Martin Sehwarz, gunner, bailed out. Uffz Franz Witte, radio operator-gunner found dead in the wreckage.
24/25.4.43	XII		85 Sqn	Ju 88	nr Bromley, Kent	F/O J. P. M. Lintott-Sgt G. G. Gilling-Lax (Ju 88A-14 3E+HS of *8./KG6* disintegrated in the air and the wreckage fell in Bromley, Kent)
4/5.5.43	II		605 Sqn	Do 217K1 x 2	Eindhoven	F/O B. Williams-P/O D. Moore (Do 217K-I U5+AA W/Nr 4415 of *6./KG2*. Lt Ernst Andres, pilot, seriously injured, Maj Walter Bradel, *Kommodore* of *KG2* KIA in the crash at Landsmere, near Amsterdam. Flg Wernerker also killed, although may have died in the Mosquito attack and rest of crew injured. All recovered, Andres promoted to Oblt and receiving the *Ritterkreuz* 20 April 1944. KIA with *5./NJG4* 11 February 1945)

DATE	TYPE	SERIAL	SQN	ENEMY A/C	DETAILS	PILOT-NAVIGATOR/RADAR OP
13/14.5.43	II		157 Sqn	Do 217E-4	10mls NE Colchester	P/O R. Watts-Sgt J. Whewell. Do 217E-4 of II/KG2 intercepted by Watts and Whewell and shot down after an exchange of fire. A fire started in the Dornier's starboard engine and it crashed about 10 mls NE of Colchester at 0207 hrs. (Near Norwich, a Do 217K-1 of 4./KG2 flown by Uffz Erhard Corty was claimed at about 0250 hrs. 157 Squadron shot down two Do 217E-4s of KG2 piloted by Lt Stefan Szamek and Lt Gerd Strufe)
16/17.5.43	XII	'A'	85 Sqn	Fw 190A-4/U-8	nr Dover	S/L W. P. Green-F/Sgt A. Grimstone
16/17.5.43	XII	'G'	85 Sqn	Fw 190A-4/U-8	15mls S Hastings	F/L G. L. Howitt-F/O G. Irving
16/17.5.43	XII	'L'	85 Sqn	Fw 190A-4/U-8	Dover Straits	F/O B. J. Thwaites-P/O W. P. Clemo DFM*
16/17.5.43	XII	'L'	85 Sqn	Fw 190A-4/U-8 (prob)		F/O B. J. Thwaites-P/O W. P. Clemo DFM*
16/17.5.43	XII	'D'	85 Sqn	Fw 190A-4/U-8	off Gravesend	F/O J. D. Shaw-P/O A. C. Lowton
18/19.5.43	XII	'Z'	85 Sqn	Fw 190A-5	Kent	F/O J. P. M. Lintott-Sgt G. G. Gilling-Lax
21/22.5.43	XII	'V'	85 Sqn	Fw 190A	25mls NW Hardelot	S/L E. Crew DFC*-F/O F. French
29/30.5.43	XII	'S'	85 Sqn	Ju 88A-14	Isfield nr Lewes	F/O J. P. M. Lintott-Sgt G. G. Gilling-Lax (3Z+SZ of I/KG66)
5.6.43	XII		29 Sqn	Ju 88A-14	off Ostend	
11.6.43	XII		256 Sqn	Do 217	S of Ford	F/O Burnett
11.6.43	II		25 Sqn	Ju 88	Bay of Biscay	F/L J. Singleton-F/O W. G. Haslam
13/14.6.43	XII	DZ302 'R'	85 Sqn	Fw 190A-5	Wrotham	W/C J. Cunningham DSO* DFC*-F/L C. F. Rawnsley DFC DFM* (Cunningham, CO 85 Squadron, who had shot down 16 enemy aircraft while flying Beaufighters, pursued Fw 190A-5 CO+LT of 3./SKG10 flown by Lt Ullrich over his own airfield and shot it down. Fw 190 crashed at Nettlefold Farm, Borough Green near Wrotham but incredibly, Ullrich had been catapulted through the canopy in the death dive of the aircraft and he was taken prisoner)
14/15.6.43	XVII	HK315	219 Sqn	Ju 88	Harwich area	F/L M. J. Gloster DFC-F/L J. F. Oswold DFC
17/18.6.43	XII		85 Sqn	Fw 190 (prob)		Lt Räd RNWAF
19.6.43	II		151 Sqn	Ju 88	Bay of Biscay	F/L H. E. Bodien DFC
21/22.6.43	XII	'E'	85 Sqn	Fw 190	River Medway	F/L W. H. Maguire-F/O W. D. Jones (Fw 190GP+LA of 2./SKG 10)
2/3.7.43	XII	HK166	FIU	Ju 88D-1	45mls S Bognor	W/C R. A. Chisholm DFC-F/O N. L. Bamford DFC
3/4.7.43	II	DD739	157 Sqn	Do 217	St Trond	F/L J.G. Benson DFC-F/L L. Brandon DFC
9.7.43	XII	'Z'	85 Sqn	Do 217K-1	nr Detling	F/O J. P. M. Lintott-Sgt G. G. Gilllng-Lax (Lintott's 4th victory: Do 217K-1 U5+FP, piloted by Oblt Hermann Zink of 6./KG2. Zink and his crew were all KIA. The GCI controller who had put Lintott onto the raider saw two blips on his CRT merge and stay together for 7 minutes: then they had faded. 2 mls from where the Dornier fell the Mosquito crew were also found dead in the wreckage of their aircraft)
11/12.7.43	II	HJ944	410 Sqn	Do 217	10mls E Humber	S/L A. G. Lawrence DFC RCAF-F/Sgt H. J. Wilmer DFM
13/14.7.43	XII	'T'	85 Sqn	Me 410A-1	off Felixstowe	F/L E. N. Bunting-F/O F. French (Me 410A-1 U5+KG flown by Fw Franz Zwißler (pilot) and Ofw Leo Raida (bordfunker) of 16./KG2. Bunting closed to within 200 yds but the Mosquito got caught in the Germans' slipstream and he could not aim his guns. Diving below and closing in again before firing two short bursts, the Me 410 burst into flames at once and fell into the sea 5 mls off Felixstowe. First Me 410 shot down over Britain.
13/14.7.43	II	HJ944	410 Sqn (RCAF)	Do 217	off Humber Estuary	(Do 217M-I, U5+EL of 3./KG2, flown by Uffz Willy Spielmanns)
13/14.7.43	II		605 Sqn	Do 217M-1	nr Eindhoven	F/O R. R Smart-F/O J. K. Sutcliffe on Intruder over Holland. (Do 217M-1 U5+CK of 2./KG2. Uffz Hauck and his crew cr in vicinity of Eindhoven)
15/16.7.43	XII	'G'	85 Sqn	Me 410 A-1	off Dunkirk	F/L B. J. Thwaites-P/O W. P. Clemo DFM* (Me 410 U5+CJ of V/KG2. Hptm Friederich-Wilhelm Methner (P) and Uffz Hubert Grube)
18.7.43	XII		256 Sqn	Fw 190	Channel	
25/26.7.43	II		605 Sqn	Do 217M-1	Soesterberg	F/L C. Knowles-F/O A. Eagling (Do 217M-1 U5+KL flown by Lt Manfred Lieddert of 3./KG2)
26/27.7.43	XII	VY-A	85 Sqn	Ju 88	25mls E Ramsgate	S/L W. P. Green DFC-F/Sgt A. R. Grimstone DFM
29/30.7.43	XII		256 Sqn	Me 410A-1	20mls S Beachy Head	W/C G. R. Park (Me 410A-1 U5+BJ of V/KG2. Oblt Helmut Biermann and Uffz Willi Kroger fell into the sea 20 mls S of Beachy Head)
15/16.8.43	XII		256 Sqn	2 x Do 217M-1	30mls SE Selsey	W/C G. R. Park (Uffzs Karl Morgenstern and Franz Bundgens' Do 217M-Is of KG2 in the sea off Worthing. Park's third claim (Uffz Walter Kayser's Do 217M-I) amended to 'damaged')
15/16.8.43	XII		256 Sqn	2 x Do 217M-1	France	F/Sgt Brearley (Fw Theodor Esslinger fell near Evreux and Lt Franz Bosbach crashed near St André)
15/16.8.43	VI	HP849	410 Sqn	Do 217M	17mls off Beachy Hd	P/O R. D. Schultz-F/O V. A. Williams (Do 217M-1 U5+GT of 9./KG2 flown by Uffz Josef Schultes and crew, all KIA)
17/18.8.43	VI	'O'	605 Sqn	Bf 109	E Schleswig	F/L D. H. Blomely-F/O R. 'Jock' Birrel
22/23.8.43	XII	'V'	85 Sqn	Me 410A-1	Chelmondiston	S/L G. E. Howitt DFC-P/O J. C. O. Medworth (Me 410A-1, U5+AF of 15./KG2 crewed by Fw Walter Hartmann and Obgefr Michael Meurer. Meurer bailed out and came down at Stratton Hall. Hartman's body later found in a field - parachute unopened)
22/23.8.43	XII	'R'	85 Sqn	Fw 190	nr Dunkirk	
22/23.8.43	XII	HK197	29 Sqn	Me 410A-1	E of Manston	F/L C. Kirkland-P/O R. C. Raspin
22/23.8.43	XII	HK175	29 Sqn	Me 410A-1	nr Dunkirk	
22/23.8.43	XII	HK164	29 Sqn	Me 410A-1	N of Knocke	
23/24.8.43	XII	DZ302 'R'	85 Sqn	Fw 190	off Dunkirk	W/C J. Cunningham DSO* DFC*-F/L C. F. Rawnsley DFC DFM*
24/25.8.43	XII	'G'	85 Sqn	Me 410A-1		Capt J. Räd RNWAF-Capt L. Lövestad RNWAF DFM* (Me 410A-1 U5+EG of 16./KG2, flown by Fw Werner Benner with Uffz Hermann Reimers). Victory was officially shared with W/C R. E. X. Mack DFC in a XII of 29 Sqn
6/7.9.43	XII	'K'	85 Sqn	Fw 190A-5	France	
6/7.9.43	II	'V'	85 Sqn	Fw 190A-5	3mls E Clacton	S/L G. E. Howitt DFC-F/L C. Irving DFC

DATE	TYPE	SERIAL	SQN	ENEMY A/C	DETAILS	PILOT-NAVIGATOR/RADAR OP
8/9.9.43	XV	DZ302 'R'	85 Sqn	Fw 190A-5	off Aldborough	W/C J. Cunningham DSO* DFC*-F/L C. F. Rawnsley DFC DFM*
8/9.9.43	XII	'L'	85 Sqn	2 x Fw 190A-5 of I/SKG10	off N Foreland	F/L B. J. Thwaites-P/O W. P. Clemo DFM*
15/16.9.43	XII	'T'?	85 Sqn	Ju 88A-14	Tenterden	F/O E. R. Hedgecoe-P/O J. R. Witham (Ju 88A-14 3E+FP of 6./KG6. Mosquito was crippled by return fire and the crew bailed out, their aircraft crashing at Tenterden, Kent)
15/16.9.43	XII	'T'?	85 Sqn	Ju 88A-14	off Boulogne	F/L E. N. Bunting-F/O F. French (Ju 88A-14 of II/KG6)
15/16.9.43	XII	HK204	488 Sqn	Do 217M	E of Foreness	F/L Watts (9./KG2 Do 217M-1, flown by Ofw Erich Mosler shot down into the sea SE of Ramsgate)
15/16.9.43	XII	HK203	488 Sqn	He 111	North of Bradwell	
15/16.9.43	XII	HK189	29 Sqn	Me 410	off Beachy Head	F/O Jarris. (Ofw Horst Muller and Uffz Wolfgang Dose in Me 410A-1 U5+AF of 15./KG2 during a raid on Cambridge)
21.9.43	VI	'C'	605 Sqn	2 x Ju 88	W Skaggerak	S/L D. H. Blomely-F/O R. 'Jock' Birrel
22.9.43	XI		85 Sqn	Me 410	off Orfordness	
26.9.43	II	DZ757	410 Sqn	Do 217	Dutch coast	F/L W. A. Cybulski DFC-F/O H. H. Ladbrook DFC
27/28.9.43	VI	'R'	605 Sqn	Do 217	Dedelsdorf	W/C B. R. O'B. Hoare DSO DFC*-W/C J. F. Potter
2/3.10.43	XII		85 Sqn	2 x Do 217K	off Humber Est.	P/O T. Weisteen RNWAF-F/O F. French
6.10.43	XII		488 Sqn	Do 217M-1	Canterbury	
7/8.10.43	II	DZ260	157 Sqn	Me 410A-1 (Dam?)	off Shoeburyness	F/Sgt Robertson
7/8.10.43	XII	'E'	85 Sqn	Me 410A-1	15mls off Hastings	F/L W. H. Maguire-Capt L. Lövestad RNWAF. (Me 410A flown by Fw Georg Slodczyk and Uffz Fritz Westrich of 16./KG2. (Westrich's body was picked up off Dungeness on 13 October and buried at sea)
7/8.10.43	XII		85 Sqn	Me 410A-1		F/L B. J. Thwaites-P/O W. P. Clemo. (Me 410A flown by Fw Wilhelm Sohn and Uffz Günther Keiser of 14./KG2, which crashed at Ghent)
8/9.10.43	XII		85 Sqn	Ju 88S-1	off Foulness	F/O S. V. Holloway-W/O Stanton (Ju 88S-1 3E+US of 8./KG6)
8/9.10.43	XII		85 Sqn	Ju 88S-1	10mls S Dover	F/L E. N. Bunting-F/O F. French (Ju 88S-1 3E+NR of 7./KG6 into the sea 10 miles S of Dover at 2020 hrs; Fw W. Kaltwasser, Obgefr J. Jakobsen and Uffz J. Bartmuss KIA)
12.10.43	XII		151 Sqn	Me 410	NE of Cromer	
15/16.10.43	XII	'K'	85 Sqn	Ju 188E	Birchington	F/O H. B. Thomas-W/O C. B. Hamilton
15/16.10.43	XII	'E'	85 Sqn	Ju 188E-1	Hemley, Suffolk	F/L W. H. Maguire-F/O W. D. Jones (Ju 188 3E+BL of 1./KG6, the first Ju 188 down on land in the UK)
15/16.10.43	XII	'E'	85 Sqn	Ju 188E-1	S of Clacton	F/L W. Maguire-F/O W. D. Jones (Ju 188 3E+RH of 1./KG6)
17/18.10.43	XII	'V'	85 Sqn	Me 410A-1	Hornchurch/Little Warley	F/L E. N. Bunting-F/O F. French (Me 410 U5+LF of 15./KG2 flown by Ofw Lothar Bleich FF (pilot) (k) and Uffz Ernst Greiecker (inj))
20.10.43	XII		29 Sqn	Fw 190A-1	S of Beachy Head	
20.10.43	XII		29 Sqn	Me 410A-1	over Channel	
22.10.43	XII		29 Sqn	Fw 190A	E of Beachy Head	
20/21.10.43	XII	HK163	29 Sqn	Me 210 (prob)	Dungeness-Ashford	F/L R. C. Pargeter-F/L R. L. Fell.
30/31.10.43	XII	'G'	85 Sqn	Ju 88S-1	20mls SE of Rye	F/L R. L. T. Robb-F/O R. C. J. Bray. (Ju 88S of III./KG6 either WNr 1404853E+KS, or W/Nr 140585 3E+AS)
30/31.10.43	XII	'J'	85 Sqn	Ju 88S-I	20mls S of Shoreham	F/O H. B. Thomas-W/O C. B. Hamilton
1.11.43	XII		29 Sqn	Ju 88S-1?	nr Andover	
2/3.11.43	XII	'K'	85 Sqn	Fw 190	S of Canvey Island	F/O E. R. Hedgecoe-P/O J. R. Witham
5/6.11.43	II	HJ917	410 Sqn	Me 410	10mls S of Dungeness	F/O C. F. Green-P/O E. G. White
6/7.11.43	XII	'W'	85 Sqn	Fw 190A	2–3mls S of Hastings	
8/9.11.43	XII	HK163	29 Sqn	Me 410A-1	nr Beachy Head	F/O Russell-Steward-F/O G. K. Main
8/9.11.43	XII	'E'	85 Sqn	Me 410A-1	nr Eastbourne	S/L W. H. Maguire DFC-F/O W. D. Jones. (WNr 10244 U5+BF of 15./KG2. Major Wilhelm Schmitter, Ritterkreuz mit Eichenlaub (Knight's Cross with Oak leaves), and his bordfunker, Uffz Felix Hainzinger, both killed when the a/c crashed into Shinewater Marsh)
8/9.11.43	XIII	HK367	488 Sqn	Me 410A-1	off Clacton	F/O Reed-P/O Bricker
9.11.43	VI	'O'	605 Sqn	Bf 110	20mls W Aalborg	F/L D. H. Blomely DFC- R. 'Jock' Birrel
18/19.11.43	II	HJ705	FIU	Bf 110	Mannheim	W/C R. A. Chisholm DFC-F/L P. C. Clarke
20.11.43	II		157 Sqn	Ju 290	8mls N Estaca Point	W/C J. A. Mackie-F/O L. Scholefield
20.11.43	II		157 Sqn	Ju 88 (prob)	15-40mls N Cape Ortegal	F/L Dyke-W/O C. R. Aindow
20/21.11.43	XIII	HK403	29 Sqn	Fw 190	Broadbridge Heath	F/L R. C. Pargeter-F/L R. L. Fell
20/21.11.43	XII	HK177	151 Sqn	Me 410	off Esparto Point	
22.11.43	II	HJ651	307 Sqn	Fw 200	120mls NE Shetlands	F/Sgt Jaworski
25/26.11.43	XII	HK228	488 Sqn	Me 410	off Calais	F/L P. F. L. Hall-F/O R. D. Marriott
9.12.43	II	EW-R	307 Sqn	Ju 88D-1		
10/11.12.43	II	DZ29	410 Sqn	3 x Do 217M-1	Clacton-Dunkirk	F/O R. D. Schultz-F/O V. A. Williams (Do 217Ms of KG2)
10/11.12.43	II	HJ944	410 Sqn	Do 217	nr Chelmsford	
19/20.12.43	XIII	HK457	488 Sqn	Me 410A-1	nr Rye	P/O D.N. Robinson RNZAF
20/21.12.43	VI		418 Sqn	UEA	Delune a/f nr Metz	P/O J. T. Caine RCAF-P/O E. W. Boal RCAF
22/23.12.43	VI	HX812 'T'	418 Sqn	UEA (prob)	Orleans a/f	F/L D. A. MacFadyen RCAF-F/L Wright
23/24.12.43	VI	'H'	605 Sqn	UEA	Fassberg airfield	F/L A. D. Wagner DFC-P/O E. T. 'Pip' Orringe
2.1.44	XIII	HK461	488 Sqn	Me 410	Straits of Dover	
2/3.1.44	XIII	HK374	85 Sqn	Me 410	Sandwich	W/C J. Cunningham DSO* DFC*-F/L C. F. Rawnsley DFC DFM*
2/3.I.44	II		96 Sqn	Fw 190	Rye	F/L N. S. Head-F/O A. C. Andrews
4/5.1.44	XII		85 Sqn	Ju 88	off Dieppe	F/O E. R. Hedgecoe-P/O J. R. Witham DFM*"
4/5.1.44	XIII		96 Sqn	Ju 188-1	3mls S of Hastings	W/C E. D. Crew DFC-W/O W. R. Croysdill
10/11.1	VI	'E'	605 Sqn	Ju 188	4mls E Chieves	W/C B. R. O'B. Hoare DSO DFC*-W/O J. F. Potter
15/16.1.44	XIII		96 Sqn	Fw 190	Dungeness	S/L A. Parker-Rees-F/L Bennett
21/22.1.44	XII	HK197	29 Sqn	Fw 190	S of Beachy Head	
21/22.1.44	XII	HK168	29 Sqn	Ju 88	S of Beachy Head	
21/22.1.44	XII	'N'	85 Sqn	Ju 88	off Rye	
21/22.1.44	XIII	HK414	96 Sqn	Ju 88	Paddock Wood Stn	Sub-Lt J. A. Lawley-Wakelin-Sub-Lt H. Williams
21/22.1.44	XIII	HK372	96 Sqn	2 x Ju 88 (prob)	S of Bexhill	F/L N. S. Head-F/O A. C. Andrews

DATE	TYPE	SERIAL	SQN	ENEMY A/C	DETAILS	PILOT-NAVIGATOR/RADAR OP
21/22.1.44	XII	HK193	151 Sqn	He 177A-3	nr Hindhead	W/O H. K. Kemp-F/Sgt J. R. Maidment. (He 177A-5 Werk Nr 15747 of I/KG40, first He 177 to be shot down over British Isles, crashing at Whitmore Vale, nr Hindhead, Surrey. Only tail assembly about 3ft forward of the fin survived relatively undamaged)
21/22.1.44	XIII	HK425	96 Sqn	Ju 88	Tonbridge	
21/22.1.44	XI		85 Sqn	He 177A-3	6mls SE of Hastings	F/O C. K. Nowell-F/Sgt F. Randall (He 177 of 2./KG40)
21/22.1.44	XIII	HK380/Y	488 Sqn	Do 217M-1	13mls off Dungeness	F/L J. A. S. Hall-F/O J. P. W. Cairns
21/22.1.44	XIII	HK380/Y	488 Sqn	Ju 88A-14	Sellindge, Kent	F/L J. A. S. Hall-F/O J. P. W. Cairns
21/22.1.44	VI	'D'	418 Sqn	Bf 110	20mls SW Wunsdorf	I/Lt J. F. Luma US-F/O A. Eckert
27.1.44	VI		418 Sqn	Ju 88	Clermont-Ferrand a/f	F/L J. R. F. Johnson RCAF
27.1.44	VI		418 Sqn	Ju W34 x 2	10mls SE Bourges	F/L J. R. F. Johnson RCAF
27.1.44	VI		418 Sqn	Ju 88	Clermont-Ferrand a/f	P/O J. T. Caine RCAF-P/O E. W. Boal RCAF
27.1.44	VI		418 Sqn	Ju W34 x 2	10mls SE Bourges	P/O J. T. Caine RCAF-P/O E. W. Boal RCAF
27.1.44	VI	'R'	418 Sqn	Fw 200	SE Avord a/f	F/L C. C. Scherf RAAF
28/29.1.44	XIII	HK432	410 Sqn	Ju 88		
28/29.1.44	XIII	HK397	96 Sqn	Ju 88	nr Biddenden	F/O S. A. Hibbert-F/O G. D. Moody
28/29.1.44	II	HJ941 'X'	141 Sqn	Bf 109	nr Berlin	F/O H. E. White DFC-F/O M. S. Allen DFC
28/29.1.44	II	HJ644	239 Sqn	Bf 110	nr Berlin	F/O N. Munro-F/O A. R. Hurley
30/31.1.44	II	HJ712 'R'	141 Sqn	Bf 110	nr Berlin	F/L G. J. Rice-F/O J. G. Rogerson
30/31.1.44	II	HJ711 'P'	169 Sqn	Bf 110	Brandenburg area	S/L A. H. Cooper-F/L R. D. Connolly. (Bf 110G-4 W/Nr 740081 D5+LB of Stab III/NJG3, which cr at Werneuch-en, 20 km E of Berlin. Oblt Karl Loeffelmaan (p) KIA. Fw Karl Bareiss (radar op and Ofw Oscar Bickert, both WIA, bailed out)
3/4.2.44	XIII	'P'	85 Sqn	Do 217	20mls E The Naze	F/O H. B. Thomas-W/O C. B. Hamilton
3/4.2.44	XIII		410 Sqn	Do 217		F/O E. S. P. Fox RCAF-F/O C. D. Sibett RCAF
3/4.2.44	XIII	HK463	410 Sqn	Do 217	off Orfordness	
3/4.2.44	XIII	HK367	488 Sqn	Do 217	off Foulness Point	F/Sgt C. J. Vlotman-Sgt J. L. Wood
4/5.2.44	VI		605 Sqn	UEA (prob)	Chièvres	W/C B. R. O'B. Hoare DSO DFC*-W/O J. F. Potter
5/6.2.44	II	HJ707 'B'	169 Sqn	Bf 110	North Sea off England	P/O W. H. Miller-P/O F. C. Bone
8.2.44	II		157 Sqn	Bv 222	Lake Biscarosse	S/L H. E. Tappin DFC-F/O I. H. Thomas
12.2.44	II	687 'A'	157 Sqn	Fw 200	on Instep Criegal	F/O R. D. Doleman-F/L J. S. V. McAllister DFM
12/13.2.44			29 Sqn	Me 410	off Fécamp	
13.2.44	VI	'X'	418 Sqn	He 177	3mls S Bordeaux	1/Lt J. F. Luma US-F/O C. Finlayson
13/14.2.44	XIII	HK426	96 Sqn	Ju 188	nr Whitstable	W/C E. D. Crew-W/O W. R. Croysdill
13/14.2.44	XIII	HK466	410 Sqn (RCAF)	Ju 88S-1	nr Romford	S/L J. D. Somerville-F/O G. D. Robinson. (Ju 88S-1 Z6+HH of I/KG66)
13/14.2.44	XIII	HK429	410 Sqn	Ju 188	10–20mls off E Anglia	F/O R. D. Schultz-F/O V. A. Williams
15/16.2.44	II	DZ726 'Z'	141 Sqn	He 177	Berlin	F/O H. E. White-F/O M. Allen
18/19.2.44	VI	'S'	605 Sqn	Ju 188	Brussels-Melsbroek	F/O I. Williams-F/O F. Hogg
18/19.2.44	VI		418 Sqn	2 x Me 410	Juvincourt a/f	S/L R. A. Kipp DFC RCAF-F/L P. Huletsky RCAF
19.2.44	II		157 Sqn	Ju 290	Instep patrol	F/L R. J. Coombs-F/O G. H. Scobie-F/L R. D. Doleman-F/L L. Scholefield
19/20.2.44	XIII	HK396	96 Sqn	Me 410	S of Dungeness	
20/21.2.44	II	DZ270	239 Sqn	Bf 110	nr Stuttgart	F/O T. Knight-F/O D. P. Doyle
20/21.2.44	XVII	HK285	25 Sqn	Ju 188	E Essex	P/O J. R. Brockbank-P/O D. McCausland. (Ju 188E-1 U5+LN flown by Lt Ewald Bohe of 5/KG2, which, blazing curiously, commenced a deep death dive through the clouds to crash at Park Farm, Wickham St Paul, Essex. The time of the 'kill', 2203 hrs, was logged; the first 'kill' attributed to a Mosquito NFXVII. Bohe, Ofw Karl Bittgen (BO), Uffz Günther Güldner (BF) Uffz Wilhelm Pyttel (BM) and Gftr Hugo Schweitzer (BS) KIA)
20/21.2.44	XVII	HK255	25 Sqn	Do 217K-10	50mls E Lowestoft	F/L J. Singleton DFC-F/O W. G. Haslam. (Victim either Do 217K-1 U5+AR of 7./KG2, which was shot down at 2236 hrs Oblt Wolfgang Brendel, Fw Bruno Preker, Ofw Bruno Schneider and Uffz Heinz Grudßus all posted as 'Missing'. Or, Do 217M1 of 9.KG2. Uffz Walter Schmidt, (pilot) Uffz Fritz Frese, Ogfr Siegfried Briesning and Ogfr Heinz Bodzien (all KIA)
20/21.2.44	XVII		85 Sqn	Ju 188 (prob)	Lydd	S/L B. J. Thwaites DFC-F/O W. P. Clemo DFM*
22/23.2.44	XVII	HK285	25 Sqn	He 177A-3	nr Yoxford	F/L W. Baillie-F/O Simpson. (He 177A-3 of 3./KG100. Ofw Wolfgang Ruppe fflugzeugfuhrer (pilot), Uffz Ernst Werner bordschutze (gunner), Uffz Friedrich Beck, bordfunker (radio operator) Uffz Georg Lobenz, kampf beobachter (observer), Bordschutzen Obgefr Georg Markgraf, and Obgefr Bordwart (ground crew) KIA. Emil Imm, heck schutz (tail gunner) survived).
22/23.2.44	XVII	'Y'	85 Sqn	Me 410	off Dungeness	F/L B. Burbridge-F/L F. S. Skelton
22/23.2.44	XVII		85 Sqn	Me 410	35mls S Dungeness	F/O E. R. Hedgecoe-P/O J. R. Witham
22/23.2.44	XIII	HK370	96 Sqn	Me 410	W Uckfield	S/L G. L. Caldwell-F/O Rawling
22/23.2.44	XIII	HK521	410 Sqn	Ju 88A-4	N Sea	S/L C. A. S. Anderson-F/Sgt C. F. A. Bodard
22/23.2.44	XIII	HK521	410 Sqn	Ju 188E-1	nr Rochford	S/L C. A. S. Anderson-F/Sgt C. F. A. Bodard
22/23.2.44	VI		605 Sqn	E/a	Melsbroek	Flt Off B. F. Miller USAAF-F/O J. C. Winlaw RCAF
23/24.2.44	XVII		25 Sqn	Do 217	off E. Anglia	
23/24.2.44	XVII	HK293	25 Sqn	Ju 188	off Yarmouth	
23/24.2.44	XVII	'O'	85 Sqn	Ju 88 (prob)	Beachy Head	W/C J. Cunningham DSO* DFC*-F/O C. F. Rawnsley DFC DFM*
23/24.2.44	VI		605 Sqn	Ju 88	Chièvres airfield	F/O L. Williams-F/O F. Hogg
24/25.2.44	VI		418 Sqn	Me 410	Würzburg a/f	F/L D. A. MacFadyen RCAF-F/L Wright
24/25.2.44	VI	'R'	418 Sqn	2 x Ju 88	Ansbach a/f	F/L C. C. Scherf RAAF
24/25.2.44	XIII	HK413	29 Sqn	Do 217M	Dorking Hills, Surrey	S/L C. Kirkland-F/O R. C. Raspin
24/25.2.44	XIII	HK515	29 Sqn	Ju 188	E Framfield, Sussex	F/O W. W. Provan-W/O Nicol
24/25.2.44	XIII	HK422	29 Sqn	Ju 88A-4	Withyham, Sussex	F/L R. C. Pargeter-F/L R. L. Fell. (Ju 88A-4 of 8./KG6)
24/25.2.44	XIII	HK422	29 Sqn	Ju 188		F/L R. C. Pargeter-F/L R. L. Fell (Ju 188 fell at Thame?)
24/25.2.44	XII	HK168	29 Sqn	Do 217M	Willesborough, Kent	F/O J. E. Barry-F/O G. Hopkins

DATE	TYPE	SERIAL	SQN	ENEMY A/C	DETAILS	PILOT-NAVIGATOR/RADAR OP
24/25.2.44	XII	HK168	29 Sqn	Me 410 (prob)		F/O J. E. Barry-F/O G. Hopkins
24/25.2.44	XII		29 Sqn	He 177	30–35mls S of Ford-Beachy Hd area	F/L E. Cox-W/O Kershaw
24/25.2.44	XIII	HK370	96 Sqn	Me 410	off Beachy Head	F/L D. L. Ward-F/L E. D. Eyles (Me 410 of 2/KG54 B3+CK; crew PoW)
24/25.2.44	XIII	HK415	96 Sqn	He 177 (prob)	Sussex	S/L A. Parker-Rees-F/L Bennett
24/25.2.44	XII	HK228	488 Sqn	He 177A-3	Lamberhurst.	F/L P. F. L. Hall-F/O R. D. Marriott (He 177A-3 of 3./KG)
24/25.2.44			FIU	He 177	at sea (prob)	
25/26.2.44	II	DZ254 'P'	169 Sqn	Bf 110	SW Mannheim	F/L R. G. Woodman-F/O P. Kemmis
25/26.2.44	XVII	HK293	25 Sqn	Ju 188	off Yarmouth	
26.2.44	VI		418 Sqn	Bo 242	St Yan	S/L H. D. Cleveland RCAF-F/Sgt F. Day DFM
26.2.44	VI	'F'	418 Sqn	Go 242/He 111Z	Dole/Tavaux a/f	F/L C. C. Scherf RAAF
29.2/1.3.44	XVII	'S'	85 Sqn	He 177	English Channel	
29.2/1.3.44	XIII	HK469	96 Sqn	Fw 190	off Dieppe	
1/2.3.44	XIII	HK499	96 Sqn	Me 410	50mls SE Beachy Head	F/L W. J. Gough-F/L Matson
1/2.3.44	XIII	HK377	151 Sqn	He 177A-3	cr Hammer Wood	W/C G. H. Goodman-F/O W. F. E. Thomas
1/2.3.44	XIII	MM448	151 Sqn	Ju 188	at sea	S/L Harrison
1/2.3.44	XIII	HK232	151 Sqn	Ju 88	at sea	F/L Stevens
5.3.44	VI	LR364 'E'	613 Sqn	He 177	Chateaudun	W/C J. R. D. Braham DSO* DFC**-F/L W. J. Gregory DFC
5.3.44	VI		515 Sqn	He 177	Bretigny? Melun	W/C E. F. F. Lambert DFC-F/L E. W. M. Morgan DFM. (He 177A-3 W/.Nr 332214 5J+RL of 3./KG100 cr near Châteaudun/France. Lt Wilhelm Werner (pilot); Uffz Kolemann Schoegl (WOp); Uffz Gustav Birkebmaier (Flt Eng); Uffz Alfred Zwieselsberger (AG); Uffz Josef Kerres (AG) all KIA)
5/6.3.44	VI	'J'	605 Sqn	Fw 190 + 2 Me 410	Gardelegen a/f	F/L A. D. Wagner DFC-F/O E. T. 'Pip' Orringe
6.3.44	VI	'Y'	418 Sqn	Fw 190	Pau	1/Lt J. F. Luma US-F/O C. Finlayson
14/15.3.44	XIII	HK406	96 Sqn	Ju 88A-4	Hildenborough	F/L N. S. Head-F/O A. C. Andrews
14/15.3.44	XIII	HK406	96 Sqn	Ju 188	Channel	F/L N. S. Head-F/O A. C. Andrews
14/15.3.44	XIII	HK466	410 Sqn	Ju 88	off East Coast	
14/15.3.44	XIII	HK521	410 Sqn	Ju 88A-4	Hildenborough	1/Lt A. A. Harrington US-Sgt D. G. Tongue (Ju 88A-14 B3+CK of 2./KG54I)
14/15.3.44	XIII	HK432	410 Sqn	Ju 88	off East Coast	
14/15.3.44	XIII	MM476 'V'	410 Sqn	Ju 188E-1		S/L E. N. Bunting DFC-F/L C. P. Reed DFC (Ju 188E-l U5+BM, flown by Lt Horst Becker of 4./KG6 broke up in the air and crashed in flames at White House Farm, Great Leighs, nr Chelmsford. Becker, Uffz G. Bartolain, Uffz A. Lange, Uffz G. Goecking and Ofw H. Litschke, killed)
14/15.3.44	XIII		488 Sqn	Ju 188E-1		
14/15.3.44	XIII	NK523	410 Sqn	Ju 88		S/L W. P. Green DFC-F/Sgt A. R. Grimstone DFM
14/15.3.44	XVII	HK255	25 Sqn	Ju 88	E Southwold	F/L J. Singleton DFC-W/O W. G. Haslam (Ju 88 of KG30)
18/19.3.44	II	HJ710 'T'	141 Sqn	2 x Ju 88	near Frankfurt	F/O H. E. White DFC-F/O M. S. Allen DFC
18/19.3.44	II	DZ761 'C'	141 Sqn	Ju 88	near Frankfurt	F/O J. C. N. Forshaw-P/O F. S. Folley (Ju 88C-6 W/Nr 750014 R4+CS of 8./NJG2, shot down by Mosquito of 141 Squadron, cr at Arheilgen near Darmstadt, 25 km S of Frankfurt. Ofw Otto Müller (pilot); Ogfr Erhard Schimsal (radar op); Gefr Gunter Hanke (AG) all KIA)
19/20.3.44	XVII	HK255	25 Sqn	3 x Ju 88	50mls NNE Cromer	F/O J. Singleton DFC-F/O W. G. Haslam
19/20.3.44	XVII	HK278	25 Sqn	Do 217	NNW Cromer	F/L D. H. Greaves DFC-F/O T. M. Robbins DFC
19/20.3.44	XVII	HK278	25 Sqn	He 177A-3	off Skegness	F/L D. H. Greaves DFC-F/O T. M. Robbins DFC
19/20.3.44	XII	HK119 'J'	307 Sqn	He 177	nr Humber Estuary	P/O J. Bruchoci-F/L Ziolkowski
19/20.3.44	XII		264 Sqn	Do 217M-1	Cr Alford, S Lincs	F/O R. L. J. Barbour-F/O O. G. Paine
19/20.3.44	VI	'U'	418 Sqn	Ju W34+Ju 52/3mls	Luxeuil a/f	1/Lt J. F. Luma USA-F/O C. Finlayson
21/22.3.44	XVII	HK322	25 Sqn	Ju 188	35mls SE Lowestoft	F/L R. L. Davies-F/O B. Bent
21/22.3.44	XVII	HK322	25 Sqn	Ju 88	25mls SE Lowestoft	F/L R. L. Davies-F/O B. Bent
21/22.3.44	XIII	HK456	410 Sqn	Ju 88A-4	Latchington, Essex	F/O S. B. Huppert-P/O J. S. Christie (Ju 88A-4 of 4./KG30)
21/22.3.44	XIII	HK365	488 Sqn	Ju 188	at Sea	F/Sgt C. J. Vlotman-Sgt J. E. Wood
21/22.3.44	XIII	HK365	488 Sqn	Ju 88	nr Herne Bay	F/Sgt C. J. Vlotman-Sgt J. E. Wood
21/22.3.44	XIII	HK380 'Y'	488 Sqn	Ju 88A-14		F/L J. A. S. Hall-F/O J. P. W. Cairns (Ju 88A-14 3E+GS of 8./KG6 from Melsbroek fell on Earls Colne airfield where the aircraft and one of its 500kg HE bombs exploded, damaging three B-26 Marauders of the 323rd BG, US 9th AF)
21/22.3.44	XIII	MM476	488 Sqn	Ju 88A-4		S/L E. Bunting DFC-F/L C. P. Reed DFC (Ju 88A-4 4D+AT flown by Ofw Nikolaus Mayer of 9./KG30 from Varêl-busch cr at Blacklands Hall, Cavendish, Suffolk where the bomber's fuel tanks exploded. Fw K. Maser and Fw Karl-Heinz Elmhorst had bailed out and were taken prisoner. Mayer and Ofw W. Szyska died in the crash)
21/22.3.44	XIII	MM476	488 Sqn	Ju 188E-1		S/L E. Bunting DFC-F/L C. P. Reed DFC (Ju 188E-1 3E+BK of 2./KG6, flown by Lt G. Lahl hit the ground and exploded near Butlers Farm, Shopland, Essex shortly after 0110 hrs. Lahl, Uffz J. Fromm, Uffz R. Budrat and Obgefr Schiml were killed. Uffz E. Kosch bailed out, injured, and was taken prisoner)
21/22.3.44	XVII	HK359	456 Sqn	Fw 190	off S Coast	
21/22.3.44	XVII	HK297 'V'	456 Sqn	Ju 88	Rye	F/L K. A. Roediger RAAF-F/L R. J. H. F. Dobson
21/22.3.44	XIII		604 Sqn	Ju 88A-4	Chelmsford	F/L J. C. Surman-F/Sgt C. E. Weston
22/23.3.44	II		239 Sqn	Bf 110	Frankfurt	S/L E. W. Kinchin-F/L D. Sellers
22/23.3.44	XIII	MM451	96 Sqn	Fw 190	SE of Pevensey	F/L N. S. Head-F/O A. C. Andrews
22/23.3.44	XVII	HK286 'A'	456 Sqn	Ju 88A-4	nr Arundel	W/C K. M. Hampshire DSO RAAF-F/L T. Condon
23/24.3.44	XII	VY-R	85 Sqn	Fw 190	off Hastings	S/L B. J. Thwaites DFC-F/O W. P. Clemo DFM*
24.3.44	VI	LR374 'W'	613 Sqn	Ju 52/3mls	15mls S Aalborg	W/C J. R. D. Braham DSO* DFC**-S/L Robertson
24.3.44	VI	LR374 'W'	613 Sqn	Ju 64	6mls S Aalborg	W/C J. R. D. Braham DSO* DFC**-S/L Robertson
24/25.3.44	XVII	HK293	25 Sqn	Ju 188E-1		F/L V. P. Luinthune DFC-F/O A. B. Cumbers DFC (Ju 188E-1, U5+AN, flown by Uffz Martin Hanf of 5./KG2. Hanf and his four crew died in a watery grave 45 miles SE of Lowestoft)
24/25.3.44	XII	'O'	85 Sqn	Ju 188	off Hastings	F/O E. R. Hedgecoe-F/O N. L. Bamford

DATE	TYPE	SERIAL	SQN	ENEMY A/C	DETAILS	PILOT-NAVIGATOR/RADAR OP
24/25.3.44	XVII	'M'	85 Sqn	Do 217+Ju 88	Straits	F/L B. Burbridge-F/L F. S. Skelton
24/25.3.44	XVII	HK286 'A'	456 Sqn	Ju 88	Walberton, Sussex	W/C K. M. Hampshire DSO RAAF-F/L T. Condon
24/25.3.44	VI	'R'	605 Sqn	Bf 109	Stendal-Burg	W/C B. R. O'B. Hoare DSO DFC*-F/O Robert C. Muir
24/25.3.44	II	DD717 'M'	141 Sqn	Fw 190	Berlin	F/L H. C. Kelsey DFC*-F/O E. M. Smith DFC DFM
27/28.3.44	XIII	HK425	96 Sqn	Fw 190	at Sea	
27/28.3.44	XVII	HK260	219 Sqn	Ju 88	Hestar Combe	S/L Ellis-F/L Craig
27/28.3.44	XVII	HK286 'A'	456 Sqn	Ju 88A-4	nr Beer	W/C K. M. Hampshire DSO RAAF-F/L T. Condon
27/28.3.44	XVII	HK286 'A'	456 Sqn	Ju 88A-14	nr Ilminster	W/C K. M. Hampshire DSO RAAF-F/L T. Condon
27/28.3.44	XVI	HK323		Ju 88	nr Beer	S/L B. Howard-F/O J. R. Ross
30/31.3.44	II	DZ661	239 Sqn	Ju 88	Nuremberg	F/Sgt J. Campbell DFM-F/Sgt R. Phillips. (Ju 88C-6 W/Nr360272 D5+ of 4./NJG3, cr 10 km SW of Bayreuth. Oblt Ruprecht Panzer (pilot) WIA; radar op and AG bailed out safely)
4.4.44	VI	LR355 'H'	613 Sqn	Bucker 131	St Jean-d'Angely	W/C J. R. D. Braham DSO* DFC**-F/L W. J. Gregory DFC
5.4.44	VI	'F'	418 Sqn	Bf 110/Fw 58	Lyon	F/L C. C. Scherf RAAF
6.4.44	XIII	MM448	151 Sqn	Ju 88	off St Nazaire	W/C G. H. Goodman-F/O W. F. Thomas DFM
11/12.4.44	II	DZ263	239 Sqn	Do 217	Aachen	S/L N. E. Reeves DFC*-W/O A. A. O'Leary DFC** DFM
12.4.44	VI		418 Sqn	Fw 190	12mls SE Verdun	F/L C. M. Jasper-F/L O. A. J. Martin
13.4.44	VI	LR313 'B'	(613 Sqn)	He 111/Fw 58	Esbjerg/Aalborg	W/C J. R. D. Braham DSO*DFC** F/L W. J. Gregory DFC
13/14.4.44	XIII	MM497	96 Sqn	Ju 88	nr Le Touquet	P/O Allen? DFM
13/14.4.44	XIII	HK497	96 Sqn	Ju 88	off Dungeness	S/L A. Parker-Rees-F/L Bennett
13/14.4.44	XIII	HK415	96 Sqn	Me 410	at Sea	S/L A. Parker-Rees-F/L Bennett
13/14.4.44	XIII			Me 410	off Dungeness	F/L D. L. Ward-F/L E. D. Eyles
14.4.44	VI		418 Sqn	2 x Ju 52/3mls	Kattegat	P/O J. T. Caine RCAF-P/O E. W. Boal RCAF
14.4.44	VI		418 Sqn	2 x Ju 52/3mls	Kattegat	S/L R. A. Kipp DFC RCAF-F/L P. Huletsky RCAF
16.4.44	VI		418 Sqn	Caudron Goeland	Luxeuil a/f	F/L C. M. Jasper-F/L O. A. J. Martin
18/19.4.44	XVII	'B'	85 Sqn	Ju 88	Sandgate	F/L B. Burbridge-F/L F. S. Skelton
18/19.4.44	XVII	HK349 'R'	85 Sqn	Ju 188E-1	nr Dymchurch	W/C C. M. Miller DFC**-Capt L. Lövestad RNWAF (5./KG2 Ju 188E-1 U5+KN, piloted by Fw Helmuth Richter)
18/19.4.44	XIII	MM499	96 Sqn	Me 410-1	Brighton	W/C E. D. Crew DFC*- W/O W. R. Croysdill. (Me 410A-1 of 1./KG51. Oblt Richard Pohl (k) Fw Wilhelm Schubert (k) KG2?)
18/19.4.44	XIII	MM495	96 Sqn	Ju 88A-4	nr Margate	S/L W. P. Green DFC-F/Sgt A. R. Grimstone DFM
18/19.4.44	XIII		96 Sqn	Ju 88A-4	Cr nr Cranbrook	P/O Allen-F/Sgt Patterson
18/19.4.44	XIII	MM551 'X'	488 Sqn	Ju 88	60mls E Bradwell	F/L J. A. S. Hall-F/O J. P. W. Cairns
18/19.4.44	XIII	MM813	488 Sqn	Ju 88	at sea	W/O R. F. D. Bourke
18/19.4.44	XVII	HK237	25 Sqn	Me 410	off Southwold	F/L R. M. Carr-F/L Saunderson
18/19.4.44	XIII	MM456 'D'	410 Sqn	He 177		F/O S. B. Huppert-P/O Christie (He 177 of 3./KG100 flown by Fw Heinz Reis, which fell near Saffron Walden)
18/19.4.44	XIII		410 Sqn	Ju 88		F/O Snowdon-F/Sgt McLeod
18/19.4.44	XVII		456 Sqn	Me 410-1	nr Horsham	F/L C. L. Brooks-W/O R. J. Forbes
18/19.4.44	II	DD799	169 Sqn	Bf 110	Compiègne	F/O R. G. Woodman-F/O P. Kemmis
20.4.44	XVII	HK354	25 Sqn	Ju 188	at sea	
20.4.44	XIII	HK480	264 Sqn	He 177	40mls ENE Spurn Head	F/O J. H. Corre-P/O Bines
20.4.44	XIII	MM446 'Q'	151 Sqn	Ju W34	N Biscarosse	W/C G. H. Goodman-F/O W. F. Thomas
20/21.4.44	II	DD732 'S'	141 Sqn	Do 217	N of Paris	F/L H. E. White DFC*-F/L M. S. Allen DFC*. (Either Do 217N-1 W/Nr 51517 of 5/NJG4, which cr near Meulan N of Paris. Ofw Karl Kaiser, pilot and Uffz Johannes Nagel, radar op both WIA, bailed out. Gefr Sigmund Zinser (AG) (KIA). Or Do 217E-5 W/Nr 5558 6N+EP of 6./KG100, crash place u/k. Fw Heinz Fernau (pilot), Hptm Willi Scholl (observer), Uffz Josef Bach (WOp), Ofw Fritz Wagner (Flt Eng), all MIA)
20/21.4.44	II		169 Sqn	Bf 110	Ruhr	F/L G. D. Cremer-F/O B. C. Farrell
22/23.4.44	II	W4085	169 Sqn	Bf 110	Bonn area	F/L R. G. Woodman-F/O P. Kemmis
22/23.4.44	II	W4076	169 Sqn	Bf 110	Köln	P/O W. H. Miller-P/O F.C. Bone
23/24.4.44	II	HJ712 'R'	141 Sqn	Fw 190	Flensburg	F/L G. J. Rice-P/O R. S. Mallett
23/24.4.44	XVII	HK355	125 Sqn	Ju 88A-14	4mls S Melksham	W/C E. G. Barwell DFC-F/L D. A. Haigh
23/24.4.44	XVII	HK299	125 Sqn		off SW Coast	
23/24.4.44	XVII	HK301	125 Sqn		off SW Coast	
23/24.4.44	XVII	HK286 'A'	456 Sqn	Ju 88	in sea, nr Swanage	W/C K. M. Hampshire DSO RAAF-F/L T. Condon
25/26.4.44	XVII	'B'	85 Sqn	Me 410	S Selsey Bill	F/L B. Burbridge-F/L F. S. Skelton
25/26.4.44	XVII	HK299	125 Sqn	Do 217	at sea	
25/26.4.44	XVII	HK353	456 Sqn	Ju 88	S Selsey	F/L K. A. Roediger RAAF-F/L R. J. H. F. Dobson
26.4.44	VI		515 Sqn	UEA	Gilze a/f	S/L H. B. Martin DSO DFC-F/O J. W. Smith
26.4.44	VI		515 Sqn	UEA	Le Culot a/f	W/O T. S. Ecclestone-F/Sgt J. H. Shimmon
26.4.44	VI		515 Sqn	UEA	Brussels Evere	W/O T. S. Ecclestone-F/Sgt J. H. Shimmon
26/27.4.44	II	W4078	239 Sqn	Bf 110	Essen	F/O W. R. Breithaupt-F/O J. A. Kennedy DFM
26/27.4.44	XVII	HK286 'A'	456 Sqn	Ju 88	at sea	
26/27.4.44	XVII	HK297 'V'	456 Sqn	Ju 88	at sea	
26/27.4.44	XVII	HK264	456 Sqn	Ju 88	at sea	
26/27.4.44	XVII	HK346 'D'	125 Sqn	Ju 188	S St Catherines Pt	W/C J. G. Topham DFC*-F/L H. W. Berridge DFC
27/28.4.44	II	W4076	169 Sqn	Bf 110	SE of Strasbourg	P/O P. L. Johnson-P/O M. Hopkins
27/28.4.44	II		239 Sqn	Bf 110/Ju 88	Montzon-Aulnoye	F/O R. Depper-F/O G. C. Follis
27/28.4.44	II	DD622	239 Sqn	Bf 110	Montzon-Aulnoye	S/L N. E. Reeves DFC*-W/O A. A. O'Leary DFC** DFM
27/28.4.44	VI		605 Sqn	UEA (prob)	Couron	F/O R. E. Lelong RNZAF-P/O J. A. McLaren
27/28.4.44	VI		418 Sqn	UEA	Toul /Croix de Metz	S/L H. D. Cleveland RCAF-F/Sgt F. Day DFM
28/29.4.44	XVII	HK346 'D'	125 Sqn	Ju 88	off Cherbourg	W/C J. G. Topham DFC*-F/L H. W. Berridge DFC
28/29.4.44	XVII	HK286 'A'	456 Sqn	Do 217(prob)	86mls off Curmington	W/C K. M. Hampshire DSO RAAF-F/L T. Condon
29.4.44	VI	MM422 'H'	613 Sqn	Fw 190	NW Poitiers	W/C J. R. D. Braham DSO* DFC**-F/L W. J. Gregory DFC
29/30.4.44	XII	'O'	406 Sqn	2 x Do 217	off Plymouth	W/C D. J. Williams DFC RCAF-F/O Kirkpatrick DFM
2.5.44	VI	'X'	418 Sqn	Ju 86P (+4 on ground)	Griefswald	F/O C. C. Scherf RAAF

DATE	TYPE	SERIAL	SQN	ENEMY A/C	DETAILS	PILOT-NAVIGATOR/RADAR OP
2/3.5.44	VI		418 Sqn	4 x Fw 190	SW Saarbourg	S/L R. A. Kipp DFC RCAF-F/L P. Huletsky RCAF
4.5.44	XIII	MM446 'Q'	151 Sqn	4 x He 111	Dijon area	W/C G. H. Goodman-F/O W. F. Thomas
6/7.5.44	VI		605 Sqn	Me 210	St Dizier airfield	W/C N. J. Starr DFC
7.5.44	VI	'G'	21 Sqn	Ju 188	Roskilde, 30mls N Copenhagen	W/C J. R. D. Braham DSO* DFC**-F/L D. Walsh DFC
8/9.5.44	II	DD709	169 Sqn	Bf 110	Braine-le-Comte	S/L R. G. Woodman DFC-F/O P. Kemmis. (Bf 110 of I./NJG4 crewed by Lt Wolfgang Martstaller and his radar operator/air gunner who had taken off from Florennes at 0300 hrs shot down Lancaster ND587 of 405 Squadron before their combat with Woodman. The Bf 110 belly-landed in a field. Martstaller was KIA in a crash at St Trond aerodrome in August 1944)
8/9.5.44	VI		605 Sqn	Ju 88	Creilsham	F/O R. E. Lelong RNZAF-P/O J. A. McLaren
10/11.5.44	II	W4078	239 Sqn	Bf 110	nr Courtrai	F/O V. Bridges DFC-F/Sgt D. G. Webb DFM. (Bf 110 3C+F1 W/Nr 740179 of I./NJG4, which cr at Ellezelles, Belgium. Oblt Heinrich Schulenberg, pilot and Ofw Hermann Meyer, radar operator, bailed out near Flobeq. Meyer was wounded and badly concussed and spent 3 weeks in hospital and 4 more weeks at home)
11/12.5.44	II	DZ726 'Z'	141 Sqn	Ju 88	N of Amiens	F/L H. E. White DFC*-F/L M. S. Allen DFC*
11/12.5.44	II	DZ240 'H'	141 Sqn	Ju 88	SW of Brussels	F/L L. J. G. LeBoutte-F/O R. S. Mallett. (Ju 88 of 6./NJG2. Wilhelm Simonsohn, pilot, Uffz Franz Holzer, flight engineer and Uffz Günther Gottwick, wireless operator-air gunner all bailed out. A/c cr near Mechlen, north east of Brussels)
12.5.44	VI	NS885 'B'	21 Sqn	Fw 190	Herning 10mls WSW W/C Aalborg	J. R. D. Braham DSO* DFC**-F/L W. J. Gregory DFC
12/13.5.44	II	W4078	239 Sqn	Bf 110	Hasselt-Louvain	F/O W. R. Breithaupt-F/O J. A. Kennedy DFM
12/13.5.44	II	W4092	239 Sqn	Ju 88	Belgium	F/O V. Bridges DFC-F/Sgt D. G. Webb DFM. (Ju 88C-6 Wrk Nr 750922 D5+ of 5./NJG3 cr at Hoogcruts nr. Maastricht. Uffz Josef Polzer, Ogfr Hans Klünder, radar op, KIA. Gefr Hans Becker (AG) WIA)
14.5.44	VI		418 Sqn	He 111	Nancy-Croix Metz	F/L C. M. Jasper-F/L O. A. J. Martin
14/15.5.44	XVII	HK325	125 Sqn	Ju 88	off Cherbourg	
14/15.5.44	XVII	HK318	125 Sqn	Me 410	N of Portland Bill	
14/15.5.44	III	'D'	406 Sqn	Ju 88	20mls SE Portland	W/C R. C. Fumerton DFC*-nav u/k
14/15.5.44	XVII	HK246	456 Sqn	Ju 188A-2	cr Larkhill, Wilts	F/O A. S. McEvoy-F/O M. N. Austin
14/15.5.44	XIII	MM551 'X'	488 Sqn	Ju 188A-2		F/L J. A. S. Hall-F/O J.P W. Cairns (Henstridge, Somerset)
14/15.5.44	XIII	HK381	488 Sqn	Ju 88	at sea	F/O R. W. Jeffs-F/O E. Spedding
14/15.5.44	XIII	HK381	488 Sqn	Do 217K1	cr nr Yeovilton	F/O R. W. Jeffs-F/O E. Spedding
14/15.5.44	XIII	HK527	604 Sqn	Do 217	at sea	F/L J. C. Surman-P/O C. E. Weston
14/15.5.44	XIII		264 Sqn	Ju 188	nr Alton	F/L C. M. Ramsay DFC-F/O J. A. Edgar DFM. Crew bailed out and Edgar was killed
14/15.5.44	VI		418 Sqn	He 177	Mont de Marson a/f	S/L R. A. Kipp DFC RCAF-F/L P. Huletsky RCAF
15/16.5.44	XIII		264 Sqn	Me 410	over the Channel	S/L P. B. Elwell-F/O F. Ferguson
15/16.5.44	XIII	MM526	604 Sqn	Ju 188	SW Isle of Wight	W/C M. H. Constable-Maxwell DFC
15/16.5.44	II	DZ748	169 Sqn	Bf 110/2 x Ju 88	Cuxhaven area	P/O W. H. Miller-P/O F.C. Bone
15/16.5.44	XVII	HK297	456 Sqn	Ju 88A-4	Medstead	F/O D. W. Arnold-F/O J. B. Stickley
16.5.44	VI		418 Sqn	He 111	Kiel Bay area	S/L H. D. Cleveland RCAF-F/Sgt F. Day DFM (KIA)
16.5.44	VI	'U'	418 Sqn	He 111/Fw 190/ He 177/Hs 123/ Ju 86P		S/L C. C. Scherf DFC* RAAF
19/20.5.44	VI		605 Sqn	He 219	Florennes	W/C N. J. Starr DFC-P/O J. Irvine
22/23.5.44	XVII	HK316	125 Sqn	Ju 188	S St Catherine's Pt	F/O K. T. A. O'Sullivan
22/23.5.44	XVII	HK252	125 Sqn	Ju 88	nr Southampton	
22/23.5.44	XVII	HK286 'A'	456 Sqn	Ju 88	S Isle of Wight	W/C K. M. Hampshire DSO DFC RAAF-F/L T. Condon
22/23.5.44	XVII	HK353 'M'	456 Sqn	Ju 88	nr Southampton	
22/23.5.44	II	DZ309	239 Sqn	Bf 110	Dortmund	F/L D. L. Hughes-F/O R. H. Perks
22/23.5.44	II		169 Sqn	Bf 110	Groningen area	W/C N. B. R. Bromley OBE-F/L P. V. Truscott. (Bf 110G-4 Wrk Nr 720050 D5 of 3.NJG3 cr at Hoogeveen S of Groningen. Fw Franz Müllebner (FF), Uffz Alfons Josten (radar op); Gefr Karl Rademacher (AG) all WIA and bailed out)
24/25.5.44	II	DZ265	239 Sqn	Bf 110	Aachen	F/L D. J. Raby DFC-F/Sgt S. J. Flint DFM
24/25.5.44	II	DZ309	239 Sqn	Bf 110	Aachen	F/L D. L. Hughes-F/O R. H. Perks (Bf 110G-4 W/Nr 730106 2Z+AR of 7./NJG6 poss. shot down by either of these two crews at 0230 hrs in forest between Zweifall and Mulartshuette SE of Aachen. Oblt Helmut Schulte (FF) bailed out, Uffz Georg Sandvoss (radar op) KIA, Uffz Hans Fischer (AG) bailed out. Bf 110G-4 W/Nr 720387 2Z+HR of 7./NJG6, poss. shot down by Raby/Flint or Hughes/Perks, cr at 0235 hrs at the Wesertalsperre near Dipen, S of Aachen. Crew: Uffz Oskar Voelkel (pilot); Uffz Karl Hautzenberger (radar op); Uffz Günther Boehxne (AG) all bailed out)
24/25.5.44	II	DZ297	239 Sqn	Ju 88	15mls ESE of Bonn	F/O W. R. Breithaupt-F/O J. A. Kennedy DFM
24/25.5.44	XVII	HK345	219 Sqn	Ju 88 (prob)	55mls E Orfordness	F/O D. T. Tull
27.5.44	XVII	HK346	456 Sqn	Me 410	nr Cherbourg	
27/28.5.44	II	DD622	239 Sqn	Bf 110F	Aachen	S/L N. E. Reeves DFC*-P/O A. A. O'Leary DFC** DFM. (Bf 110F Wrk.Nr. 140032 G9+CR of 7./NJG1 cr at Spannum in Friesland Province/Neth. at 0115 hrs. Uffz Joachim Tank (pilot, 26), slightly wounded. Uffz Günther Schroe-der (radar op, 19) and Uffz Heinz Elwers (AG, 24), KIA)
27/28.5.44	II	HJ941 'X'	141 Sqn	Bf 109	W of Aachen	F/L H. E. White DFC*-F/L M. S. Allen DFC*
28.5.44	XIII	HK462 'E'	410 Sqn	Ju 88	nr Lille	
28.5.44			605 Sqn	Ju 52	off Sylt	F/L Welch-F/L L. Page DFM
28/29.5.44	XVII	HK257	25 Sqn	Me 410	50mls off Cromer	W/C C. M. Wight-Boycott DSO-F/L D. W. Reid (Me 410 Hornisse 9K+KP of KG51 flown by Fw Dietrich (KIA) and Uffz Schaknies (KIA))
29.5.44	XVII	HK286 'A'	456 Sqn	Me 410		

DATE	TYPE	SERIAL	SQN	ENEMY A/C	DETAILS	PILOT-NAVIGATOR/RADAR OP
31.5/1.6.44	II	DZ297	239 Sqn	Bf 110	nr Trappes	F/O V. Bridges DFC-F/Sgt D. C. Webb DFM
31.5/1.6.44	II	DZ256 'U'	239 Sqn	Bf 110	W of Paris	F/L D. Welfare DFC*-F/O D. B. Bellis DFC*
1/2.6.44	II	DZ265	239 Sqn	Bf 110	Northern France	F/L T. L. Wright-P/O L. Ambery
1/2.6.44	XIX	'K'	85 Sqn	Ju 88 (prob)	Ipswich	F/L B. A. Burbridge DFC-F/L F. S. Skelton DFC
3/4.6.44	XVII	HK248	219 Sqn	He 219	Dutch Islands	F/O D. T. Tull
5/6.6.44	VI		605 Sqn	Me 410	7mls SE Evreux a/f	F/O R. E. Lelong RNZAF-P/O J. A. McLaren
5/6.6.44	II	DD789	239 Sqn	Ju 88	off Friesians	F/O W. R. Breithaupt-F/O J. A. Kennedy DFM. (Ju 88 G-1 Wrk.Nr. 710454 of 5./NJG3, cr 20km N of Spiekeroog. Uffz Willi Hammerschmitt (pilot), Uffz Friedrich Becker (radar op) and Fw Johannes Kuhrt (AG) all KIA)
5/6.6.44	II	DZ256 'U'	239 Sqn	Bf 110	N of Aachen	F/L D. Welfare-F/O D. B. Bellis. Poss. (Bf 110 W/Nr 440272 G9+NS of 8./NJG1 shot down at great height, cr at 0054 hrs on Northern beach of Schiermonnikoog. Uffz Adolf Stuermer (22), pilot, KIA; Uffz Ludwig Serwein (21) Radar Op MIA; Gefr Otto Morath (23) AG, KIA)
5/6.6.44	XIII		409 Sqn	Ju 188 (prob)	S Coast	F/O H. F. Pearce-F/O Moore
6/7.6.44	VI		418 Sqn	3 x Ju 52 & 1 Ju 188	Orleans & Châteaudun a/f	F/L S. H. R. Cotterill DFC RCAF-Sgt McKenna
6/7.6.44			29 Sqn	Ju 52/3m & UEA	over Coulommiers	F/L Allison-F/O Stanton
6/7.6.44	XVII	HK286 'A'	456 Sqn	He 177	3mls S Barfleur?	W/C K. M. Hampshire DSO DFC RAAF-F/L T. Condon
6/7.6.44	VI		605 Sqn	Ju 88	Orleans-Bricy a/f	F/L E. L. Williams DFC*-F/O S. Hatsell
6/7.6.44	VI	HR155 'X'	418 Sqn	Ju 52/3m	3mls N Coulommiers a/f	F/L D. A. MacFadyen DFC RCAF-F/L Wright
7/8.6.44	XVII	HK319	219 Sqn	Me 410	10mls E Harwich	F/O D. T. Tull
7/8.6.44	XVII	HK248	219 Sqn	Ju 188	15mls ESE Harwich	W/C P. L. Burke AFC*
7/8.6.44	XVII	HK290 'J'	456 Sqn	2 x He 177	off Normandy coast	S/L B. Howard-F/O J. R. Ross
7/8.6.44	XVII	HK302	456 Sqn	He 177	off Normandy	P/O Hodgen
7/8.6.44			29 Sqn	Ju 188 & Ju 88	S of Paris	F/L J. E. Barry-S/L Porter
7/8.6.44			29 Sqn	UEA	Dreux	F/O F. E. Pringle-P/O W. Eaton
7/8.6.44	XVII	HK354	25 Sqn	Me 410	nr Happisburgh	F/L D. H. Greaves DFC-F/O T. M. Robbins DFC
8/9.6.44	XIII	MM500	604 Sqn	Bf 110	NE of Laval	F/L J. C. I. Hooper DFC-F/O Hubbard DFM
8/9.6.44	II	DD741	169 Sqn	Do 217	Paris area	W/C N. B. R. Bromley OBE-F/L P. V. Truscott. (Poss. Do 217K-3 W/Nr 4742 6N+OR of Stab III./KG100 claimed in Paris area but crash-place u/k. Oblt Oskar Schmidtke (pilot); Uffz Karl Schneider (Observer); Uffz Helmuth Klinski (WOp); Uffz Werner Konzett (Flt. Eng), all MIA)
8/9.6.44	II	DD303 'E'	141 Sqn	UEA	Rennes	F/O A. C. Gallacher DFC-W/O G. McLean DFC
8/9.6.44			29 Sqn	Ju 88		F/O Wigglesworth-Sgt Blomfield
9/10.6.44	XII	MK403	29 Sqn	Ju 88	8mls S Beachhead	F/L R. C. Pargeter-F/L R. L. Fell
9/10.6.44			29 Sqn	Ju 188		Lt Price
9/10.6.44	XVII	HK353 'M'	456 Sqn	He 177	off Cap Levy	S/L R. B. Cowper DFC RAAF-F/L W. Watson
9/10.6.44	XVII	HK353 'M'	456 Sqn	Do 217	off Cap de la Hague	S/L R. B. Cowper DFC RAAF-F/L W. Watson
9/10.6.44	XIII	MM460	409 Sqn	Ju 188	40mls SE Le Havre	S/L R. S. Jephson-F/O C. D. Sibbett
9/10.6.44			410 Sqn	Ju 188		F/O Snowden-Lt Wilde
10/11.6.44	XIII		264 Sqn	Ju 88/Fw 190 (prob)		F/L J. H. Corre
10/11.6.44	XIII	MM453	409 Sqn	Ju 188		F/O R. L. Fullerton-F/O Castellan
10/11.6.44			409 Sqn	2 x Ju 88		P/O C. J. Preece-F/O Beaumont
10/11.6.44	XVII	HK249 'B'	456 Sqn	He 177 (prob)	40mls S Brighton	S/L G. E. Howitt DFC-F/L G. Irving DFC
10/11.6.44	XIII	MM547	409 Sqn	Fw 190		F/Sgt S. H. J. Elliott-F/L R. A. Miller
10/11.6.44	VI		605 Sqn	Ju 188	SE Coulommiers	F/O R. E. Lelong RNZAF-P/O J. A. McLaren
10/11.6.44	VI		605 Sqn	Me 410	Chateaudun	W/C N. J. Starr DFC
11/12.6.44	II	DZ256 'U'	239 Sqn	Bf 110	N of Paris	F/L D. Welfare DFC*-F/O D. B. Bellis DFC*
11/12.6.44	XIII	MM555	409 Sqn	Ju 188	over France	F/O K. Livingstone
11/12.6.44	XIII	MM523	409 Sqn	Do 217E	over France	F/O A. W. Sterrenberg
11/12.6.44	XIX	MM642 'R'	85 Sqn	Bf 110	10mls NE Melum a/f	W/C C. M. Miller DFC**-F/O R. O. Symon
12/13.6.44	XIII	HK512	264 Sqn	Ju 188	over beaches	F/L M. M. Davison DFC-F/O A. C. Willmott DFC
12/13.6.44	XIII	HK475	264 Sqn	Ju 188	over beaches	F/L Beverley-F/O Sturley
12/13.6.44	XVII	HK286'A'	456 Sqn	Ju 88		W/C K. M. Hampshire DFC DSO RAAF-F/L T. Condon
12/13.6.44	XIX	MM630 'E'	157 Sqn	Ju 188	Fôret De Compiègne	F/L J. G. Benson DFC-F/L L. Brandon DFC
12/13.6.44	XIX		85 Sqn	Bf 110	nr Paris	F/L M. Phillips-F/L D. Smith
12/13.6.44	XIII	MM526	604 Sqn	He 177	15mls NE Cherbourg	F/L R. A. Miller DFC-P/O P. Catchpole
12/13.5.44	XIII	MM500	604 Sqn	Ju 88		F/L J. C. I. Hooper DFC-F/O Hubbard DFM
12/13.6.44	VI		605 Sqn	Ju 88 (prob)	Chièvres a/f	F/L E. L. Williams DFC-F/O S. Hatsell
12/13.6.44	XIII	HK366 '0'	410 Sqn	2 x Do 217	over Beachhead	W/O W. F. Price
12/13.6.44	XIII	HK459 'A'	410 Sqn	He 177	over Channel	P/O L. J. Kearney-F/O Bradford
12/13.6.44	XIII	HK466 'J'	410 Sqn	Ju 88	10mls off Le Havre	F/O R. L. Snowden-F/O Wilde
12/13.6.44	XIII	MM476 'V'	488 Sqn	Ju 88	Caen-Bayeux	S/L E. N. Bunting DFC*-F/L C. P. Reed DFC*
13/14.6.44	XIII	HK502	264 Sqn	He 177	over Channel	S/L I. H. Cosby-F/L E. R. Murphy
13/14.6.44	XIII	MM560 'F'	409 Sqn	He 177	10mls E of Le Havre	W/C J. W. Reid-F/L J. W. Peacock
13/14.6.44	II	DZ254 'P'	169 Sqn	Ju 88	nr Paris	W/O L. W. Turner-F/Sgt F. Francis
14/15.6.44	XVII	HK282	456 Sqn	He 177	off Fécamp	
14/15.6.44	XIII		410 Sqn	Ju 88		S/L I. A. March-F/L Eyolfson
14/15.6.44			604 Sqn	Fw 190 (prob)	Carentan	F/O Wood-F/L Elliott
14/15.6.44			604 Sqn	He 177		F/L F. C. Ellis
14/15.6.44	VI		418 Sqn	He 111	S end Sagnkop Isle	S/L R. A. Kipp DFC RCAF-F/L P. Huletsky RCAF
14/15.6.44	XIII	HK476 'O'	410 Sqn	Mistel (Ju 88A-4/ piggyback Bf 109F-4 guided bomb)	25mls SE of Caen	F/L W. G. Dinsdale RCAF-P/O J. E. Dunn RCAF
14/15.6.44	XVII	HK356 'D'	456 Sqn	Ju 88	at sea	S/L R. B. Cowper DFC RAAF-F/L W. Watson
14/15.6.44	XIII	HK502	264 Sqn	Mistel (Ju 88A-4/ piggyback Bf 109F-4 guided bomb)	off Normandy	F/L J. H. Corre-P/O C. A. Bines
14/15.6.44	XIII	MM513 'D'	488 Sqn	Ju 88	10mls SW St Lô	F/O P. F. L. Hall-F/O R. D. Marriott
14/15.6.44	VI		418 Sqn	Bf 110	Avord a/f	S/L R. Bannock RCAF-F/O R. R. Bruce
14/15.6.44	II	DZ240 'H'	141 Sqn	Me 410	N of Lille	W/O H. W. Welham-W/O E. J. Hollis
14/15.6.44	XIX	MM671 'C'	157 Sqn	Ju 88	nr Juvincourt	F/L J. Tweedale-F/O L. I. Cunningham

DATE	TYPE	SERIAL	SQN	ENEMY A/C	DETAILS	PILOT-NAVIGATOR/RADAR OP
14/15.6.44	XIX	'Y'	85 Sqn	Ju 188	SW Nivelles	F/L B. A. Burbridge DFC-F/L F. S. Skelton DFC. (Ju 188 flown by Major Wilhelm Herget, *Kommandeur I./NJG4*. By the end of the war 58 of the 73 victories Herget gained were at night)
14/15.6.44	XIX	'J'	85 Sqn	Ju 88	near Creil	F/L H. B. Thomas-P/O C. B. Hamilton
14/15.6.44	XVII	HK315	219 Sqn	Ju 88	Harwich area	F/L M. J. Gloster DFC-F/L J. P. Oswold DFC
15/16.6.44	FIU		564 Sqn	Ju 88	at Laôn	Lt P. Twiss RN-F/O R. J. Lake AFC
15/16.6.44	XIX	'C'	85 Sqn	Bf 110	St Trond a/f	S/L F. S. Gonsalves-F/L B. Duckett. (Bf 110 W/Nr 5664 G9+IZ of *12./NG1* cr 9 km W of Tongres (between St. Trond and Maastricht). Uffz Heinz Bärwolf (pilot, injured, bailed out); Uffz Fischer (WOp/Radar op) bailed out. Ogfr Edmund Kirsch (23, AG) KIA)
15/16.6.44	XIX	MM671 'C'	157 Sqn	Ju 88	Creil-Beauvais	F/L J. O. Mathews-W/O A. Penrose
15/16.6.44	VI		605 Sqn	Bf 110/Fw 190	Le Culot	F/L E. L. Williams DFC-F/O S. Hatsell
16/17.6.44	XIII		410 Sqn	Ju 88	SE of Valongues	F/O I. S. Girvan-Lt Cardwell
16/17.6.44	XVII	HK344	219 Sqn	Me 410		F/O Faraday
16/17.6.44	XIII		29 Sqn	UEA & Do 217		F/O Crone
16/17.6.44	XIII		264 Sqn	Ju 188	La Haye de Pais	F/L M. M. Davison DFC-F/L A. C. Willmott DFC
16/17.6.44	II	W4076	169 Sqn	Ju 88	Pas de Calais	F/O W. H. Miller-F/O F. Bone. (Poss. Ju 88 W/Nr 710590 of *1./NJG2* cr in Pas de Cancale/France. Hptm Herbert Lorenz (pilot), Fw Rudolf Scheuermann (radar op.) and Flg Harry Huth (AG) all KIA)
16/17.6.44	XIII	MM476 'V'	488 Sqn	Fw 190	St Lô	S/L E. N. Bunting DFC*-F/O C. P. Reed DFC*
17/18.6.44	XIX		85 Sqn	Bf 110	Eindhoven	F/O P. S. Kendall DFC*-F/L C. R. Hill. (Bf 110 of *NJG1* shot down at 0230 hrs and cr at Soesterberg airfield. Müller and 2(?) others KIA
17/18.6.44	II	W4092	239 Sqn	Ju 88	nr Eindhoven	F/O G. F. Poulton-F/O A. J. Neville. (Ju 88G-1 W/Nr 710866 R4+NS of *8./NJG2*, which crashed at Volkel airfield. Lt Harald Machleidt (pilot) (k). Uffz Kurt Marth (radar op) WIA, Gefr Max Rinnerthaler (AG) KIA)
17/18.6.44	XIII	HK466 'J'	410 Sqn	Ju 188	6mls off Le Havre	F/L C. E. Edinger-F/O C. C. Vaessen
17/18.6.44	XIII	MM499 'C'	410 Sqn	Ju 188	nr Caen	S/L I. A. March-F/L Eyolfson
17/18.6.44	XIII	MM439	488 Sqn	Fw 190	Quinville area	F/O D. N. Robinson RNZAF-F/O K. C. Keeping
17/18.6.44	XIII	MM558 '5'	488 Sqn	Ju 88	30mls S Radox Mather	F/L P. F. L. Hall-F/O R. D. Marriott
17/18.6.44	XVII	HK250	219 Sqn	Ju 88 (*prob*)	18mls N Ostend	F/O G. R. I. Parker DSM-W/O D. L. Godfrey
17/18.6.44	XIII		264 Sqn	Ju 88	Domtront-Argentan	F/L M. M. Davison DFC-F/L A. C. Willmott DFC
17/18.6.44	XIII	HK473	264 Sqn	Fw 190		F/L I. H. Cosby-F/L E. R. Murphy
17/18.6.44	XIII		264 Sqn	2 x Ju 188	over Beachhead	F/O J. P. de L. Brooke-P/O J. Hutchinson
17/18.6.44	XIII		264 Sqn	Ju 188		F/O J. C. Duffy-F/Sgt Newhouse
17/18.6.44	XIII		29 Sqn	Ju 88		F/Sgt Johnson
18/19.6.44	XIII	HK470 'X'	410 Sqn	Ju 88	over Beachhead	F/O G. E. Edwards-F/Sgt Georges
18/19.6.44	XIII	MM571 'Y'	410 Sqn	Ju 88	Vire area	1/Lt A. A. Harrington USAAF-Sgt D. G. Tongue
18/19.6.44	XVII	HK346 'D'	125 Sqn	2 x Ju 88	Beachhead area	W/C J. G. Topham DFC*-F/O H. W. Berridge DFC
19/20.6.44			488 Sqn	Fw 190	S Falaise	P/O C. J. Vlotman-F/Sgt Wood
19/20.6.44	XIII		264 Sqn	Ju 88	over Channel	S/L F. J. A. Chase-F/O A. P. Watson
20/21.6.44	XIII	MM573 'B'	409 Sqn	Ju 88 (*prob*)		F/L M. C. Taylor-W/O Mitchell
20/21.6.44	XIII		29 Sqn	Bf 110	Coulommiers	F/L Price-S/L Armitage
20/21.6.44	XIII		29 Sqn	Ju 188 (*prob*)	Bourges	F/Sgt Benyon-F/Sgt Pearcy
21/22.6.44	II	DZ2950	239 Sqn	He 177	Ruhr	F/O R. Depper-F/O R. G. C. Follis
21/22.6.44	XIII	MM552	604 Sqn	Ju 188 (*prob*)	SSE Ventnor IoW	F/L P. V. G. Sandeman-F/O Coates
21.6.44	VI	PZ203 'X'	515 Sqn	Bf 110F		S/L P. W. Rabone DFC-F/O F. C. H. Johns. (Bf 110G W/Nr 440076G9+NS of *8./NJG1*, which had just taken off from Eelde a/f, shot down at 1519 hrs. Uffz Herbert Beyer (21) pilot, Uffz Hans Petersmann (21) radar op, and Ogfr Franz Riedel (20) AG, all KIA)
22/23.6.44			488 Sqn	Ju 188	E Bayeux	P/O O. J. McCabe-W/O Riley
22/23.6.44	XVII	HK23?	125 Sqn	3 x Ju 88	at sea	F/O W. J. Grey
22/23.6.44	XVII	HK262	125 Sqn	2 x Ju 88	at sea	Sub Lt H. J. Petrie RNZVR-Lt F. A. Noyes RNZVR
22/23.6.44	XIII	MM527	604 Sqn	Ju 88	NW Le Havre	F/O J. S. Smith-F/O Roberts
22/23.6.44	XIII		264 Sqn	Ju 88	N Rouen	F/O J. C. Trigg-F/L Smith
23/24.6.44	XVII	HK257	25 Sqn	Ju 88	NW Orfordness	W/C C. M. Wight-Boycott DSO-F/O D.W. Reid
23/24.6.44	XVII	HK257	25 Sqn	Ju 188F1	Cr Chillesford	W/C C. M. Wight-Boycott DSO-F/O D.W. Reid
23/24.6.44	XIII	MM554?	409 Sqn	Ju 188		F/O W. H. Vincent-F/L Thorpe
23/24.6.44	XIX	'Y'	85 Sqn	Ju 88		F/L B. A. Burbridge DFC-F/L F.S. Skelton DFC
23/24.6.44	XIII	HK500 'T'	410 Sqn	Ju 188	15mls NW Beachhead	W/O R. Jones-W/O Gregory
23/24.6.44	XIII		264 Sqn	2 x Fw 190 (*prob*)		S/L P. B. Elwell-F/O F. Ferguson
24.6.44	XVII	HK262	125 Sqn	Ju 88	Isle de St Marcouf	
24.6.44	XVII	HK310	125 Sqn	Ju 88	W of Le Havre	
24/25.6.44	II	DD759 'R'	239 Sqn	Ju 88	Paris-Amiens	F/L D. Welfare-F/O D. B. Bellis
24/25.6.44	XIII	MM554?	409 Sqn	Ju 188		W/O W. G. Kirkwood-W/O Matheson
24/25.6.44	XIII	MM466	488 Sqn	Me 410	20mls SW Bayeux	F/L G. E. Jameson DFC RNZAF-F/O A. N. Crookes
24/25.6.44	XVII	HK355	125 Sqn	Ju 88	W St Marcouf	W/C E. G. Barwell DFC-F/L D. A. Haigh
25/26.6.44	XVII	HK287	125 Sqn	Ju 88	E Le Havre area	F/L Simcock
25/26.6.44	XIII	MM518	409 Sqn	Ju 188/Do 217		F/L D. T. Steele-F/O Storrs
27.6.44	VI		418 Sqn	Ju 88	2mls N Rostock	F/L C. M. Jasper-F/L O. A. J. Martin
27/28.6.44	II	HJ911 'A'	141 Sqn	Ju 88	Cambrai	S/L G. J. Rice-F/O J. G. Rogerson
27/28.6.44		DZ240 'H'	141 Sqn	Ju 88	S of Tilburg	W/O H. Welham-W/O E. Hollis. (Poss Ju 88G-1 W/Nr 710455 of *4./NJG3*, cr at Arendonk/Belgium. Uffz Eügen Wilfert (pilot), KIA; Ogfr Karl Martin (radar op.), KIA; Gefr Rudolf Scherbaum (AG), KIA)
27/28.6.44	II	DD759 'R'	239 Sqn	Me 410	E of Paris	F/L D. Welfare-F/O D. B. Bellis
27/28.6.44	II		239 Sqn	Fw 190	Near Brussels	W/C P. M. J. Evans-F/O R. H. Perks DFC
27/28.6.44	II	DD749	239 Sqn	Ju 88	Near Brussels	F/L D. R. Howard-F/O F. A. W Clay
27/28.6.44	VI	PZ188 'J'	515 Sqn	Ju 88	Eindhoven	P/O C. W. Chown RCAF-F/Sgt D. G. N. Veitch. (Ju 88 W/Nr 300651 B3+LT of *9./NJG54* during landing approach at Welschap (after a mine-laying operation in the invasion area) at 0213 hrs. Ju 88 crashed into a house, killing 3 children and Uffz Gotthard Seehaber, pilot, Gefr Kurt Voelker, Ogfr Walter Oldenbruch and Ogfr Hermann Patzel)
27/28.6.44	XIII		264 Sqn	Ju 188	Seine estuary	F/L Turner-F/O T V. Arden

DATE	TYPE	SERIAL	SQN	ENEMY A/C	DETAILS	PILOT-NAVIGATOR/RADAR OP
28/29.6.44	VI	NT150	169 Sqn	Bf 110	nr Mucke	P/O H. Reed-F/O S. Watts
28/29.6.44	XIII	MM589	409 Sqn	Ju 188		W/O W. G. Kirkwood-W/O Matheson
28/29.6.44	XIII	MM466	488 Sqn	Ju 88	10mls NE Caen	F/L G. E. Jameson DFC RNZAF-F/O A. N. Crookes
29/30.6.44	XIII		264 Sqn	Ju 188	Seine Bay	F/O R. Barbour-F/O G. Paine
30.6.44	VI	PZ203 'X'	515 Sqn	He 111	Jagel/Schleswig	S/L P. W. Rabone DFC-F/O F. C. H. Johns
30.6.44	VI	PZ188 'J'	515 Sqn	Ju 34		P/O C. W. Chown RCAF-F/Sgt D. G. N. Veitch
30.6/1.7.44	VI	DZ265	239 Sqn	Ju 88	Le Havre	F/L C. J. Raby DFC-F/Sgt S. J. Flint DFC (Probably Ju 88 W/Nr 711114 of 5./NJG2 cr SE of Dieppe/France. Uffz Erich Pollmer WIA. Other crew details u/k)
2/3.7.44	XIII	MM526	604 Sqn	Ju 188	15mls W of Le Havre	F/L R. A. Miller DFC-P/O P. Catchpole
2/3.7.44	XIII	MM465	604 Sqn	Ju 88	10mls N Ouistreham?	W/C M. H. Constable-Maxwell DFC-F/L Quintin
2/3.7.44			488 Sqn	Ju 188		W/O T. G. C. Mackay
2/3.7.44	XIII	MM517	604 Sqn	Ju 88	15mls N of Le Havre	S/L D. C. Furse-F/L Downes
3/4.7.44	XIII	MM447	410 Sqn	Ju 188	NE Raz de la Pierce	F/L C. E. Edinger RCAF-F/O C. C. Vaessen
3/4.7.44	XIII	MM570 'B'	410 Sqn	Ju 188/Me 410		F/L S. B. Huppert-F/O Christie (a/c FTR)
3/4.7.44	XIII	HK479	264 Sqn	Ju 188		S/L I. H. Cosby-F/L E. R. Murphy
4.7.44	XVII	HK325	125 Sqn	Do 217 (Poss Ju 188)	Le Havre	
4/5.7.44	XVII	HK356 'D'	456 Sqn	He 177	30mls S Selsey Bill	S/L R. B. Cowper DFC RAAF-F/L Watson
4/5.7.44	XVII	HK249 'B'	456 Sqn	He 177	N of Cherbourg	
4/5.7.44	XVII	HK282	456 Sqn	He 177	over Channel	
4/5.7.44	XVII	HK282	456 Sqn	Do 217	at sea	
4/5.7.44	II		169 Sqn	Bf 110	Villeneuve	F/L J .S. Fifield-F/O F. Staziker
4/5.7.44	XIII		264 Sqn	Ju 88/Me 410	Normandy	F/L C. M. Ramsay DFC-F/L D. J. Donnet DFC
4/5.7.44	II		239 Sqn	Bf 110	NW Paris	S/L N. E. Reeves DFC*-P/O A. A. O'Leary DFC** DFM
4/5.7.44	VI	PZ163 'C'	515 Sqn	Ju 88	nr Coulommiers	W/O R. E. Preston-F/Sgt F. Verity
4/5.7.44	II	DD725 'G'	141 Sqn	Me 410	nr Orleans	F/L J. D. Peterkin-F/O R. Murphy
5/6.7.44	II	DZ298	239 Sqn	Bf 110	nr Paris	S/L N. E. Reeves DFC*-W/O A. A. O'Leary DFC** DFM
5/6.7.44	II	W4097	239 Sqn	2 x Bf 110	Paris	S/L J. S. Booth DFC*-F/O K. Dear DFC. (Bf 110G-4 W/Nr 110028 C9+HK of 2./NJG5, which crashed near Compiègne, believed to be one of the two aircraft shot down by Booth and Dear. Lt Joachim Hanss, pilot and Fw Kurt Stein, bordschütz, were killed. Uffz Wolfgang Wehrhan, radar operator, was wounded)
5.7.44	XVII	HK312 'G'	456 Sqn	He 177	over Channel	
5/6.7.44	XIII	MM552	604 Sqn	Me 410	15mls SW of Caen	W/O J. E. Moore-W/O J. A. Hogg
5/6.7.44	VI	NT121	169 Sqn	Ju 88	S of Paris	F/O P. G. Bailey-F/O J. O. Murphy. (Ju 88 W/Nr 751065 R4+ of 5./NJG2, cr near Chartres/France. Ofw Fritz Farrherr (pilot) KIA; Gefr Josef Schmid (Radar op) WIA bailed out; Ogfr Heinz Boehme (AG) KIA)
5/6.7.44	XIII		264 Sqn	Ju 188		F/O Trigg-F/L G. E. Smith
7/8.7.44	XIII	MM504	409 Sqn	Ju 188		F/O Pearce-P/O Smith
7/8.7 44	II	HJ911 'A'	141 Sqn	Bf 110	NW of Amiens	S/L G. J. Rice-F/O J. G. Rogerson. (Poss. Bf 110G-4 Wrk.Nr. 730006 D5+ of 2./NJG3 cr 5 km W of Chièvres/Belgium. Pilot u/k and Gefr Richard Reiff WIA, bailed out. Ogfr Edmund Hejduck KIA)
7/8.7.44	II	DD789	239 Sqn	Fw 190	Pas de Calais	W/C P. M. J. Evans-F/L T. R. Carpenter
7/8.7.44	II	DZ29S8	239 Sqn	Bf 110	nr Charleroi	F/L V. Bridges DFC-F/Sgt D. G. Webb DFM
7/8.7.44	XIII		410 Sqn	Me 410	nr Paris	S/L I. A. March-F/L Eyolfson
7/8.7.44	XIII		410 Sqn	Ju 88		F/L S. B. Huppert-F/O Christie
7/8.7.44	XIII		29 Sqn	UEA		F/O Bennett-W/O Gordon
8/9.7.44	XIII	MM465	604 Sqn	Ju 88	10mls W Le Havre	W/C M. H. Constable-Maxwelll
8/9.7.44	XIII	MM465	604 Sqn	Do 217 (prob)	S bank Seine	W/C M. H. Constable-Maxwell
9/10.7.44	XIII		264 Sqn	Ju 88	25mls NE Bayeux	S/L F. J. A. Chase-F/O A. F. Watson
10.7.44	VI	PZ188 'J'	515 Sqn	Ju 88	Zwishilnahner a/f	F/O R. A. Adams-P/O F. H. Ruffle shared
10.7.44	VI	PZ420 'O'	515 Sqn			F/O D. W. O. Wood-F/O K. Bruton shared
10/11.7.44	XIII		264 Sqn	Do 217 (prob)		S/L Elwell-F/O Ferguson
11/12.7.44	XVII		219 Sqn	Ju 88	20mls ENE Rouen	F/O D. T. Tull
11/12.7.44	XVII	HK248	219 Sqn	Ju 188		W/C P. L. Burke AFC
12/13.7.44	XIII	HK451	264 Sqn	Ju 88	Seine Estuary	F/O R. Barbour-F/O G. Paine
12/13.7.44	XIX	TA401 'D'	157 Sqn	Ju 88	SE Étampes	F/L J. O. Mathews-W/O A. Penrose
14.7.44	VI	RS993 'T'	515 Sqn	Ju 34	Stralsund, NE Germany	F/L A. E. Callard-F/Sgt E. D. Townsley
14/15.7.44	XIX		157 Sqn	Bf 110	20mls NE Juvincourt	Lt Sandiford RNVR-Lt Thompson RNVR (anti Diver)
14/15.7.44	VI	NT112 'M'	169 Sqn	Bf 109	Auderbelck	W/O L. W. Turner-F/Sgt F. Francis
14/15.7.44	XVII	HK248	219 Sqn	Ju 188	SW Caen	W/C P. L. Burke AFC
17/18.7.44	VI		605 Sqn	UEA	Schwabish Hall	W/C N. J. Starr DFC-P/O J. Irvine
17/18.7.44	VI		418 Sqn	UEA	Altenburg a/f	S/L R. Bannock RCAF-F/O R. R. Bruce
17/18.7.44	XIII		604 Sqn	Ju 88		F/L G. A. Hayhurst-W/O Gosling
18/19.7.44	XIII	MM512	409 Sqn	Do 217		F/O McPhail-P/O Smith
18/19.7.44	XIII	MM589	409 Sqn	Ju 88		W/O Kirkwood-W/O Matheson
18/19.7.44	XIII		29 Sqn	UEA		W/O A. Cresswell
19.7.44	XXX		219 Sqn	Ju 188	over Beachhead	
20/21.7.44	VI	NT113	169 Sqn	Bf 110G-4	nr Courtrai	W/C N. B. R. Bromley OBE-F/L R. Truscott DFC. (Bf 110G- W/Nr 7302-18 G9+EZ of 12./NJG1 cr near Moll, Belgium. Ofw Karl-Heinz Scherfling (25) pilot, a Ritterkreuztraeger since 8 April 1944 and who had 33 night victories, KIA. Fw Herbert Winkler (31, AG), Fw Herbert Scholz (25, radar op), bailed out seriously injured. Fw Herbert Winkler (31, AG) KIA)
20/21.7.44	VI	NT146	169 Sqn	Ju 88	Homburg area	P/O H. Reed-F/O S. Watts
20/21.7.44	VI	NTl21	169 Sqn	Bf 110	Courtrai	F/L J. S. Fifield-F/O F. Staziker
21.7.44	XXX	MM731	406 Sqn	2 x Do 217		W/C D. J. Williams DFC RCAF
23/24.7.44	II	DZ661	239 Sqn	Bf 110	Kiel	F/O N. Veale-F/O R. D. Comyn. (Bf 110G-4 730117 G9+GR of 7./NJG1 shot down N of Deelen airfield at 0125 hrs. Lt Josef Hettlich, pilot and Fw Johann Treiber, (RO) the air gunner all bailed out safely)

DATE	TYPE	SERIAL	SQN	ENEMY A/C	DETAILS	PILOT-NAVIGATOR/RADAR OP
23/24.7.44	II	HJ710 'T'	141 Sqn	Ju 88	SW of Beauvais	P/O I. D. Gregory-P/O D. H. Stephens. (Poss. Bf 110G-4 W/Nr 730117 G9+GR of *7./NJG1*, shot down by Mosquito NF at 0125 hrs, cr 5km N of Deelen a/f. Lt Josef Hettlich (pilot); Fw Johann Treiber (WOp/ Radar Op.) both slightly injured and bailed out. AG also bailed out. Or, Bf 110 W?Nr 441083 G9+OR of *III./NJG1* or *7./NJG1*, shot down by Mosquito NF at 0147 hrs during landing at Leeuwarden a/f, cr at Rijperkerk N of Leeuwarden. Hptm Siegfried Jandrey (30, pilot) and Uffz Johann Stahl (25, Radar op) KIA. Uffz Anton Herger (24, AG) injured)
23/24.7.44	VI	NS997 'C'	169 Sqn	Bf 110G-4	nr Kiel	F/L R. J. Dix-F/O A. J. Salmon. (Bf 110G-4 W/Nr 730036 0 G9+ER of *7./NJG1* shot down at very low level around midnight and cr near Balk, Friesland Province, Holland. Fw Heinrich-Karl Lahmann (25, pilot) and Uffz Günther Bouda (21 AG) both bailed out. Uffz Willi Huxsohl (21, radar op) KIA
23/24.7.44	XIII		29 Sqn	Bf 110	nr Leeuwarden a/f	F/L A. C. Musgrove-F/O G. Egerton-Hine. (441083 G9+OR of *7./NJG1*, shot down at 0147 hours during landing at Leeuwarden airfield and crashed at Rijperkerk, just to the N of the base. Hptm Siegfried Jandrey (30, pilot) and Uffz Johann Stahl (25, radar operator) killed. Uffz Anton Herger (24, air gunner) injured)
24/25.7.44	XIII	MM504	409 Sqn	Ju 88		W/O MacDonald-F/Sgt King
25/26.7.44	XIII	MM587	409 Sqn	Ju 88		W/C Reid-F/L Peacock
25/26.7.44	VI	RS961 'H'	515 Sqn	Me 410	Knocke, Belgium	S/L H. B. Martin DSO DFC-F/O J. W. Smith
25/26.7.44	VI	PZ178	23 Sqn	UEA	Laon Pouvron	F/L D. J. Griffiths-F/Sgt S. F. Smith
25/26.7.44	XVII		219 Sqn	Ju 88	50mls ENE La Havre	F/O D. T. Tull
26/27.7.44	XIII	HK462	409 Sqn	Ju 88	over Caen	S/L Jephson-F/O Roberts (Mos FTR)
26/27.7.44	XIII		29 Sqn	Ju 188	Melun	F/O F. E. Pringle-F/O Eaton
26/27.7.44	XIII		604 Sqn	Ju 88	Granville	F/O J. C. Truscott-F/O Howarth
28/29.7.44	XIII	MM500	604 Sqn	Ju 88	Lisieux-Bernay	F/L J. P. Meadows-F/O McIlvenny
28/29.7.44	XIII	MM526	604 Sqn	Ju 88	3mls E Bretal	F/L R. A. Miller DFC-P/O P. Catchpole
28/29.7.44	XIII	MM513 'D'	488 Sqn	2 x Ju 88	10mls NW Vire	F/L R. F. L. Hall-F/O R. D. Marriott
28/29.7.44	XIII	MM439	488 Sqn	Ju 188	10–15mls N Mayenne	F/O D. N. Robinson RNZAF-F/L W. T. M. Clarke DFM
28/29.7.44	II	HJ712 'R'	141	2 x Ju 88	Metz/Neufchâteau	F/L H. E. White DFC*-F/L M. S. Allen DFC*
28/29.7.44	II	HJ741 'Y'	141 Sqn	Ju 88	Metz area	P/O I. D. Gregory-P/O D. H. Stephens. (Ju 88G-1 W/Nr 713649 R4+KT of *9./NJG2*, possibly shot down by Mosquito of 141 Sqn (White and Allen or Gregory/ Stephens), cr 20km SSW of Toul, France. Hptm August Speckmann (pilot), KIA; Ofw Arthur Boos (radar op) WIA. Ofw Wilhelm Berg (Flt Eng) and Uffz Otto Brueggenkamp (AG) both KIA
28/29.7.44	XIII		410 Sqn	Ju 88	Beachhead	F/L W. A. Dexter-Lt Richardson
29/30.7.44	XIII	MM466	488 Sqn	3 x Ju 88	5–6mls S Caen	F/L G. E. Jameson DFC RNZAF-F/O A. N. Crookes DFC
29/30.7.44	XIII	MM466	488 Sqn	Do 217	5–6mls S Lisieux	F/L G. E. Jameson DFC RNZAF-F/O A. N. Crookes DFC
29/30.7.44	XIII		264 Sqn	Ju 188 (or 88)	15mls SE St Lô	S/L F. J. A. Chase-F/O A. F. Watson
29/30.7.44	XIII	MM621	604 Sqn	Ju 88	30mls S of Cherbourg	F/L Miller
30/31.7.44	XIII	MM589	409 Sqn	Ju 88		W/O Kirkwood
30/31.7.44	XIII	MM501	410 Sqn	Ju 88		P/O Mackenzie-P/O C. F. A. Bodard
30/31.7.44	XIII		29 Sqn	Ju 88	nr Paris	F/O Pringle
30/31.7.44	XIII		604 Sqn	Ju 88	SE of Caen	S/L B. Maitland-Thompson-W/O Pash
31.7.44	XXX		219 Sqn	Ju 188		
31.7/1.8.44	XIII		410 Sqn	Ju 88		F/O J. Maday-F/O J. R. Walsh
1/2.8.44	XIII	MM498	488 Sqn	Ju 88	10mls E of St Lô	F/L P. F. L. Hall-F/O R. D. Marriott
1/2.8.44	XIII	MM477 'U'	410 Sqn	Ju 188	NE Tessy	S/L J. D. Somerville-F/O G. D. Robinson RCAF
1/2.8.44	XIII		604 Sqn	Ju 188	SE Caen	F/L F.C. Ellis-F/O P.C. Williams
2/3.8.44	XIII	HK532	488 Sqn	Do 217	4mls S of Avranches	F/L A. S. Browne-W/O T. F. Taylor
2/3.8.44	XIII	MM439	488 Sqn	Ju 188	8mls S of Avranches	W/O T. G. C. Mackay-F/Sgt A. A. Thompson
2/3.8.44	XIII	MM477'U'	410 Sqn	Do 217	6mls NW Pontorson	S/L J. D. Somerville-F/O G. D. Robinson RCAF
2/3.8.44	XIII		264 Sqn	Ju 188 (or 88)	10mls W Argentan	S/L F. J. A. Chase-F/O A. F. Watson
2/3.8.44	XIII		410 Sqn	Ju 188		F/L B. E. Plumer-F/O V. W. Evans
3/4.8.44	XXX		219 Sqn	2 x Ju 188	Seine Estuary	F/L P. G. K. Williamson DFC RAAF-F/O F. E. Forrest
3/4.8.44	XIII	MM466	488 Sqn	Ju 88	8mls N St Lô	F/L G. E. Jameson DFC RNZAF-F/O A. N. Crookes DFC (*Claim 2nd Ju 88*)
3/4.8.44	XIII	HK504	488 Sqn	Ju 88	ENE of Vire	
3/4.8.44	XIII	MM513	488 Sqn	Do 217	NW of Barnes	
3/4.8.44	XIII	MM502	488 Sqn	Do 217	W of Angers	
3/4.8.44	XIII	HK420	488 Sqn	Ju 88	W Avranches	W/O G. S. Patrick-F/Sgt J. J. Concannon
3/4.8.44	XIII	MM552	604 Sqn	Do 217	5mls S of Granville	F/L R. J. Foster DFC-F/L M. F. Newton DFC
3/4.8.44	XIII	'S'	264 Sqn	Ju 88		S/L I. H. Cosby DFC-F/L E. R. Murphy
3/4.8.44	XIII		264 Sqn	Ju 88		F/L Beverley-F/O P. C. Sturling (Mos FTR crew bailed out)
3/4.8.44	XIII		604 Sqn	Do 217	S Granville	F/L R. J. Foster DFC-F/O M. F. Newton
3/4.8.44	XIII	MM554?	409 Sqn	Ju 188		F/L E. Spiller-F/O Donaghue
3/4.8.44	XIII	MM508?'K'	409 Sqn	Ju 188		W/O MacDonald-W/O Colborne
3/4.8.44	XIII		410 Sqn	Bf 110	NE Avranches	F/L W. G. Dinsdale-P/O J.E. Dunn
4/5.8.44	XIII	MM512	409 Sqn	Ju 188		W/O Joss-W/O Lailey
4/5.8.44	XIII		409 Sqn	Ju 88 (*prob*)		P/O Haley
4/5.8 44	XIII	MM514 'B'	604 Sqn	Ju 188 & Ju 88	nr Barnes	F/L J. A. M. Haddon-F/O R. J. McIlvenny
4/5.8.44	XIII	MK403	29 Sqn	Ju 188	Orly a/f	F/L C. Pargeter-F/L R. L. Fell
4/5.8.44	XIII	HK504 'M'	488 Sqn	Ju 88	ENE Vire	W/C R. C. Haine DFC-F/L A. P. Bowman
4/5.8.44	XIII		488 Sqn	Ju 188	NE St Lô	F/O A. L. Shaw-F/Sgt L. J. Wyman
5/6.8.44	XII)	MM513 'D'	488 Sqn	Do 217K-2	20mls from Beacon	F/L P. F. L. Hall-F/O R. D. Marriott
5/6.8.44	XIII		488 Sqn	Do 217K-2		F/Sgt T. A. Mackan
5/6.8.44	XIII	MM514	604 Sqn	Ju 188/Ju 88	Rennes area	F/L J. A. M. Haddon-F/O R. J. McIlvenny
6/7.8.44	XIII	MM466	488 Sqn	Ju 88	15mls S Avranches	F/L G. E. Jameson DFC RNZAF-F/O A. N. Crookes DFC

DATE	TYPE	SERIAL	SQN	ENEMY A/C	DETAILS	PILOT-NAVIGATOR/RADAR OP
6/7.8.44	XIII	MM500	604 Sqn	Ju 188		F/O R. M. T. MacDonald-F/Sgt C.G. Baird
6/7.8.44	XIII	HK420	488 Sqn	Ju 188	SW Avranches	F/L A. E. Browne-W/O T. F. Taylor ((+2 UEA flew into ground trying to evade) One of these poss. Hptm Helmut Bergmann of 8/NJG4 MIA Invasion area)
6/7.8.44	XIII	MM465	604 Sqn	Ju 88	S Avranches	W/C F. D. Hughes DFC**-F/L L. Dixon DFC*
6/7.8.44	XIII	MM449 'B'	604 Sqn	2 x Do 217 & Bf 110		F/L J. C. Surman-P/O C. E. Weston
6/7.8.44	XXX		219 Sqn	Ju 188	Argentan area	F/L P. G. K. Williamson DFC RAAF-F/O F. E. Forrest
6/7.8.44	XIII	MM566 'R'	410 Sqn	Ju 88	St Hilaire	S/L J. D. Somerville-F/O G. D. Robinson RCAF
7.8.44	XIII		410 Sqn	Ju 88		F/L R. M. Currie-F/O A. N. Rose. Hptm Helmut Bergmann, St.Kapt 8./NJG4 (36 night victories, Knight's Cross 9.6.44, MIA 6/.8.44 in Bf 110G-4 W/Nr 140320 3C+CS from sortie to Invasion Front area Avranches-Mortain, poss shot down by Mosquito NF)
7.8.44	XIII	MM550 FIU		Ju 88	Melun-Bretigny	Lt P. Twiss RN-F/O R. J. Lake AFC
7/8.8.44	XIII	MM555	409 Sqn	Ju 188		W/O Henke-F/Sgt Emmerson
7/8.8.44	XIII	MM429	604 Sqn	2 x Do 217	nr Rennes	F/O J. S. Smith-F/O L. Roberts
7/8.8.44	XIII	HK525	604 Sqn	Ju 188	S of Nantes	F/O R. M. T. MacDonald-F/L S. H. J. Elliott
7/8.8.44	XIII	MM517	604 Sqn	Ju 188	E of Falaise	F/L J. R. Cross-W/O H. Smith
7/8.8.44	XIII	MM517	604 Sqn	Ju 88	nr Conde	F/L J. R. Cross-W/O H. Smith
7/8.8.44	XIII	HK524	29 Sqn	Bf 110	Melun, W Orly	F/O W. W. Provan-W/O Nicol
7/8.8.44	XXX		219 Sqn	2 x Ju 188	W Vire	F/L M. J. Gloster DFC-F/L J. F. Oswold DFC
7/8.8.44	XIII		264 Sqn	Ju 88		F/L Davidson-F/O Willmott
8/9.8.44	II	DZ256 'U'	239 Sqn	Fw 190	St Quentin	F/L D. Welfare-F/O B. Bellis
8/9.8.44	II		239 Sqn	Bf 109	N France	F/L D. J. Raby DFC-F/Sgt S. J. Flint DFM
8/9.8.44	VI	NT156 'Y'	169 Sqn	Fw 190	E Abbeville	F/L R. G. Woodman DFC-F/L P. Kemmis
8/9.8.44	XIII	MM528 'H'	604 Sqn	Do 217		F/O T. R. Wood-F/O R. Leafe
8/9.8.44	XXX		219 Sqn	2 x Ju 188		
9/10.8.44	XXX		219 Sqn	Fw 190	E Evreux	F/L M. J. Gloster DFC-F/L J. F. Oswold DFC
10/11.8.44	XIII		264 Sqn	Ju 188	Caen	S/L F. J. A. Chase-F/O A. F. Watson
10/11.8.44	XXX		219 Sqn	Ju 88	10mls SW Le Havre	F/L G. R. I. Parker DSM-W/O D. L. Godfrey
10/11.8.44	XXX		219 Sqn	Fw190	5mls S Le Havre	F/L G. R. I. Parker DSM-W/O D. L. Godfrey
10/11.8.44	XIII	MM504	409 Sqn	Fw 190		S/L Hatch-F/O Eames
10/11.8.44	XIII	MM523	409 Sqn	Do 217		F/O Collins-F/O Lee
10/11.8.44	VI	NT176 'H'	169 Sqn	Bf 109	Over Dijon	F/O W. H. Miller DFC-F/O F. C. Bone DFC
10/11.8.44	XIII		264 Sqn	Ju 188		F/O Daker-F/Sgt J. A. Heathcote
10/11.8.44	XIII		410 Sqn	Ju 88		W/C G. A. Hiltz-F/O J. R. Walsh
11/12.8.44	XXX		219 Sqn	Ju 88		
11/12.8.44	XIII	HK429	604 Sqn	Do 217 (prob)		F/L R. A. Miller DFC-P/O P. Catchpole
11/12.8.44	XIII	MM619	409 Sqn	Fw 190		W/O Henke-F/Sgt Emmerson
12/13.8.44	VI	NT173	169 Sqn	He 219	nr Aachen	F/O W. H. Miller DFC-F/O F. C. Bone DFC
14/15.8.44	XIII	MM477 'U'	410 Sqn	Ju 88	15mls W Le Havre	S/L J. D. Somerville-F/O G. D. Robinson
14/15.8.44	XIII	MM491	409 Sqn	Ju 88		F/O Collins-F/O Lee
14/15.8.44	XIII	MM466 'B'	488 Sqn	Ju 88	20–30mls S of Caen	F/L J. A. S. Hall DFC-F/O J. P. W. Cairns
15/16.8.44	XXX		219 Sqn	Ju 88	15mls W Le Havre	F/L G. R. I. Parker DSM-W/O D. L. Godfrey
15/16.8.44	XIII	HK377	488 Sqn	Ju 88	SE of Caen	P/O McCabe-W/O F. Newman
16/17.8.44	XIII	MM590 'H'	409 Sqn	Ju 188		W/O MacDonald-W/O Colborne
16/17.8.44	XXX		219 Sqn	Ju 188	nr Caen	F/L M. J. Gloster DFC-F/L J. F. Oswold DFC
16/17.8.44	VI	HB213 'G'	141 Sqn	Bf 110	Ringkobing Fjord	W/O E. A. Lampkin-F/Sgt B. J. Wallnutt
18/19.8.44	XIII	MM560 'F'	409 Sqn	Ju 88/Ju 188		S/L Hatch-F/O Eames
18/19.8.44	XIII	MM622	488 Sqn	Do 217		F/O M. G. Jeffs-F/O A. N. Crookes DFC
19/20.8.44	XIII	MM589	409 Sqn	Do 217		S/L R. Hatton-F/L Rivers
19/20.8.44	XXX	MM744	410 Sqn	2 x Ju 88		F/O J. Fullerton-F/O B.E. Gallagher
20/21.8.44	XIII	MM439	488 Sqn	Ju 188	15mls S of Caen	F/L D. N. Robinson RNZAF-W/O W. N. Addison DFC DFM
26/27.8.44	VI	NT146 'T'	169 Sqn	Ju 88	nr Bremen	W/O L. W. Turner-F/Sgt T. Francis. (Ju 88G-1 W/Nr 710542 D5+BR of 7./NJG. cr nr Mulsum 42km E of Bremen. Lt Achim Woeste (pilot), KIA. Uffz Heinz Thippe, WIA, bailed out. Gefr Karl Walkenberger, WIA, bailed out. Uffz Anton Albrecht KIA)
27.8.44.44	XIII	HK304	25 Sqn	Bf 109	Northern France	
28/29.8.44	VI		605 Sqn	UEA	Chièvres airfield	F/O R. E. Lelong RNZAF-P/O J. A. McLaren
29/30.8.44	II	W4097	239 Sqn	Ju 88	nr Stettin	F/L D. L. Hughes-F/L R. H. Perks
1/2.9.44	XIII		410 Sqn	Fw 190		F/L I. E. Mactavish-F/O A. M. Grant
1/2.9.44	XIII	MM566 'A'	488 Sqn	Ju 188	10–15mls W Le Havre	W/C R. C. Haine DFC-F/L A. P Bowman
6/7.9.44	VI	PZ338 'A'	515 Sqn	Bf 109	Odder, Denmark	W/C F. F. Lambert DFC-F/O R. J. Lake AFC
11/12.9.44	XVII	FIU		Ju 88	10mls S Bonn	F/O D. T. Tull-F/O P. J. Cowgill
11/12.9.44	XIX	'Y'	85 Sqn	Ju 188	Baltic Sea	S/L B. A. Burbridge DFC-F/L F. S. Skelton DFC
11/12.9.44	VI	HR180 'B'	141 Sqn	Bf 110	SW of Mannheim	F/L P. A. Bates-P/O W. G. Cadman
11/12.9.44	XIX	MM630 'E'	157 Sqn	2 x Ju 188	Zeeland	S/L J. G. Benson DFC-F/L L. Brandon DFC
11/12.9.44	XIX	'A'	85 Sqn	Bf 109G	Limburg area	F/L P. S. Kendall DFC*-F/L C. R. Hill DFC*
12/13.9.44	XIX	MM643 'F'	157 Sqn	Bf 110	Frankfurt	F/L R. D. Doleman-F/L D. C. Bunch DFC
12/13 9.44	II		239 Sqn	Bf 110	Ranschhack	F/O W. R. Breithaupt DFC-F/O J. A. Kennedy DFC DFM
12/13.9.44	XIII	HK469	29 Sqn	Bf 110	SE Frankfurt	F/L W. W. Provan-W/O Nicol
12/13.9.44	VI		418 Sqn	UEA	Kitzingen	S/L R. Bannock RCAF-F/O R. R. Bruce
12/13.9.44	XXX		219 Sqn	Ju 88	Dutch border	F/L L. Stephenson DFC-F/L G. A. Hall DFC
13/14.9.44	XIX	'D'	85 Sqn	Bf 110	nr Koblenz	F/L W. House-F/Sgt R. D. McKinnon. (Bf 110G-4 W/Nr 440384 G9+EN of 5./NJG1 which took off from Düsseldorf A/F at 2234 hrs cr at Birresborn in the Eiffel at 2335 hrs. Oblt Gottfried Hanneck, pilot, bailed out WIA. Uffz Thdch Sacher (radar op) and Uffz Willi Wurschitz (radar op/AG) both KIA)
16/17.9.44	XXX	MM743	410 Sqn	UEA		F/L C. E. Edinger RCAF-F/O C. C. Vaessen
16/17.9.44	XIII		FIU	UEA	Ardorf a/f	F/O E. R. Hedgecoe DFC-F/O N. L. Bamford
17/18.9.44	XIX	'J'	85 Sqn	2 x Bf 110		F/O A. J. Owen-F/O J. S. V. McAllister DFM. (Bf 110G-4 W/Nr 740358 G9+MY of 11./NJG1 cr E of Arnhem/Holland. Uffz Walter Sjuts KIA;

DATE	TYPE	SERIAL	SQN	ENEMY A/C	DETAILS	PILOT-NAVIGATOR/RADAR OP
						Uffz Herbert Schmidt KIA; Uffz Ernst Fischer KIA. Bf 110G-4 W/Nr. 740757 G9+GZ of *12./NJG1* cr E of Arnhem/Holland. Uffz Heinz Gesse, Uffz Josef Kaschub and Ogfr Josef Limberg all KIA)
23/24.9.44	XVII		FIU	Bf 110	10mls SE Munster	F/O D. T. Tull-F/O P. J. Cowgill DFC
23/24.9.44	XXX		219 Sqn	Bf 110	7–10mls NE Cologne	S/L W. P. Green DFC-F/L D. Oxby DFM**
24/25.9.44	XIII	MM462 'T'	604 Sqn	He 219	55mls S Nijmegen	F/L R. J. Foster DFC-F/L M. F. Newton DFC. (He 219 of *I/NJG1*?)
25/26.9.44	XIII	MM589	409 Sqn	He 111H-22	over N Sea	W/O Fitchett-F/Sgt Hardy
25/26.9.44	XVII		125 Sqn	He 111H-22	over N Sea	F/O Beadle
26/27.9.44	VI	PZ301 'N'	515 Sqn	He 111	Zellhausen a/f	S/L H. F. Morley-F/Sgt R. A. Fidler
26/27.9.44	XXX	MM743	410 Sqn	Ju 87	12mls N Aachen	1/Lt A. A. Harrington USAAF-P/O D. G. Tongue
26/27.9.44	XVII	HK257	25 Sqn	Ju 188	40mls S Harwich	W/C C. M. Wight-Boycott DSO-F/L D. W. Reid
27/28.9.44	VI		418 Sqn	2 x Bf 108	Barrow airfield/sea	S/L R. Bannock RCAF-F/O R. R. Bruce
27/28.9.44	XIX	'J'	85 Sqn	Ju 188 *(prob)*	SW Kaiserlautern	F/O A. J. Owen-F/O J. S. V. McAllister DFM
28/29.9.44	XXX		219 Sqn	Ju 87	over Low Countries	F/L G. R. I. Parker DSM-W/O D. L. Godfrey
28/29.9.44	XIX	'Y'	85 Sqn	Ju 88		F/L M. Phillips-F/L D. Smith
28/29.9.44	XVII	HK357	25 Sqn	2 x He 111H-22	over N Sea	W/C L. J. C. Mitchell-F/L D. L. Cox
29/30.9.44	XIX		157 Sqn	Me 410 *(prob)*	10mls ESE Yarmouth	F/L Vincent-F/O Money
2/3.10.44	VI		605 Sqn	Bv 138	Jasmunder Bay	F/O R. E. Lelong RNZAF-P/O J. A. McLaren
2/3.10.44	XXX		219 Sqn	3 x Ju 87	E Nijmegen	S/L W. P. Green DFC-F/L D. Oxby DFM**
5/6.10.44	XVII	HK239	25 Sqn	He111H-22	over N Sea	
5/6.10.44	XIII		409 Sqn	Bf 110		S/L S. J. Fulton-F/O A. R. Ayton
5/6.10.44	XXX	MM760	410 Sqn	Ju 88	16mls NE Namur	F/L C. S. Edinger RCAF-F/O C. C. Vaessen
6/7.10.44	XIII	MM560	409 Sqn	Bf 110	over Peer, Belgium	F/O R. H. Finlayson-F/O J. A. Webster. (Bf 110 G9+MN of *5./NJG1*. Fw Robert Kock, on his 70th operation bailed out and was slightly inj. Uffz Heinz Forster, bordfunker and Uffz Ernst Darg, gunner were both KIA)
6/7.10.44	XIII		409 Sqn	Ju 88		P/O F. S. Haley-P/O S. J. Fairweather *(bailed out)*
6/7.10.44	XVII	HK317 'Y'	456 Sqn	Ju 188	20mls NW of Nijmegen	
6/7.10.44	XXX		219 Sqn	Bf 110	N Arnhem	F/L G. R. I. Parker DSM-W/O D. L. Godfrey
6/7.10.44	XXX		219 Sqn	Ju 87		F/L J. C. E. Atkins-F/O D. R. Mayo
6/7.10.44	VI	NT234 'W'	141 Sqn	Ju 88	S of Leeuwarden	F/L A. C. Gallacher DFC-P/O D. McLean DFC. (Ju 88G-1 W/Nr 710639 D5+EV of *10./NJG3* cr near Groningen. Oblt Walter Briegleb (pilot) WIA; Fw Paul Kowalewski (radar op) KIA; Uffz Brandt (Flt. Eng) WIA; Uffz Bräunlich (AG) WIA)
6/7.10.44	XVII	HK257	25 Sqn	He 111H-22	40mls S Southwold	F/L A. E. Marshall DFC DFM
6/7.10.44	XIII		410 Sqn	Bf 110		F/L Plumer-F/L Hargrove
7/8.10.44	XIII			Ju 188		F/O Fullerton-F/O Gallagher
7/8.10.44	XIX	MM671 'C'	157 Sqn	Bf 110	W of Neumünster	F/L J. O. Mathews DFC-W/O A. Penrose DFC
8.10.44	VI	PZ181 'E'	515 Sqn	Bf 109	Eggebek, Denmark	F/L F. T. L'Amie-F/O J. W. Smith
11.10.44	II	DZ256 'U'	239 Sqn	Seaplane	Tristed	F/L D. Welfare DFC-F/O D. B. Bellis DFC (on the water)
14.10.44	XVII	HK245	125 Sqn	He 219	nr Duisburg	
14/15.10.44	XIX	'Y'	85 Sqn	2 x Ju 88G	Gütersloh a/f	S/L B. A. Burbridge DFC*-F/L F. S. Skelton DFC*
14/15.10.44	VI	PZ245	239 Sqn	Fw 190	Meland	F/L D. R. Howard-F/O F. A. W. Clay
14/15.10.44	XIX		FIU	Ju 88G	W Kassel	F/O D. T. Tull-F/O P. J. Cowgill DFC
15/16.10.44	XIX	'D'	85 Sqn	Bf 110		F/L C. K. Nowell-W/O Randall
19/20.10.44	XXX	NT250 'Y'	141 Sqn	Ju 88	SE of Karlsruhe	F/L G. D. Bates-F/O D. W. Field. (Poss. Ju 88G-1 W/Nr 712312 2Z+EB of *I./NJG6*, which cr at Vaihirgen/ Marksdorf ENE of Pforzheim/ Germany. Oblt Wilhelm Engel (pilot) WIA; radar op safe)
19/20.10.44	VI	PZ175 'H'	141 Sqn	Ju 88	NW of Nuremberg	F/O J. C. Barton-F/Sgt R. A. Kinnear
19/20.10.44	XIX	TA404 'M'	157 Sqn	Ju 88	nr Mannheim	S/L R. D. Doleman DFC-F/L D. C. Bunch DFC. (Poss. Ju 88G-1 W/Nr 714510 2Z+CM of *4./NJG6*, which cr at Murrhardt, SE of Heilbronn/Germany. Uffz Georg Haberer (pilot) and Uffz Ernst Dressel (radar op) both KIA)
19/20.10.44	XIX	'Y'	85 Sqn	Ju 188	Metz	S/L B. A. Burbridge DFC*-F/L F. S. Skelton DFC*
19/20.10.44	VI	PZ275	239 Sqn	Bf 110	Strasbourg	W/O P. C. Falconer-F/Sgt W. C. Armour
22/23.10.44	XXX	MM792	219 Sqn	Ju 88	Verviers area	S/L W. P. Green DFC-F/L D. Oxby DFM**
25.10.44	XVII	HK310	125 Sqn	He 111	over N Sea	
28/29.10.44	II	PZ245	239 Sqn	He 111	Dummer Lake	F/L D. R. Howard-F/O F. A. W. Clay
29.10.44	VI	PZ344 'E'	515 Sqn	Fw 190 + Ju W34		F/L P. T. L'Amie-F/O J. W. Smith
29.10.44	VI	PZ217 'K'	515 Sqn	Bf 110		P/O T. A. Groves-F/Sgt R. B. Dockeray
29/30.10.44	XXX	MM767	410 Sqn	Fw 190	nr St Antonis	I/Lt A. A. Harrington USAAF-F/O D. G. Tongue
30/31.10.44	XVII	HK240	125 Sqn	He 111H-22	over N Sea	S/L L. W. G. Gill-F/L D. A. Haigh. (He 111H-22 of *4./KG53*. Fw Warwas and crew KIA)
1/2.11.44	XIX	'R'	85 Sqn	Ju 88	20mls S Mülhouse	F/O A. J. Owen-F/O J. S. V. J. S. V. McAllister DFM
2/3.11.44	XIII	HK469	29 Sqn	Bf 110	Handorf a/f	F/O W. W. Provan-W/O Nicol
4/5.11.44	XIX	TA401 'D'	157 Sqn	Bf 110	Osnabrück	W/C K. H. P. Beauchamp-P/O Money
4/5.11.44	II		239 Sqn	Bf 110	Bochum	F/O J. N. W. Young-F/O R. H. Siddons
4/5.11.44	XIX	TA401 'D'	85 Sqn	Bf 110	Bochum	S/L R. G. Woodman DFC-F/O A. F. Witt
4/5.11.44	XXX	MM820	488 Sqn	Bf 110		W/O J. W. Marshall-F/O P. P. Prestcott (4/5.11.44. Bf 110 of *II./NFG1*, shot down by Mosquito NF at 1900 hrs at 20,000ft. Uffz Gustav Sario (pilot) injured and bailed out; Uffz Heinrich Conrads (radar op) and Ogfr Roman Talarowski (AG) both KIA. Bf 110G-4 W/Nr 440648 G9+PS of *8./NJG1* possibly shot down by Mosquito NF, cr at Bersenbrueck, 30km N of Osnabrück/Germany. Fw Willi Ruge (pilot) WIA, bailed out; Uffz Helmut Kreibohm (radar op) and Ogfr Anton Weiss (AG) both KIA. Bf 110 W/Nr 730272 G9+E2 of *IV./NJG1* shot down by Mosquito NF SW of Wezel/Germany. Lt Heinz Rolland (26, pilot, 15 night victories); Fw Heinz Krüger (25, WOp/Radar Op); Uffz Karl Berger (22, AG) all KIA)
4/5.11.44	XIX	'B'	85 Sqn	Ju 88	SE Bielefeld	F/O A. J. Owen-F/O J. S. V. McAllister DFM
4/5.11.44	XXX	MM802	151 Sqn	Ju 87		P/O Oddie-F/L Gibbs
4/5.11.44	XIX	'Y'	85 Sqn	Ju 88G	30mls S Bonn	S/L B. A. Burbridge DSO DFC*-F/O P. S. Skelton DSO DFC*

DATE	TYPE	SERIAL	SQN	ENEMY A/C	DETAILS	PILOT–NAVIGATOR/RADAR OP
4/5.11.44	XIX	'Y'	85 Sqn	Ju 88	5mls SE Bonn	S/L B. A. Burbridge DSO DFC*-F/O P. S. Skelton DSO DFC*
4/5.11.44	XIX	'Y'	85 Sqn	Ju 88	N of Hangelar	S/L B. A. Burbridge DSO DFC*-F/O P. S. Skelton DSO DFC*
4/5.11.44	XIX	'Y'	85 Sqn	Bf 110	N of Hangelar	S/L B. A. Burbridge DSO DFC*-F/O P. S. Skelton DSO DFC*. (Bf 110 of *II./NJG1*, which crashed into the River Rhine nr Hangelar airfield at 2150 hrs. Oblt Ernst Runze, pilot, KIA. Ogfr Karl-Heinz Bendfield, radar operator and air gunner bailed out)
5/6.11.44	XIX	TA389	68 Sqn	He 111H-22	over N Sea	F/Sgt Neal-F/Sgt Eastwood
6/7.11.44	XIX	'N'	85 Sqn	Ju 188		S/L F. S. Gonsalves-F/L B. Duckett
6/7.11.44	XXX	'Y'	85 Sqn	Bf 110	S Bonn a/f	F/O B. R. Keele DFC-F/O H. Wright
6/7.11.44	XIX	TA391 'N'	157 Sqn	Ju 188 (*prob*)	Osnabrück/Minden	F/O H. P. Kelway-Sgt Bell
6/7.11.44	XIX	TA404 'M'	157 Sqn	Bf 110	S of Koblenz	S/L R. D. Doleman DFC-F/L D. C. Bunch DFC
6/7.11.44	II	DD789	239 Sqn	Ju 188	Osnabrück	F/O G. E. Jameson-F/O L. Ambery
6/7.11.44	XXX	MM726	151 Sqn	Ju 188		F/O Turner-F/O Partridge
6/7.11.44	XIX	'A'	85 Sqn	Ju 88 (*prob*)		Capt T. Weisteen RNWAF. (Ju 88G-6 W/Nr 620396 R4+KR of *Stab/IV./NJG3*, shot down by Mosquito and cr at Marienburgh Germany. Hptm Ernst Schneider (pilot) KIA; Ofw Mittwoch (radar op) and Uffz Kaase (AG) bailed out. Ju 88G-6 W/Nr 620583 R4+TS of *11./NJG3*, shot down by a Mosquito NF and cr SW of Paderborn/ Germany. Oblt Josef Förster (pilot), safe; Fw Werner Moraing (radar op) and Fw Heinz Wickardt (AG) both WIA)
9/10.11.44	VI		605 Sqn	2 x Ju 87		F/O R. H. Smart-P/O P. O. Wood
9/10.11.44	VI			He 111		F/O Lomas-F/O Fleet
10/11.11.44	XVII		125 Sqn	He 111H-22 (*prob*)	over N Sea	F/O G. F. Simcock-F/O N. E. Hoijne
10/11.11.44	XVII		68 Sqn	He 111H-22	over N Sea	F/Sgt A. Brooking-P/O Finn
10/11.11.44	XXX	MT492	25 Sqn	He 111H-22	70mls S Lowestoft	F/O D. H. Greaves DFC-F/O T. M. Robbins DFC
10/11.11.44	XIX	TA402 'F'	157 Sqn	Ju 88	Frankfurt-Koblenz	S/L J. G. Benson DFC*-F/L L. Brandon DFC*
10/11.11.44	XXX	PZ247	169 Sqn	Ju 188	NE Germany	S/L R. G. Woodman DFC-F/O A. F. Witt
11/12.11.44	XIX	MM671	157 Sqn	Ju 88 (*prob*)	Bonn	F/O J. O. Mathews DFC-W/O A. Penrose DFC. (Ju 88 W/Nr 712268 of *1./NJG4*, cr near Giessen/Germany. Pilot and radar op bailed out. Gefr Alfred Graefer (AG) KIA)
11/12.11.44	XIX	'B'	85 Sqn	Fw 190	30mls SE Hamburg	F/O A. J. Owen-F/O J. S. V. McAllister DFM
18/19.11.44	XXX	MM813	219 Sqn	Ju 87		F/O Atkinson-F/O Mayo
19.11.44	XVII		456 Sqn	He 111H-22	over N Sea	F/O D. W. Arnold-P/O J. B. Stickley
21/22.11.44	XIX	'N'	85 Sqn	Bf 110 & Ju 88	nr Würzburg/over Bonn	S/L B. A. Burbridge DSO DFC*F/L F. S. Skelton DSO DFC*
25/26.11.44	XXX	MM767	410 Sqn	3 x Ju 88G	Muntz	I/Lt A. A. Harrington USAAF-F/O D. G. Tongue (Jacberath and N of Hunxe)
25/26.11.44	XIII	HK425 'D'	409 Sqn	Ju 52	Rheindahlen	F/O R. I. E. Britten RCAF-F/L L. E. Fownes
25.11.44	XVII	HK298 'J'	456 Sqn	He 111H-22	75mls S Lowestoft	F/O F. S. Stevens-W/O W. A. H. Kellett
29/30.11.44	XIII	MM622	409 Sqn	2 x Ju 88		W/O S.F. Cole-F/O W.S. Martin
?.11.44			FIU	He 111H-22		S/L W. H. Maguire DFC-F/L W. D. Jones DFC
30.11.44	VI	HR242	169 Sqn	He 177	Liegnitz (on ground)	W/C H. C. Kelsey DFC*-F/O E. M. Smith DFC DFM
30.11/1.12.44	XIX		85 Sqn	Ju 88		S/L F. S. Gonsalves-F/L B. Duckett
30.11/1.12.44			157 Sqn	Ju 188	5030N 0920E	F/O R. J. V. Smythe-F/O Waters
30.11/1.12.44	XIII		410 Sqn	Ju 88		F/O Mackenzie-F/O C. F. A. Bodard
2/3.12.44	XIX	'A'	85 Sqn	Bf 110		Capt T. Weisteen RNWAF. (Bf 110G-4 W/Nr 180382 of *12./NJG4* took off Bonninghardt at 2047 hrs, cr at 2145 hrs near Lippborg (near Hamm/Germany). Lt Heinz-Joachim Schlage (pilot) safe. Fiebig and Uffz Kundmüller KIA)
2/3.12.44	XIX		157 Sqn	Ju 88	Osnabrück	F/L W. Taylor-F/O J. N. Edwards. (Poss. Ju 88 W/Nr 714819 3C+WL of *3./NJG4*, which cr at Rheine. Ofhr Erhard Pfisterhammer (pilot) WIA; Uffz Wolfgang Sode (radar op) WIA; AG u/k probably safe)
4.12.44	XXX	MM790	219 Sqn	Bf 110	nr Krefeld	F/O L. Stephenson DFC-F/L G. A. Hall DFC
4/5.12.44	XXX	'B'	85 Sqn	Bf 110	50mls ENE Heilbronn	Capt S. Heglund DFC-F/O R.O. Symon
4/5.12.44	XIX	MM671 'C'	157 Sqn	Ju 88	Dortmund a/f	F/L J. O. Mathews DFC-W/O A. Penrose DFC
4/5.12.44	XIX		157 Sqn	Bf 110	Limburg	F/L W. Taylor-F/O J. N. Edwards
4/5.12.44	XXX	'C'	85 Sqn	2 x Bf 110	Germesheim	F/L R. T Goucher-F/L C. H. Bulloch
4/5.12.44	XXX	'H'	85 Sqn	Ju 88	nr Krefeld	F/O A. J. Owen-F/O J. S. V. McAllister DFM. (Prob. Ju 88G-1 W/Nr 714152 of *6./NJG4* (85 Squadron's 100th victory), which cr nr Krefeld/Germany. Uffz Wilhelm Schlutter (pilot) WIA; Uffz Friedrich Heerwagen (radar op) and Gefr Friedrich Herbeck (AG) both KIA)
6/7.12.44	XXX	'O'	85 Sqn	Bf 110	W of Münster	F/O E. R. Hedgecoe D FC-F/Sgt J. R. Whitham. (Poss. Bf 110G-4 W/Nr 140078 G9+HZ of *12./NJG1*, shot down by Mosquito and cr 10km NW of Münster-Handorf/Germany. Hptm Hans-Heinz Augenstein Knight's Cross 9.6.44 (*St.Kpt 12./NJG1*, 46 night victories, of which 45 were four-engined RAF bombers) KIA. Fw Gunther Steins (radar op) KIA; Uffz Kurt Schmidt (AG) WIA, bailed out)
6/7.12.44	XIX	MM671 'C'	157 Sqn	Bf 110	nr Limburg	F/L J. O. Mathews DFC-W/O A. Penrose DFC
6/7.12.44	XIX	MM671 'C'	157 Sqn	Ju 88	15mls SW Giessen	F/L J. O. Mathews DFC-W/O A. Penrose DFC
6/7.12.44	XIX	TA404 'M'	157 Sqn	Bf 110	Giessen	S/L R. D. Doleman DFC-F/L D. C. Bunch DFC
6/7.12.44	XIX	MM638 'G'	BSDU	Bf 110	W of Giessen	S/L N. E. Reeves DSO DFC*-F/O M. Phillips
12/13.12.44	XIX	'A'?	85 Sqn	Ju 88		Capt E. P. Fossum-F/O S. A. Hider
12/13.12.44	XXX	'O'	85 Sqn	2 x Bf 110	20mls S Hagen/Essen	F/L E. R. Hedgecoe DFC-F/Sgt J. R. Whitham (with FIU)
12/13.12.44	XXX	'Z'	85 Sqn	Ju 88	Gütersloh a/f	S/L B. A. Burbridge DSO DFC**-F/L F. S. Skelton DSO DFC**. (Ju 88G-1 W/Nr 714530 of *6./NJG4*, cr at Gütersloh airfield. Uffz Heinrich Brune, pilot, Uffz Emil Hoftharth, radar op and Uffz Wolfgang Rautert (AG) all KIA)
12/13.12.44	XXX	'Z'	85 Sqn	Bf 110	2mls W of Essen	S/L B. A. Burbridge DSO DFC**-F/L F. S. Skelton DSO DFC**
17/18.12.44	XIX	MM627 'H'	157 Sqn	Bf 110	5112N 0635E	W/O D. A. Taylor-F/Sgt Radford
17/18.12.44	XIX	MM653 'L'	157 Sqn	Bf 110		F/Sgt J. Leigh
17/18.12.44	XXX	'J'	85 Sqn	Bf 110	40mls from Ülm	F/L R. T. Goucher-F/L C. H. Bullock
18/19.12.44	XIII	MM569	409 Sqn	Bf 110		P/O Haley-W/O McNaughton
18/19.12.44	XIII	HK415	409 Sqn	Ju 88		F/O Finlayson-F/O Webster

DATE	TYPE	SERIAL	SQN	ENEMY A/C	DETAILS	PILOT-NAVIGATOR/RADAR OP
18/19.12.44	XIII	MM456 'M'	409 Sqn	Ju 88	Kaiserworth area	W/C J. O. Somerville DFC-F/O G. D. Robinson DFC
18/19.12.44	XIX	MM640 'I'	157 Sqn	He 219	Osnabrück area	F/L W. Taylor-F/O J. N. Edwards. (Poss. He 219A-0 W/Nr 190229 G9+GH of I./NJG1. Uffz Scheuerlein (pilot) bailed out, Uffz Günther Heinze (radar op) KIA. Taylor and Edwards were killed 22/23 December trying to land at Swannington)
18/19.12.44	XXX	MV527	410 Sqn	Ju 88	S Bonninghardt	F/O G. E. Edinger RGAF-F/O C. C. Vaessen
18/19.12.44	XXX	MV549	85 Sqn	Bf 110		F/O D. T. Tull DFC (KIA)-F/O P. J. Cowgill DFC (KIA) (accidentally rammed Bf 110 G9+CC of Stab IV/NJG1, flown by Hptm Adolf Breves (Fw Telsnig (radar op) Uffzs Ofers (AG) as the latter was landing at Dusseldorf a/f at 22.30 hrs. Breves managed to land safely but Tull and Cowgill were killed in the crash of their Mosquito)
21/22.12.44	XIX	TA401 'D'	157 Sqn	Ju 88	N of Frankfurt	W/C K. H. P. Beauchamp DSO DFC-F/L L. Scholefield
22/23.12.44	XXX	MM792	219 Sqn	Ju 88		W/C W. P. Green DSO DFC-F/O D. Oxby DFM**
22/23.12.44	XXX	'B'	85 Sqn	2 x Ju 88 + Bf 110	Saarbrücken area	F/O A. J. Owen-F/O J. S. V. McAllister DFM. (Ju 88 W/Nr 621441 2Z+HK of 2./NJG6 cr at Larxistuhl/Germany. Ofw Max Hausser (pilot) KIA; Ofw Fritz Steube (radar op) KIA; Fw Ernst Beisswenger (AG) WIA. Ju 88G-6 Wrk.Nr. 621436 2Z+DC of II./NJG6 cr at Lebach, N of Saar-brücken/Germany. Uffz Werner Karau, aircrew function unknown, KIA; 2 others safe?)
22/23.12.44	XXX	'P'	85 Sqn	Bf 110	Koblenz-Gütersloh	S/L B. Burbridge DSO*DFC*-F/O F. S. Skelton DSO* DFC*
22/23.12.44	XIX	TA404 'M'	157 Sqn	Ju 88	5mls W Limburg	S/L R. D. Doleman DFC-F/L D. C. Bunch DFC
23/24.12.44	XXX	MM702?	219 Sqn	Ju 88		F/O W. B. Allison-W/O Mills
23/24.12.44	XXX	NT297?	219 Sqn	Ju 88		F/O R. L. Young-F/O N. C. Fazan
23/24.12.44	XXX	MM706	219 Sqn	Ju 88	S Huy	S/L W. P. Green DSO DFC-F/L D. Oxby DFM**
23/24.12.44	XXX	NT263	488 Sqn	Ju 188		W/C R. G. Watts-F/O I. C. Skudder
23/24.12.44	XXX	MM822	488 Sqn	Ju 88/188	10mls W Maeseyck	F/L K. W. Stewart-F/O H. E. Brumby
23/24.12.44	XXX	MT570 'P'	488 Sqn	Me 410	US Sector	F/L J. A. S. Hall DFC-F/O J. P. W. Cairns DFC
23/24.12.44	XVII	HK247	125 Sqn	He 111H-22	over N Sea	F/L R. W. Leggett-F/O E. J. Midlane. (He 111H22 of 7./ KG53 Legion Kondor cr Holland. Four crew KIA. 1 gunner survived)
23/24.12.44	XVII		68 Sqn	He 111H-22	over N Sea	F/Sgt Bullus-F/O Edwards
23/24.12.44	XIII	MM461	409 Sqn	Ju 188		F/L McPhail-F/O Donaghue
23/24.12.44	XXX		157 Sqn	Ju 88	nr Koblenz	F/L R. J. V. Smythe-F/O Waters
23/24.12.44	XIX	'N'	85 Sqn	Bf 110	Mannheim-Mainz	F/L G. C. Chapman-F/L J. Stockley
23/24.12.44	XIII		410 Sqn	2 x Ju 88		F/O Mackenzie-F/O C. F. A. Bodard
24/25.12.44	XIII	MM462 'T'	604 Sqn	He 219		F/L G. R. I. Parker DFC DSM-W/O D. L. Godfrey DFC DFM
24/25.12.44	XXX	MM698	219 Sqn	Ju 188	12mls S Eindhoven	F/L G. R. I. Parker DFC DSM-W/O D. L. Godfrey DFC DFM
24/25.12.44	XXX	MM698	219 Sqn	Ju 188	34mls E Arnhem	F/L L. Stephenson DFC-F/L G. A. Hall DFC
24/25.12.44	XXX	MM790	219 Sqn	Bf 110	nr Hasselsweiler	S/L Mactavish-F/O Grant
24/25.12.44	XXX		410 Sqn	Ju 87		F/L C. E. Edinger DFC RCAF-F/O C. Vaessen DFC
24/25.12.44	XXX	MV527	410 Sqn	Ju 87	Wassemberg area	F/O J. A. Watt-F/L Collis
24/25.12.44	XXX		410 Sqn	Ju 88		F/L J. O. Mathews DFC-W/O A. Penrose DFC
24/25.12.44	XIX	MM671 'C'	157 Sqn	Ju 88G	3mls SW Köln	S/L R. D. Doleman DFC-F/L D. C. Bunch DFC. (Bf 110G-4 G9+CT W/Nr 740162 of 9./NJG1 flown by Hptm Heinz Strüning, Ritterkreuz mit Eichenlab (Knight's Cross with Oak Leaves) and 56 night victories in NJG1 and NJG2 cr at Bergisch Gladbach/. Bordfunker and bordschütze bailed out safely. Strüning hit the tail of his Bf 110 and was killed. 2nd Bf 110 was G9+GR of 7./NJG1, which crashed nr. Soppenrade at 1922 hrs. Pilot and bordfunker survived. Gfr Wilhelm Ruffleth inj)
24/25.12.44	XIX	TA404 'M'	157 Sqn	2 x Bf 110	Köln/Duisburg	
24/25.12.44	XIX	MM676 'W'	157 Sqn	Bf 110	5038N 0752E	S/L J. G. Benson DFC*-F/L L. Brandon DFC*
24/25.12.44	XXX	'A'	85 Sqn	Bf 110	20mls N Frankfurt	Capt S. Heglund DFC-F/O B. C. Symon
24/25.12.44	XXX	MM693	406 Sqn	Ju 88	nr Paderborn	W/C R. Bannock DFC* RCAF-F/L R. R. Bruce DFC
25/26.12.44	XXX	MM706	219 Sqn	Bf 110		F/L E. A. Campbell-W/O G. Lawrence
26/27.12.44	XXX	MM792	219 Sqn	Ju 87	S Huy	S/L W. P. Green DSO DFC-F/L D. Oxby DFM**
26/27.12.44	XXX		488 Sqn	Ju 188 (prob)		F/L H. D. C. Webbe-F/O I. Watson DFC
27/28.12.44	XXX		410 Sqn	Ju 88G	Helchteren area	F/L W. G. Dinsdale-F/O J. E. Dunn
27/28.12.44	XIII	MM466 'G'	409 Sqn	2 x Ju 88G	Kaltenkirchen	F/O R. I. E. Britten RCAF-F/L L. E. Fownes
30/31.12.44	XIII	MM560 'F'	409 Sqn	Ju 88G		S/L Hatton-F/O Rivers
31.12.44	XIX	TA389	68 Sqn	He 111	over N Sea	
31.12.44/ 1.1.45	XIII	MM569 'J'	604 Sqn	2 x Ju 87		
31.12.44/ 1.1.45	VI	RS518 'L'	515 Sqn	Ju 88	Lovns Bredning	S/L C. V. Bennett DFC-F/L R. A. Smith. (Ju 88 of 4./NJG2. Oblt August Gyory (k). Enemy spun in and dropped into Lim Fijord)
31.12.44/ 1.1.45	XIX	MT491 'E'	169 Sqn	He 219	Köln area	F/L A. P. Mellows-F/L S. L. Drew (att 85 Sqn) (He 219A-2 W/Nr 290194 G9+KL of 3./NJG1, cr at Schleiden, 50 km SW of Köln. Oblt Heinz Oloff (pilot) and Fw Helmut Fischer (radar op) both WIA and bailed out)
31.12.44/ 1.1.45	VI	RS507 'C'	239 Sqn	Ju 88	Alhorn area	S/L J. Tweedale-F/O L. I. Cunningham
31.12.44/ 1.1.45	XIX	'R'	169 Sqn	He 219		F/L L. F. Endersby (att 85 Sqn)
31.12.44/ 1.1.45	XXX		410 Sqn	Ju 188	nr Antwerp	S/L Currie-F/L Rose
31.12.44/ 1.1.45	XXX		410 Sqn	Ju 88G		F/L Dexter-F/O D. G. Tongue
31.12.44/ 1.1.45	XXX		219 Sqn	2 x Ju 188		S/L J. P. Meadows-F/L H. M. Friend
1/2.1.45	XXX	MM790	219 Sqn	Bf 110		F/L F. T. Reynolds-F/O F. A. van den Heuvel
1/2.1.45	XIII	HK529	604 Sqn	He 219	Munchen Gladbach	S/L D. C. Furse-F/L J. H. Downes
1/2.1.45	XIII	HK526 'U'	604 Sqn	3 x Ju 88		F/L R. J. Foster DFC-F/L M. F. Newton DFC
1/2.1.45	XXX	'R'	85 Sqn	Ju 188	10mls N of Münster	F/L R. T. Goucher-F/L C. H. Bullock
1/2.1.45	XXX	'R'	85 Sqn	Ju 88G-6	10mls E of Dortmund	F/L R. T. Goucher-F/L C. H. Bullock. (Ju 88G-6 W/Nr 621364 2Z+CP of 5./NJG6, which cr at Dortmund killing Oblt Hans Steffen, pilot and Uffzs Josef Knon, Helmut Uttler and Friedrich Krebber)

DATE	TYPE	SERIAL	SQN	ENEMY A/C	DETAILS	PILOT-NAVIGATOR/RADAR OP
1/2.1.45	XXX		85 Sqn	Ju 88		F/O L. J. York
2/3.1.45	XXX	'N'	169 Sqn	Ju 188	nr Frankfurt	F/L R. G. Woodman DFC-F/L B. J. P. Simpkins DFC (85 Sqn)
2/3.1.45	XIX	TA393 'C'	157 Sqn	Ju 88	3mls W Stuttgart	F/L J. O. Mathews DFC-W/O A. Penrose DFC
2/3.1.45	XXX	'X'	85 Sqn	Ju 88	15mls SW Ludwigshafen	S/L B. A. Burbridge DSO DFC* F/L F. S. Skelton DSO DFC*
4.1.45	XIII	MM563	604 Sqn	Ju 88	W Hostmar	F/O P. W. Nicholas-F/O W .M. G. Irvine
5/6.1.45	XXX	NT283 'Y'	406 Sqn	He 111	Josum a/f	W/C R. Bannock DFC* RCAF-F/L R. R. Bruce DFC
5/6.1.45	XXX	'B'	85 Sqn	Bf 110	25mls N Münster	Capt S. Heglund DFC-F/O R. O. Symon
5/6.1.45	XIX	TA394 'A'	157 Sqn	He 219	S Hanover	S/L J. G. Benson DFC*-F/L L. Brandon DFC*. (He 219A-0 W/Nr 190188 G9-CK of 2./NJG1 cr 5km S of Wesendorf/Germany. Ofw Josef Stroelein (pilot) KIA. Uffz Kenne (radar op) bailed out safely)
5/6.1.45	VI	RS881 'C'	515 Sqn	Ju 88	Jagel a/f	F/L A. S. Briggs-F/O Rodwell. (Poss. Ju 88 W/Nr 620513 R4+CD of III./NJG2 which cr in Denmark (at Jagel airfield?) Oblt Bruno Heilig (pilot), Uffz Günther Kulas (radar op), Gefr Johann Goliasch (Flt Eng) and Ogfr Horst Jauernig (AG) all KIA)
6.1.45	XVII	HK296	68 Sqn	He 111H-22	over N Sea	W/O A. Brooking-P/O Finn (FTR)
6.1.45	XXX		488 Sqn	Bf 110	Holland	F/L F. A. Campbell-W/O G. H. Lawrence
7.1.45	XXX	MM792	219 Sqn	2 x Ju 87		
13/14.1.45	XIII	MM459	604 Sqn	Ju 188	Rotterdam area	W/C P. O. Hughes DFC*-F/O Dixon
14/15.1.45	XXX	'Y'	85 Sqn	Ju 188	Frankfurt	F/L K. D. Vaughan-F/L R. D. MacKinnon
14/15.1.45	VI	HR294 'T'	141 Sqn	UEA	Jüterborg	F/L B. Brearley-F/O J. Sheldon
16/17.1.45	VI	RS507 'C'	239 Sqn	Bf 109	Fassberg	F/L T. Smith-F/O A. Cockayne
16/17.1.45	XXX	'Y'	85 Sqn	He 219	Ruhr	F/L K. D. Vaughan-F/Sgt R. D. MacKinnon. (Poss. Ju 88G-1 W/Nr 710818 D5+EP of Stab/NJG3 which cr 3km SE of Friedberg (N of Frankfurt). Ofw Johann Fels (pilot), Uffz Richard Zimmer (radar op) and Gefr Werner Hecht (AG) all KIA)
16/17.1.45	VI	HR200 'E'	141 Sqn	Bf 110	Magdeburg	F/L D. H. Young-F/O J. J. Sanderson
16/17.1.45	VI	HR213 'G'	141 Sqn	Bf 110	SW Magdeburg	F/O R. C. Brady-F/L M. K. Webster
16/17.1.45	XIX	TA446 'Q'	157 Sqn	Ju 188	Fritzlar	F/L A. Mackinnon-F/O Waddell
17/18.1.45	XXX	MM696	219 Sqn	Ju 88	10mls E Aachen	F/L P. G. K. Williamson DFC RAAF-F/O F. E. Forrest
22/23.1.45	XXX	MM703	219 Sqn	2 x Ju 87		F/L G. R. I. Parker DFC DSM-W/O D. L. Godfrey DFC DFM
23/24.1.45	XIII	MM466 'G'	409 Sqn	Ju 88	over Scheldt	P/O M.G. Kent-P/O Simpson
23/24.1.45	XIII	MM456 'M'	409 Sqn	Ju 188E-1	3mls W Dienst	W/C J. D. Somerville DFC-P/O A.C. Hardy. (Ju 188E-1 A3+QD W/Nr 260452 of Kommando Olga crewed by FF (pilot) Ogfr Heinz Hauck, Observer Gfr Kurt Wuttge, Uffz Max Grossman (BF) and Fw Heinrich Hoppe (dispatcher) shot down after dropping 2 Leute (trusted people) in Holland. Crew all PoW)
26.1.45	VI		FIU	Bf 109		F/L E. L. Williams
26.1.45	VI		FIU	Bf 109		F/L P. S. Crompton
1/2.2.45	XIX		157 Sqn	Bf 110 (prob)	Oberolm	S/L Ryall-P/O Mulroy
1/2.2.45	XXX	NT252	169 Sqn	Bf 110	Stuttgart	F/L A. P. Mellows DFC-F/L S. L. Drew DFC. (Prob. Bf 110 W/Nr 7303-70 2Z+EL of 3./NJG6, which cr 25km S of Stuttgart. Oblt Willy Rathmann (pilot), Fw Erich Berndt (radar op) and Uffz Alfred Obry (AG) all KIA)
1/2.2.45	XXX	NT309 'C'	239 Sqn	Bf 110G-4	Mannheim	W/C W. F. Gibb DFC-F/O R. C. Kendall DFC. (Bf 110G-4 W/Nr 730262 G9+CN of 5./NJG1, probably shot down by Mosquito of 157 or 239 Sqn, belly-landed 2km W of Kettershausen. Oblt Gottfried Hanneck (pilot) WIA. Fw Pean (radio/radar op) and Uffz Gloeckner (AG) bailed out safely)
1/2.2.45	XXX	MM792	219 Sqn	Ju 88	2mls SW Rheydt	W/C W. P. Green DSO DFC-F/L D. Oxby DFC DFM**
2/3.2.45	XXX	MV548 'Z'	85 Sqn	Ju 88		W/C W. K. Davison
2/3.2.45	VI	RS575 'V'	515 Sqn	Ju 88	Vechta	W/C H. C. Kelsey DFC*-F/L E. M. Smith DFC DFM
3/4.2.45	XXX		219 Sqn	Ju 88		P/O M. G. Kent-P/O Simpson
3/4.2.45	XXX		410 Sqn	He 219		F/L B. E. Plumer DFC-F/L Hargrave
7/8.2.45	XXX	NT330 'P'	239 Sqn	Bf 110	Ruhr	F/L A. J. Holderness-F/L W. Rowley DFC
7/8.2.45	XXX	NT361 'N'	239 Sqn	Bf 110	Ruhr	F/L D. A. D. Cather DFM-F/Sgt L. J. S. Spicer DFM. (Bf 110G-4 W/Nr 730322 G9+HR of 7./NJG1 cr W of Soest (Ruhr). Fw Heinz Amsberg (pilot) and Uffz Matthias Dengs (radar op) both KIA. Gefr Karl Kopperberg (AG) WIA bailed out)
13/14.2.45	XIX	MM684 'H'	BSDU	2 x Bf 110	Frankfurt area	F/L D. R. Howard DFC-F/L F. A. W. Clay DFC. (Bf 110 W/Nr 480164 C9+ of 5./NJG5 cr nr Bodenbach (Frankfurt area). Fw Heinrich Schmidt (pilot), Uffz Erich Wohlan (radar op) and Uffz Adam Zunker (AG) all KIA)
14/15.2.45	XXX	MV532 'S'	85 Sqn	Ju 88	Schwabish Hall a/f	F/L F. D. Win RNZAF-F/O T. P. Ryan RNZAF
20/21.2.45	XXX	NT361 'N'	239 Sqn	Fw 190	Worms	W/C W. F. Gibb DFC-F/O R. C. Kendall DFC DFM
21/22.2.45	XXX	NT263	488 Sqn	Ju 88	Groenlo	F/L K. W. Stewart-F/O H. E. Brumby
21/22.2.45	XXX	NT325 'N'	406 Sqn	Bf 110	E Stormede a/f	F/L D. A. MacFadyen DFC RCAF
24/25.2.45	XXX	MM792	219 Sqn	Ju 87		W/C W. P. Green DSO DFC-F/O D. Oxby DFC DFM**
24/25.2.45	VI		605 Sqn	2 x Fw 190	Ludwigslost a/f	F/O R. E. Lelong DFC RNZAF-P/O J. A. McLaren DFC
28.2.45	XXX	NT325 'N'	406 Sqn	UEA (prob)	Hailfingen	S/L D. A. MacFadyen DFC RCAF
3/4.3.45	XXX	NT368	68 Sqn	Ju 188	at sea	F/L D. B. Wills
3/4.3.45	XXX	NT381	68 Sqn	Ju 188	at sea	F/L R. B. Miles
3/4.3.45	XXX	NT415	125 Sqn	Ju 188	at sea	W/C Griffiths
5/6.3.45	XXX	NT361 'N'	239 Sqn	2 x Ju 88	Chemnitz/Nuremberg	W/C W. F. Gibb DFC-F/O R. C. Kendall DFC DFM. (Ju 88G 6 W/Nr 622319 C9+GA of Stab/NJG5 flown by Obstlt Walter Borchers KIA (Kommodore NJG5, (59 victories -16 by day, 43 by night) Knight's Cross 29.10.44 KIA. Lt Friedrich Reul (radar op) KIA (cr nr Altenburg 25km NW of Chemnitz in Thuringia). Ju 88G-6 W/Nr 622318 C9+NL of 3./NJG5 cr near Chemnitz. Uffz H. Dorminger (FF), Uffz Max Bartsch (BF), Ogfr Franz Wohlschlögel (BMF); Uffz Friedrich Rullmann (BS) all MIA)
5/6.3.45	XXX	NT325 'N'	406 Sqn	Ju 88G	Gerolzhofen	F/L D. A. MacFadyen DFC RCAF

DATE	TYPE	SERIAL	SQN	ENEMY A/C	DETAILS	PILOT-NAVIGATOR/RADAR OP
7/8.3.45	VI	'S'	23 Sqn	Fw 190	Stendahl	F/O E. L. Heath-F/Sgt J. Thompson
8/9.3.45	XXX	MV555	85 Sqn	Ju 188		F/L I. A. Dobie-W/O A. R. Grimstone
12/13.3.45	XXX		410 Sqn	Ju 88 (prob)	Dunkirk area	F/L J. W. Welford-F/O R. H. Phillips
14/15.3.45	VI	HR213 'G'	141 Sqn	UEA	Lachen, Germany	F/O (2/Lt) R. D. S Gregor-F/Sgt P. S. Baker
14/15.3.45	XIX	TA397 'R'	157 Sqn	Ju 88G	Lützkendorf	S/L R. D. Doleman DSO DFC-F/L D. C. Bunch DFC
15/16.3.45	XXX	NT309	85 Sqn	Ju 88	Hanover area	Capt E. P. Fossum-F/O S. A. Hider
15/16.3.45	XIX	TA393 'C'	157 Sqn	Ju 88	20mls S Würzburg	F/L J. O. Mathews DFC*-W/O A. Penrose DFC*
16/17.3.45	XXX	NT330	239 Sqn	Ju 188	Nuremberg	S/L D. L Hughes DFC-F/L R. H. Perks DFC. (Pilot Maj Werner Hoffmann?)
18/19.3.45	XXX	NT364 'K'	157 Sqn	Ju 88	Hanau	W/O D. Taylor-F/Sgt Radtord
18/19.3.45	XXX	NT271 'M'	239 Sqn	He 219	Witten	W/C W. F. Gibb DFC-F/L R. C. Kendall DFC DFM. (Prob. He 219 of NJG1 Hptm Baake (Kommandeur I./NJG1) and Uffz Bettaque (radar op) both safe)
18/19.3.45	XXX	MV548 'Z'	85 Sqn	Bf 110		F/L F. D. Win RNZAF-F/O T. P. Ryan RNZAF
20/21.3.45	XXX	NT450	125 Sqn	Ju 188	at sea	F/L Kennedy
20/21.3.45	XXX	NT324 'T'	85 Sqn	Bf 110		F/L G. C. Chapman-F/Sgt J. Stockley. (Poss. He 219V-14 Wrk.Nr. 190014 of 3./NJG1. Oblt Heinz Oloff (pilot and St.Kpt. 3./NJG1); radar op u/k)
21/22.3.45	XIII	MM466 'G'	604 Sqn	Bf 110	Dhunn area	F/O R. I. E. Britten DFC RCAF-F/O L. E. Fownes DFC
21/22.3.45	XIII		409 Sqn	Bf 110		F/O K. Fleming-F/O K. L. Nagle
21/22.3.45	XXX		488 Sqn	Bf 110		F/O Atkins-F/O Mayo
23/24.3.45	XXX		219 Sqn	Fw 190		F/L A. D. Wagner DFC-F/L E. T. 'Pip' Orringe
24/25.3.45	VI		605 Sqn	Ju 88	Erfurt	F/L L. J. Leppard-F/L Houghton
24/25.3.45	XIII		604 Sqn	Bf 109	Haltern	F/L G. R. Leask-F/L J. W. Rolf
24/25.3.45	XXX		410 Sqn	Bf 110		S/L Mactavish-F/O Grant
24/25.3.45	XXX		410 Sqn	Ju 88G		F/O R. I. E. Britten DFC RCAF-F/O L. E. Fownes DFC
25/26.3.45	XIII	MM513 'J'	409	Ju 88	Dortmund area	F/L C. M. Ramsay DFC-F/L D. J. Donnet DFC
25/26.3.45	XIII		264 Sqn	Ju 88	25mls NNE Wesel	F/O A. Recina-F/Sgt R. A. W. Smith
25/26.3.45	XIII		264 Sqn	Ju 88 (prob)		F/L Ruffley-F/O Fagan
25/26.3.45	XXX		219 Sqn	2 x Bf 110		F/O T. R. Wood-F/O R. Leafe
26/27.3.45	XIII	MM497	604 Sqn	Ju 88	8mls NW Bocholt	F/L K. W. Stewart-F/O H. E. Brumby
26/27.3.45	XXX	NT263	488 Sqn	Bf 110	20mls N Emmerich	F/L J. A. S. Hall DFC-P/O Taylor (Mos Cr landed)
26/27.3.45	XXX	NT314 'P'	488 Sqn	Ju 88		F/O Reed-F/O Bricker
26/27.3.45	XXX		219 Sqn	Ju 188		F/L B. E. Plumer DFC-F/L Bradford
26/27.3.45	XXX		410 Sqn	Bf 110		F/O Reed-F/O Bricker
27/28.3.45	XXX		219 Sqn	He 177		W/C E. S. Smith AFC-F/L P. C. O'Neil-Dunne
30/31.3.45	XIII		264 Sqn	Fw 190	SE Münster	S/L D. L. Hughes DFC-F/L R. H. Perks DFC
3.4.45	XXX		239 Sqn	Ju 188		S/L R. G. Woodman DFC-F/L A. J. Neville DFC
4/5.4.45	XXX	NT540 'C'	BSDU	Bf 109	W Magdeburg	F/L C. W. Turner-F/Sgt G. Honeyman
4/5.4.45	XXX	'C'	85 Sqn	Ju 188	nr Magdeburg	W/C W. K. Davison DFC-F/L D. C. Bunch DFC (85/157 Sqns)
7/8.4.45	XXX	'Q'	85 Sqn	Fw 190	NW Mobiis	F/L K. W. Stewart-F/O H. E. Brumby
7/8.4.45	XXX	NT263	488 Sqn	UEA	20mls SE Osnabrück	F/L H. B. Thomas DFC-F/O C. B. Hamilton
8/9.4.45	XXX	NT494 'N'	85 Sqn	Ju 88	20mls W Lützkendorf	W/C H. C. Kelsey DFC*-F/L E. M. Smith DFC DFM
9/10.4.45	VI	RS575 'V'	515 Sqn	Ju 188	SE Hamburg	F/O Lang-F/O Fagan
9/10.4.45	XXX		219 Sqn	He 177	Ruhr	F/L R. D. Schultz DFC-F/O J. S. Christie DFC
10/11.4.45	XXX	MM744	410 Sqn	Ju 188	Damme area	W/C P. O. Falconer-F/Sgt W. G. Armour
10/11.4.45	XXX		239 Sqn	He 111		F/L F. R. L. Mellersh DFC* (Dest 39-42 V-1s 20.6.44-23.9.44 in 96 Sqn)
11/12.4.45	XXX		FIDS	Ju 88	20mls NNW Berlin	F/L K. D. Vaughan-F/Sgt R. D. MacKinnon
13/14.4.45	XXX	NT334 'S'	85 Sqn	He 219	Kiel	S/L D. J. Raby DFC-F/O S. J. Flint DFM
14/15.4.45	XXX		239 Sqn	Ju 88	Potsdam	P/O L. G. Holland-F/Sgt R. Young
15/16.4.45	VI	PZ398 'C'	515 Sqn	Ju 52/3M	nr Schleissheim	W/C W. K. Davison DFC-F/L D. C. Brunch DFC (85/157 Sqns)
17/18.4.45	XXX	MV557	85 Sqn	Ju 88	Munich area	F/L D. R. Howard DFC-F/L F. A. W. Clay DFC
19/20.4.45	XXX	NT276 'B'	BSDU	Ju 88	S Denmark	F/O P. N. Lee-F/O R. Thomas
20/21.4.45	XIII	MM521	264 Sqn	Ju 88	20mls W Berlin	W/O East-F/Sgt Eames
21.4.45	VI		23 Sqn	Ju 188		F/O J. Daber-W/O J. A. Heathcote
21/22.4.45	XIII		264 Sqn	2 x Ju 290	20mls W Berlin	W/O A. S. Davies-F/Sgt C. T. Fisher
21/22.4.45	XIII		264 Sqn	Ju 188		P/O G. S. Patrick-W/O J. J. Concannon
21/22.4.45	XXX		488 Sqn	Ju 52		F/L R. D. Schultz DFC-F/O J. S. Christie
21/22.4.45	XXX	MV527	410 Sqn	2 x Ju 188	Ferrbellen area	F/O C. M. Ramsay DFC-F/L D. J. Donnet DFC
21/22.4.45	XIII		264 Sqn	Ju 88 (prob)	35mls NW Berlin	F/O W. A. Craig-F/L A. Tauwhare
21/22.4.45	XIII		264 Sqn	He 111		F/L C. M. Ramsay DFC-F/L D. J. Donnet DFC
22/23.4.45	XIII		264 Sqn	Ju 88G	20mls W Berlin	F/O W. H. Foster-F/O F. H. Dagger
23/24.4.45	XIII		264 Sqn	He 111	between Elbe-Berlin	
23/24.4.45	XXX	NT512	488 Sqn	Ju 52		
23/24.4.45	XXX	NT327	488 Sqn	Ju 88		
23/24.4.45	XIII	HK506 'H'	409 Sqn	2 x Ju 52		F/O J. H. Skelly-P/O P. J. Linn
23/24.4.45	XIII	HK429 'D'	409 Sqn	2 x Ju 87/Fw 190		F/O E. E. Hermansen-F/L D. J. T. Hamm
23/24.4.45	XIII	MM588 'T'	409 Sqn	Ju 52		P/O J. Leslie-P/O C. M. Turgood
23/24.4.45	XXX	NV548 'Z'	406 Sqn	Ju 88	Witstock	W/C R. Bannock DFC* RCAF-F/L R. R. Bruce DFC
23/24.4.45	XIII	MM517 'S'	409 Sqn	Ju 29		W/C R. F. Hatton-F/L R. N. Rivers
24/25.4.45	XIII		409 Sqn	Ju 52		P/O L. E. Fitchett-P/O A. C. Hardy (Mos cr land/Basle
24/25.4.45	VI		605 Sqn	Ju 88	Neuburg a/f	F/L A. D. Wagner DFC*-F/L E. T. 'Pip' Orringe DFC
24/25.4.45	XXX		488 Sqn	Ju 52		S/L F. W. Davison-F/L E. Hickmore
24.4.45	XXX		29 Sqn	Me 262a		W/O Dallinson
24/25.4.45	VI	RS575 'V'	515 Sqn	Do 217	6mls N Libeznice	W/C H. C. Kelsey DFC*-F/L E. M. Smith DFC DFM
24/25.4.45	VI	RS575 'V'	515 Sqn	Do 217	Prague, Czech	W/C H. C. Kelsey DFC*-F/L E. M. Smith DFC DFM
25/26.4.45	XIII	HK466	264 Sqn	Fw 190	W Berlin	P/O J. Hutton-P/O H. E. Burraston
25/26.4.45	XXX	NT527	488 Sqn	Fw 189		F/O J. W. Marshall-P/O P. F. Prestcott
2/3.5.45	VI	'K'	605 Sqn	Fw 190	Lecke, Denmark	F/O B. Williams DFC-W/O S. Hardy